FEDERAL DISABILITY LAW

IN A NUTSHELL®

FIFTH EDITION

RUTH COLKER
Distinguished University Professor and
Heck-Faust Memorial Chair in
Constitutional Law
Professor of Law, The Ohio State University

Nutshell Series, In a Nutshell and the Nutshell Logo are trademarks registered in the U.S. Patent and Trademark Office.

COPYRIGHT © 1994, 1998 WEST PUBLISHING CO.
© West, a Thomson business, 2004
© 2010 Thomson Reuters
© 2016 LEG, Inc. d/b/a West Academic
        444 Cedar Street, Suite 700
        St. Paul, MN 55101
        1-877-888-1330

West, West Academic Publishing, and West Academic are trademarks of West Publishing Corporation, used under license.

Printed in the United States of America

ISBN: 978-1-63460-115-3

PREFACE

The objective of this book is to help law students, lawyers and others recognize and understand the federal laws protecting people with disabilities from discrimination. Students taking courses on disability law, education law, employment law and health law are among the intended beneficiaries. The book will also benefit other students as well, such as those taking courses on civil rights issues and disabilities studies. In addition the book will assist lawyers, educators, employers, disabled persons and others who have direct or indirect interests in these significant federal laws, either on their own behalf or on behalf of those they represent or work with.

As with all Nutshells, a word of caution is required. This book presents an *overview* of the major federal laws pertaining to discrimination against people with disabilities. It is not intended to provide a comprehensive analysis of those laws. Case citations are limited save for a few leading or significant illustrative examples, and secondary sources are not mentioned. Emphasis is placed on the statutes, regulations and significant points of substantive and procedural law. With a few exceptions there is relatively little discussion of policy issues, although the statutes, regulations and case law are placed in historical perspective for clarity. In addition, major issues of dispute have been noted throughout.

RUTH COLKER

August 2015

OUTLINE

Chapter 18. Disciplining Students with
Disabilities 523

Conclusion 539

TABLE OF CASES

References are to Pages

FEDERAL DISABILITY LAW

IN A NUTSHELL®

FIFTH EDITION

CHAPTER 1
INTRODUCTION AND OVERVIEW

§ 1.1   BACKGROUND

When Congress passed the Americans with Disabilities Act (ADA) in 1990, it estimated there were 43 million Americans with physical or mental disabilities and noted that this number is increasing as the population grows older. When Congress amended the ADA in 2008, it abandoned trying to estimate the number of individuals with disabilities. Instead, it stated that "historically, society has tended to isolate and segregate individuals with disabilities, and, despite some improvements, such forms of discrimination against individuals with disabilities continue to be a serious and pervasive social problem." In 1990, and again in 2008, Congress observed that discrimination persisted in critical areas such as employment, housing, public accommodations, transportation, communication, education, recreation, institutionalization, health services, voting, and access to public services. This discrimination occurs in various forms including

outright intentional exclusion, the discriminatory effects of architectural, transportation, and communication barriers, overprotective rules and policies, failure to make modifications to existing facilities and practices, exclusionary qualification standards and criteria, segregation, and relegation to lesser services, programs, activities, benefits, jobs, or other opportunities.

42 U.S.C.A. § 12101(5).

Discrimination based on disability differs in some respects from discrimination based on other factors such as race or sex. Factors like race, and in most cases sex, generally do not create any rational differences between individuals regarding the ability to do a job or qualification to perform in a program. Thus, there is rarely, if ever, a reason to treat persons of different races or sexes differently. Conversely, an individual's disability *may*—to differing degrees—affect his or her ability to perform, and thus *may*—to differing degrees—constitute a permissible reason for treating that individual in a different manner. Because in many cases there are meaningful differences between disabled and nondisabled individuals, it cannot automatically be assumed that *all* disparate treatment of persons with disabilities is discriminatory. Moreover, because of the differences between disabled and nondisabled individuals, the underlying premise of discrimination based on disability differs in some respects from that based on other factors such as race. Racial discrimination is often premised on an irrational and hostile animus. Disability discrimination is also sometimes based on animus, but it is frequently premised on other factors:

First, "able-bodied" members of our society often feel discomfort and embarrassment around people with disabilities and do not know how to react toward them. Some able-bodied people may even feel actual aversion to some people with disabilities. These feelings may cause nondisabled people to treat people with disabilities differently.

Second, nondisabled people often patronize and pity people with disabilities and thus treat them in a paternalistic fashion based on unfounded stereotypes about their purported incapabilities. While this form of different treatment is based on compassion, such benevolent paternalism displays a lack of respect for, and fails to recognize the dignity of, people with disabilities. As the court recognized in *Pushkin v. Regents of the University of Colorado*, 658 F.2d 1372 (10th Cir. 1981), discrimination against people with disabilities "often occurs under the guise of extending a helping hand or a mistaken, restrictive belief as to the limitations of [disabled] persons."

Third, our society has attached unpleasant stigmas to disabling conditions. Many Americans view disabilities as very negative, undesirable characteristics, and thereby treat people adversely when they have a disability.

Finally, the Supreme Court in *Alexander v. Choate*, 469 U.S. 287 (1985) recognized that discrimination against people with disabilities is "most often the product of benign neglect." It noted that "[f]ederal agencies and commentators on the plight of [people with disabilities] . . . have found that discrimination against [people with disabilities] is primarily the result of apathetic attitudes rather than affirmative animus." All of these factors contribute to the second-class citizenship status of Americans with disabilities.

§ 1.2   RELEVANT LEGISLATION

As a result of the concentrated lobbying activities of persons with disabilities and their advocates, Congress passed several laws geared to protect people with disabilities in the late 1960s and early 1970s. Among the most prominent were Sections 501, 503, and 504 of the Rehabilitation Act of 1973, 29 U.S.C.A. §§ 791, 793, 794; the Individuals with Disabilities Education Act (IDEA), 20 U.S.C.A. §§ 1400 *et seq.* (originally entitled the Education of all Handicapped Children Act); and the Architectural Barriers Act (ABA), 42 U.S.C.A. §§ 4151–4157. Sections 501, 503 and 504 prohibit federal agencies, federal contractors and recipients of federal financial assistance from discriminating against otherwise qualified persons with disabilities on the basis of disability; the ABA requires that federally owned, leased or financed buildings be accessible to people with disabilities; and the IDEA requires states to provide all children with disabilities who require special education and related services with a free, appropriate public education.

Subsequently, Congress passed laws aimed at alleviating some of the additional inequities faced by persons with disabilities. These include the Air Carriers Access Act of 1986, 49 U.S.C.A. § 1374(c), which prohibits air carriers from discriminating on the basis of disability; the Fair Housing Act

Amendments of 1988, 42 U.S.C.A. §§ 3601 *et seq.*, which expanded the coverage of the Fair Housing Act to prohibit discrimination based on disability in private and public real estate transactions; and the Child Abuse Amendments of 1984, 42 U.S.C.A. §§ 5101 *et seq.*, which are intended to prevent the withholding of medical treatment to infants with disabilities.

Despite these laws, as of early 1990 no federal statute prohibited the majority of employers, program administrators, owners and managers of places of public accommodation and others from discriminating against people with disabilities. In the late 1980s, studies showed that only two-thirds of working age Americans with disabilities who were able to be employed had jobs, and many of those who did have jobs were working in positions below their capabilities. This was so because many employers refused to hire people with disabilities, and because those people with disabilities who were employed were often left in entry-level positions and not promoted in accord with their abilities. In 1990, over eight million Americans with disabilities who wanted to work were denied jobs and thus were forced to depend on government subsidies—to the disadvantage of *all* Americans.

Americans with disabilities also face discrimination in transportation. Generally, public bus and train transportation is the only mode of travel available to poor or rural Americans, and Americans with disabilities are more likely than nondisabled persons to live in poverty and in rural areas. Moreover, people with disabilities often rely heavily upon public transportation to conduct their daily lives because they have low incomes and are unable to afford the cost of private cars (much less the cost of specially equipped private cars for some mobility-impaired persons) and because some disabilities (blindness, for example) preclude driving. As of early 1990, however, very few rail cars and only approximately one-third of the public buses in this country were accessible to riders with disabilities.

In 1990, Congress enacted the ADA, 42 U.S.C.A. §§ 12101–12213, to assist in remedying the problems relating to access by persons with disabilities to public facilities, employment and transportation services. In 2008, Congress enacted a sweeping amendment of the 1990 Act, entitled the ADA Amendments Act of 2008 ("ADAAA"). The purpose of this amendment was to reverse various court decisions that had narrowly construed the coverage of the ADA. The ADAAA sought to "carry out the ADA's objectives of providing 'a clear and comprehensive national mandate for the elimination of discrimination' and 'clear, strong, consistent, enforceable standards addressing discrimination' by reinstating a broad scope of protection to be available under the ADA." 29 U.S.C. § 705 NOTE (b)(1). Specifically, Congress rejected the Supreme Court's decisions in *Sutton v. United Air Lines, Inc.*, 527 U.S. 471 (1999) and *Toyota Motor Manufacturing, Kentucky, Inc. v. Williams*, 534 U.S. 184 (2002) and sought to reinstate the reasoning of the Supreme Court in *School Board of Nassau County v. Arline*, 480 U.S. 273 (1987).

§ 1.3   EDUCATION

Americans with disabilities also faced discrimination in the field of education. Although the Supreme Court ruled in *Brown v. Board of Education of Topeka*, 347 U.S. 483 (1954), that *racially* segregated schools are prohibited by the United States Constitution, automatic segregation of children with disabilities was not barred by federal law until the enactment of the IDEA in 1975. Federal intervention was deemed necessary because over half of the more than eight million children with disabilities in this country were not receiving "appropriate educational services which would enable them to have full equality of opportunity," 20 U.S.C.A. § 1400(c)(2)(B), and one million of those children were excluded entirely from the public school system. *Id.*, § 1400(c)(2)(C). The IDEA was amended in 1991 to address several substantive concerns arising under the Act, as well as to change the name from the Education for All Handicapped Children Act to the Individuals with Disabilities Education Act. The IDEA was again amended in 1997 and 2004 to address further concerns arising under the Act.

§ 1.4   OVERVIEW

This *Nutshell* provides a general overview of the major federal laws enacted by Congress to aid in eliminating the discrimination confronted by Americans with disabilities.

A word of caution, however: This book is *not* intended to serve as a substitute for thorough analysis and examination of the very complex laws at issue. It should be used as guidance only, for a very broad background of the subject matter.

CHAPTER 2
CONSTITUTIONAL RIGHTS

§ 2.1   EQUAL PROTECTION

In *City of Cleburne v. Cleburne Living Center, Inc.*, 473 U.S. 432 (1985), the Supreme Court concluded that persons with intellectual disabilities (then called "mental retardation") do not constitute a "suspect class" that has historically suffered unequal treatment (like racial minorities) or a "quasi-suspect class" (like women). The Court thus held that the judicial review of state legislation or state action impacting persons with intellectual disabilities would be reviewed under a "rational basis" standard and not the "strict scrutiny" standard used for issues impacting race or national origin or the "heightened scrutiny" standard used for gender questions. The Court's opinion was premised primarily on the fact that people who are intellectually disabled, unlike people of different races or sex, have a reduced ability to cope with and function in the everyday world. Thus, people with intellectual disabilities are immutably different from others, and states have a legitimate interest in promulgating statutes and regulations dealing with the treatment of such persons. In addition, the Court stated that if it were to attribute quasi-suspect status to persons with intellectual disabilities "it would be difficult to find a principled way to distinguish a variety of other groups . . . [including] the disabled. . . ." Accordingly, although the *Cleburne* case involved only persons with intellectual disabilities, the implications of the Court's decision are much broader.

Despite the invocation of rational basis scrutiny in *Cleburne,* the Court did strike down the zoning ordinance at issue in the case as one founded on irrational and unconstitutional stereotypes about individuals with intellectual disabilities. Some scholars thought that the Court's decision in *Cleburne* therefore signaled a willingness to invoke a sort of heightened rational basis scrutiny in this area. Nonetheless, the Supreme Court revisited the *Cleburne* holding in *Board of Trustees v. Garrett*, 531 U.S. 356 (2001) and rejected the contention that *Cleburne* established a special kind of rationality review for disability claims.

§ 2.2   EDUCATION

The Supreme Court has held that, while education is one of the most important services performed by the state, it is not among the rights afforded explicit or implicit protection under the Federal Constitution. Accordingly, it has analyzed constitutional challenges to educational decisions under the rational basis test. *See, e.g.*, *San Antonio Independent School District v. Rodriguez*, 411 U.S. 1 (1973). Nevertheless, the Court recognized the pivotal role that education plays in our society, and implicitly applied a heightened scrutiny standard in *Plyler v. Doe*, 457 U.S. 202 (1982), when it held that "the discrimination contained . . . [in a state law governing education] can hardly be considered rational unless it furthers some substantial goal of the State."

Two lower court decisions addressing the question of what constitutional rights are applicable to students with disabilities recognized constitutional principles that have since been embodied in the IDEA: *Pennsylvania Association for Retarded Children (PARC) v. Pennsylvania*, 343 F.Supp. 279 (E.D.Pa. 1972), and *Mills v. Board of Education*, 348 F.Supp. 866 (D.D.C. 1972).

In *PARC*, children with intellectual disabilities (then called "mental retardation") sued the state, claiming that they were denied the right to a public education. The suit was based upon three claims: (1) a violation of due process because there was no notice or hearing provided before children with intellectual disabilities were excluded from public education or their educational assignments were changed; (2) a violation of equal protection due to the lack of a rational basis for assuming that children with intellectual disabilities were uneducable and untrainable; and (3) a violation of due process because it was arbitrary and capricious to deny children with intellectual disabilities a right to the education guaranteed by state law. The parties in *PARC* entered into an interim stipulation that provided:

> no child who is mentally retarded or thought to be mentally retarded can be assigned initially (or re-assigned) to either a regular or special educational status, or excluded from a public education without a prior recorded hearing

before a special hearing officer. At that hearing, parents have the right to representation by counsel, to examine their child's records, to compel the attendance of school officials who may have relevant evidence to offer, to cross-examine witnesses testifying on behalf of school officials and to introduce evidence of their own.

Thereafter, a consent agreement was submitted to the court providing that "it is the Commonwealth's obligation to place each mentally retarded child in a free, public program of education and training appropriate to the child's capacity." This language is the forerunner to the free appropriate public education (FAPE) guarantee to every child with a disability under the IDEA.

The district court in *PARC* found that the plaintiffs possessed colorable claims under both the Due Process and Equal Protection Clauses of the Fourteenth Amendment, but the consent agreement effectively resolved the case.

The *Mills* case involved students with disabilities—labeled mentally retarded, emotionally disturbed, hyperactive or as having behavior problems—who were denied admission to, or excluded from, the public school system. The defendants admitted that they had a duty to provide students with disabilities with a publicly supported education suited to each child's needs, as well as a constitutionally proper prior hearing and periodic program reviews. The defendants' admission—like the agreement in *PARC*—made it unnecessary for the court to actually rule on the plaintiffs' constitutional claims. Since the plaintiffs claimed that the defendants failed to comply with court orders and agreements between the parties, however, the plaintiffs applied for, and were granted, summary judgment. The summary judgment granted by the district court provided in part:

(1) That no child eligible for a publicly supported education . . . shall be excluded from a regular public school assignment . . . unless such child is provided (a) adequate alternative educational services suited to the child's needs, which may include special education or tuition grants, and (b) a constitutionally adequate prior hearing and periodic review of the child's status, progress, and the adequacy of any educational alternative. . . .

(3) The District of Columbia shall provide to each child of school age a free and suitable publicly-supported education regardless of the degree of the child's mental, physical or emotional disability or impairment. Furthermore, defendants shall not exclude any child resident in the District of Columbia from such publicly-supported education on the basis of a claim of insufficient resources.

As these cases illustrate, the constitutional rights and protections extended to children with disabilities by the Equal Protection and Due Process Clauses of the Fourteenth Amendment are considerably greater in the area of education than in many other areas of human activity. Moreover, the limited case law on point reflects strong protections for students with disabilities.

§ 2.3 EMPLOYMENT

A. EQUAL PROTECTION

Under the rationale of *City of Cleburne*, a job applicant or employee with a disability will not succeed on a claim that, based on his or her disability, he or she is a member of a constitutionally protected class. Moreover, under the prevailing view, courts do not consider employment to be a fundamental right. *See, e.g., United Bldg. & Constr. Trades Council v. Mayor & Council of Camden*, 465 U.S. 208 (1984) ("there is no fundamental right to government employment"); *Nicholas v. Pennsylvania State University*, 227 F.3d 133 (3d Cir. 2000). Thus, equal protection claims of persons with disabilities relating to employment will be analyzed under the rational basis test.

B. DUE PROCESS

Terminated employees have no due process rights if they have no right or interest under state law to continued employment. *See, e.g., Board of Regents v. Roth*, 408 U.S. 564 (1972). Employees do have due process rights, however, if they have a state law right to continued employment or the right to continued employment unless sufficient cause is shown. The scope of such due process rights includes the right to notification of the grounds for non-retention and an opportunity to challenge the sufficiency or legitimacy of the basis for non-retention. *See, e.g., Perry v. Sindermann*, 408 U.S. 593 (1972); *Cleveland Bd. of Educ. v. Loudermill*, 470 U.S. 532 (1985). However, a public employee dismissable only for cause is entitled only to a very limited hearing prior to termination, to be followed by a more comprehensive post-termination hearing. *See, e.g., Gilbert v. Homar*, 520 U.S. 924 (1997).

C.   IRREBUTTABLE PRESUMPTION

An employee may successfully claim a violation of due process when his or her right to employment is impaired because the employer applies an irrebuttable presumption—a presumed fact or set of facts that, although not necessarily true, is held unassailable by the employer. For example, a prospective employer might believe an applicant's disability indicates an inability to perform the essential elements of a job. An irrebuttable presumption that the disability would preclude performance of the job violates due process. *See, e.g., Gurmankin v. Costanzo*, 556 F.2d 184 (3d Cir. 1977).

D.   SUMMARY OF EMPLOYMENT ISSUES

The constitutional rights available to job applicants with disabilities are limited to violations of equal protection analyzed under the rational basis test or violations of due process—including reliance on an irrebuttable presumption. The Constitution offers actual employees similar protections under the Equal Protection and Due

Process Clauses. In addition, an employee who has a property interest in continued employment is entitled to additional due process rights including an explanation and informal hearing before a termination of employment.

§ 2.4   SUMMARY

In most cases, with the exception of the educational arena, people with disabilities seeking to utilize constitutional means to redress discriminatory conduct have obtained little relief—in both employment and non-employment contexts. Constitutional claims based on equal protection and due process theories will only rarely provide relief for persons with disabilities because of the lack of suspect class status or of a fundamental right. Accordingly, the federal laws enacted specifically to assist people with disabilities in avoiding discrimination and entering the mainstream of society are of crucial importance.

CHAPTER 3

DEFINITION OF "DISABILITY"?

§ 3.1 GENERAL DEFINITION

The federal laws discussed in this *Nutshell* (with the exception of the Individuals with Disabilities Education Act discussed in Chapters 12–18), define an individual with a disability as one who: (1) has a physical or mental impairment that substantially limits one or more of the individual's major life activities; (2) has a record of such impairment (*e.g.*, someone with a past history of cancer); or (3) is regarded as having such an impairment (*e.g.*, an individual who has been misclassified as disabled or who is treated as being disabled irrespective of whether the individual is disabled). *See, e.g.*, 29 U.S.C.A. § 705(9) (Rehabilitation Act); 42 U.S.C.A. § 12102(2) (ADA); 42 U.S.C.A. § 3602(h) (Fair Housing Act Amendments Act of 1988); 49 U.S.C.A. § 41705(a)) (Air Carrier Access Act). Under the first part of this definition, merely having an impairment does not make one "disabled"; the individual must also demonstrate that the impairment *substantially* limits one or more *major* life activities. Thus, courts apply a three-part analysis to determine whether an individual has a disability: 1) does the person's condition constitute a mental or physical "impairment"; 2) does the impairment impact one or more "major life activities"; and 3) does the impairment "substantially limit" the major life activities identified. The courts typically conduct an individualized inquiry on this issue, and the existence of a disability is determined in a case-by-case manner. Nonetheless, the EEOC has provided a list in its regulations of impairments that covered entities should "easily conclude" constitute disabilities without such an individualized inquiry. *See* 29 C.F.R. § 1630.2(j)(3)(iii) (predictable assessments).

§ 3.2   PHYSICAL IMPAIRMENT

When the ADA was enacted in 1990, and amended in 2008, it did not include a definition of "physical or mental impairment." The EEOC defined that term in its regulations drafted to interpret the 1990 Act. Following adoption of the 2008 Amendments, the EEOC proposed new regulations that were similar to the previous regulations on this subject except for substituting the term "intellectual disability" for "mental retardation" in defining a physical or mental impairment, and adding "immune and circulatory" in the first part of what became a two-part definition. Hence, the federal regulations define "physical or mental impairment" as including: "Any physiological disorder, or condition, cosmetic disfigurement, or anatomical loss affecting one or more of the following body systems: neurological, musculoskeletal, special sense organs, respiratory (including speech organs), cardiovascular, reproductive, digestive, genitourinary, immune, circulatory, hemic and lymphatic, skin, and endocrine." 29 C.F.R. § 1630.2(h)(1).

To fall within the parameters of a physical "impairment," an individual's physical characteristic must be the result of a "physical disorder." Thus, such characteristics as eye color, hair color, left-handedness, or height, weight, or muscle tone that are within the normal range and are not the result of a physiological disorder. A normal condition, such as pregnancy, is not an impairment but a pregnancy-related impairment can constitute an impairment under the ADA.

Before the enactment of the 2008 Amendments, some courts had taken the position that the ADA did not cover transitory or temporary impairments. The 2008 Amendments state that "transitory and minor" impairments are not covered under the "regarded as" prong but do not except such impairments from the "actually disabled" prong. See 42 U.S.C. § 12102(3)(B). The EEOC has therefore taken the position that transitory or temporary impairments *are* covered under the "actually disabled" prong of the ADA. *See* 29 C.F.R. § 1630.2(j)(1)(vii) ("An impairment that is episodic or in remission if it would substantially limit a major life activity when active.")

Presumptively covered physical impairments include: deafness, blindness, partially or completely missing limbs, mobility impairments requiring the use of a wheelchair, autism, cancer, cerebral palsy, diabetes, epilepsy, HIV, multiple sclerosis, and muscular dystrophy. *See* 29 C.F.R. § 1630.2(3)(iii).

In addition, the Supreme Court recognized in *School Board of Nassau County v. Arline*, 480 U.S.

273 (1987), that a contagious disease—in that case tuberculosis—constitutes a physical impairment. It has also held that Human Immunodeficiency Virus (HIV) is a "physical impairment" within the meaning of the ADA from the moment of infection and throughout every stage of the disease because it is a physiological disorder with a constant and detrimental effect on the infected person's hemic and lymphatic systems. *Bragdon v. Abbott*, 524 U.S. 624 (1998). That holding has been codified in the EEOC regulations regarding "predictable assessments." *See* 29 C.F.R. § 1630.2(3)(iii).

As previously noted, however, even if an individual has a physical impairment, that does not mean that the individual is disabled under the federal laws, since the physical impairment might not substantially limit a major life activity of the individual. The 2008 ADA Amendments, however, broadened the definition of disability and instructed courts to construe the statute in "favor of broad coverage," thereby lessening the likelihood that an individual with a physical or mental impairment will be found not to be disabled under the ADA. *See* 42 U.S.C. § 12102(4). That issue is discussed later in this chapter.

§ 3.3 MENTAL OR PSYCHOLOGICAL IMPAIRMENT

The regulations define a "mental or psychological impairment" as "[a]ny mental or psychological disorder, such as intellectual disability (formerly termed mental retardation), organic brain syndrome, emotional or mental illness, and specific learning disabilities." *See* 29 C.F.R. § 1630.2(h)(2). Many mental or psychological impairments are now listed in the "predictable assessments" regulation, such as intellectual disability, major depressive disorder, post-traumatic stress disorder, obsessive compulsive disorder, and schizophrenia, lessening the likelihood that courts will question their inclusion under the ADA.

Again, however, an individual who has a mental impairment will not be considered disabled under the federal law unless the mental impairment substantially limits one or more of the individual's major life activities.

In 1997, the EEOC issued an Enforcement Guidance on the ADA and Psychiatric Disabilities to assist *inter alia*, in determining what constitutes a psychiatric disability under the ADA. *EEOC Guidance on the Americans with Disabilities Act and Psychiatric Disabilities* http://www.eeoc.gov/policy/docs/psych.html (March 25, 1997). It is not known at this time whether the EEOC will update the Enforcement Guidance in light of the 2008 Amendments.

§ 3.4   SPECIFICALLY EXCLUDED CRITERIA

Both the ADA and the Rehabilitation Act provide that the following conditions or criteria do not constitute physical or mental impairments: homosexuality; bisexuality; transvestism, transsexualism, pedophilia, exhibitionism, voyeurism, gender identity disorders not resulting from physical impairments, or other sexual behavior disorders; compulsive gambling; kleptomania; pyromania; and psychoactive substance use disorders resulting from current illegal use of drugs. 29 U.S.C.A. § 705(20)(E) (Rehabilitation Act); 42 U.S.C.A. § 12211 (ADA). Other federal laws do not specifically address this question, but the same exclusions will likely apply.

§ 3.5   ALCOHOLICS AND DRUG ABUSERS

Generally, rehabilitated drug abusers (or those currently undergoing rehabilitation), are considered individuals with disabilities under the federal laws. Similarly, alcoholics—both rehabilitated and non-rehabilitated—are protected by the statutes. *See, e.g., Mararri v. WCI Steel, Inc.*, 130 F.3d 1180 (6th Cir. 1997) (recognizing that the ADA treats drug addiction and alcoholism differently, and an alcoholic is not automatically excluded from ADA protection because of current use of alcohol). There are some limitations to this general rule, however.

While current alcoholics are protected individuals under federal law, an employer may prohibit use of alcohol (or drugs) at the workplace and may hold an alcoholic employee (or one who engages in the illegal use of drugs) to the same standards of performance required of other employees "even if any unsatisfactory performance or behavior is related to the drug use or alcoholism of such employee." 42 U.S.C.A. § 12214(c)(4) (ADA); *see also* 29 U.S.C.A. § 705(20)(C)(ii) (Rehabilitation Act) (an individual with a disability does not include an alcoholic whose current use of alcohol prevents performance of the job or whose current alcohol abuse would pose a direct threat to property or to the safety of others in the workplace). An employer may also require that employees comply with standards relating to alcohol and drug use established by the Department of Defense, the Nuclear Regulatory Commission and the Department of Transportation. 42 U.S.C.A. § 12114(c)(5) (ADA).

Current drug addicts, unlike current alcoholics, are not considered individuals with disabilities under the federal laws. But both the ADA and the Rehabilitation Act provide that rehabilitated drug abusers, those participating in a supervised rehabilitation program who are no longer engaging in illegal drug use, and those who are erroneously regarded as engaging in illegal drug use, are protected as individuals with disabilities. Both Acts further provide, however, that employers may adopt policies, including drug testing, to ensure that an employee is no longer using illegal drugs. 42 U.S.C.A. § 12214(b)(3) (ADA); 29 U.S.C.A. § 705(20)(C)(ii) (Rehabilitation Act).

The protection for alcoholics and rehabilitated drug abusers is not intended to restrain school districts from implementing rules and policies prohibiting the use or possession of drugs or alcohol at educational institutions. Thus, the Rehabilitation Act provides that local educational agencies may take disciplinary action pertaining to the use or possession of illegal drugs or the use of alcohol to the same extent that such disciplinary action is taken against non-disabled students. 29 U.S.C.A. § 705(20)(C)(iv).

It is important to note, however, that the ADA expressly provides that a covered entity may not deny health or drug rehabilitation services to a drug abuser if that individual would otherwise be entitled to such services. 42 U.S.C.A. § 12210(c). This applies with respect to both Titles II and III of the Act, discussed in chapter 7 of this *Nutshell*.

It is also important to note that mere status as an alcoholic or substance abuser does not necessarily imply a "limitation" as defined in the disability statutes; to prevail, a recovering drug addict or alcoholic must demonstrate not only that he or she was actually addicted to drugs or alcohol in the past, but also that this addiction substantially limits one or more of his or her major life activities.

§ 3.6   HAVING A RECORD OF
AN IMPAIRMENT

The federal laws are intended to protect individuals who had a physical or mental disability in the past but who no longer suffer from that disability. Thus, the second prong of the definition of an individual with a disability encompasses individuals with a prior history of a physical or mental impairment, such as mental illness, cancer or heart disease, as well as individuals who have been misclassified as having such an impairment, such as one who was improperly classified as intellectually disabled. To satisfy this prong, the individual must show both that (1) he has a record or history of impairment and (2) the impairment substantially limits a major life activity. In the 2008 Amendments, Congress stated its expectation that the term "disability" should be construed broadly. See 42 U.S.C. § 12102(4)(A). That rule of construction applies to each of the three ways that disability is defined under the statute. Hence, the EEOC regulations state that the "record of" test should "be construed broadly to the maximum extent permitted by the ADA and should not demand extensive analysis." 29 C.F.R. § 1630.2(k).

Before the ADA was amended in 2008, there was some confusion about whether an individual covered under the "record of" prong could seek a reasonable accommodation. By excluding reasonable accommodations *only* for individuals covered under the "regarded as" prong, Congress clarified that "record of" plaintiffs are also entitled to reasonable accommodations. *See* 42 U.S.C. § 12201(h). The EEOC regulations take the position that individuals with "record of" impairments "may be entitled, absent undue hardship, to a reasonable accommodation if needed and related to the past disability" such as a schedule change to attend follow-up appointments with a health care provider. *See* 29 C.F.R. § 1630.2(k)(3).

§ 3.7   REGARDED AS HAVING A DISABILITY

The third prong of the definition of an individual with a disability protects individuals who are "regarded as having such an impairment." The 2008 Amendments provide a definition of this prong which, in turn, overturns some case law interpreting the "regarded as" prong. The 2008 Amendments state that: "(A) an individual meets the requirement of 'being regarded as having such an impairment' if the individual establishes that he or she has been subjected to an action prohibited under this Act because of an actual or perceived physical or mental impairment whether or not the impairment limits or is perceived to limit a major life activity. (B) Paragraph (1)(C) [regarded as prong] shall not apply to impairments that are transitory and minor. A transitory impairment is an impairment with an actual or expected duration of 6 months or less." 42 U.S.C. § 12102(3). In the Miscellaneous Provisions, the 2008 Amendments also provide that reasonable accommodations are not available to individuals who qualify for statutory coverage under the "regarded as" prong. See 42 U.S.C. § 12201(h).

Under this revised definition of "regarded as" disabled, the proof required by an individual to attain statutory coverage is that the individual was subjected to a prohibited action because of an impairment, so long as the impairment is not transitory and minor. The individual need *not* demonstrate an actual or perceived limitation on a major life activity.

In the purpose section of the 2008 Amendments, Congress stated that a purpose of the Amendments is "to reject the Supreme Court's reasoning in *Sutton v. United Air Lines, Inc.*, 527 U.S. 471 (1999) with regard to coverage under the third prong of the definition of disability and to reinstate the reasoning of the Supreme Court in *School Board of Nassau County v. Arline,* 480 U.S. 273 (1987) which set forth a broad view of the third prong of the definition of handicap under the Rehabilitation Act of 1973." 42 U.S.C. § 12101 NOTE (b)(3). Congress has dispensed with the requirement in employment discrimination cases for the plaintiff to demonstrate that the employer believed that he or she was unqualified in a broad class of jobs due to an impairment rather than merely unqualified for the specific job requested in order to invoke statutory protection.

It is important to remember that the "regarded as" prong does *not* require the plaintiff to demonstrate a substantial limitation of a major life activity. Thus, the EEOC has stated that claimants, who do not request reasonable accommodations, can proceed under the "regarded as" prong to be covered by the ADA *without* "a showing of an impairment that substantially limits a major life activity or a record of such an impairment." *See* 29 C.F.R. § 1630.2(g)(3).

§ 3.8   MAJOR LIFE ACTIVITY

To be protected as a person with a disability, it is not enough that an individual has a physical or mental impairment or has a record of such an impairment. The physical or mental impairment at issue must also cause the individual to be *substantially limited* in a major life activity. As discussed above, the major life activity rule no longer applies to "regarded as" cases.

The 2008 Amendments provide a broad definition of "major life activities." Major life activities are defined as:

"(A) In general. For purposes of paragraph (1) [the definition of disability], major life activities include, but are not limited to, caring for oneself, performing manual tasks, seeing, hearing, eating, sleeping, walking, standing, lifting, bending, speaking, breathing, learning, reading, concentrating, thinking, communicating, and working.

(B) Major bodily functions. For purposes of paragraph (1), a major life activity also includes the operation of a major bodily function, including but not limited to, functions of the immune system, normal cell growth, digestive, bowel, bladder, neurological, brain, respiratory, circulatory, endocrine, and reproductive functions." 42 U.S.C. § 12102(2).

The purpose of this broad definition of "major life activity" is to overturn some Supreme Court precedents. A purpose of the 2008 Amendments is: "to reject the standards enunciated by the Supreme Court in *Toyota Motor Manufacturing, Kentucky, Inc. v. Williams*, 534 U.S. 184 (2002), that the terms 'substantially' and 'major' in the definition of disability under the ADA 'need to be interpreted strictly to create a demanding standard for qualifying as disabled,' and that to be substantially limited in performing a major life activity under the ADA 'an individual must have an impairment that prevents or severely restricts the individual from doing activities that are of central importance to most people's daily lives." 42 U.S.C. § 12101 NOTE (b)(4).

The 2008 Amendments also specify that an individual only need demonstrate a substantial limitation in *one* major life activity to attain statutory coverage. "An impairment that substantially limits one major life activity need not limit other major life activities in order to be considered a disability." 42 U.S.C. § 12102(4)(C).

Prior to the adoption of the 2008 Amendments, lower courts had ruled that individuals with cancer, HIV infection, hearing impairments, learning disabilities, ADHD, missing limbs and various visual impairments were not disabled because they were not able to identify a major life activity that was substantially limited. This broad list of major life activities makes such determinations unlikely under the 2008 Amendments. Because of the inclusion, for example, of "learning" and "concentrating," students with learning disabilities or ADHD are likely to meet the statutory definition of disability.

The EEOC regulations have also been modified to include more discussion of how the factors of "condition, manner, or duration" should be used to determine if an individual's performance of a major life activity is substantially limited. *See* 29 C.F.R. § 1630.2(j)(4). In understanding this language, it is important to remember that the regulations say "or" rather than "and." The regulations state that it may be helpful, in determining if a major life activity is substantially limited, to consider, "as compared to most people in the general population: the condition under which the individual performs the major life activity; the manner in which the individual performs the major life activity; and/or the duration of time it takes to perform the major life activity, or for which the individual can perform the major life activity." 29 C.F.R. § 1630.2(j)(4)(i).

The "condition, manner or duration" regulation has spawned some confusion with respect to students with learning disabilities. Does the "as compared to most people in the general population" language mean that students with high levels of academic achievement cannot also have a learning disability if, for example, they manage to read at a level that is typical of their age? The EEOC Section by Section Analysis answers that question in the affirmative. It says: "Thus, someone with a learning disability may achieve a high level of academic success, but may nevertheless be substantially limited in the major life activity of learning because of the additional time or effort he or she must spend to read, write or learn compared to most people in the general population." 29 C.F.R. § 1630.2(j)(4)(i) App. These regulations may therefore cause courts to reject the pre-2008 reasoning found in cases, such as *Price v. National Bd. of Medical Examiners,* 966 F.Supp. 419 (S.D. W. Va. 1997) and *Gonzales v. National Board of Medical Examiners,* 225 F.3d 620 (6th Cir. 2000), in which courts held that high levels of achievement precluded these individuals from being considered disabled.

§ 3.9   SUBSTANTIAL LIMITATION AND MITIGATING MEASURES

To fall within the protection of the federal laws, a person must have an impairment that causes the individual to be *substantially limited* in the ability to perform a major life activity. Prior to the adoption of the 2008 Amendments, the Supreme Court had interpreted this requirement quite stringently. Congress amended the ADA in 2008 to overturn these decisions. A purpose of the 2008 Amendments is: "to convey congressional intent that the standard created by the Supreme Court in the case of *Toyota Motor Manufacturing, Kentucky, Inc. v. Williams*, 534 U.S. 184 (2002) for 'substantially limits', and applied by lower courts in numerous decisions, has created an inappropriately high level of limitation necessary to obtain coverage under the ADA, to convey that it is the intent of Congress that the primary object of attention in cases brought under the ADA should be whether entities covered under the ADA have complied with their obligations, and to convey that the question of whether an individual's impairment is a disability under the ADA should not demand extensive analysis." 42 U.S.C. § 12101 NOTE (b)(5).

One way that the Supreme Court had made the substantial limitation test quite rigorous is by taking into account the ameliorative effects of mitigating measures when determining whether an individual was disabled. The 2008 Amendments overturned those decisions by stating that:

> The determination of whether an impairment substantially limits a major life activity shall be made without regard to the ameliorative effects of mitigating measures such as—
>
> (I) medication, medical supplies, equipment, or appliances, low-vision devices (which do not include ordinary eyeglasses or contact lenses), prosthetics including limbs and devices, hearing aids and cochlear implants or other implantable hearing devices, mobility devices, or oxygen therapy equipment and supplies:
>
> (II) use of assistive technology;
>
> (III) reasonable accommodations or auxiliary aids or services; or
>
> (IV) learned behavioral or adaptive neurological modifications.

42 U.S.C. § 12102(4)(E)(i).

The "ameliorative effect" language clearly overturns those cases in which courts had asked whether an individual was substantially limited *after* he or she took advantage of mitigating measures. Now, that inquiry takes place *before* those effects take place. An individual who uses a hearing aid would be considered disabled if his hearing is substantially limited in comparison with most people in the population *before* he uses the hearing aid.

Nonetheless, Congress created one exception to this ameliorative effect rule. "The ameliorative effects of the mitigating measures of ordinary eyeglasses or contact lenses shall be considered in determining whether an impairment substantially limits a major life activity." 42 U.S.C. § 12102(4)(E)(ii). Hence, if someone wears eyeglasses, one would determine if that individual is substantially limited in the major life activity of seeing *after* the person puts on her eyeglasses. A final twist to this rule occurs in the employment situation in which an employer insists that an individual demonstrate that she is qualified for employment *without* the use of corrective lenses. If a covered entity makes an employment decision based on an individual's uncorrected vision then the entity must demonstrate that "the standard, test, or other selection criteria, as used by the covered entity, is shown to be job-related for the position in question and consistent with business necessity." 42 U.S.C. § 12113(c). In other words, eyeglasses are treated differently than other mitigating measures and must be addressed under the eyeglass exception and the further exception for the situation in which an employer insists on testing someone without the use of corrective lenses.

§ 3.10   SUBSTANTIAL LIMITATION OF THE ABILITY TO WORK

Before Congress passed the 2008 Amendments, there was considerable confusion about whether "working" should be considered a "major life activity" for ADA purposes and, if so, what legal standard should apply. Congress resolved that controversy by explicitly listing "working" as a major life activity in the 2008 Amendments. See 42 U.S.C. § 12101(2). Congress also made it clear that an individual only needs to demonstrate a substantial limitation in *one* major life activity in order to be covered by the ADA. See 42 U.S.C. § 12102(4)(C). Hence, if an individual has a physical impairment that precludes the individual from lifting more than twenty pounds, and the individual is terminated from employment due to an inability to lift such weight, then that individual would be covered under the ADA as someone with a physical impairment that substantially limits the major life activity of working. The person would not need to demonstrate that the lifting restriction precludes him or her from engaging in any other activities of daily living.

In addition, before the adoption of the 2008 Amendments, the Supreme Court required evidence that an individual was substantially limited in a broad "class of jobs" to invoke the major life activity of "working." *See Sutton v. United Airlines*, 527 U.S. 471 (1999). Hence, the plaintiffs in *Sutton* were unable to meet that rule because they showed they were not able to work as "global airline pilots" but could still work for regional air carriers. The EEOC's regulations had also endorsed this "class of jobs" perspective.

The 2008 Amendments are silent on this "class of jobs" requirement while explicitly listing "working" as a major life activity. In the purpose section, the

2008 Amendments make no reference as to whether they intend to overrule this "class of jobs" requirement. Nonetheless, the 2008 Amendments do indicate that "the definition of disability in this Act shall be construed in favor of broad coverage of individuals under this Act, to the maximum extent permitted by the terms of this Act." 42 U.S.C. § 12102 (4)(A). This language would appear to override the *Sutton* decision's discussion of the "class of jobs" rule. The EEOC had considered drafting a special regulation on the meaning of "working" but, ultimately, abandoned that approach, explaining: "This is consistent with the fact that no other major life activity receives special attention in the regulation, and with the fact that, in light of the expanded definition of disability established by the Amendments Act, this major life activity will be used in only very targeted situations." *See* 29 C.F.R. § 1630.2(j)(5) and (6) App.

CHAPTER 4

THE REHABILITATION ACT OF 1973

§ 4.1 OVERVIEW

Three sections of the Rehabilitation Act of 1973 are especially relevant in federal disability discrimination law: Section 501 (29 U.S.C.A. § 701), Section 503 (29 U.S.C.A. § 703), and Section 504 (29 U.S.C.A. § 794). This chapter will provide a brief overview of the parameters and procedural requirements of those sections. The substantive requirements under them, however, are addressed in later chapters of this text dealing with specific forms of discrimination (*e.g.*, employment discrimination, discrimination in post-secondary educational settings, etc.).

§ 4.2 SECTION 504: INTRODUCTION

Section 504 of the Rehabilitation Act of 1973 constituted the first national declaration of the rights of people with disabilities. It states:

No otherwise qualified individual with a disability in the United States, as defined in section 705(20) [29 U.S.C.A. § 705(20)] of this title, shall, solely by reason of her or his disability, be excluded from the participation in, be denied the benefits of, or be subjected to discrimination under any program or activity receiving Federal financial assistance or under any program or activity conducted by any

Executive agency or by the United States Postal Service.

29 U.S.C.A. § 794(a).

This section prohibits recipients of federal financial assistance from discriminating on the basis of disability in numerous aspects of life, including employment, education, architectural accessibility, and health, welfare and social services. Section 504 required the head of each federal executive agency to promulgate regulations necessary to carry out the Act's purposes.

Congress uses the same definition of disability under Section 504 as under the ADA. Hence, when it amended the ADA in 2008, it also amended Section 504.

§ 4.3   SECTION 504: PROCEDURAL ISSUES

A.   PRIVATE RIGHT OF ACTION

Although Section 504 provides that the various Offices of Civil Rights within each of the federal executive agencies may file suit (through the United States Department of Justice) against a recipient of federal financial assistance to enforce the statute, it does not specifically provide that a private individual has the right to do so. In 1978, however, Congress amended the Rehabilitation Act to provide that the remedies, procedures and rights set forth in Title VI of the Civil Rights Act, which bars race discrimination, apply with respect to actions under Section 504. 29 U.S.C.A. § 794a. There was initially some question if there was a private right of action under this section, but in *Alexander v. Sandoval*, 532 U.S. 275 (2001) the Court stated it was "beyond dispute that private individuals may sue to enforce" Title VI. And in *Barnes v. Gorman*, 536 U.S. 181 (2002) the court applied this reasoning to Section 504 and to Title II of the ADA (which states that the rights and remedies available under it are those found in Section 504). The remedies under Title II are discussed in more detail in § 7.28 of this *Nutshell*.

The circuit courts have unanimously recognized the availability of monetary damage claims in suits under Section 504 against private entities and state and local governments, but have limited them to cases involving *intentional* discrimination. Some courts have held that the "deliberate indifference" standard applies in determining if this standard is met. "Deliberate indifference" requires both (1) knowledge that an action is substantially likely to harm a federally-protected right and (2) a failure to act upon that likelihood. The first element is met when the defendant has notice that an accommodation is required. The second element is met if the defendant's "failure to act" is "a result of conduct that is more than negligent, and involves an element of deliberateness." *Duvall v. County of Kitsap*, 260 F.3d 1124 (9th Cir. 2001). *See also Barber ex rel. Barber v. Colorado Dept. of Revenue*, 562 F.3d 1222 (10th Cir. 2009) (using that test to determine that state did not engage in deliberate indifference when it required a parent, stepparent or guardian to supervise a child's driving practices; requirement adversely affected blind mother).

In *Barnes v. Gorman*, 536 U.S. 181 (2002), however, the Court held that *punitive* damages are *not* available under Section 504 and Title II of the ADA. The Court noted that it had often characterized statutes involving the provision of federal funding to be "much in the nature of a *contract:* in return for federal funds, the [recipients] agree to comply with federally imposed conditions." Punitive damages, unlike compensatory damages and injunction, are generally not available for breach of contract, and the Court reasoned they should also not be available to enforce Section 504 and other federal funding statutes.

The Supreme Court has also held that monetary damages are not available against the *federal* government for violations of the Rehabilitation Act's prohibition of discrimination on the basis of disability "under any program or activity conducted by any Executive agency." *Lane v. Pena*, 518 U.S. 187 (1996). The Court held that Congress has not waived the *federal* government's sovereign immunity in enacting Section 504.

A more difficult question arises when a private individual, rather than filing suit against the recipient of federal financial assistance, wants to sue the *federal agency* that provides the funding based on the agency's purported failure to investigate or review decisions relating to Section 504 complaints. The vast majority of courts have held that such actions against federal agencies are prohibited. The courts have reasoned that obtaining direct relief from the funding agency that allegedly failed to *enforce* Section 504, as opposed to obtaining direct relief from the federal funds recipient who purportedly violated the statute, would disrupt the federal agency's enforcement efforts in a manner inconsistent with the Act's overall framework. They have also noted that the remedial purpose of Section 504 would not be undermined by such a holding because the plaintiff could still pursue an action directly against the federal funds recipient. *See, e.g., Bennett v. New York City Housing Authority*, 248 F.Supp.2d 166 (E.D.N.Y. 2002); *Jersey Heights Neighborhood Ass'n v. Glendening*, 174 F.3d 180 (4th Cir. 1999). Although the Ninth Circuit reached a somewhat different conclusion in *Doe v. Attorney Gen'l of the U.S.*, 941 F.2d 780 (9th Cir. 1991) and *J.L. v. Social Sec. Admin.*, 971 F.2d 260 (9th Cir. 1992), those rulings are likely invalidated by the Supreme Court's reasoning in *Lane v. Pena.*

Finally, the decision in *Alexander v. Sandoval*, 532 U.S. 275 (2001) *may* have an impact on Section 504 claims. In *Sandoval*, the Supreme Court held that plaintiffs could not pursue a private right of action for *disparate impact* claims under Title VI because that cause of action is not included in the statute's language; it is only recognized in the regulations promulgated to enforce Title VI. This decision was grounded on the conclusion that Title VI only bars intentional discrimination, and disparate impact claims do not constitute intentional discrimination. The Court suggested that the general principle of there not being a cause of action to enforce regulations also applies to Section 504.

Lower courts interpreting the *Sandoval* decision, however, have distinguished Title VI from Section 504 and held that disparate impact claims are still viable for disability discrimination. They acknowledge that Congress modeled Section 504 on Title VI but note that in *Alexander v. Choate*, 469 U.S. 287 (1985) the Court rejected the argument that Section 504 only barred intentional discrimination. Courts distinguishing *Sandoval* also note, as did the *Choate* Court that, by the time Congress enacted Section 504, model enforcement regulations for Title VI had incorporated a disparate-impact standard, and every Cabinet Department and about 40 federal agencies had adopted standards in which Title VI was interpreted to bar programs with a discriminatory impact. "Thus, while the conduct regulated by section 601 of Title VI is limited to intentional discrimination . . . the same cannot be said for section 504. With section 504, Congress clearly sought to remedy a problem of a different, and for these purposes broader, nature." *Frederick L. v. Department of Public Welfare*, 157 F.Supp.2d 509 (E.D.Pa. 2001) (overruled on other grounds); *see also Robinson v. State of Kansas*, 295 F.3d 1183 (10th Cir. 2002).

In addition, several courts have allowed Title VI claims to proceed by amending the complaint to convert the cause of action into a claim under 42 U.S.C.A. § 1983, which allows a person to sue for the violation of any federal law. *See, e.g., Robinson v. State of Kansas*, 295 F.3d 1183 (10th Cir. 2002) (allowing disparate impact claims to be brought under Section 1983); *Lucero v. Detroit Public Schools*, 160 F.Supp.2d 767 (E.D.Mich. 2001) (same). In *South Camden Citizens in Action v. New Jersey Department of Environmental Protection*, 274 F.3d 771 (3d Cir. 2001), however, the Third Circuit disallowed disparate impact claims under Section 1983 which were based on a violation of Title VI.

The Supreme Court's recent decision in *Texas Department of Housing and Community Affairs v. Inclusive Communities Project*, 576 U.S. ___, 135 S.Ct. 2507 (2015) may add some clarity to this area of the law. The Court affirmed the use of the disparate impact theory under the Fair Housing Act, with strong language regarding the importance of that cause of action under various civil rights statutes. That decision, however, was limited to a discussion of race discrimination even though disability discrimination is also prohibited by the Fair Housing Act.

B.   EXHAUSTION OF ADMINISTRATIVE REMEDIES

Section 504 complainants do not need to exhaust their remedies with the federal agency providing the funds before filing suit because Section 504's administrative procedures do not provide any direct relief to individual victims. *See, e.g., Freed v. Consolidated Rail Corp.*, 201 F.3d 188 (3rd Cir. 2000); *Tuck v. HCA Health Serv. of Tennessee, Inc.*, 7 F.3d 465 (6th Cir. 1993); *Smith v. Barton*, 914

F.2d 1330 (9th Cir. 1990). The courts recognize that if an individual does file an administrative proceeding, the only remedy available against a federal funds recipient is termination, suspension or deferment of the funding. That remedy, rather than assisting a person with a disability, would in fact harm the individual, since a cutoff of federal financial assistance would remove the individual's ability to invoke Section 504's non-discrimination mandate. Further, to the extent that the individual was receiving some, albeit inadequate, services, discontinuing the federal funds might result in the termination of those services.

The Section 504 administrative procedures do not allow individual complainants to participate in the administrative hearings. The only parties are the recipient and the governmental agency responsible for enforcing Section 504 against that recipient. *See*, *e.g.*, 45 C.F.R. §§ 80.7–80.11. In reality, therefore, administrative proceedings are often ineffective as a remedy for an individual complainant.

However, when an individual with a disability brings a Section 504 claim in conjunction with a claim under another federal law that *does* require administrative remedies to be exhausted before suit is filed, the individual must exhaust the administrative steps prescribed by the second law. Similarly, if an individual with a disability files an action claiming employment discrimination under both Sections 504 and 501 of the Rehabilitation Act, the administrative procedures prescribed under Section 501 must be pursued before suit is filed. For example, if an individual files an action claiming educational discrimination under both Section 504 and the Individuals with Disabilities Education Act (IDEA) (discussed later in this *Nutshell*), the administrative procedures prescribed under the IDEA must be followed prior to filing the IDEA action in state or federal court. Some courts have even held that one cannot bring the Section 504 claim until one exhausts the IDEA claim because the rights protected under both statutes overlap substantially. The 2008 Amendments to the ADA (and Section 504), however, now result in Section 504 having broader coverage than the IDEA. It is not clear at this time whether courts will continue to require Section 504 claimants to exhaust their IDEA administrative remedies before bringing a Section 504 lawsuit.

C.   ELEVENTH AMENDMENT IMMUNITY

In *Atascadero State Hospital v. Scanlon*, 473 U.S. 234 (1985), the Supreme Court held that, in enacting Section 504, Congress did not intend to overturn the states' Eleventh Amendment immunity from suit. The Court held that Congress's general authorization in Section 504 permitting suits in federal court was not the kind of unequivocal statutory language necessary to abrogate Eleventh Amendment immunity. Further, the Court held that a state did not consent to being sued under Section 504 by accepting funds under the Rehabilitation Act.

In response to the resulting public outcry over the decision, Congress passed the Rehabilitation Act Amendments of 1986. Section 1003 of those Amendments, entitled "Civil Rights Remedies Equalization," provides that a state shall not be immune under the Eleventh Amendment from suit in federal court for a violation of Section 504, Title VI of the Civil Rights Act, or the provisions of any other federal law prohibiting discrimination by recipients of federal financial assistance. 42 U.S.C.A. § 2000d–7. That section further provides that remedies at law and in equity are available in a suit against a state for a violation of any such federal statute to the same extent that such remedies are available against private parties or entities.

Accordingly, most circuit courts have held that states have waived such immunity as a condition of receiving federal funds. *See, e.g., Miranda B. v. Kitzhaber*, 328 F.3d 1181 (9th Cir. 2003); *Nihiser v. Ohio Environmental Protection Agency*, 269 F.3d 626 (6th Cir. 2001); *Koslow v. Pennsylvania*, 302 F.3d 161 (3d Cir. 2002); *Jim C. v. United States*, 235 F.3d 1079 (8th Cir. 2000). The court in *Garcia v. S.U.N.Y. Health Sciences Center of Brooklyn*, 280 F.3d 98 (2d Cir. 2001), however, found that a state had not waived its sovereign immunity when it accepted federal funds, but the opinion is a complicated one. The result of its approach is that a waiver is not valid if the state agreed to the condition before the Supreme Court issued its opinion in *Seminole Tribe of Florida v. Florida*, 517 U.S. 44 (1996).

Despite these sovereign immunity issues, individuals with disabilities can still sue state governments for *injunctive* relief pursuant to *Ex parte Young*, 209 U.S. 123 (1908). Moreover, they will still be able to sue *municipal or local governments* for damages, because the principle of sovereign immunity applies to states, not local governments.

D.   STATUTES OF LIMITATION

Section 504 does not contain a specific statute of limitations defining the time frame during which the plaintiff must file suit under the Act. Accordingly, courts have generally held that the applicable statute of limitations is found in the state statute that most closely applies in similar types of actions. *See, e.g., Faibisch v. University of Minnesota*, 304 F.3d 797 (8th Cir. 2002).

Because Section 504 complaints are grounded on federal statutes and regulations, however, federal law will determine when a claim under Section 504 accrues. Generally, under federal law a cause of action accrues, and the statute of limitations begins to run, where a plaintiff knows or had reason to know of the injury upon which the complaint is premised.

In appropriate situations the statute of limitations will toll. For example, in *Board of Educ. of City of Chicago v. Wolinsky*, 842 F.Supp. 1080 (N.D. Ill. 1993) the court held the statute of limitations applicable to Rehabilitation Act discrimination claims was tolled while the parties were involved in administrative hearings under the IDEA. In *Andrews v. Consolidated Rail Corp.*, 831 F.2d 678 (7th Cir. 1987), however, the Seventh Circuit held that the statute of limitations did *not* toll for a private action under Section 504 while the plaintiff pursued a claim under Section 503, which does not provide for a private right of action. Similarly, in *Cheeney v. Highland Community College*, 15 F.3d 79 (7th Cir. 1994) the court held that the Illinois two-year statute of limitations applicable to Rehabilitation Act claims was not tolled during the pendency of administrative proceedings filed by the plaintiffs. *See also Raggi v. Wegmans Food Markets, Inc.*, 779 F.Supp. 705 (W.D.N.Y. 1991) (statute of limitations was not tolled by filing of complaint with state human rights commission objecting to same conduct); *Estrada v. Trager*, 2002 WL 31053819 (E.D.Pa. 2002) (same), *Repp v. Oregon Health Sciences University*, 972 F.Supp. 546 (D.Or. 1997) (statute of limitations was not tolled while student pursued the university's internal grievance procedures).

Courts have held that when a continuing violation is alleged, and some of the discriminatory acts took place during the applicable limitations period, the plaintiff's complaint may be premised on all of the discriminatory acts, even those that would otherwise have been time barred. *See, e.g., Harris v. City of New York*, 186 F.3d 243 (2d Cir. 1999).

E.   RIGHT TO JURY TRIAL

The statute does not specifically state whether a plaintiff has a right to a jury trial under Section 504. In *George v. Brock*, 1987 WL 16038 (E.D.Pa. 1987), however, the court held that a Section 504 plaintiff has no right to a jury trial where the defendant is a *federal* agency.

Courts are split on the issue of whether there is a right to a jury trial for Section 504 suits brought against *state* government and private entities. In *Smith v. Barton*, 914 F.2d 1330 (9th Cir. 1990), the Ninth Circuit ruled that blind plaintiffs had a Seventh Amendment right to a jury trial when they sought monetary damages under Section 504 against the state Commission of the Blind for allegedly illegally restructuring the Commission and causing the plaintiffs to lose their jobs. The court held that, under Supreme Court precedent, the Seventh Amendment requires a jury trial in actions that are analogous to common law actions. Other courts have held that a jury trial is available under Section 504 where the plaintiff alleges *intentional* discrimination and seeks legal relief in the form of monetary damages, but a jury trial is not constitutionally required in every Section 504 action. *See, e.g., Panzardi-Santiago v. University of Puerto Rico*, 200 F.Supp.2d 1 (D.Puerto Rico 2002) (citing cases). Still other courts, however, have simply stated that there is no right to a jury trial for Section 504 claims. *See, e.g., Tyler v. City of Manhattan*, 849 F.Supp. 1442 (D.Kan. 1994); *Gauthreaux v. Baylor University Medical Center*,

879 F.Supp. 634 (N.D.Tex. 1994). The trend in recent cases is to allow a jury trial. *See, e.g., Vazquez v. Municipality of Juncos,* 756 F.Supp.2d 154 (D. Puerto Rico 2010).

Although a jury trial may not be a matter of right, at least when the federal government is the defendant, jury trials may nevertheless be available in Section 504 cases if the parties agree. Moreover, a jury trial may be available for a Section 504 claim if it is appended to other federal or state law claims that may be tried to a jury. *See, e.g., Hart v. Mayor and City Council of Baltimore,* 625 F.2d 13 (4th Cir. 1980) (jury heard the plaintiff's claims under Sections 504, 1981 and 1983); *Ross v. Beaumont Hospital,* 687 F.Supp. 1115 (E.D.Mich. 1988) (jury heard the plaintiff's employment discrimination claim premised on Section 504 and a Michigan state statute prohibiting employment discrimination on the basis of disability).

F.   STANDING TO SUE

Generally, individuals who are not themselves disabled lack standing to sue under Section 504. Courts have, however, accorded standing to non-disabled individuals suing due to retaliation against them for attempts to vindicate the rights of a person with a disability. For example, in *Whitehead v. School Board for Hillsborough County*, 918 F.Supp. 1515 (M.D.Fla.1996), the court granted standing to the parents of a child with Down's Syndrome who sought damages under Section 504 for retaliation against them in their capacity as parents. *See also*

Davis v. Flexman, 109 F.Supp.2d 776 (S.D.Ohio 1999) (holding that a non-disabled marriage counselor had standing to sue a medical clinic under Section 504 where she alleged the clinic retaliated for her complaints regarding the clinic's refusal to provide a sign language interpreter for a hearing impaired patient); *Vives v. Fajardo*, 472 F.3d 19 (1st Cir. 2007) (holding that parents of autistic student could bring retaliation claim under Section 504 even though neither parent was disabled).

Organizations made up of persons with disabilities generally have standing to sue under Section 504. But if there is an insufficient nexus between the organization and the injury claimed, standing will be denied. Further, an association will probably not be held to have standing to maintain a suit on behalf of its members when the suit requires participation of individual members.

To have standing to seek *injunctive* relief under Section 504, a plaintiff must show a real or immediate threat of *future* injury. A past injury is insufficient to gain standing to seek injunctive relief. Moreover, merely stating an intent to go back to a place where the individual previously experienced a lack of accommodations or accessibility is not enough; there must be "concrete plans" to return. Accordingly, some courts have dismissed ADA and/or Section 504 actions where the plaintiffs alleged they had been injured by discriminatory practices in the past but could not prove any potential harm in the future. *See, e.g., Schroedel v. New York Univ. Med. Ctr.*, 885 F.Supp.

594 (S.D.N.Y. 1995) (holding that an individual who was deaf and was not provided an interpreter while in a hospital emergency room did not have standing to sue because it was mere speculation that the plaintiff would need emergency room assistance again, that she would use the defendant hospital again, or that she would be discriminated against if she did); *Romano v. SLS Residential, Inc.*, 246 F.R.D. 432 (S.D.N.Y. 2007) (holding that patients of a psychiatric treatment facility alleging a pattern of abuse under the ADA lacked standing to sue for injunctive relief because they were no longer patients at the facility, lived in a different state, and had expressed no interest in returning). Other courts, however, have held that a single past incident of discrimination can provide grounds for a plaintiff's standing as long as the lack of accommodation continues to exist. *See, e.g., Majocha v. Turner*, 166 F.Supp.2d 316 (W.D.Pa. 2001) (holding that the parents of an infant allegedly denied treatment by a pediatric ear, nose, and throat specialist (ENT) based on the infant's father's hearing impairment had standing to sue the ENT under the ADA; injunctive relief may be available "where a public accommodation in the health care field adheres to its policies of refusing to provide the requested auxiliary aid or has denied treatment altogether to an individual who seeks to receive treatment at the facility"); *Dudley v. Hannaford Bros. Co.*, 333 F.3d 299 (1st Cir. 2003) (holding that a disabled customer of a liquor store had standing to sue under the ADA where there is no absolute certainty that the plaintiff would be denied the right

to purchase alcoholic beverages during a future visit to the store but the likelihood of a denial seems substantial).

G.   ATTORNEY'S FEES

The prevailing party may obtain its attorney's fees in a Section 504 suit. For a more detailed discussion of the attorney's fees issue, see § 11.5 of this *Nutshell*.

§ 4.4   SECTION 504: RECIPIENTS OF FEDERAL FINANCIAL ASSISTANCE

Section 504 prohibits discrimination against people with disabilities only in those "programs or activities" that receive "federal financial assistance." The Department of Justice (DOJ) and the Department of Health and Human Services (DHHS) regulations define the term "federal financial assistance" as:

any grant, loan, contract (other than a procurement contract or a contract of insurance or guaranty), or any other arrangement by which the [agency] provides or otherwise makes available assistance in the form of:

(1)   Funds

(2)   Services of federal personnel; or

(3)   Real and personal property or any interest in or use of such property, including:

(i)   Transfers or leases of such property for less than fair market value or for reduced consideration; and

(ii) Proceeds from a subsequent transfer or lease of such property if the federal share of its fair market value is not returned to the Federal Government.

28 C.F.R. § 41.3(e); 45 C.F.R. § 84.3(h). Notwithstanding these regulatory attempts to define the "programs or activities" who are "recipients" of "federal financial assistance," the precise meaning or scope of these terms has been the subject of much dispute.

A.   PROGRAM SPECIFICITY

In *Consolidated Rail Corp. v. Darrone*, 465 U.S. 624 (1984), the Court held that Section 504's prohibition against discrimination by a "program or activity receiving Federal financial assistance" extended only to the specific program or activity receiving the federal funds. The *Consolidated Rail* decision relied on *Grove City College v. Bell*, 465 U.S. 555 (1984), which interpreted the ban on sex discrimination in any "program or activity receiving Federal financial assistance" under Title IX of the Education Act Amendments of 1972. The college in *Grove City* did not receive direct federal aid to its programs, but a large number of its students received federal Basic Educational Opportunity Grants. The Supreme Court held that Grove City College was a "recipient of federal financial assistance" because the term includes those who receive both direct and indirect aid from the federal government. The Court further held, however, that *only* the specific program within an entity or institution that receives direct or indirect federal financial assistance must comply with Title IX. It ruled that, since only the student financial aid office at Grove City College received the indirect federal financial assistance, only the financial aid program—but not the entire college—was required to comply with Title IX's antidiscrimination provision.

To overturn the effects of *Grove City*, Congress passed the Civil Rights Restoration Act of 1987, which is codified in 20 U.S.C.A. § 1687, 42 U.S.C.A. § 2000d–4a, 42 U.S.C.A. § 6107(4) and 29 U.S.C.A. § 794(b). This Act added a section to Title IX, Title VI of the Civil Rights Act, Section 504 and the Age Discrimination Act to define the phrase "program or activity" in each statute to make it clear that discrimination is prohibited throughout entire agencies or institutions if any part of an agency or institution receives federal financial assistance.

With respect to educational institutions, the Civil Rights Restoration Act provides that where federal aid is extended anywhere within a college, university or public system of education, the entire university or system is covered under the applicable federal statute. 29 U.S.C.A. § 794(b)(2). For private corporations, if the federal aid is extended to the corporation as a whole, or if the corporation provides a public service (such as social services, education or housing), the entire corporation is covered. If the federal aid is extended to only one plant or geographically separate facility, however, only that plant is covered. *Id.* § 794(b)(3). With respect to all other entities, the entire entity is covered if it receives any federal aid. *Id.* § 794(b)(1), (4).

B.   SCOPE OF THE TERM "PROGRAM OR ACTIVITY"

The scope of the term "program or activity" has raised controversy in several areas. Courts are split as to whether a state or local government itself, as opposed to an individual agency, is a proper defendant in a Section 504 claim. For example, in *Innovative Health Sys., Inc. v. City of White Plains*, 117 F.3d 37 (2d Cir. 1997) the court held that the allegation that the city received federal financial assistance was sufficient to sustain a claim that the zoning and planning boards discriminated under the Rehabilitation Act. Other courts, however, have held that the amendment to the Rehabilitation Act's "program or activity" definition is not intended to "sweep in the whole state or local government;" only the department or agency which receives the aid is covered. *See, e.g., Schroeder v. City of Chicago*, 927 F.2d 957 (7th Cir. 1991). *See also Bacon v. City of Richmond*, 475 F.3d 633 (4th Cir. 2007) (city not liable for violations of Section 504 where the School Board was vested sole power in running the schools and there was no evidence to show that the city was liable for any statutory violation; nexus required between federal funds received and discriminatory practice for liability to accrue).

While some courts have held that the activities of prisons do not constitute a "program or activity" under Section 504 (*see, e.g., Williams v. Meese*, 926 F.2d 994 (10th Cir. 1991)), most courts have ruled to the contrary. *See, e.g., Bonner v. Lewis*, 857 F.2d 559 (9th Cir. 1988); *Bane v. Va. Dep't of Corr.*, 267 F.Supp.2d 514 (W.D. Va. 2003); *Harris v. Thigpen*, 941 F.2d 1495 (11th Cir. 1991). Moreover in *Pennsylvania Dept. of Corrections v. Yeskey*, 524 U.S. 206 (1998) the Court held that Title II of the ADA, prohibiting a "public entity" from discriminating against a "qualified individual with a disability" on account of that individual's disability, applied to inmates in state prisons. Similarly, the Supreme Court found in favor of a state prisoner in *United States v. Georgia*, 546 U.S. 151 (2006), a case brought under ADA Title II.

In *Barnes v. Gorman*, 536 U.S. 181 (2002), the Court applied the ADA and Section 504 to actions by a police department *after* an arrest. However, courts have reached varying conclusions on whether investigative and arrest procedures are programs or activities under Section 504 and the ADA. For example, some courts have held that the ADA does not apply to actions taken by police officers during an arrest. *See, e.g., Patrice v. Murphy*, 43 F.Supp.2d 1156 (W.D.Wash. 1999); *Foley v. Klickitat County*, 2009 WL 5216992 (E.D. Wash. 2009). The Tenth Circuit, however, has read the ADA definition of "program or activity" broadly to include police activity occurring prior to arrests and "investigations potentially involving arrests." *Gohier v. Enright*, 186 F.3d 1216 (10th Cir. 1999); *see also*

Calloway v. Boro of Glassboro Dept. of Police, 89 F.Supp.2d 543 (D.N.J. 2000) (relying on *Yeskey* to place station-house investigative questioning within the ambit of ADA activity). Still other courts have held that police activity is a government program under the ADA, but only when the circumstances surrounding the activity is "secure" and there is "no threat to human safety." *See, e.g., Hainze v. Richards*, 207 F.3d 795 (5th Cir. 2000); *Walling v. City of Largo*, 2008 WL 2782687 (M.D. Fla 2008); *Rada v. Miami-Dade County*, 2006 WL 4033817 (S.D. Fla. 2006).

C.   "RECIPIENTS" VERSUS "BENEFICIARIES"

In *United States Department of Transportation v. Paralyzed Veterans of America*, 477 U.S. 597 (1986), the Supreme Court held that commercial airlines are not recipients of federal financial assistance. The plaintiffs in *Paralyzed Veterans* argued that commercial airlines are subject to Section 504 since they indirectly receive federal financial assistance in several forms, including the use of the air traffic control system furnished by the government. The Supreme Court disagreed.

The Supreme Court held that the federal government's direct financing of an extensive air traffic control system, which the Court acknowledged is indispensable to the existence of commercial airline companies, does not constitute federal financial assistance *to the airlines*. The Court held that the scope of Section 504 is limited to those who actually *choose to receive* federal financial assistance, as opposed to those who merely *benefit* from such assistance. According to the Court, only airports or airport operators choose whether to receive, and do receive, the federal assistance provided in the form of an air traffic control system. The airlines merely benefit from that assistance.

A point of possible confusion between the Supreme Court's rulings in *Grove City* and *Paralyzed Veterans* should be noted. In *Grove City*, the Court held that recipients of federal financial assistance within the meaning of Section 504 are not limited to institutions that apply for federal aid or receive checks directly from the federal government. Rather, *indirect* recipients of federal financial assistance are bound by the act. In *Paralyzed Veterans*, the Court explained its statement in *Grove City* by noting that "we made [that] statement[ ] in the context of determining whom Congress intended to receive the federal money". The Court explained that in *Grove City* Congress intended colleges to receive the money from student grants, rather than the individual students to whom the checks were sent. According to the Court, *Grove City* holds that recipients of federal financial assistance are the *intended*, even if indirect, recipients of the assistance. Airlines are not the *intended*, even if indirect, recipients of the assistance (the air traffic control system), however, but are merely the beneficiaries of assistance that is intended to be given to airports.

The DHHS regulations are in accord with the Supreme Court's ruling that ultimate beneficiaries, rather than intended beneficiaries, do not fall within the coverage of Section 504. 45 C.F.R. § 84.3(f). Similarly, the Civil Rights Restoration Act contains a rule of construction that leaves intact the then existing exemption from coverage of the civil rights laws for ultimate beneficiaries of federal financial assistance. 29 U.S.C.A. § 794 note.

The complexity of this issue is illustrated when attempting to determine whether recipients of Medicare or Medicaid funds are recipients of federal financial assistance. Hospitals, physicians or other health-care providers who receive Medicare or Medicaid funds from the federal governments have been held by several courts to be recipients of federal financial assistance, thereby requiring that they comply with Section 504. *See, e.g., Frazier v. Board of Trustees*, 765 F.2d 1278 (5th Cir. 1985). The DHHS regulations, however, take the position that Medicare providers are not such recipients, because "no federal financial assistance flows from the Department [of HHS] . . . under the program, since Medicare Part B—like other social security programs—is basically a program of payments to direct beneficiaries." 45 C.F.R. Pt. 84, App. A. And, at least one court has stated that where a Section 504 defendant is not the health care provider *per se*, but is instead the holding company or affiliate of the health-care provider, the affiliated health care provider is an "ultimate beneficiary" of such funds rather than a "recipient" under Section 504. *Eivins v. Adventist Health System/Eastern & Middle America*, 651 F.Supp. 340 (D.Kan. 1987).

For another example of the complexity of this issue, compare *Moore v. Sun Bank of North Florida*, 923 F.2d 1423 (11th Cir. 1991) (holding Sun Bank was a recipient, rather than a beneficiary, of federal assistance under the Small Business Administration's Guaranteed Loan Program because the bank was able to make more attractive loans as a result of its participation in the program), with *McCullough v. Branch Banking and Trust Company*, 844 F.Supp. 258 (E.D.N.C. 1993) (holding that a bank that participated in the SBA's Guaranteed Loan Program was *not* a recipient of federal financial assistance). *See also Gallagher v. Croghan Colonial Bank*, 89 F.3d 275 (6th Cir. 1996) (holding bank did not receive "federal financial assistance" for purposes of the Rehabilitation Act by disbursing loans to students pursuant to federal student loan legislation).

Several courts have held that the mere receipt of a federal license does not constitute federal financial assistance. And the Supreme Court has held that an entity that receives dues from recipients of federal funds does not thereby become a recipient itself. *National Collegiate Athletic Ass'n v. Smith*, 525 U.S. 459 (1999).

D. PROCUREMENT, INSURANCE OR GUARANTY CONTRACTS

The Section 504 *regulations* promulgated by the DHHS and DOJ provide that "contracts of insurance or guaranty" do not constitute federal financial assistance. In *Moore v. Sun Bank of North Florida*,

923 F.2d 1423 (11th Cir. 1991), however, the court held that those regulatory provisions were invalid because, unlike Title VI and other federal statutes, this exclusion was not specifically mentioned in the *statutory* language of the Rehabilitation Act. Other courts, however, have followed the regulations' definition that "procurement contracts" do not constitute federal financial assistance. *See, e.g., Cook v. Budget Rent-A-Car Corporation*, 502 F.Supp. 494 (S.D.N.Y. 1980); *Jones v. Alabama Power Co.*, 6 NDLR ¶ 145 (N.D. Ala. 1995); *Gallagher v. Croghan Colonial Bank*, 89 F.3d 275 (6th Cir. 1996).

E.   SUBSIDIES

The DHHS and DOJ Section 504 regulations provide that federal financial assistance does not include contracts in which goods or services are sold or purchased by the government at fair market value (procurement contracts). However, the regulations provide that transfers or leases of property at less than fair market value or for reduced consideration do constitute federal financial assistance. In interpreting these provisions, courts have held that payments that constitute a subsidy *do* constitute federal financial assistance. Several courts have held that the deciding factor in determining whether federal financial assistance constitutes a subsidy is whether the government *intended* to give a subsidy. *See, e.g., DeVargas v. Mason & Hanger-Silas Mason Co.*, 911 F.2d 1377 (10th Cir. 1990).

Some courts have held that exemption from taxation is not a form of federal financial assistance. *See, e.g., Martin v. Delaware Law Sch. of Widener Univ.*, 625 F.Supp. 1288 (D. Del. 1985) (stating, under Rehabilitation Act, that "'assistance' connotes transfer of government funds by way of subsidy, not merely exemption from taxation"); *Stewart v. New York Univ.*, 430 F.Supp. 1305 (S.D.N.Y. 1976) (finding tax benefits insufficient to create federal financial assistance under Title VI). *But see M.H.D. v. Westminster Schools*, 172 F.3d 797 (11th Cir. 1999) (holding that contention that a private school's tax-exempt status constituted federal financial assistance so as to make it subject to Title IX was neither immaterial nor wholly frivolous).

§ 4.5   SECTION 504: DISCRIMINATION SOLELY ON THE BASIS OF DISABILITY

Unlike the ADA, Section 504 prohibits only such discrimination against otherwise qualified individuals that is "solely" on the basis of disability.

A difficult interpretive problem arises when an individual with a disability is denied employment, advancement in employment, or admission to programs or services based on two factors: one related to the disability and one not. For example, an individual who is blind may be denied admission to college because the admissions committee erroneously believed that people who are blind are incapable of performing well in college, *and* because the blind applicant's college grades were not quite as high as those of other applicants. A technical reading of the Section 504 "solely" on the basis of disability requirement would lead to the conclusion that the individual who is blind had not been impermissibly discriminated against within the meaning of Section 504. Accordingly, some courts apply the "but for" test applied in Section 504 cases where an employer has mixed motives for refusing to hire or promote an employee protected by Section 504. Under that test, a covered entity is held to violate Section 504 if it is found that *but for* an individual's disability the entity would have acted differently.

The ADA does not include the word "solely" in its causation requirement. 42 U.S.C.A. § 12112(a) ("No covered entity shall discriminate against a qualified individual with a disability because of the disability of such individual . . . "). In *Parker v. Columbia Pictures Industries*, 204 F.3d 326 (2d Cir. 2000) the court stated that "[t]he elimination of the word 'solely' from the causation provision of the ADA suggests forcefully that Congress intended the statute to reach beyond the Rehabilitation Act to cover situations in which discrimination on the basis of disability is one factor, but not the only factor, motivating an adverse employment action." *See also Baird v. Rose*, 192 F.3d 462 (4th Cir. 1999); *McNely v. Ocala Star-Banner Corp.*, 99 F.3d 1068 (11th Cir. 1996) (both ruling that the ADA did not impose a "solely because of" standard of causation). In 1992, Congress amended the Rehabilitation Act and explicitly incorporated the ADA's standards for complaints alleging *employment* discrimination. 29

U.S.C.A. § 794(d). In *Soledad v. U.S. Dept. of Treasury*, 304 F.3d 500 (5th Cir. 2002), however, the Fifth Circuit held that Congress did not intend to adopt the ADA standard for causation when it amended Section 504 in 1992. It ruled that liability can still only be found in Section 504 actions when the alleged discrimination was "solely by reason" of her or his disability.

In order for a recipient of federal financial assistance to be liable under Section 504, of course, the recipient must know of the plaintiff's disability or be aware of facts sufficient to put the recipient on notice of the plaintiff's disability. Absent such knowledge or awareness, a recipient cannot have discriminated against a person solely on the basis of his or her disability. Knowledge of an obvious disability (such as the fact an individual uses a wheelchair) will be imputed to the recipient.

A recipient of federal financial assistance may not avoid Section 504's mandate against discrimination on the basis of disability by simply claiming that there is a rational basis for the rejection of an applicant with a disability or for a rule that discriminates against persons with disabilities. As the Tenth Circuit noted in *Pushkin v. Regents of the University of Colorado*, 658 F.2d 1372 (10th Cir. 1981):

> [Section 504] by its very terms does not provide that a recipient of federal financial assistance may act in an unreasonable manner to promote legitimate ... means, even if discrimination should be the result. Rather, the statute

provides that a recipient of federal financial assistance may not discriminate on the basis of handicap, regardless of whether there is a rational basis for so discriminating. . . .

Moreover, a recipient of federal financial assistance may not avoid the mandate of Section 504 by claiming that it did not *intentionally* discriminate against a person with a disability. In *Alexander v. Choate*, 469 U.S. 287 (1985), the Supreme Court recognized that discrimination against persons with disabilities is often the result of benign indifference or paternalistic attitudes, rather than a result of hostile animus. The Court held, therefore, that it is not necessary to find discriminatory intent before a cause of action may lie under Section 504; rather, Section 504 prohibits both disparate treatment and disparate impact discrimination.

§ 4.6   SECTION 501: INTRODUCTION

Section 501 of the Rehabilitation Act, 29 U.S.C.A. § 791(a), establishes a federal Interagency Committee on Employees who are Individuals with Disabilities. Committee members are appointed by the President and include the following persons or their designees (whose positions must be executive level IV or higher): The Chairman of the Equal Employment Opportunity Commission (EEOC), the Director of the Office of Personnel Management (OPM), the Secretary of Veterans Affairs, and the Secretaries of Labor, Education, and Health and Human Services. The Committee is to be co-chaired by the EEOC Chairman and the OPM Director, or the two may determine that either may serve as sole Chair. The Committee's purposes and functions are

(1) to provide a focus for Federal and other employment of individuals with disabilities, and to review, on a periodic basis, in cooperation with the [Equal Employment Opportunity] Commission, the adequacy of hiring, placement, and advancement practices with respect to individuals with disabilities, by each department, agency, and instrumentality in the executive branch of Government, and to insure that the special needs of such individuals are being met; and (2) to consult with the Commission to assist the Commission to carry out its responsibilities under subsections (b), (c) and (d) of this section.

Subsection (b) of Section 501 requires federal agencies to establish affirmative action plans for the hiring, placement and advancement of individuals with disabilities; subsection (c) requires the EEOC to develop policies and procedures for state agencies to follow to facilitate the hiring, placement and employment of individuals with disabilities; subsection (d) requires the Commission to submit yearly reports to Congress with respect to the practices of and achievements of the hiring, placement and employment of persons with disabilities in all federal agencies.

The hub of Section 501 is subsection (b), which requires all federal agencies to submit affirmative action plans for the "hiring, placement, and advancement of individuals with disabilities." This section was enacted to make it clear that the federal government is to be an equal opportunity employer and to require that it act as the model employer of persons with disabilities and take affirmative action to hire and promote such individuals.

Notwithstanding the broad legislative purpose underlying Section 501, it did not expressly prohibit the federal government from discriminating against employees or applicants with disabilities. Rather, it merely required submission of affirmative action plans. Moreover, Section 501, as initially enacted, did not provide an express remedy for federal employees or applicants for federal jobs who claimed that they were discriminated against on the basis of disability. Thus, many courts ruled that Section 501 neither expressly nor implicitly created a private right of action against a federal agency that allegedly violated the Act. And, while Section 504 *was* held to imply a private right of action, employees of federal agencies were held not to be protected under Section 504 because federal agencies were not viewed as programs or activities that received federal financial assistance. Moreover, the Act did not expressly provide any authority for the promulgation of regulations to define the duties of federal employers under Section 501. Thus, in 1978 Congress amended the Rehabilitation Act to correct the inadequacies in Section 501.

First, Congress amended Section 504 of the Rehabilitation Act specifically to encompass programs and activities conducted by federal agencies. Second, Congress amended Section 501 to require federal agencies to draft regulations to carry out the non-discrimination mandate. Finally, Congress added a remedies provision to the Rehabilitation Act, Section 505(a) (29 U.S.C.A. § 794a), which provides, *inter alia*, that any federal employee or job applicant who has a complaint against a federal employer under Section 501 is entitled to the same rights and remedies provided by Title VII of the Civil Rights Act of 1964.

§ 4.7   SECTION 501: PROCEDURAL ISSUES

A.   PRIVATE RIGHT OF ACTION

Section 505(a) of the Rehabilitation Act provides that an individual has a private right of action under Section 501 against a federal employer. 29 U.S.C.A. § 794a(a)(1).

B.   EXHAUSTION OF ADMINISTRATIVE REMEDIES

Prior to filing suit under Section 501, an individual is required to exhaust his or her administrative remedies. The administrative procedures that must be followed are those set forth under Title VII of the Civil Rights Act. Basically, those procedures are set forth in 42 U.S.C.A. § 2000e–16(c) and 29 C.F.R. § 1614.101 *et seq*.

An employee or applicant who feels that he or she has been discriminated against on the basis of disability by a federal employer must initiate contact with an Equal Employment Opportunity counselor within 45 days of the allegedly discriminatory action at issue. That time limit may be extended if the: (i) plaintiff was never notified or made aware of it; (ii) the plaintiff was prevented by circumstances beyond his/her control from contacting a counselor within the time period; or (iii) for other reasons deemed sufficient by the agency or the EEOC. 29 C.F.R. § 1614.105.

If the complainant is not satisfied with the agency's resolution of the dispute, he or she may appeal the agency's decision to the EEOC. 29 C.F.R. §§ 1614.401–1614.403. Alternatively, within 90 days of receipt of notice of the agency's final decision the complainant may file suit in federal district court without appealing to the EEOC. If the complainant does appeal to the EEOC, he or she may file suit in federal court within 90 days of the EEOC's final decision. In any event, if the agency or the EEOC has not taken final action within 180 days after the filing of the complaint, the complainant may file a civil action in federal district court at the expiration of that 180-day period. 29 C.F.R. § 1614.407.

A claim that is not first presented to the agency cannot be brought before the federal courts. To ensure that discrimination charges are not dismissed due to mere technicalities, however, an administrative complaint should be "liberally construed [by courts] to encompass all charges 'reasonably expected to grow out of the charge of discrimination.'" *Haithcock v. Frank*, 958 F.2d 671 (6th Cir. 1992) (overruled on other grounds). This rule has been followed in *Tisdale v. Federal Express Corp.*, 415 F.3d 516 (6th Cir. 2005).

Several courts have held that a plaintiff who is offered and declines full relief in the administrative process is barred from pursuing a Section 501 claim in federal court.

C.   RIGHT TO JURY TRIAL

At least one court has held that there is no right to a jury trial under Section 501. *George v. Brock*, 1987 WL 16038 (E.D.Pa. 1987). On November 21, 1991, however, the Civil Rights Act of 1991 was enacted. That Act provides for awards of compensatory and punitive damages in Section 501 actions involving *intentional* discrimination, and further provides that: (1) a plaintiff who seeks damages for intentional discrimination may demand a trial by jury, and (2) the court may not inform the jury of statutory limitations to damages under the Act. 42 U.S.C.A. § 1981a. Courts citing this statute have allowed a jury trial for Section 501 claims based on actions which occurred after November 21, 1991. *See, e.g., Lussier v. Runyon*, 1993 WL 434078 (D.Me. 1993); *O'Brien v. Frank*, 1994 WL 440730 (S.D.N.Y 1994); *Miller v. Runyon*, 88 F.Supp.2d 461 (M.D.N.C. 2000).

D.   JUDICIAL REVIEW OF AGENCY ACTION

An individual who seeks judicial review of the action taken at the administrative level under Section 501 is entitled to *de novo* consideration of his or her discrimination claim by the federal district court. *See, e.g., Reisiger v. Gober*, 1999 WL 674751 (N.D.Ill. 1999).

§ 4.8 RELATIONSHIP BETWEEN SECTIONS 501 AND 504

While both Sections 501 and 504 prohibit federal agencies from discriminating on the basis of disability, the courts are in some disagreement as to whether an individual may sue a federal agency under *both* sections. Some courts have allowed individuals to file actions under both sections under the reasoning that when two laws cover the same subject both laws should be given effect if possible. *See, e.g., Spence v. Straw*, 54 F.3d 196 (3rd Cir. 1995). Other courts have held that individuals may sue federal agencies under only one federal law— Section 501. *See, e.g., Boyd v. United States Postal Serv.*, 752 F.2d 410 (9th Cir. 1985); *Spencer v. United States Postal Service*, 2009 WL 5217981 (Col. 2009). In many cases this distinction may make little difference. When an individual files suit under both Sections 501 and 504 he or she must first exhaust the Section 501 administrative remedies. *See, e.g., Spence v. Straw*, 54 F.3d 196 (3rd Cir. 1995). Thus, the only possible advantage to being able to assert causes of action under both Sections 504 *and* 501 is that the damages available for intentional discrimination under Section 504 may be greater than those available under Section 501. This issue is addressed later in this *Nutshell*.

§ 4.9   RELATIONSHIP BETWEEN
SECTION 501 AND THE ADA

Following the enactment of the ADA in 1990, Congress passed the Rehabilitation Act Amendments of 1992 which state that "[t]he standards used to determine whether [Section 501] ... has been violated in a complaint alleging nonaffirmative action employment discrimination" are to be those found in the employment sections of the ADA. 29 U.S.C.A. § 791(g); *see also* 29 C.F.R. § 1614.203.

§ 4.10   SECTION 503: INTRODUCTION
AND OVERVIEW

Section 503 of the Rehabilitation Act, 29 U.S.C.A. § 793(a), requires every contract of $10,000 or more with any federal department or agency to "contain a provision requiring that the party contracting with the United States shall take affirmative action to employ and advance in employment qualified individuals with disabilities." Basically, this section extends the non-discrimination mandates of Section 504 (as applied to recipients of federal financial assistance) and Section 501 (as applied to federal agencies) to persons or companies having existing contracts (or subcontracts) of $10,000 or more with the federal government. The regulations promulgated by the Office of Federal Contract Compliance Programs (OFCCP) under Section 503 require that contractors refrain from discriminating against persons with disabilities. 41 C.F.R. § 60–741.1 *et seq.*

Section 503 applies to all government *contracts and subcontracts* for $10,000 or more for the furnishing of supplies or services or for the use of real or personal property (including construction). Upon request by the contractor (or subcontractor), the Deputy Assistant Secretary for Federal Contract Compliance of the United States Department of Labor, or his or her designee, may waive the affirmative action requirements with respect to facilities that are separate and distinct from those at which the federal contract is to be performed. To do so, he or she must find that such a waiver will not interfere with or impede the effectuation of Section 503. 41 C.F.R. § 60–741.4(b)(3). The Deputy Assistant Secretary may also waive all or part of a contractor's affirmative action requirements under Section 503 if "special circumstances in the national interest so require". Specifically he or she may grant waivers "to groups or categories of contracts or subcontracts of the same type" where it is in the national interest; where it is found impracticable to act upon each request individually; and where such waiver will substantially contribute to convenience in administration of the act. *Id.* § 60–741.4(b)(2). The requirements can also be waived "whenever the head of the contracting agency determines that such contract is essential to the national security." *Id.* § 60–741.4(b)(2).

Contractors having federal contracts or subcontracts of less than the statutory amount of $10,000 are not covered by Section 503. Further a contractor is exempt from Section 503 if: (1) the contracting agency has reason to believe that the amount to be ordered under an indefinite delivery-type contract or subcontract will be less than $10,000 in one year; or (2) work under the contract (or subcontract) is to be performed outside the United States by employees who were not recruited in the United States. *Id.* § 60–741.4(a)(3), (4).

A determination as to whether Section 503 applies with respect to contracts for indefinite quantities will be made at the time the contract is awarded and reassessed on an annual basis during succeeding years. If the contract is found to be initially subject to Section 503, it will continue to be subject to that section throughout its term, regardless of the amounts ordered or expected to be ordered in any year. *Id.* § 60–741.4(a)(3). In the absence of a general or master contract between the government and the contractor, however, individual purchase orders will be viewed as individual contracts with Section 503 coverage to be assessed independently. *See, e.g., Burnett v. Brock,* 806 F.2d 265 (11th Cir. 1986).

Section 503 also governs contracts between the federal government and state and local governments. Agencies, subdivisions or instrumentalities of state and local governments that do "not participate in work on or under the contract or subcontract," however, are exempt from Section 503's requirements. 41 C.F.R. § 60–741.4(a)(5).

§ 4.11   RELATIONSHIP BETWEEN SECTION 503 AND THE ADA

The Rehabilitation Act Amendments of 1992 provide that the standards used to determine whether Section 503 has been violated shall be the same as those applied under Title I of the ADA (dealing with employment discrimination). 29 U.S.C.A. § 793(d); *see also* 41 C.F.R. § 60–741.1(b), ("except as otherwise provided" Section 503 "does not apply a lesser standard than the standards applied" under ADA Title I or the EEOC regulations issued pursuant to that title (29 C.F.R. part 1630)).

§ 4.12   SECTION 503: PROCEDURAL ISSUES

A.   PRIVATE RIGHT OF ACTION

The courts are virtually unanimous in their conclusion that no private right of action exists under Section 503, since Section 503 does not confer a right on the benefitted class of disabled persons, nor does it create a duty upon contractors. *Clemmer v. Enron Corp.*, 882 F.Supp. 606 (S.D.Tex. 1995). Rather, Section 503 simply creates a duty upon federal agencies to make and enforce contracts containing the required affirmative action language.

B.   THIRD PARTY BENEFICIARY ACTIONS

In several cases plaintiffs have attempted to circumvent the "no private right of action" rule by claiming that they had the right to sue federal contractors as third party beneficiaries of contracts between such contractors and the government.

Courts have generally rejected this claim. *See, e.g., Howard v. Uniroyal, Inc.*, 719 F.2d 1552 (11th Cir. 1983); *D'Amato v. Wisconsin Gas Co.*, 760 F.2d 1474 (7th Cir. 1985).

C.   SECTION 1983 ACTIONS

In a few cases plaintiffs have filed actions under Section 1983 to protest the deprivation of a right secured by Section 503. It has been held that a plaintiff may not circumvent the "no private right of action rule" by asserting a Section 501 claim via a Section 1983 action against a state agency.

D.   ACTIONS TO ENFORCE
CONCILIATION AGREEMENTS

At least one court has held that an employee with a disability who is named as a beneficiary of a conciliation agreement entered into between a federal contractor and the Department of Labor's Office of Federal Contract Compliance Programs (OFCCP) pursuant to a Section 503 investigation could assert a cause of action against the contractor for failure to abide by the terms of the agreement. In *McBee v. Mack Trucks, Inc.*, 655 F.Supp. 1459 (D.Md. 1987), the court noted that the plaintiff was not seeking to enforce the affirmative action clauses of the original government contract, but was seeking to enforce the conciliation agreement.

§ 4.13   SECTION 503: ADMINISTRATIVE PROCEDURES AND REMEDIES

Pursuant to the Section 503 regulations, 41 C.F.R. Part 60, the only recourse for a person with a disability against a government contractor under Section 503 is to file a written complaint with the OFCCP within 300 days of the purported violation. The OFCCP is required to investigate the complaint and attempt to resolve the matter. If the OFCCP finds that the contractor violated Section 503, the OFCCP shall invite the contractor to participate in conciliation discussions. If the contractor and the OFCCP reach a conciliation agreement, that agreement must be in writing and must specify the remedial action to be taken and dates for completion. The time period to remedy violations of the Act should be no longer than minimally necessary to make the changes. The term "conciliation agreement" does not include "letters of commitment," which are only appropriate for resolving minor technical differences.

If the OFCCP is not able to informally resolve the matter with the contractor through conciliation and persuasion, it may refer the matter for administrative or judicial action. If a formal administrative hearing is held, and a violation established, the OFCCP may order the contractor to comply with the Section 503 regulations and to take corrective action, such as offering employment to a complaining applicant and also awarding back pay. Other options available to the OFCCP upon establishing a violation are to file suit against the contractor in federal court, withhold payments due on existing federal contracts, terminate existing federal contracts with the contractor in whole or in part, and/or bar the contractor from receiving future federal contracts. If the OFCCP chooses to file suit in federal court, it may seek appropriate injunctive relief to ensure that the contractor fulfills its affirmative action requirements towards people with disabilities.

If no violation is found by the OFCCP, or if the Director of the OFCCP declines to initiate proceedings against the contractor, the complainant must be given notice of the OFCCP's conclusion. The complainant may request review of the OFCCP's findings or decision within 30 days. Courts have held that the OFCCP's decision not to take action against a contractor is immune from judicial review. *See, e.g., Andrews v. Consolidated Rail Corporation*, 831 F.2d 678 (7th Cir. 1987).

§ 4.14   SECTION 503: ACTIONS AGAINST THE OFCCP

At least one court has held that an individual with a disability may sue the Department of Labor under the Administrative Procedure Act (APA), 5 U.S.C.A. §§ 704, 706, to compel institution of Section 503 administrative enforcement proceedings against a federal contractor-employer. *Moon v. Secretary, United States Department of Labor*, 747 F.2d 599 (11th Cir. 1984). And in one case the court held that blind employees terminated from their positions could file suit under the federal

Mandamus Act, 28 U.S.C.A. § 1361, to compel the Secretary of Labor and the OFCCP to require their employer to rehire them or lose its federal contracts but must show that the defendants acted in an arbitrary and capricious manner. *Pace v. Donovan*, 35 F.E.P.Cas. (BNA) 255 (D.D.C. 1984). Another court, however, declined to follow the decision in *Moon* and said it was inconsistent with a subsequent Supreme Court decision. *Andrews v. Consolidated Rail Corporation*, 831 F.2d 678 (7th Cir. 1987).

§ 4.15   SECTION 503: AFFIRMATIVE ACTION PLANS

Although Section 503 requires contractors having government contracts of $10,000 or more to undertake "affirmative action" to employ and advance in employment people with disabilities, the OFCCP notes that non-discrimination and affirmative action are different concepts and that the term "affirmative action" as used in Section 503 does not require federal contractors to grant *preference* in the hiring process to people with disabilities. *See* 61 *Fed. Reg.* 19343 (May 1, 1996) (discussion of Subpart C of the OFCCP's regulations). The OFCCP views the "affirmative action" language in Section 503 as being analogous to the "equal opportunity" concept underlying the Americans with Disabilities Act, which requires the provision of reasonable accommodations to persons with disabilities.

The OFCCP's 1996 regulations, however, require larger contractors to have "affirmative action plans." 41 C.F.R. § 60–741.40 *et seq.* Each government contractor having 50 or more employees and a contract of $50,000 or more is required to prepare and maintain an affirmative action plan. The plan must be established within 120 days of commencement of a contract, must set forth the contractor's policies and procedures, must be reviewed and updated annually, and must be submitted to the OFCCP within 30 days of a request to do so (unless the OFCCP specifies otherwise), and must be available on-site upon OFCCP's request. The plan must be available to any employee or applicant upon request.

After making an offer to a job applicant, the contractor shall invite the applicant to self-identify as being covered by Section 503 and wishing to benefit from it. The contractor may invite self-identification *prior* to making a job offer only when: (1) the contractor is undertaking affirmative action for people with disabilities at the pre-offer stage; or (2) a federal or state law requires affirmative action for individuals with disabilities. The contractor must notify the individual that the information is being requested on a voluntary basis, that it will be kept confidential, and that it will not adversely affect the individual. If an individual declines to self-identify, that does not relieve the contractor from its affirmative action obligations under Section 503 with respect to an individual whom it knows to be disabled. 41 C.F.R. § 60–741.42

Under this affirmative action obligation, covered contractors must "take affirmative action to employ and advance in employment qualified individuals with disabilities at all levels of employment, including the executive level." *Id.* § 60–741.43

CHAPTER 5
EMPLOYMENT DISCRIMINATION

§ 5.1 INTRODUCTION AND OVERVIEW

Four major federal laws prohibit employment discrimination against persons with disabilities: Sections 501, 503 and 504 of the Rehabilitation Act (29 U.S.C.A. §§ 791, 793 and 794), and Title I of the Americans with Disabilities Act (42 U.S.C.A. §§ 12101–12117). The Rehabilitation Act prohibits federal agencies (§ 501), federal contractors having contracts of $10,000 or more with the federal government (§ 503), and recipients of federal financial assistance (§ 504) from discriminating on the basis of disability in any aspect of the employment setting. The Americans with Disabilities Act (ADA) prohibits private employers having 15 or more employees, and *all* state and local government entities (regardless of the number of employees), from discriminating on the basis of disability in any aspect of the employment setting.

While employers governed by Sections 503–504 and the ADA may not refuse to hire or promote an individual because of that individual's disability, such employers are *not* required to affirmatively seek to hire or promote disabled persons. Employers governed by Section 501 (federal agencies), however, must *affirmatively* seek to hire (and promote where appropriate) people with disabilities; under this section, preference toward people with disabilities *is* required.

Under the Rehabilitation Act Amendments of 1992, the standards used in employment actions brought under Sections 501, 503 and 504 are to be those found in ADA Title I. *See* 29 U.S.C.A. §§ 791(g), 793(d), 794(d). Thus, this chapter will discuss the requirements under all four laws simultaneously. It will then explain the remedies available under the four laws for employment discrimination, and the differences between the applicable remedies.

§ 5.2 ENTITIES SUBJECT TO THE ADA

The previous chapter of this *Nutshell* discussed the entities covered by Sections 501, 503 and 504 of the Rehabilitation Act. This section will describe the entities covered under the ADA's employment provisions. 42 U.S.C.A. §§ 12111–12117.

Title I of the ADA provides that "covered entities" may not discriminate against qualified individuals with disabilities with respect to any aspect of the employment setting. The statute defines "covered entity" to include employers, employment agencies, labor organizations or joint labor-management committees. This broad definition includes some exceptions. Religious organizations are not precluded under the Act from giving preference in hiring decisions to members of their own religion. Moreover, the Act provides that a religious entity "may require that all applicants and employees conform to the religious tenets . . . " of the entity. In addition, the term "employer" does not include the

United States or a private membership club that is exempt from ordinary tax rules.

When an employer controls a corporation whose place of incorporation is a foreign country, any discriminatory practice under the ADA engaged in by the corporation is presumed to be engaged in by the employer. Thus, American citizens working in foreign countries will be protected under Title I of the ADA if the employer is an American-owned or-controlled company. The ADA does not apply, however, with respect to the foreign operations of a foreign employer not controlled by an American employer, even if the employee is an American. 42 U.S.C.A. § 12112(c)(2).

Under the ADA, an "employee" is one who is employed by an employer. That term includes United States citizens employed in a foreign country. 42 U.S.C.A. § 12111(4). For foreign employment, however, an employer may take an action affecting an employee with a disability that would otherwise constitute discrimination under the ADA if compliance with the ADA would violate the foreign country's law. 42 U.S.C.A. § 12112(c)(1). The Equal Employment Opportunity Commission (EEOC) has published enforcement guidelines describing the extraterritorial application of ADA Title I. *Enforcement Guidance on Application of Title VII and the Americans with Disabilities Act to Conduct Overseas and to Foreign Employers Discriminating in the United States.* http://www. eeoc.gov/policy/docs/extraterritorial-vii-ada.html (Oct. 20, 1993).

For state and local government employers, Title II of the ADA, 42 U.S.C.A. §§ 12131–12132, prohibits *all* departments, agencies, special purpose districts or other instrumentalities of any state or local government from discriminating in any aspect of the employment setting. Basically, Title II obligates state and local government entities to comply with the mandates set forth in Title I of the ADA.

Title I also prohibits discrimination in employment against *associates* of people with disabilities as well as against people with actual or perceived disabilities. Thus, an employer may not discriminate against a nondisabled individual who lives with someone with AIDS, for example, or who has a disabled family member who the employer fears will cause the nondisabled applicant or employee to incur excessive absences from work.

Courts tend to use a four-part test to analyze claims of associational discrimination. Under that test, the plaintiff must show that (1) she was qualified for her job at the time of the adverse employment action; (2) she was subjected to an adverse employment action; (3) she was known by her employer at the time to have a relative or associate with a disability; and (4) the adverse employment action occurred under circumstances raising a reasonable inference that the disability of the relative or associate was a determining factor in the employer's decision. *Den Hartog v. Wasatch Academy,* 129 F.3d 1076, 1085 (10th Cir.1997). If the plaintiff meets such a burden, the court then applies the remainder of the *McDonnell Douglas* burden-shifting framework. *See, e.g., Walker v. Wal-Mart Stores,* 2014 WL 3940662 (N.D. Miss. 2013).

§ 5.3   FIFTEEN EMPLOYEE THRESHOLD

All employers having 15 or more employees (including part-time employees) are covered under Title I. The U.S. Supreme Court has held that the "payroll" method of counting employees applies in cases under Title VII of the Civil Rights Act of 1964. *EEOC v. Metropolitan Educational Enterprises, Inc.,* 519 U.S. 202 (1997). Similar reasoning will apply under ADA Title I, which is premised on Title VII and uses the same 15-employee threshold. 42 U.S.C.A. § 12111(5)(a). This method looks at the number of employees on the employer's payroll during a given week. The result of this approach is that all hourly and part-time employees count toward the jurisdictional minimum even though they are not present at work on each day of the workweek. If the number is at least 15 for 20 weeks, the 15-employee threshold is satisfied, regardless of whether every employee on the payroll actually works every day of those weeks.

In *Clackamas Gastroenterology Associates P.C. v. Wells,* 538 U.S. 440 (2003), the Supreme Court clarified the meaning of the word "employees" under ADA Title I. The question in the case was whether four physicians actively engaged in a medical practice as shareholders and directors of a professional corporation should be counted as "employees." The court of appeals had concluded that the physicians should be counted as employees and, when they were included in the count, the corporation was over the 15-employee threshold. The Supreme Court reversed and remanded, stating that, on remand, the court of appeals should apply the common law's definition of the master-servant relationship. Under this definition, it is highly unlikely that the physicians would be deemed "employees," and the corporation would, therefore, be under the 15-employee threshold.

Courts are split on the issue of whether ADA Title I's 15-employee threshold applies to entities covered under Section 504, which does not use the term "employer" but rather imposes liability upon programs or activities who receive federal assistance. Some courts have held that the ADA definition of "employer" is not applicable to the Rehabilitation Act based on the plain language of the statute and Congress's intent that Section 504 provide a broader prohibition than the ADA. *See, e.g., Schrader v. Ray*, 296 F.3d 968 (10th Cir. 2002). Other courts, however, have stated that the ADA's definition of "employer" also applies to the Rehabilitation Act. *See, e.g., Romand v. Zimmerman*, 881 F.Supp. 806 (N.D.N.Y. 1995).

With respect to employment, ADA Title II covers *all* state and local government entities, not just those having 15 or more employees. State and local government employers having fewer than 15 employees, while subject to Title II of the ADA, must follow regulations promulgated under Section 504 rather than the ADA Title I regulations. State and local government employers having in excess of

15 employees must comply with the ADA Title I regulations. The Rehabilitation Act Amendments of 1992, however, require Section 504 and the ADA to be interpreted in identical fashion with respect to employment,   29   U.S.C.A.   § 794(a),   so   this distinction should be irrelevant.

§ 5.4   FORMER EMPLOYEES

Courts are in dispute over the question of whether former employees are covered under ADA Title I when they sue to challenge limitations placed on post-employment fringe benefits. Some have held they are. *See, e.g. Ford v. Schering-Plough Corp.*, 145 F.3d 601 (3d Cir. 1998) (holding that a former employee who was no longer able to perform the functions of her former position due to her mental disorder could bring an action against the employer and its insurer carrier alleging that the disparity in disability benefits for mental and physical disabilities violated the ADA). Others, however, have held that a former employee who cannot perform the essential functions of the employment position with or without reasonable accommodations cannot be a qualified individual entitled to sue for employment discrimination under ADA Title I. *See, e.g., Weyer v. Twentieth Century Fox Film Corp.*, 198 F.3d 1104 (9th Cir. 2000).

The Supreme Court ruled in *Robinson v. Shell Oil Co.*, 519 U.S. 337 (1997) that the term "employees" as used in the anti-retaliation provision of Title VII of the Civil Rights Act of 1964 includes former employees. In an opinion that was later vacated, the

Eleventh Circuit ruled that the decision in *Robinson* applies to the ADA, finding that an ADA claim could be brought by a former employee challenging limitations on post-employment benefits. *Johnson v. K Mart Corp.*, 273 F.3d 1035 (11th Cir. 2001), rehearing en banc granted, opinion vacated, 273 F.3d 1070 (11th Cir. 2001). Although the vacated opinion holds no precedential value, it may signal the appropriate legal analysis of this issue.

§ 5.5   QUALIFIED INDIVIDUAL WITH A DISABILITY

Only a "qualified individual with a disability" is protected from discrimination under the federal laws. A "qualified individual with a disability" is generally defined as an individual with a disability who, with or without reasonable accommodation, can perform the essential functions of the position. The EEOC's ADA Title I regulations divide this inquiry into two parts: (1) whether the individual has the requisite skill, experience, education and other job-related requirements of the position sought, and (2) whether the individual, with or without reasonable accommodation, can perform the essential functions of that position. 29 C.F.R. § 1630.2(m). The term "other job-related requirements" is intended to recognize that other factors, in addition to skill, experience and education, may be relevant to determining whether an individual is qualified for a position.

A two-step procedure should be followed when determining whether an individual with a disability is qualified. The first step is to determine whether the individual satisfies the job prerequisites. The second step is to determine whether the individual can perform the essential functions of the job with or without reasonable accommodations. The determination as to whether the individual is qualified should be based on the individual's capabilities at the time of the employment decision, and should not be based on speculation about future inability to perform the job or fear that future health insurance premiums or workers' compensation costs may arise. This determination is to be made by the employer, relying on all relevant information, and not by medical personnel.

§ 5.6   INCONSISTENT STATEMENTS/WAIVERS

After the ADA was passed there was a split among the lower courts on the question of whether an individual who claims to be completely disabled (and therefore unable to work) for purposes of receiving Social Security or other disability benefits can be a qualified individual with a disability under Title I (which applies to people who can work without or without a reasonable accommodation). The Supreme Court resolved this issue in *Cleveland v. Policy Mgmt. Sys. Corp.*, 526 U.S. 795 (1999), holding that a plaintiff's statement in an application for Social Security benefits that she was "totally disabled" did not automatically bar her from bringing an ADA claim (which required that she prove she could perform essential functions of her job) if she could provide a "sufficient explanation" for the inconsistencies. The Court recognized that the Social Security Administration (SSA) does *not* take the possibility of "reasonable accommodation" into account when it determines whether an individual is disabled for Social Security Disability Insurance (SSDI) purposes. Where a plaintiff has stated in one forum that she is "totally disabled," she must provide an explanation "sufficient to warrant a reasonable juror's concluding that, assuming the truth of, or the plaintiff's good-faith belief in, the earlier statement, the plaintiff could nonetheless 'perform the essential functions' of her job, with or without 'reasonable accommodation.'"

Another issue that remains in dispute is an individual's ability to waive, such as in an employment contract, his or her right to file a claim under the federal discrimination laws. The Supreme Court has held that the Federal Arbitration Act (FAA) mandates enforcement of valid, written arbitration agreements. *Circuit City Stores v. Adams*, 532 U.S. 105 (2001). And several circuit courts have held that employment discrimination claims arising under Title VII may be referred to arbitration. *See, e.g., Tinder v. Pinkerton Security*, 305 F.3d 728 (7th Cir. 2002) (citing cases). The terms of such arbitration agreements, however, are still a fertile source of litigation, and courts have refused to enforce them when they limit an employee's statutory rights. *See, e.g., Ingle v. Circuit City Stores, Inc.*, 328 F.3d 1165 (9th Cir. 2003); *Morrison v. Circuit City Stores, Inc.*, 317 F.3d 646 (6th Cir. 2003). *See also Kirleis v. Dicie, McCamey & Chilcote, P.C.*, 560 F.3d 156 (3rd Cir. 2009) (denying law firm's motion to compel arbitration in a complaint filed by a shareholder/director at the law firm). *But see Musnick v. King Motor Co. of Fort Lauderdale*, 325 F.3d 1255 (11th Cir. 2003) (mere existence of a fee-shifting provision in an arbitration agreement providing for mandatory arbitration of employment discrimination claims did not automatically render the agreement unenforceable). For more on the enforceability of arbitration agreements, see § 11.12 of this *Nutshell*.

The Supreme Court has also had to determine whether an agreement between an employer and an employee to arbitrate employment-related disputes barred the Equal Employment Opportunity Commission (EEOC) from pursuing a claim on the employee's behalf for specific judicial relief, such as backpay, reinstatement, and damages. The Court concluded that the arbitration agreement did not preclude an EEOC enforcement action. *EEOC v. Waffle House, Inc.*, 534 U.S. 279 (2002).

§ 5.7   ESSENTIAL FUNCTIONS

The term "essential functions" means "job tasks that are fundamental and not marginal." 29 C.F.R. § 1630.2(n)(1). Suppose, for example, that a counselor at a juvenile hall has epilepsy and does not have a driver's license. Suppose, further, that in emergencies counselors are required to transport juveniles to the hospital or for court appearances. Although it would be necessary for *some* counselors to be able to drive, it would not be essential that *all* counselors be able to drive. Thus, possession of a driver's license would not constitute an essential function of a counselor's job, and it would violate the federal laws to fire or to refuse to hire the counselor with epilepsy based on his or her lack of a driver's license. *See, e.g., Milton v. Scrivner, Inc.*, 53 F.3d 1118 (10th Cir. 1995) ("The initial inquiry in determining whether a job requisite is essential is whether an employer actually requires all employees in the particular position to perform the allegedly essential function."); *Hawkins v. George F. Cram Co.*, 397 F.Supp.2d 1006 (S.D. Indiana 2005) (denying a motion for summary judgment to defendant employer in a case where a disabled employee alleged a loss of 29 percent hand function due to a work related accident).

Moreover, the term "essential functions" refers only to the tasks to be performed, and not to the manner in which those tasks are performed. Thus, for example, if the job requires some telephone use, the essential function is the ability to receive and provide information over the telephone lines. It is not essential that a person be able to hear via ordinary telephone receivers. Adaptive equipment, such as amplifiers or telephone devices for the deaf (TDDs) and relay services, as explained in chapter 11 of this *Nutshell*, may enable a person with impaired hearing to receive and provide information over telephone lines.

Consideration will be given to the employer's judgment as to what functions of a job are essential. Written job descriptions prepared before advertising or interviewing applicants for the job are to be considered as relevant evidence. Other factors to review when addressing the essential functions issue include: (1) the amount of time spent performing the function; (2) the consequences of not requiring one employee to perform the function; (3) the terms of an applicable collective bargaining agreement; and (4) the work experience of past and present people in that and similar jobs. 29 C.F.R. § 1630.2(n)(3). None of these factors is determinative of the issue, but all are relevant.

The essential functions requirement is not intended to provide a means by which applicants or employees (or courts) may second guess an employer's business judgment regarding production standards, nor does this requirement obligate employers to lower their employment standards. Thus, if an employer requires its typists to be able to type 75 words per minute, it will not be called upon to explain why a typing speed of 65 words per minute is inadequate. Of course, to be valid under the federal laws the production standards imposed by the employer must be actually *imposed* on employees and not just stated on paper. Moreover, an employer could not select a particular production level for the purpose of excluding individuals with disabilities from a job. And, to the extent that production standards exclude persons with disabilities, such standards would have to be job related and satisfy the business necessity test. 29 C.F.R. Pt. 1630, App. § 1630.2(n).

Further, the essential functions requirement does not limit an employer's ability to establish or alter the content, nature, or functions of a job. Once the employer does change the parameters of a job, however, it must define the essential functions of that job and provide reasonable accommodations where necessary.

The question of what functions are essential to a particular job is very complex and is fact specific. For example, many courts have held that regular, predictable attendance at the workplace is an essential function of most jobs. *See, e.g., Hypes v. First Commerce Corp.*, 134 F.3d 721 (5th Cir. 1998). In some cases, however, absenteeism does not render an employee unqualified for a job. It has been noted that "the necessary level of attendance and regularity is a question of degree depending on the circumstances of each position." *Vera v. Williams Hospitality Group, Inc.*, 73 F.Supp.2d 161 (D.Puerto Rico 1999). For example, one court held there where fact issues regarding whether a regular and predictable schedule was an essential function of a data entry clerk position and whether providing an employee with a flexible schedule was a reasonable accommodation. *Ward v. Massachusetts Health Research Institute, Inc.*, 209 F.3d 29 (1st Cir. 2000). In some situations it may constitute a reasonable accommodation to permit an employee to work scheduled part-time hours at the workplace or to work regular hours at home rather than in the workplace (in cases in which full time participation in the job site is not deemed an essential function). "Courts that have rejected working at home as a reasonable accommodation focus on evidence that personal contact, interaction, and coordination are needed for a specific position." *Kvorjak v. Maine*, 259 F.3d 48 (1st Cir. 2001) (quoting EEOC *Enforcement Guidance: Reasonable Accommodation and Undue Hardship Under the Americans with Disabilities Act* (March 1, 1999)).

Another permutation of the attendance issue is whether an employee should be permitted to telework as a reasonable accommodation. The Sixth Circuit recently vacated an opinion that had said that technology has advanced such that attendance at the workplace no longer is assumed to mean attendance at the employer's physical location. *See EEOC v. Ford Motor Co.*, 752 F.3d 634 (6th Cir. 2014), opinion vacated; rehearing en banc granted (August 29, 2014). By contrast, in the en banc opinion, the Sixth Circuit said: "with few exceptions, 'an employee who does not come to work cannot perform any of his job functions, essential or otherwise.'" EEOC v. Ford Motor Co., No. 12–2484 (6th Cir. April 10, 2015). It therefore found, as a matter of law, that the plaintiff's request for up to four days each week of telecommuting to perform her job as a resale buyer was unreasonable because of the strong evidence that her job required some face-to-face interactions. Those "few exceptions" would appear to be jobs with virtually no requirements of face-to-face interactions. In this case, the Sixth Circuit ruled (over a vigorous dissent) that there was not sufficient evidence to send to the jury the issue of whether this job could be performed with limited face-to-face interactions. Plaintiff was therefore not considered to be a qualified individual with a disability because she could not perform the essential functions of the job even with accommodations.

Rather than work from home, some employees request a flexible work schedule. In a case that proceeded under Section 501 of the Rehabilitation Act, Linda Solomon argued that the Department of Agriculture should have allowed her to have a flexible work schedule, which the Department called a "maxiflex" schedule, as an accommodation for her disability (depression). The district court judge ruled that a maxiflex work schedule is unreasonable as a matter of law. The D.C. Circuit reversed, finding that the question of whether an accommodation is reasonable is contextual and fact-specific. Further, the Court found that she had offered sufficient factual evidence that she was able to complete her work when given flexibility and that other nondisabled employees were allowed to work flexible schedules to survive summary judgment. *See Solomon v. Vilsack*, 763 F.3d 1 (D.C. Cir. 2014)

§ 5.8   SCOPE OF THE FEDERAL LAWS

The federal mandate against employment discrimination on the basis of disability applies to every aspect of the employment setting. Thus, Title I of the ADA defines the term "discriminate" in the context of employment actions as including: (1) limiting, segregating, or classifying job applicants or employees in a manner that adversely affects the status or opportunities of a disabled person; (2) participating in a contractual or other arrangement/relationship that has the effect of discriminating against a person with a disability; (3) utilizing administrative criteria or procedures that have the effect of discriminating on the basis of disability; (4) denying equal jobs or benefits to a disabled person; (5) failing to make reasonable accommodations to allow disabled persons to perform in the workplace; (6) using selection criteria, standards or tests that screen out or tend to screen out one or more individuals with a disability; (7) failing to select and administer employment tests in a manner that will reflect the factor the test purports to measure as opposed to an applicant's disability. 42 U.S.C.A. § 12112(b).

The EEOC's ADA Title I regulations provide that covered entities may not discriminate on the basis of disability with regard to:

(a) Recruitment, advertising, and job application procedures;

(b) Hiring, upgrading, promotion, award of tenure, demotion, transfer, layoff, termination, right of return from layoff, and rehiring;

(c) Rates of pay or any other form of compensation and changes in compensation;

(d) Job assignments, job classification, organizational structures, position descriptions, lines of progression, and seniority lists;

(e) Leaves of absence, sick leave, or any other leave;

(f) Fringe benefits available by virtue of employment, whether or not administered by the covered entity;

(g) Selection and financial support for training, including: apprenticeships, professional meetings, conferences, and other related activities, and selection for leave of absence to pursue training;

(h) Activities sponsored by a covered entity including social or recreational programs; and

(i) Any other term, condition, or privilege of employment.

29 C.F.R. § 1630.4.

§ 5.9   DISPARATE TREATMENT/DISPARATE IMPACT

The federal laws prohibit employment actions that have a discriminatory *effect* on disabled persons even when the employer has no *intent* to discriminate. Thus, the laws prohibit both disparate treatment of persons with disabilities and the implementation of policies that have a disparate impact.

The use of qualification standards, tests, or selection criteria that screen out or tend to screen individuals with disabilities are permissible, however, if shown to be job-related and consistent with business necessity, and performance of the required conduct cannot be accomplished with reasonable accommodation. 42 U.S.C.A.

§§ 12112(b)(6), 12113(a). Courts have held that the employer has the burden of proving that its discriminatory qualification standards satisfy the ADA's business necessity defense and stated "[t]he business necessity standard is quite high, and is not [to be] confused with mere expediency." *See, e.g., Conroy v. New York State Dept. of Correctional Services*, 333 F.3d 88 (2d Cir. 2003). *See also Cripe v. City of San Jose*, 261 F.3d 877, 890 (9th Cir. 2001) (using same language).

With respect to disparate treatment discrimination, the Civil Rights Act of 1991 provides that an unlawful employment practice is established under Title VII (and thus ADA Title I, which follows Title VII rules) when the plaintiff proves that a discriminatory reason was "a motivating factor" for the practice, "even though other factors also motivated the practice." 42 U.S.C.A. § 2000e–2(m). Thus, disability is not permitted to play any part in the decision making process under Title I. That Act further provides, however, that when more than one motivating factor for the alleged discriminatory practice is established, the employer is allowed to prove that it would have taken the same action even without the impermissible motivating factor. If the employer does so, the court may grant declaratory or injunctive relief and attorneys' fees and costs directly attributable to pursuit of the claim but may *not* "award damages or issue an order requiring any admission, reinstatement, hiring, promotion, or payment." 42 U.S.C.A. § 2000e–5(g)(2)(A). This rule will also apply under ADA Title I. The Supreme Court has held that direct evidence of discrimination is not required in order to prove employment discrimination in mixed-motive cases under Title VII; the statute imposes no special or heightened evidentiary burden on a plaintiff in a mixed-motive case. *Desert Palace, Inc. v. Costa*, 539 U.S. 90 (2003).

§ 5.10   REASONABLE ACCOMMODATIONS

Employers governed by the ADA and the Rehabilitation Act must make "reasonable accommodations" for "otherwise qualified" individuals with disabilities.

The term "reasonable accommodation" is generally defined as: (1) a modification or adjustments to the job application process, to the work environment, or to the manner or circumstances under which the job is performed, or (2) a modification or adjustment that allows a disabled employee to enjoy the same benefits and privileges enjoyed by non-disabled employees, as long as such modification or adjustment does not impose an undue hardship on the employer's business. 29 C.F.R. § 1630.2(*o*).

Employers are only required to accommodate individuals who make their disabilities *known* to their employers and let their employers know that some accommodation is required. Moreover, if an employee requests an accommodation, the employer may request documentation of the employee's disability if the disability is not obvious.

Suggested "reasonable accommodations" under the federal laws include (but are not limited to): (1) making existing facilities readily accessible to and usable by people with disabilities (including both work areas and non-work areas, such as lunch-rooms, restrooms and training rooms); (2) job restructuring (by reallocating or redistributing non-essential job functions); (3) development of part-time or modified work schedules; (4) reassignment to a vacant position (when accommodation within an employee's current job cannot satisfactorily be made); (5) acquisition or modification of equipment or devices; (6) modification or adjustment of examinations, training materials or policies; and (7) the provision of auxiliary aids such as qualified readers or interpreters for blind or deaf employees. 29 C.F.R., Pt. 1630, App. § 1630.2(*o*)(2).

This list of suggested accommodations is not exhaustive, nor would all of the suggested accommodations be "reasonable" in every situation. What constitutes an appropriate accommodation in a given case must be determined by utilizing a fact based case-by-case approach, considering all relevant factors. The reasonable accommodation mandate does not require an employer to provide personal items for an employee's use, such as eyeglasses, wheelchairs or prosthetic limbs, unless such items are specifically designed or required to meet job-related rather than personal needs. 29 C.F.R. Pt. 1630, App. § 1630.9.

An employer need not create a new job—such as a "light duty" job—for an employee who becomes disabled, unless the "heavy duty" tasks the employee can no longer perform are marginal job functions that can be allocated to co-workers. The EEOC's *Technical Assistance Manual* provides specific guidance on light-duty jobs: "[I]f an employer already has a vacant light duty position for which an injured worker is qualified, it might be a reasonable accommodation to reassign the worker to that position. If the position was created as a temporary job, a reassignment to that position need only be for a temporary period." EEOC, *A Technical Assistance Manual on the Employment Provisions (Title I) of the Americans with Disabilities Act* § 9.4. Courts have held that the temporary and limited nature of a light-duty program does not violate the ADA. *See, e.g., Hendricks-Robinson v. Excel Corp.*, 154 F.3d 685 (7th Cir. 1998). *See also Thompson v. E.I. DuPont deNemours & Co.*, 2003 WL 21771959, 70 Fed.Appx. 332 (6th Cir. 2003) (holding the defendant was not liable for not placing a disabled worked in a temporary position due to the fact that doing so would effectively transform a temporary position into a permanent position).

An employer has no obligation toward individuals who are currently using illegal drugs, regardless of whether such individuals are addicts or casual users of drugs, and regardless of whether the illegal drug use impacts upon the individuals' behavior or job performance. Such individuals are not protected under the federal laws. Employers do have obligations toward employees who are rehabilitated drug abusers—or those undergoing rehabilitation— and to both rehabilitated and *current* alcoholics, as long as the employee is able to perform the duties of the job and does not constitute a threat to the health or safety of persons or property. The ADA's coverage of alcoholics and drug users is discussed in more detail in Section 3.5 of this *Nutshell*.

The extent of an employer's obligation to provide reasonable accommodations for rehabilitated drug abusers (or those undergoing rehabilitation) and alcoholics whose job performance is not impaired remains unclear. The EEOC has noted that reasonable accommodations, such as modified work schedules to permit an employee to attend an ongoing self-help program, may be required in appropriate circumstances. The EEOC has also stated, however, that the ADA "does not *require* an employer to provide an opportunity for rehabilitation in place of discipline or discharge" to employees who abuse drugs or alcohol. EEOC, *A Technical Assistance Manual on the Employment Provisions (Title I) of the Americans with Disabilities Act* § 8.7 (emphasis in original). Again, each case will require individual consideration.

Employers may always terminate employees for misconduct, and most courts hold that this is so even if the misconduct at issue is related to an employee's disability, such as alcoholism.

Prior to the enactment of the ADA and the Rehabilitation Act Amendments of 1992, numerous courts held that, due to the affirmative action requirement under Section 501, federal employers have a greater obligation to accommodate employees under Section 501 than do employers governed by

Section 504. Whether the same precept applies in light of the mandate in the Rehabilitation Act Amendments of 1992 that all four laws be interpreted in the same manner with respect to employment discrimination remains unclear, but some courts have stated that heightened responsibility under Section 501 continues after the Amendments. *See, e.g., Woodman v. Runyon*, 132 F.3d 1330 (10th Cir. 1997).

When a qualified individual with a disability asks for a reasonable accommodation, the employer should initiate an informal, interactive process with the individual. 29 C.F.R. § 1630.2(*o*)(3). In this interactive process, the employer should use a problem-solving approach to analyze the job, determine its essential functions, consult with the person with a disability regarding the limitations imposed by the disability and possible accommodations to overcome those limitations, consider the preferences of the individual with the disability, and select and implement the most appropriate accommodation. If consultation with the individual with a disability does not uncover potential appropriate accommodations, the employer should seek technical assistance from the EEOC, from state or local rehabilitation agencies, or from disability constituent organizations. Failure to obtain technical assistance, however, will not relieve the employer from the obligation to provide reasonable accommodations. 29 C.F.R. Pt. 1630, App. § 1630.9.

Ultimately, after following this problem-solving approach, the employer has the discretion to choose the accommodation to be provided, and may choose the less expensive accommodation or the accommodation that is easier to provide, so long as the accommodation provided is effective. *Id.* Title I does not provide a time frame in which an employer must provide an accommodation, and courts have considered the following factors in determining if a delay in providing one violates the ADA: the length of the delay, the reasons for the delay, whether the employer has offered any alternative accommodations while evaluating a particular request, and whether the employer has acted in good faith. *See, e.g., Selenke v. Medical Imaging of Colorado*, 248 F.3d 1249 (10th Cir. 2001). Further, since Title I contemplates an interactive process between employers and employees, *both* have responsibilities in this regard. Thus, it has been held that employees who fail to fulfil their responsibilities in this process cannot prevail in an action under Title I.

A person with a disability may, of course, refuse to accept a proffered accommodation. But the result of such refusal may be that the applicant or employee with a disability is not qualified for the position at issue.

The 2008 Amendments make clear that individuals who qualify for ADA coverage by virtue of being "regarded as" disabled do *not* receive reasonable accommodation protection. *See* 42 U.S.C. § 12201(h).

§ 5.11 UNDUE HARDSHIP

An accommodation is *not* reasonable if it would impose an "undue hardship" on the employer's business. The term "undue hardship" is defined as "an action requiring significant difficulty or expense." 42 U.S.C.A. § 12111(10)(A). Factors to be considered when determining in each individual case whether an accommodation would constitute an undue hardship include the nature and cost of the accommodation at issue; the overall financial resources, size and impact of the accommodation on the facility involved and any applicable parent entity; the type of operation involved; and the impact of the accommodation upon the operation of the facility, including the impact on the ability of the facility to conduct business and the ability of other employees to perform their jobs. *Id.* § 12111(10)(B). The circuit courts disagree on whether the burdens of production and persuasion on the issues of reasonable accommodation and undue burden are properly placed on the plaintiff or the defendant, or are divided between them. *See, e.g., Reed v. LePage Bakeries, Inc.*, 244 F.3d 254 (1st Cir. 2001) (explaining the various approaches).

Only the employer's *net* costs are to be considered when determining whether providing an accommodation is reasonable (*i.e.*, whether the undue hardship test is satisfied). Government and other benefits, such as tax credits and rehabilitation agency grants, must be subtracted before the employer's costs are calculated. Further, an employer must pay for that portion of an accommodation that would not cause an undue hardship if other funding sources are available to pay for the remainder. If no such funding is available, the individual with a disability requesting the accommodation should be given the option of providing the accommodation on her own or of paying that portion of the cost which constitutes the undue hardship on the operation of the business. 29 C.F.R. Pt. 1630, App. § 1630.2(p).

The cost for an employer must be more than *de minimus* before the undue hardship test will be satisfied. Further, when enacting the ADA Congress refused to apply a presumption that any accommodation that cost more than ten percent of a disabled individual's salary would constitute an undue hardship. Each case must be decided on an individual basis.

With respect to the impact on other employees, the undue hardship test will not be satisfied if the disruption to them results from fears or prejudices toward the individual's disability and not from the provision of the accommodation. Nor is there an undue hardship if the accommodation negatively impacts on the morale of other employees but does not affect those employees' abilities to perform their jobs. 29 C.F.R. Pt. 1630, App. § 1630.15(d).

§ 5.12   COLLECTIVE BARGAINING AGREEMENTS

Courts interpreting Section 501 have consistently held that an accommodation was not reasonable if it would contravene the terms of an otherwise applicable collective bargaining agreement (CBA). In enacting the ADA, however, Congress stated that a CBA will not necessarily serve as a defense to an employer who fails to accommodate an employee with a disability. The House Report to the ADA notes, for example, that "if a collective bargaining agreement reserves certain jobs for employees with a given amount of seniority, it may be considered as a factor in determining whether it is a reasonable accommodation to assign an employee with a disability without seniority to that job. However, the agreement would not be determinative on the issue." H.R. Rep. 101–485, part 2, 101st Cong., 2d Sess. 63 (1990). That report further notes that if the CBA lists job duties, such a list may be taken into account in determining whether a given task is an essential function of the job. "Again, however, the agreement would not be determinative on the issue." *Id.*

The EEOC's ADA Title I regulations list the terms of an applicable CBA as just one of many factors to be considered when determining whether the undue hardship test is satisfied. Pursuant to the 1992 requirement that the ADA and the Rehabilitation Act be interpreted in the same manner with respect to employment discrimination, the Section 501 caselaw on this subject should be outmoded. Nevertheless, there remains controversy over the questions of: (i) whether an employee who is a member of a union must pursue grievance procedures under an applicable CBA before filing a claim under Title I; (ii) the extent to which the National Labor Relations Act requires employers to bargain with the union when selecting reasonable accommodations for employees with disabilities, and (iii) whether an employer can unilaterally (without union approval) provide a reasonable accommodation for an individual with a disability that contravenes an applicable CBA. For a discussion of the first of these issues, see the section on alternative dispute resolution in Section 11.12 of this *Nutshell*.

On the third issue, unilaterally providing a reasonable accommodation which goes against a CBA, the Seventh Circuit held in *Winfrey v. City of Chicago*, 259 F.3d 610 (7th Cir. 2001) that "[c]omplying with the collective bargaining agreement is a legitimate, nondiscriminatory policy, and the City was not required to abandon it in order to accommodate Winfrey's disability." In *Cripe v. City of San Jose*, 261 F.3d 877 (9th Cir. 2001), however, the court held that modifying the non-seniority requirements of a CBA in order to permit disabled police officers to compete for specialized assignments would not impose an undue hardship on the city and the difficulties of doing so did not support the city's business necessity defense to an ADA claim; permitting the disabled officers to compete would not give them a benefit denied to able-bodied officers.

The Supreme Court's decision in *US Airways, Inc. v. Barnett*, 535 U.S. 391 (2002), as discussed in Section 5.13, provides further guidance on this issue. Although this case did not involve a collective bargaining agreement, the Court held that ordinarily the ADA does not require reassignment of an employee with a disability to a position in contravention of an established seniority system. A collective bargaining agreement is the typical manner in which a seniority agreement becomes "established."

A union may be liable under the ADA for failing to take an employee's grievance against an employer under a CBA if the union breached its duty of fair representation. *See, e.g., Wood v. Crown Redi-Mix, Inc.*, 218 F.Supp.2d 1094 (S.D.Iowa 2002).

§ 5.13   SENIORITY SYSTEMS

The lower courts have unanimously found that *collectively bargained* seniority systems trump conflicting reasonable accommodation requests in the context of the Rehabilitation Act. *See Eckles v. Consolidated Rail Corp.*, 94 F.3d 1041 (7th Cir. 1996) (collecting cases). Several Circuits have reached a similar conclusion in the context of seniority and the ADA. *See, e.g., Smith v. Midland Brake, Inc.*, 180 F.3d 1154 (10th Cir. 1999); *Feliciano v. Rhode Island*, 160 F.3d 780 (1st Cir. 1998). In *US Airways, Inc. v. Barnett*, 535 U.S. 391 (2002) the Court examined a system *unilaterally imposed* by management. It held that a seniority system will prevail over a disabled employee's reasonable accommodation request "in the run of cases." More specifically:

The statute does not require proof on a case-by-case basis that a seniority system should prevail. That is because it would not be reasonable in the run of cases that the assignment in question trump the rules of a seniority system. To the contrary, it will ordinarily be unreasonable for the assignment to prevail.

Nonetheless, the Court held that a disabled employee could "show that special circumstances warrant a finding that, despite the presence of a seniority system (which the ADA may not trump in the run of cases), the requested 'accommodation' is 'reasonable' on the particular facts." For example, the plaintiff might show that an employer which created a *unilaterally-imposed* seniority system (as opposed to one created through a CBA) exercised the right to change it fairly frequently, "reducing employee expectations that the system will be followed—to the point where one more departure, needed to accommodate an individual with a disability, will not likely make a difference." Or, "[t]he plaintiff might show that the system already contains exceptions such that, in the circumstances, one further exception is unlikely to matter." *See also Dilley v. SuperValu, Inc.,* 296 F.3d 958 (10th Cir. 2002) (holding that allowing an employee with a 60-pound lifting restriction for back problems to return to a truck driver position with no lifting requirements was a "reasonable accommodation" under the ADA despite the fact that driving positions were subject to a seniority system under the union's collective bargaining agreement with the employer; any potential violation of agreement was speculative and remote because the employee ranked fifth out of 42 drivers in seniority).

§ 5.14 SAFETY DEFENSE

The federal laws recognize a "safety" defense for employers. For example, the ADA expressly provides that an individual with a disability is not qualified for a job if he or she poses a direct threat to the health or safety *of other individuals* in the workplace. 42 U.S.C.A. § 12113(b) (emphasis added). The term "direct threat" is defined as "a significant risk to the health or safety *of others* that cannot be eliminated by reasonable accommodation." 42 U.S.C.A. § 12111(3) (emphasis added).

Despite the statutory language which speaks only of a risk to "others," the EEOC regulation defines a direct threat as "a significant risk of substantial harm to the health or safety *of the individual or others* that cannot be eliminated or reduced by reasonable accommodation," and states that "[a]n employer may require, as a qualification standard, that an individual not pose a direct threat to the health or safety of *himself/herself or others*." 29 C.F.R. § 1630.2(r) (emphasis added). In *Chevron U.S.A. Inc. v. Echazabal*, 536 U.S. 73 (2002), the Court rejected an argument that the EEOC regulation impermissibly included the "threat to self" within the direct threat defense: "The EEOC was certainly acting within the reasonable zone when it saw a difference between rejecting workplace paternalism and ignoring specific and documented risks to the employee himself, even if the employee would take his chances for the sake of getting a job."

A determination that an individual with a disability poses a direct health or safety threat must be made on a case-by-case basis, through consideration of four basic factors: (1) the duration of the risk; (2) the nature and severity of the potential harm; (3) the likelihood that the potential harm will occur; and (4) the imminence of the potential harm. These factors were enumerated by the Supreme Court in *School Board of Nassau County v. Arline*, 480 U.S. 273 (1987) and subsequently adopted in the ADA and other regulations. *See, e.g.*, 29 C.F.R. § 1630.2(r).

This individualized inquiry must be based on the behavior of the particular person with a disability at issue, and not on generalizations about the disability. The safety defense is not satisfied because a particular disability may pose a statistically significant risk of harm. Thus, for example, it has been held that blanket rules prohibiting individuals with insulin-dependent diabetes from holding some jobs violate the federal laws. *See, e.g., Millage v. City of Sioux City*, 258 F.Supp.2d 976 (N.D.Iowa 2003).

Courts are divided on who bears the burden on showing a direct threat. Some have said that, because it is an affirmative defense, the employer bears the burden of proving that an employee constitutes a direct threat. *See, e.g. Nunes v. Wal-Mart Stores, Inc.*, 164 F.3d 1243 (9th Cir. 1999); *EEOC v. AIC Sec. Investigations, Ltd.*, 55 F.3d 1276 (7th Cir. 1995). Other courts, however, have placed the burden on the plaintiff to show that she does not pose risks to others as part of demonstrating her qualification for employment. *See, e.g., EEOC v. Amego, Inc.*, 110 F.3d 135 (1st Cir. 1997); *Moses v. American Nonwovens, Inc.*, 97 F.3d 446 (11th Cir. 1996); *Stafne v. Unicare Homes, Inc.*, 1999 WL 1212656 (D. Minn. 1999).

The ADA requires the Secretary of the Department of Health and Human Services (DHHS) to review all infectious and communicable diseases which may be transmitted through the handling of food and to publish an annual list of such diseases. If an individual has an infectious or communicable disease that can be transmitted through the handling of food—*as included on the DHHS list*—and the risk of transmission cannot be eliminated by the provision of reasonable accommodation, an employer may refuse to assign or continue to assign such individual to a job involving the handling of food. AIDS is not included on that list. See 74 Fed. Reg. 61152 (Nov. 23, 2009). The list has not been modified since September 26, 2006.

§ 5.15   EMPLOYMENT TESTS AND CRITERIA

To ensure that misconceptions do not bias the employee merit selection process, the federal laws prohibit employers from utilizing employment tests or criteria that tend to screen out disabled people unless such criteria are shown to be job-related and consistent with business necessity. Selection criteria that exclude disabled people and do not concern an essential function of the job are *not* consistent with business necessity. Moreover, even selection criteria that *are* consistent with business necessity, in that they *are* related to an essential job function, may not be used to exclude a disabled person if that person could satisfy the criteria with the provision of reasonable accommodations. 42 U.S.C.A. § 12112(b)(6); 29 C.F.R. Pt. 1630, App. § 1630.10.

Employers must select and administer employment tests in a manner that will ensure that such tests accurately reflect the skill or aptitude of the applicant or employee, rather than reflecting any impaired sensory, manual or speaking skills of the applicant or employee. When an applicant or employee has a disability that is *known* to the employer, the employer, where necessary, must provide reasonable accommodations for the test-taker; alternatively, the employer could choose to waive an employment test, or a portion of such test, in lieu of providing an accommodation. Where it is not possible to test in an alternative format, the employer may be required to evaluate the applicant or employee in another manner (such as via licensing or work experience requirements). If an applicant or employee does not realize that an accommodation is required and thus does not request accommodation, retesting should be performed upon request unless to do so would constitute an undue hardship to the employer. 42 U.S.C.A. § 12112(b)(7); 29 C.F.R. Pt. 1630, App. § 1630.11.

Reasonable accommodations in the testing context might include providing a test in an alternative format (such as substituting an oral test for a written test for a visually-impaired or dyslexic individual or substituting a written test for an oral test for a hearing-impaired individual); ensuring accessibility to testing sites; providing readers or interpreters for individuals with vision or hearing-impairments; allowing additional time to complete a test; simplifying test language for disabled people with limited language skills; scheduling rest breaks; and allowing a test-taker—with a disability that prevents accurate performance when there are distractions—to take a test in a separate room.

An employer may ask on a test announcement or application form that individuals who require accommodation inform the employer within a reasonable established time prior to the test. Moreover, the employer may request documentation of the need for an accommodation. 29 C.F.R. Pt. 1630, App. § 1630.14(a).

These rules do not apply, however, when employment tests are actually intended to measure the sensory, manual or speaking skill at issue. Thus, for example, if an employment test is designed to measure the ability to read, an individual with dyslexia may be required to take the written test; if speed is being tested, no extra time may be provided to the test-taker. 29 C.F.R. Pt. 1630, App. § 1630.11. Further, an employer is not required to lower job qualification standards as a reasonable accommodation, when such standards are related to essential job functions and are actually imposed on employees.

In no event may test results be utilized to exclude an applicant or employee unless the skill measured is necessary to perform an essential function of the job and no reasonable accommodation is possible to allow the individual to perform that function. *Id.*

DOJ has promulgated regulations under ADA Title III, 42 U.S.C. § 12189, to enforce the requirement that entities offer various examinations "in a place and manner accessible to persons with disabilities or offer alternative accessible arrangements for such individuals." Although these rules do not typically apply to employment applications, they may offer guidance for considering the appropriateness of such examinations. *See* 28 C.F.R. § 36.309.

The 2008 Amendments added a special rule for the situation in which an employer requires an individual to take a test based on the individual's *uncorrected* vision. Section 12113(c) states that a covered entity "shall not use qualification standards, employment tests, or other selection criteria based on an individual's uncorrected vision unless the standard, test, or other selection criteria, as used by the covered entity, is shown to be job-related for the position in question and consistent with business necessity." In other words, the job-related and business necessity standard applies in that context without the individual demonstrating that the selection criteria screens out individuals with disabilities.

§ 5.16   MEDICAL EXAMINATIONS AND INQUIRIES

A.   PRE-EMPLOYMENT

The premise of the federal laws is that employment decisions should be made based on *ability*, not *dis*ability. To further this concept, employers may not conduct pre-employment medical examinations of an applicant or make inquiries of a job applicant or employee regarding whether such individual has a disability. 42 U.S.C.A. § 12112(d). Thus, an employer may not inquire about an applicant's workers' compensation history, general health, past medical history, or the like. Similarly, employers should inform credit bureaus and other investigative agencies they use to delete references about an applicant that refer to medical problems.

Employers *may*, however, make pre-employment inquiries into the ability of an applicant to perform job-related functions, regardless of whether such job functions are essential or non-essential. As previously explained, however, an employer may *not* refuse to hire an applicant due to the applicant's inability to perform non-essential job functions.

An employer may ask *all* applicants (but not just *one* applicant) to explain or demonstrate how, with or without reasonable accommodations, they will be able to perform essential job functions. Even when all applicants are not asked to do so, however, an applicant with a disability that is *known* to the employer, and that might interfere with performance of job functions, may be asked to describe how he or she will perform the job with or without accommodation. In the latter case, however, the employer may not ask the applicant about the nature of the known disability.

The issue of what pre-employment medical examinations and inquiries are appropriate under the federal laws is enormously complex. To assist employers in following the purpose and spirit of the laws, the EEOC issued an Enforcement Guidance with respect to pre-employment medical examinations and inquiries under ADA Title I. EEOC Notice No. 915.002, October 10, 1995, *Enforcement Guidance on Preemployment Disability-Related Inquiries and Medical Examinations Under the ADA.* http://www.eeoc.gov/policy/docs/preemp.html. Although this guidance is somewhat dated, it is still the position of the EEOC.

B. POST-OFFER

An employer may require an employee with a disability to submit to a medical examination *after* he or she has been hired, and may condition a bona fide offer of employment on the results of such a medical examination when *all* entering employees in that category, regardless of disability, are subjected to such an examination. Information about the medical history or condition of the applicant or employee must be kept in separate medical files and treated as confidential, and may only be divulged in the following circumstances:

(i) supervisors and managers may be informed regarding necessary restrictions on the work or duties of the employee and necessary accommodations;

(ii) first aid and safety personnel may be informed, when appropriate, if the disability might require emergency treatment; and

(iii) government officials requesting compliance with [the federal laws] shall be provided relevant information on request.

42 U.S.C.A. § 12112(d)(3)(B). Further, the results of such examinations may not be used for any purpose inconsistent with the federal laws.

According to the EEOC, post-offer medical examinations made before an individual begins work need not focus on the individual's ability to perform the functions of a job or themselves satisfy the job-related or business necessity tests. However, the results of such examinations may not be used for any purpose inconsistent with the federal laws. If a post-offer, pre-work medical examination serves as the basis for withdrawing a conditional job offer, the employer must be able to show that: (1) the reasons for the withdrawal are job-related and consistent with business necessity, or that the rejected individual poses a direct threat to health or safety under the safety defense, and (2) no reasonable accommodation would allow the rejected individual to perform the essential functions of the job without a significant health or safety risk. 29 C.F.R. Pt. 1630, App. § 1630.14(b).

C.   POST-EMPLOYMENT

Medical examinations and inquiries may be conducted after employees have begun working if such examinations and inquiries are job related and consistent with business necessity. In all cases, however, the same restrictions noted above with respect to post-offer medical examinations and inquiries apply. This provision allows an employer, among other things, to make inquiries or require medical examinations necessary to determine what reasonable accommodations are required and may be provided to a disabled employee. 29 C.F.R. Pt. 1630, App. § 1630.14(c).

The employer may obtain voluntary medical examinations and medical histories as part of an employee health program available to employees at the worksite. Again, however, the same restrictions noted when discussing post-offer medical examinations and inquiries apply. 42 U.S.C.A. § 12112(d)(4)(B), (C).

D.   SPECIFIC ISSUES IN TESTING

Testing for illegal drugs is specifically exempted from the definition of a medical examination under the ADA. 42 U.S.C.A. § 12114(D)(1). Congress intended, however, "that the application of this provision should not conflict with the right of individuals who take drugs under medical supervision not to disclose their medical condition before a conditional offer of employment has been given." H.R. Rep. No. 101–485, part 2, *supra*. Thus, the House Report notes that pre-offer drug testing should be limited to testing for *illegal* drugs. *Id.* at 80. Pre-offer drug testing that would identify prescription drugs taken for a disability is prohibited. Because tests for illegal drugs often detect the presence of legal drugs, employers may avoid difficulties by giving drug tests after a conditional offer of employment is made.

Title I does not specifically exclude tests for alcohol from its "medical examination" definition. The EEOC has opined that certain alcohol tests might be medical tests. Thus, tests for alcohol may *not* be given prior to a conditional offer of employment. EEOC, *Enforcement Guidance: Preemployment Disability-Related Questions and Medical Examinations* (October 10, 1995).

According to the EEOC, physical agility tests are not medical tests, and thus may be given at any point in the application process. If a physical agility test screens out or tends to screen out individuals with disabilities, however, the test must be job-related and consistent with business necessity, and it must be shown that performance of the job by a disabled individual cannot be achieved with reasonable accommodation. 29 C.F.R. Pt. 1630, App. § 1630.14(a).

Whether psychological tests constitute medical tests is more problematic. If the tests are performed by medical doctors and are intended to measure mental stability, for example, they will presumably constitute medical tests which cannot be given until after a conditional job offer is made. If the tests are not performed by medical doctors, however, and are intended to measure aptitude as opposed to mental stability, arguably they should not be considered medical exams, and thus could be given before a conditional job offer is made. The EEOC has opined that psychological tests that simply concern an individual's skills or tastes are not medical tests. EEOC, *Enforcement Guidance: Preemployment Disability-Related Questions and Medical Examinations* (October 10, 1995).

The EEOC takes the position that polygraph examinations are not medical examinations, but that specific inquiries made before and during such examinations constitute prohibited pre-offer inquiries. The EEOC also opines that vision tests may or may not constitute medical examinations, depending upon the type of test and the circumstances under which the test is given. *Id.*

§ 5.17   PROVIDING A HARASSMENT-FREE ENVIRONMENT

The ADA provides that:

It shall be unlawful to coerce, intimidate, threaten, or interfere with any individual in the exercise or enjoyment of, or on account of his or her having exercised or enjoyed, or on account of his or her having aided or encouraged any other individual in the exercise or enjoyment of, any right granted or protected by [the ADA].

42 U.S.C.A. § 12203(b). This proviso will require an employer to provide a harassment-free environment for disabled employees. For example, an employer

would be responsible for prohibiting non-disabled employees on its work force from harassing disabled employees. In accord with the Rehabilitation Act Amendments of 1992, the same principle should apply under Sections 501, 503 and 504 of the Rehabilitation Act. Unlike a plaintiff in an ADA *discrimination* case, an employee need not show that she suffers from an actual disability to establish an ADA *retaliation* claim. Instead, a reasonable, good faith belief that the ADA has been violated suffices. *See, e.g., Selenke v. Medical Imaging of Colorado*, 248 F.3d 1249 (10th Cir. 2001); *Tabatchnik v. Continental Airlines*, 2008 WL 248595, 262 Fed.Appx. 674 (5th Cir. 2008). An employee may also sue under this section if he claims the employer terminated him in retaliation for a relative's actions. *Fogleman v. Mercy Hosp., Inc.*, 283 F.3d 561 (3d Cir. 2002).

§ 5.18   ENFORCEMENT OF ADA TITLE I

The EEOC is responsible for overseeing the employment discrimination provisions of the ADA. Title I of the ADA provides that the powers, remedies and procedures set forth in Title VII of the Civil Rights Act are available to the EEOC, to the Attorney General, and to "any person alleging discrimination" in violation of the employment provisions of the ADA or regulations promulgated thereunder. Thus, the Act contemplates both governmental and individual enforcement of the employment provisions. Before an individual may take judicial action against a covered entity under this section, however, administrative remedies must be pursued, just as they must be pursued under Title VII.

Final rules to coordinate the investigation and enforcement of employment discrimination complaints brought under the ADA and Section 503 were promulgated jointly by the Department of Justice (DOJ) and Department of Labor (DOL). 29 C.F.R. Pt. 1641 and 41 C.F.R. Pt. 60–742. The EEOC and DOJ have also issued regulations to coordinate the investigation and enforcement of employment discrimination complaints brought under the ADA and Section 504. 29 C.F.R. Pt. 1640 and 28 C.F.R. Pt. 37.

The EEOC is obligated to work in conjunction with the Offices of Civil Rights of all federal agencies which have enforcement authority under the Rehabilitation Act (primarily Section 504). This coordination is to ensure that administrative complaints filed under both Acts are dealt with so as to avoid duplication of effort and to prevent the imposition of inconsistent or conflicting standards for the same requirements under the two Acts.

An individual may file both a state workers' compensation claim and a charge under the ADA. "Exclusivity" clauses in state workers' compensation laws do not bar actions under the ADA. *See, e.g., Wood v. County of Alameda*, 875 F.Supp. 659 (N.D.Cal. 1995).

The Supreme Court has held that state and federal courts have concurrent jurisdiction over matters arising under Title VII. Since the ADA's

Title I enforcement provisions follow those under Title VII, this same rule should apply under ADA Title I.

Some courts have held that the individual, case-by-case analysis required by the ADA precludes the certification of class actions under Title I. *See, e.g., Davoll v. Webb,* 160 F.R.D. 142 (D.Colo. 1995), affirmed 194 F.3d 1116 (10th Cir. 1999); *Hohider v. UPS,* 574 F.3d 169 (3rd Cir. 2009). In other cases, however, courts have allowed class certification under Title I. *See, e.g., Hendricks-Robinson v. Excel Corp.,* 164 F.R.D. 667 (C.D.Ill. 1996). These courts have generally permitted some discovery before making the decision to certify a class and emphasized their discretion to tailor the scope of the class and the issues. *Delise v. Federal Express Corp.,* 2001 WL 321081 (N.D.Ill. 2001).

§ 5.19   REMEDIES FOR EMPLOYMENT DISCRIMINATION

Although the Rehabilitation Act Amendments of 1992 require that substantive issues relating to employment discrimination under the ADA and Sections 501, 503 and 504 be uniformly resolved, the remedies available for employment discrimination may vary depending upon which statute is at issue.

A.   SECTION 501

Section 505a of the Rehabilitation Act provides that the remedies available to a person with a disability who suffers employment discrimination by a federal employer are the same remedies available to an individual who suffers employment discrimination under Title VII of the Civil Rights Act. Title VII provides that an employee or job applicant who has been unlawfully discriminated against is entitled to injunctive or equitable relief, and to reinstatement and back pay if the individual was wrongfully denied employment or terminated from employment. In appropriate circumstances a court may also order an employer to promote an individual who was wrongfully denied promotion. 42 U.S.C.A. § 2000e–5(g).

Prior to the enactment of the Civil Rights Act of 1991, courts had uniformly held that plaintiffs could not recover compensatory or punitive damages resulting from employment discrimination in violation of Title VII. The Civil Rights Act of 1991, however, expressly provides for compensatory damages for *intentional* discrimination (but not for disparate impact discrimination) under both Title VII and Section 501. The 1991 Civil Rights Act provides that any plaintiff in a Section 501 (or Title VII) action may recover compensatory damages ("for future pecuniary losses, emotional pain, suffering, inconvenience, mental anguish, loss of enjoyment of life, and other nonpecuniary losses") for intentional discrimination—in addition to equitable remedies—in a maximum amount (including any amount awarded as punitive damages, where applicable) of: (1) $50,000 if the employer has 15–100 employees in each of 20 or more calendar weeks in the current or preceding year; (b) $100,000 if the employer has 101–200 employees during that period; (c) $200,000 if the employer has 201–500 employees during that period; or (d) $300,000 if the employer has more than 500 employees during that period. 42 U.S.C.A. § 1981a(b)(3). The limits on compensatory damages do not include backpay, interest on backpay, or any other type of relief authorized under Title VII. *Id.* § 1981a(b)(2).

The Civil Rights Act of 1991 further provides that compensatory damages are not available "where the covered entity demonstrates good faith efforts, in consultation with the person with the disability who has informed the covered entity that accommodation is needed, to identify and make a reasonable accommodation that would provide such individual with an equally effective opportunity and would not cause an undue hardship on the operation of the business." *Id.* § 1981a(a)(3).

Although the Civil Rights Act also provides for awards of punitive damages for intentional discrimination, such damages are not available against "a government, government agency or political subdivision," which includes the entities covered by Section 501. *Id.* § 1981a(b)(1). Moreover, it has been held that a federal government employee who, as a result of an on-the-job injury, receives workers' compensation benefits under the Federal Employees Compensation Act (FECA), may not receive additional benefits under the Rehabilitation Act. *See Alexander v. Frank*, 777 F.Supp. 516 (N.D.Tex. 1991). Another court however, disagreed with this ruling. *Karnes v. Runyon*, 912 F.Supp. 280 (S.D.Ohio 1995).

B.   THE ADA

Because the remedies available under Title I of the ADA are the same as those available under Title VII, the same damages rules that apply under Section 501 also apply under Title I of the ADA. That is, exhaustion of administrative remedies is required and only equitable remedies are available for disparate impact discrimination. [Note, however, that courts have held that employees alleging employment discrimination by an entity covered under ADA Title II do not have to exhaust administrative remedies under Title I.] In cases of intentional discrimination, however, compensatory and punitive damages are available subject to the caps explained above. Moreover, a jury trial is available when damages are sought for intentional discrimination.

Compensatory damages are defined in the 1991 Civil Rights Act as excluding "back pay, interest on back pay, or any other type of relief authorized under section 706(g) of the Civil Rights Act of 1964." 42 U.S.C.A. § 2000d–3. In *Pollard v. E.I. du Pont de Nemours*, 532 U.S. 843 (2001) the Supreme Court held that front pay was not an element of compensatory damages within the meaning of the 1991 Civil Rights Act, and, therefore was not subject to the Act's statutory cap.

Again, the 1991 Civil Rights Act expressly provides that damages may not be awarded where a discriminatory practice involves the provision of reasonable accommodation pursuant to the ADA, if the employer demonstrates good faith efforts, in consultation with the person with the disability who has informed the covered entity that accommodation is needed, to identify and make a reasonable accommodation that would provide such individual with an equally effective opportunity and would not cause an undue hardship on the operation of the business.

42 U.S.C.A. § 1981a(b)(3).

A plaintiff claiming intentional discrimination in a Title VII or ADA action may seek punitive damages but must show that the defendant acted "with malice or with reckless indifference to the federally protected rights." In *Kolstad v. American Dental Ass'n*, 527 U.S. 526 (1999) the Court stated that these terms pertain to the employer's knowledge that it may be acting in violation of federal law, not its awareness that it is engaging in discrimination. It also held that punitive damages could be imposed in a Title VII action without a showing of egregious or outrageous discrimination independent of the employer's state of mind. An employer may not be held vicariously liable, however, for punitive damages when a managerial agent's discriminatory employment decisions are contrary to the employer's good-faith efforts to comply with Title VII.

In *Board of Trustees of University of Alabama v. Garrett*, 531 U.S. 356 (2001), the Court held that state government employers have Eleventh Amendment immunity from suits for *money damages* under Title I of the ADA. The *Garrett* Court left open the question of whether monetary damages are permitted under ADA Title II. The Second Circuit has stated that an action for monetary damages under Title II is permitted under certain circumstances. In particular, "a private suit for money damages under Title II of the ADA may only be maintained against a state if the plaintiff can establish that the Title II violation was motivated by either discriminatory animus or ill will due to disability." *Garcia v. S.U.N.Y. Health Sci. Ctr. of Brooklyn*, 280 F.3d 98 (2d Cir. 2001). The Supreme Court's decision in *Tennessee v. Lane*, 541 U.S. 509 (2004) is consistent with the Second Circuit's position in *Garcia*. The Court held that monetary damages can be available under ADA Title II when the plaintiff's claim involves a fundamental right, such as access to the courts.

In *Garrett*, the Court suggested in a footnote that employees can still bring suits against state officials for injunctive relief under ADA Title II. Some earlier lower court decisions had found such relief was not available, but the courts have subsequently stated that *Garrett* abrogated those decisions. *See, e.g., Bruggeman ex rel. Bruggeman v. Blagojevich*, 324 F.3d 906 (7th Cir. 2003); *Henrietta D. v. Bloomberg*, 331 F.3d 261 (2d Cir. 2003). In addition, the federal government can still enforce ADA Title I against a state government, and employees can still sue a *municipal or local government* under ADA Title I. The principle of sovereign immunity applies to states, not local government. It applies to suits by private individuals, not to suits by the federal government.

The Supreme Court has held that an award of backpay under Title VII of the Civil Rights Act of 1964 is not excludable from gross income for tax purposes because it was not "on account of personal injury or sickness." *C.I.R. v. Schleier*, 515 U.S. 323 (1995). In addition, the Court has held that punitive damages received in tort suit for personal injuries were not excluded from taxable gross income. *O'Gilvie v. United States*, 519 U.S. 79 (1996). Congress has codified the Supreme Court's holdings: "gross income does not include . . . (2) the amount of any damages (*other than punitive damages*) received . . . on account of personal *physical* injuries or *physical* sickness. . . ." 26 U.S.C.A. § 104(a)(2) (emphasis added).

C. SECTION 504

As with the ADA and Section 501, the Civil Rights Act of 1991 provides that a plaintiff suing for employment discrimination under Section 504 can recover compensatory and punitive damages subject to the limits described above. Again, these limits do not apply to back pay, interest on back pay, or any other type of relief authorized under Title VII, and damages may not be awarded where the employer shows good faith efforts to provide a reasonable accommodation. 42 U.S.C.A. § 1981a(b)(2), (3).

In *Barnes v. Gorman*, 536 U.S. 181 (2002), however, the Court held that *punitive* damages are *not* available under Section 504. The Court noted that it had often characterized statutes involving the provision of federal funding to be "much in the nature of a *contract:* in return for federal funds, the [recipients] agree to comply with federally imposed conditions." Punitive damages, unlike compensatory damages and injunction, are generally not available for breach of contract, and the Court reasoned they should also not be available to enforce Section 504 and other federal funding statutes.

The Supreme Court has also held that monetary damages are not available against the *federal* government for violations of the Rehabilitation Act's prohibition of discrimination on the basis of disability "under any program or activity conducted by any Executive agency." *Lane v. Pena*, 518 U.S. 187 (1996). The Court held that Congress has not waived the *federal* government's sovereign immunity in enacting Section 504.

D. ATTORNEYS' FEES

Section 505(b) of the Rehabilitation Act, 29 U.S.C.A. § 794a(b), provides that the court, in its discretion, may allow the prevailing party, other than the United States, reasonable attorneys' fees in an action arising under Section 501 or Section 504. Similarly, the ADA expressly provides that, in any action or proceeding under the Act, the court or agency has discretion to award attorneys' fees to any prevailing party other than the United States. Such fees may be assessed against the United States to the same extent that they may be assessed against private individuals or entities.

Attorneys' fees are also available to plaintiffs who prevail on their claims for damages under the Civil Rights Act of 1991. Such fees include expert fees, at the court's discretion. Attorneys' fees against a *plaintiff*, however, will only be awarded if the suit is found to be "frivolous, unreasonable, or groundless."

In *Buckhannon Board and Care Home, Inc. v. West Virginia Dep't of Health and Human Resources*, 532 U.S. 598 (2001) the Court offered guidance on what it means to be the "prevailing party." The Court held that the ADA requires a party to secure either a judgment on the merits or a court-ordered consent decree in order to qualify as "prevailing party." For a more detailed discussion of the attorney's fees issue, see § 11.5 of this *Nutshell*.

E. SECTION 503

As noted in sections 4:12 and 4:13 of this *Nutshell*, damages are not available under Section 503. The only remedies available against federal contractors are termination of federal contracts in whole or in part, withholding of payment due under existing federal contracts, barring the contractor from receiving future federal contracts, or, if the Office of Federal Contract Compliance Programs (OFCCP) files suit against a contractor and prevails, appropriate injunctive relief. The individual disabled plaintiff has no personal remedies.

§ 5.20 INDIVIDUAL LIABILITY

The vast majority of courts have held that an employer's agents and supervisors cannot be held individually liable for employment discrimination in violation of ADA Title I. In *Ostrach v. Regents of the University of California*, 957 F.Supp. 196 (E.D.Cal. 1997), however, the court held that, while ADA wrongful discrimination and failure to accommodate claims cannot be maintained against an individual, the ADA's retaliation and intimidation sections permit suits against supervisors in their individual capacity. Another court has stated, however, that "virtually all other courts have disagreed with *Ostrach*" on this issue. *Van Hulle v. Pacific Telesis Corp.*, 124 F.Supp.2d 642 (N.D.Cal. 2000).

Some courts have found, however, that a person can be held liable in an individual capacity under the Rehabilitation Act if he or she was responsible for deciding whether an entity accepted or rejected federal funds. *See, e.g., Johnson v. New York Hosp.*, 903 F.Supp. 605 (S.D.N.Y. 1995); *but see Davis v. Flexman*, 109 F.Supp.2d 776 (S.D.Ohio 1999).

CHAPTER 6

ARCHITECTURAL BARRIERS

§ 6.1 THE ARCHITECTURAL BARRIERS ACT

The Architectural Barriers Act (ABA), 42 U.S.C.A. §§ 4151–4156, was the first federal law intended to ensure a barrier-free environment for persons with disabilities. The National Commission on Architectural Barriers to the Rehabilitation of the Handicapped recognized that voluntary action was insufficient and recommended to Congress that a federal agency be charged with promulgating and enforcing uniform policies, procedures and specifications to provide people with disabilities with access to government-funded or supported buildings.

As enacted in 1968, the ABA authorized three federal agencies to promulgate standards regarding the design, construction and alteration of federally owned, leased, or financed buildings to allow ready access to and use by people with disabilities: 1) The Department of Housing and Urban Development (HUD) was authorized to prescribe standards for residential structures; 2) the Department of Defense was authorized to prescribe standards for military structures; and 3) the General Services Administration (GSA) was authorized to prescribe standards for all other buildings covered under the Act. The ABA was amended in 1976 to authorize the Postal Service to promulgate standards with respect to postal facilities. As amended in 1976, the ABA *requires*, rather than simply authorizes, the four above-named federal agencies to promulgate the specified standards with respect to the buildings or facilities covered within their respective jurisdictions.

The ABA applies to buildings or facilities used in a manner requiring that they be accessible to the public or where people with disabilities work or live. But the coverage of the ABA is limited. In addition to covering the Washington, D.C. subway system, the Act covers only three types of structures: those that (1) are constructed or altered by or on behalf of the federal government; (2) were leased by the United States between 1968 and 1976 after being constructed in accord with federal plans and specifications, or any structure leased by the United States after January 1, 1977; and (3) receive a federal grant or loan for design, construction or alteration—such as college buildings or hospitals. The latter type of structure, however, only falls within the parameters of the ABA if the funding statute authorizes the imposition of standards for its *design*, *construction* or *alteration*. A building such as a hospital that receives federal funds will not be covered by the ABA unless such funds are specifically utilized for design, construction or alteration of that building.

Coverage under the ABA is further limited because, when alterations are made, only the altered portion of a covered building must be made accessible to it. Thus, for example, a building might have accessible restrooms (if the portion of the building containing the restrooms is altered) but have no accessible entry into the building. Further, if a federal agency resides in a (non-leased) building constructed prior to 1968 that has not been altered, the building need not be made accessible to people with disabilities.

§ 6.2   THE ARCHITECTURAL AND TRANSPORTATION BARRIERS COMPLIANCE BOARD

Because the ABA does not contain any provision regarding enforcement of the Act, initial compliance with the Act was inconsistent. Accordingly, to ensure compliance with the standards prescribed under the ABA, Congress created the Architectural and Transportation Barriers Compliance Board (the "Access Board"). 29 U.S.C.A. § 792. Pursuant to amendments enacted in 1992, the Access Board is composed of 25 persons. Thirteen members are appointed by the President from the general public, a majority of whom must be individuals with disabilities. The remaining members are the heads of the General Services Administration, the United States Postal Service and the Departments of Health and Human Services, Transportation, Housing and Urban Development, Labor, Interior, Defense, Justice, Veterans Administration, Education and Commerce. The heads of the named departments may select designees to represent them on the Board, but such designees must hold positions within the specified agencies at executive level IV or higher.

The chairperson and vice-chairperson of the Access Board are elected by majority vote of the Board members to serve for terms of one year. One such office must be held by a member representing the general public and the other by a federal official member; the chair must alternate between public and federal members each year. Each public member of the Access Board is appointed to serve a four-year term, with the terms of at least three public members expiring each year. The public representative members (but not the federal members) are compensated for their services.

The Access Board's primary functions are to ensure compliance with the ABA, to establish minimum guidelines and requirements for the standards issued pursuant to the ABA, to investigate alternative approaches to removing the architectural barriers confronting people with disabilities, and to make recommendations with respect to eliminating such barriers to the President and Congress. In addition, the Access Board is to examine the transportation and housing difficulties of people with disabilities and prepare plans and proposals for necessary future action.

When carrying out its functions, the Access Board is empowered to "conduct investigations, hold public hearings, and issue such orders as it deems necessary to ensure compliance with the provisions of [the ABA]." 29 U.S.C.A. § 792(e)(1). The Board is also authorized to bring a civil action in federal district court to enforce any of its final orders and to intervene or appear as amicus curiae in any civil action that relates to the ABA. *Id.* § 792(e)(2).

The Access Board's regulations for compliance hearings are codified at 36 C.F.R. Part 1150. The Board stresses voluntary compliance with the ABA; it does not generally act as a policing agency to enforce the Act. However, any person may submit a complaint to the Access Board claiming that a covered building or facility does not comply with standards issued under the ABA. The person who files such a complaint is not a party to the proceeding as a matter of course, but any person, including the complainant, may petition the administrative law judge for permission "to participate in the proceedings when he/she claims an interest in the proceedings and may contribute materially to their proper disposition." 36 C.F.R. § 1150.13(a). The Access Board is required to send copies of complaints to all interested agencies and persons. It also must apprise any person who might become a party to the compliance proceeding and give such persons a reasonable opportunity to respond or submit relevant documents. The Access Board's Executive Director is required to "seek the cooperation of persons and agencies in obtaining compliance and [to] provide assistance and guidance to help them comply voluntarily." *Id.* § 1150.41(b). In addition, the Executive Director is authorized to obtain access to all books, records and other sources of information necessary to ascertain compliance, regardless of an agency's or person's claim of privacy. *Id.* § 1150.41(d).

The Access Board must attempt to informally resolve all complaints within 180 days after all affected agencies and persons have received the complaint. Within ten days after the termination of the 180-day period, the Executive Director must either issue a citation or provide a written statement explaining why a citation is considered unnecessary. Any citation issued must specify the relief necessary to ensure compliance with the ABA; such "relief may include the suspension or withholding of funds and/or specific corrective action." *Id.* § 1150.42(a); *see also* 29 U.S.C.A. § 792(e)(1). Within 15 days of receiving a citation, a respondent must file an answer admitting or denying the allegations and attaching pertinent documents. The answering party may request a hearing if the citation does not state that a hearing will be scheduled; failure to request a hearing constitutes a waiver of the right to a hearing and consent to a decision being made on the basis of available information.

Hearings under the Act are presided over by Administrative Law Judges (ALJs). The ALJ may schedule a prehearing conference and may enter a prehearing order. The parties are empowered to exchange exhibits and are encouraged to engage in voluntary discovery procedures. The ALJ may order such discovery that he or she "considers to be consistent with and essential to the objective of securing a just and inexpensive determination of the merits of the citation without unnecessary delay." 36 C.F.R. § 1150.63(b). The ALJ also has authority to issue protective orders to shelter a party or person from "annoyance, embarrassment, oppression or undue burden or expense." *Id.* § 1150.63(c).

Hearings are conducted only to resolve issues of fact. When no issues of material fact are in dispute, the ALJ may vacate a previously set hearing date. Once a hearing has been conducted, the ALJ is required to issue a decision within 30 days (or within 30 days after the filing of posthearing briefs). The ALJ's decision must contain findings of fact, conclusions of law, and the reasons for all findings.

The Access Board is authorized to appoint as many ALJs as necessary to hear compliance proceeding under the ABA. An ALJ's decision is "deemed to be an order of the Access Board and shall be the final order for the purpose of judicial review." 29 U.S.C.A. § 792(f)(3). Any complainant or participant in a compliance proceeding may obtain judicial review of the Board's final order. Because there is no private right of action under the ABA, however, the court is limited to reviewing ALJ's opinion. Accordingly, there has been little judicial interpretation of the ABA.

At the end of each fiscal year, the Access Board is required to present a report to Congress that includes 1) an assessment of the extent of compliance with the ABA, 2) a description and analysis of investigations made and actions taken by the Access Board, and 3) reports and recommendations delineating alternative approaches to the elimination of barriers confronting people with disabilities and the measures being taken by governments and agencies to eliminate such barriers.

§ 6.3   GUIDELINES AND STANDARDS ESTABLISHED UNDER THE ABA

The Access Board is required to establish minimum guidelines and requirements for all standards issued under the ABA. In accord with that mandate, the Access Board has promulgated regulations, 36 C.F.R. § 1190.31 *et seq.*, establishing separate guidelines with respect to the accessibility of newly constructed buildings, additions to existing buildings, alterations to existing buildings, and leased buildings. In addition, the guidelines include sections dealing with technical provisions and special buildings or facilities. The minimum guidelines established by the Access Board generally follow the standards for accessibility established by the American National Standards Institute (ANSI) with respect to technical provisions; the Access Board's guidelines also contain scoping provisions that relate to which and how many spaces and elements are to be made accessible in new construction, additions, alterations, and leased facilities.

Each of the four agencies referred to in the ABA (the General Services Administration, the Postal Service, and the Departments of Defense and Housing and Urban Development) are required to promulgate accessibility *standards* (not guidelines) with respect to buildings under their respective jurisdictions. The standards promulgated by those agencies may contain additional requirements beyond the minimum guidelines established by the Access Board. In 1984 the four agencies jointly promulgated Uniform Federal Accessibility Standards (UFAS) which are to some extent more stringent than the ANSI standards originally incorporated into the Access Board's guidelines. The UFAS became effective in HUD facilities on October 4, 1984; in Department of Defense facilities on May 8, 1985; in Postal Service facilities on November 15, 1984; and in all other facilities (under the jurisdiction of the GSA) on July 31, 1984.

Each of the four standard-setting agencies is authorized to "modify or waive" any of the standards implemented by that agency on a "case by case" basis upon a finding that "such modification or waiver is clearly necessary. . . ." 42 U.S.C.A. § 4156. The Access Board is responsible for ensuring that all waivers and modifications are "based upon findings of fact and are not inconsistent with . . . [the ABA]." 29 U.S.C.A. § 792(b)(1). Because each of the agencies having authority to issue waivers is represented on the Access Board, the actions of such agencies in issuing waivers will not, as a practical matter, be subject to arm's length review.

§ 6.4   SECTION 504 AND ARCHITECTURAL BARRIERS

Section 504 provides additional protection for persons with disabilities seeking to achieve a barrier-free society. Indeed, one of the primary goals of Congress in enacting Section 504 was to eliminate architectural barriers.

Section 504 mandates accessibility for all federally assisted programs. Thus, the regulations promulgated pursuant to Section 504 generally require existing facilities to be operated so that "the program or activity, when viewed in its entirety, is readily accessible to and usable by handicapped persons." *See*, *e.g.*, 28 C.F.R. § 41.57(a) (DOJ regulation); 45 C.F.R. § 84.22(a) (DHHS regulation). The Section 504 regulations generally require that "new facilities shall be designed and constructed to be readily accessible to and usable by handicapped persons," and that "[a]lterations to existing facilities shall, to the maximum extent feasible, be designed and constructed to be readily accessible to and usable by handicapped persons." 28 C.F.R. § 41.58(a) (DOJ regulation); 45 C.F.R. § 84.23 (DHHS regulation).

Architectural accessibility may be satisfied under Section 504 in a different manner than under the ABA. A recipient may fulfill the program accessibility requirements of the Act under the DHHS regulations, for example,

through such means as redesign of equipment, reassignment of classes or other services to accessible buildings, assignment of aides to beneficiaries, home visits, delivery of health, welfare, or other social services at alternate accessible sites, alteration of existing facilities and construction of new facilities in conformance with the requirements of [45

C.F.R.] § 84.23, or any other methods that result in making its program or activity accessible to handicapped persons. A recipient is not required to make structural changes in existing facilities where other methods are effective in achieving compliance [with the accessibility requirements]. In choosing among available methods for meeting [the accessibility requirements], a recipient shall give priority to those methods that offer programs and activities to handicapped persons in the most integrated setting appropriate.

45 C.F.R. § 84.22(b).

Compliance with the ABA can only be achieved by rendering the covered building accessible. Under Section 504, however, architectural change is only one means of achieving the required accessibility. If a more expeditious method can ensure equal access to federally assisted programs, that method may be utilized. *All* federally assisted programs must be made accessible under Section 504, however, regardless of whether architectural change is possible or required.

Because Section 504 requires accessibility of *all* federally assisted activities and programs, regardless of whether such programs or activities are conducted in buildings covered by the ABA, Section 504 will often provide greater protection to people with disabilities than the ABA. Moreover, a plaintiff who files suit under Section 504 alleging the inaccessibility of a federally assisted program does not have to exhaust administrative remedies under the ABA—even where the program at issue may be conducted in a building covered by the ABA. *Disabled in Action of Pennsylvania v. Pierce*, 606 F.Supp. 310 (E.D.Pa. 1985).

Because Section 504 includes a private right of action to file suit in federal court, but no such private right exists under the ABA, a person with a disability may wish to file a claim under Section 504 rather than to file an administrative complaint with the Access Board. In such a case, however, the plaintiff must be aware that the remedy under Section 504 may not encompass architectural changes if other, less obtrusive, methods will achieve accessibility.

In some cases, however, the remedies under Section 504 and the ABA will be the same. Indeed, it has been held that in appropriate circumstances Section 504 requires compliance with the UFAS. For example, *Locascio v. St. Petersburg*, 731 F.Supp. 1522 (M.D.Fla. 1990) involved a stadium constructed by the city of St. Petersburg that the parties apparently agreed did not comply with the UFAS. The plaintiffs claimed that the city was in violation of both Section 504 and the ABA. After stating that it must determine whether either or both Section 504 and the ABA applied to the case, the court opined that regardless of whether Section 504 or the ABA applied, adherence to the UFAS was required. The court found that construction of the stadium was a "program or activity" within the meaning of Section 504. Thus, the court held that it need not determine whether the ABA applied to the case, since the ABA and Section 504 would require that the same standards be applied.

§ 6.5   INJURY DUE TO LACK OF ACCESSIBILITY

The failure to comply with accessibility standards has been cited as evidence of negligence when it led to an injury. A plaintiff alleging a building is covered by the statute, however, has the burden of proving that it has been altered since ABA's effective date; the government does not have the burden of proving the absence of such an alteration. *Poynter v. United States*, 55 F.Supp.2d 558 (W.D.La. 1999).

CHAPTER 7
ACCESS TO PROGRAMS AND SERVICES

§ 7.1   INTRODUCTION

Section 504 of the Rehabilitation Act requires that a recipient of federal funds must make all its programs and activities accessible to people with disabilities. Title III of the ADA extends that mandate to certain private entities, and Title II requires that the programs and activities of state and local government entities be similarly accessible. Finally, Section 508 of the Rehabilitation Act, 29 U.S.C. § 794d, requires federal agencies to ensure, unless it would pose an undue burden to do so, that electronic and information technology (EIT) must be accessible to federal employees with disabilities and people with disabilities who are members of the public seeking information or services from the agencies. This chapter will provide an overview of the accessibility requirements under each of these laws.

§ 7.2   SECTION 504: OVERVIEW

Section 504 prohibits disability discrimination by federal funds recipients that provide health, housing, rehabilitation or other social services or benefits to members of the public. Regulations promulgated pursuant to Section 504 by the Department of Health and Human Services (DHHS) state that such providers may not (1) deny benefits or services to qualified individuals with disabilities; (2) provide benefits or services that are "not equal to" those offered to non-disabled persons or are not "as effective" as those provided others; or (3) provide different or separate benefits or services to individuals with disabilities unless it is necessary to do so to provide services or benefits that "are as effective as those provided to others." 45 C.F.R. § 84.52(a)(1)–(5). Regulations promulgated by other federal agencies contain similar provisions.

§ 7.3   TITLE II OF THE ADA: OVERVIEW

Title II of the ADA prohibits all departments, agencies, special purpose districts or other instrumentalities of any state or local government from: (1) excluding a qualified person with a disability from participating in the programs or activities of the entity; (2) denying a qualified person with a disability the benefits of the services, programs or activities of the entity; or (3) otherwise discriminating against a qualified person with a disability. 42 U.S.C.A. §§ 12131–12133. This Title, in effect, extends the protections of Section 504 to all state and local government entities, regardless of whether they receive federal financial assistance. The DOJ states that ADA Title II's prohibition of discrimination by state and local government applies both to employment discrimination and to the accessibility of public services, programs and activities. For employment, however, Title II basically obligates state and local government entities to comply with the mandates set forth in

ADA Title I, as described in chapter 5 of this *Nutshell*.

§ 7.4   ADA TITLE II: PROGRAM AND FACILITY ACCESSIBILITY

State and local government entities must ensure that, when viewed in their entirety, all of their programs and facilities are accessible to people with disabilities. This obligation covers all programs or activities involving general public contact as part of a public entity's ongoing operations. Thus, for example, Title II requires that all events or activities at a public school be fully accessible to people with disabilities if they are open to parents or the public. This would graduation ceremonies, plays, parent-teacher meetings and adult education classes.

The regulations provide that a public entity may not discriminate "directly or *through contractual, licensing, or other arrangements*, on the basis of disability." 28 C.F.R. § 35.130(b)(1) (emphasis added). Accordingly, if a state or local government entity contracts with a private entity to provide services for the state or the public, the government entity must ensure that the private entity is operated in a manner that satisfies the government entity's Title II obligations. 28 C.F.R. Pt. 35, App. A § 35.102; *James v. Peter Pan Transit Management, Inc.*, 1999 WL 735173 (E.D.N.C. 1999). Despite these licensing rules, the Second Circuit has ruled that ADA Title II does not obligate the New York Taxi License Commission to use its licensing and regulatory authority to require that taxi owners provide meaningful access to taxis for persons with disabilities. *Noel v. New York City Taxi and Limousine Comm'n,* 687 F.3d 63 (2012).

ADA Title II only provides for equality of opportunity; it does not guarantee equality of results. Persons with disabilities need only be provided with an "equally effective opportunity to participate in or benefit from a public entity's aids, benefits, and services." Department of Justice, *Title II Technical Assistance Manual* § II–3.3000. http://www.ada.gov/taman2.html. Further, a public entity is not required to provide services for people with disabilities that it does not provide for others. For example, the DOJ notes that a city would not have to remove snow from the private driveways of residents with disabilities if the city does not provide such services for non-disabled residents. *Id.*

Public entities are precluded under Title II from making unnecessary inquiries into the existence of a disability. *Id.* § II–3.5300.

State and local government entities are required to identify and correct any policy or practice that is inconsistent with the ADA's mandate of non-discrimination on the basis of disability, and to develop plans to modify them so that they are consistent with ADA requirements. Such self-evaluations were required to be completed by January 26, 1993. Entities with 50 or more employees must keep their self-evaluations on file for at least three years. They must also establish procedures for handling complaints filed under the

ADA and must designate at least one individual to coordinate compliance efforts. 28 C.F.R. § 35.105. A public entity's decision to adopt procedures other than those outlined in its self-evaluation does not, in itself, constitute a violation of the ADA. Technological developments after the plan is developed, but before it is implemented, may make an alternative set of renovations both cheaper and more effective. *Memmer v. Marin County Courts*, 169 F.3d 630 (9th Cir. 1999).

§ 7.5   TITLE III OF THE ADA: OVERVIEW

Title III of the ADA prohibits discrimination against individuals with disabilities—or against others because of their affiliation with a disabled person—by private entities that operate places of public accommodation.

> No individual shall be discriminated against on the basis of disability in the full and equal enjoyment of the goods, services, facilities, privileges, advantages, or accommodations of any place of public accommodation by any person who owns, leases (or leases to), or operates a place of public accommodation.

42 U.S.C.A. § 12182(a).

With respect to access to services, Title III: (1) prohibits private entities from discriminating on the basis of disability in places of public accommodation; (2) requires all newly constructed and altered places of public accommodation and commercial facilities to be designed and constructed so that they are readily accessible to and usable by persons with disabilities; and (3) mandates that all examinations and courses offered with respect to licensing and certification for professional and trade purposes be accessible to disabled people. Each of these requirements will be discussed below.

§ 7.6 ADA TITLE III: DEFINITION OF PUBLIC ACCOMMODATIONS

Title III redefines a "public accommodation" as a private entity whose operations affect commerce, and that falls within at least one of the following categories:

(1) An inn, hotel, motel, or other place of lodging, except for an establishment located within a building that contains not more than five rooms for rent or hire and that is actually occupied by the proprietor of the establishment as the residence of the proprietor;

(2) A restaurant, bar, or other establishment serving food or drink;

(3) A motion picture house, theater, concert hall, stadium, or other place of exhibition or entertainment;

(4) An auditorium, convention center, lecture hall, or other place of public gathering;

(5) A bakery, grocery store, clothing store, hardware store, shopping center, or other sales or rental establishment;

(6) A laundromat, dry cleaner, bank, barber shop, beauty shop, travel service, shoe repair service, funeral parlor, gas station, office of an accountant or lawyer, pharmacy, insurance office, professional office of a health care provider, hospital, or other service establishment;

(7) A terminal, depot, or other station used for specified public transportation;

(8) A museum, library, gallery, or other place of public display or collection;

(9) A park, zoo, amusement park, or other place of recreation;

(10) A nursery, elementary, secondary, undergraduate, or postgraduate private school, or other place of education;

(11) A day care center, senior citizen center, homeless shelter, food bank, adoption agency, or other social service establishment; and

(12) A gymnasium, health spa, bowling alley, golf course, or other place of exercise or recreation.

42 U.S.C. § 12181(7). The regulation's definition of "place of public accommodation" includes the same list, 28 C.F.R. § 36.104.

To come within the coverage of Title III as a public accommodation, an entity must fall within one of these twelve categories. The examples given in each category, however, are not exhaustive, but merely illustrative.

The definition of the term "places of public accommodation" is not limited to entities of a certain size or having a certain number of employees. Thus, *all* places of public accommodation must comply with Title III's accessibility requirements. Title III covers only non-resident portions of covered entities, however; residential accommodations (places of permanent residence as opposed to temporary lodging in hotels and inns) are covered by the Fair Housing Act (FHA), which is discussed in Chapter 8 of this *Nutshell*. If residential accommodations are used as places of public accommodation, however, they will be governed by Title III. In some cases, therefore, a place of public accommodation could be covered by both the FHA and Title III.

There is considerable dispute about whether a "place of public accommodation" under Title III is limited to actual physical structures. In *Carparts Distribution Center, Inc. v. Automotive Wholesaler's Association of New England, Inc.*, 37 F.3d 12 (1st Cir. 1994), the court reasoned that the plain meaning of Title III evidences that public accommodations are *not* limited to actual structures. It noted that:

> [by] including "travel service" among the list of services considered "public accommodations," Congress clearly contemplated that "service establishments" include providers of services which do not require a person to physically

enter an actual physical structure. Many travel services conduct business by telephone or correspondence without requiring their customers to enter an office in order to obtain their services. . . . It would be irrational to conclude that persons who enter an office to purchase services are protected by the ADA, but persons who purchase the same services over the telephone or by mail are not. Congress could not have intended such an absurd result.

After noting that its interpretation was in accord with the legislative history of the ADA, the First Circuit stated:

Neither Title III nor its implementing regulations make any mention of physical boundaries or physical entry. Many goods and services are sold over the telephone or by mail with customers never physically entering the premises of a commercial entity to purchase the goods or services. To exclude this broad category of businesses from the reach of Title III and limit the application of Title III to physical structures which persons must enter to obtain goods and services would run afoul of the purposes of the ADA and would severely frustrate Congress's intent that individuals with disabilities fully enjoy the goods, services, privileges and advantages, available indiscriminately to other members of the general public.

Several courts have followed similar reasoning. Other courts, however, have taken a more

restrictive view of Title III and held it only applies
to the ability to gain access to physical structures.
*See, e.g., Stoutenborough v. National Football
League*, 59 F.3d 580 (6th Cir. 1995); *Parker v.
Metropolitan Life Ins. Co.*, 121 F.3d 1006 (6th Cir.
1997). Other courts reaching the same conclusion
note that the regulation, 28 C.F.R. § 36.104, defines
a place of public accommodation as a "facility." And
"facility is then defined as" all or any portion of
buildings, structures . . . or other real or personal
property. *See, e.g. Brown v. 1995 Tenet ParaAmerica
Bicycle Challenge.*, 959 F.Supp. 496 (N.D.Ill. 1997).
Still others have held Title III applies if there is a
"nexus" between the physical place of public
accommodation and the services or privileges denied
in a discriminatory manner. *See, e.g., Weyer v.
Twentieth Century Fox Film Corp.*, 198 F.3d 1104
(9th Cir. 2000). *Carparts*, *Parker*, and *Weyer* all
dealt with whether Title III applies to insurance
policies, so the issue of whether they are covered
under Title III thus remains in dispute. This issue is
discussed in more detail in § 11.6 of this *Nutshell*.

An emerging issue under Title III is whether
websites provided via the Internet are public
accommodations and thus must be accessible to
persons with disabilities. The courts have reached a
variety of positions on this subject, although the
developing trend is to find coverage in cases
concerning website accessibility. *See, e.g., Martin v.
Metro. Atlanta Rapid Transit Authority*, 225
F.Supp.2d 1362 (N.D. Ga. 2002); *Access Now, Inc. v.
Southwest Airlines*, 227 F.Supp.2d 1312 (S.D. Fla.
2002); *National Federation of the Blind v. Target*

Corp., 452 F.Supp.2d 946 (N.D. Cal. 2006). DOJ has not yet promulgated regulations on this topic although one might anticipate such regulations in the future.

§ 7.7 ADA TITLE III: COMMERCIAL FACILITIES

"Commercial facilities" covered by Title III are defined as facilities:

(1) Whose operations will affect commerce;

(2) That are intended for nonresidential use by a private entity; and

(3) That are not—

(i) Facilities that are covered or expressly exempted from coverage under the Fair Housing Act of 1968, as amended (42 U.S.C.A. §§ 3601–3631);

(ii) Aircraft; or

(iii) Railroad locomotives, railroad freightcars, railroad cabooses, commuter or intercity passenger rail cars (including coaches, dining cars, sleeping cars, lounge cars, and food service cars), any other railroad cars described in Section 242 of the Act or covered under [T]itle II of the Act, or railroad rights-of-way. . . .

28 C.F.R. § 36.104. This definition is intended to cover places such as factories, warehouses, office buildings, and other buildings where people work.

Only those sections of Title III and the DOJ's implementing regulations dealing with new construction and alteration apply to commercial facilities that are not places of public accommodation. The intent was to make new construction and alterations of places where people work accessible to individuals with disabilities.

§ 7.8   PRIVATE CLUBS

Private clubs or establishments that are exempt from coverage under Title II of the Civil Rights Act of 1964 are exempt from Title III's requirement. 42 U.S.C.A. § 12187. If a private club makes its facilities available to the general public (*e.g.*, if the club rents its facilities to a day care center open to the public), however, the club then becomes subject to Title III's mandates. In that case, both the private club, as a lessor, and the public accommodation lessee (*e.g.*, the day care center) will be subject to Title III. 28 C.F.R. Pt. 36, App. B § 36.201.

§ 7.9   ADA TITLE III: RELIGIOUS ENTITIES

Religious entities are exempt from Title III. 42 U.S.C. § 12187. The term "religious entity" includes any religious organization or place of worship, including entities controlled by a religious organization. Thus, for example, even if a school or social service program operated by a religious organization is governed by a lay board, the school or social service remains exempt from Title III.

Moreover, the exemption applies even if a religious organization conducts an activity that would otherwise make it a public accommodation (such as operating a day care center or nursing home that is open to the public). The test with respect to the religious entity exemption is whether the public accommodation activity (the day care center or nursing home, for example) is *operated* by the religious organization, not who benefits from the services provided. A public accommodation that leases space from a religious entity *is* subject to Title III's requirements, however, if it is not itself a religious organization and is not controlled by a religious organization. 28 C.F.R. Pt. 36, App. B § 36.104.

§ 7.10   ADA TITLES II AND III AND SECTION 504: QUALIFIED INDIVIDUAL WITH A DISABILITY

In *Southeastern Community College v. Davis*, 442 U.S. 397 (1979), the Court stated that under Section 504 "[a]n otherwise qualified person is one who is able to meet all of a program's requirements in spite of his handicap." In *School Bd. of Nassau County, Fla. v. Arline*, 480 U.S. 273 (1987), however, the Court noted that, if an individual does not meet an essential requirement of a program or activity because of his disability, it must be determined if a "reasonable accommodation" would enable the person to become "otherwise qualified." The "reasonable accommodation" rule was incorporated into ADA Titles II and III. Title II states that a "qualified individual with a disability" is one "who, with or without *reasonable modifications* to rules, policies, or practices, the removal of architectural, communication, or transportation barriers, or the provision of auxiliary aids and services, meets the essential eligibility requirements for the receipt of services or the participation in programs or activities provided by a public entity." 42 U.S.C.A. § 12131(2) (emphasis added). Similarly, Title III defines discrimination as "a failure to make *reasonable modifications* in policies practices, or procedures, when such modifications are necessary to afford such goods, services, facilities, privileges, advantages, or accommodations to individuals with disabilities." *Id.* 12182(b)(2)(A)(ii) (emphasis added).

Courts have used a three-step analysis for the "otherwise qualified" requirement under the Rehabilitation Act and the ADA. First, the disabled individual must meet all of the essential eligibility requirements in spite of his disability. Second, the rule has an "exception;" if the disabled individual cannot meet all the essential eligibility requirements because of his disability, it must be determined if he can do so with "reasonable accommodations." Third, there is an "exception to the exception;" an accommodation is not reasonable if it "fundamentally alters" the nature of the program or creates an "undue burden." As shown below, these steps are interrelated and tend to collapse into each other as courts apply the "otherwise qualified" standard.

§ 7.11 ADA TITLES II AND III AND SECTION 504: ELIGIBILITY CRITERIA

Under ADA Title III, a public accommodation may not impose or apply eligibility criteria that "that screen out or *tend* to screen out an individual with a disability or any class of individuals with disabilities from fully and equally enjoying any goods, services, facilities, privileges, advantages, or accommodations, *unless* such criteria can be shown to be necessary for the provision of the goods, services, facilities, privileges, advantages, or accommodations being offered." 42 U.S.C.A. § 12182(b)(2)(A)(i). For example, a public accommodation may not require that an individual with a disability be accompanied by an attendant, require an individual to unnecessarily identify a disability, or require presentation of a driver's license as the sole means of identification before being permitted to pay by check (since such a policy would discriminate against individuals with disabilities who were unable to obtain drivers' licenses). Moreover, a surcharge may not be assessed to an individual with a disability to cover the cost of making a facility accessible. 28 C.F.R. Pt. 36, App. B § 36.301.

The prohibition on eligibility criteria which screen out or tend to screen out people with disabilities also applies under ADA Title II and Section 504. Courts initially took two different positions on how to determine if eligibility criteria are "essential" and, thus, need not be modified. Some reasoned that the decision on whether an eligibility requirement is essential should be made prior to deciding whether the plaintiff was a "qualified individual" under the ADA. Under this approach, an individualized inquiry into whether a modification or waiver of the criteria is possible would not be made until *after* the general essentiality determination was made. Courts using this approach deferred to the defendants' reasoning on why the rule was essential and found that *any* modification would be unreasonable. *See, e.g., Pottgen v. Missouri State High Sch. Activities Ass'n*, 40 F.3d 926 (8th Cir. 1994).

Other courts, however, held that they were obligated to look at a plaintiff as an individual *before* deciding whether he or she can meet the essential requirements of an eligibility rule. If a rule could be modified without doing violence to its purposes then it cannot be "essential" to the nature of the program or activity to refuse to modify the rule. *See, e.g., Washington v. Indiana High Sch. Athletic Ass'n*, 181 F.3d 840 (7th Cir. 1999) ("To require a focus on the general purposes behind a rule without considering the effect an exception for a disabled individual would have on those purposes would negate the reason for requiring reasonable exceptions.").

The Supreme Court adopted the second approach in *PGA Tour, Inc. v. Martin*, 532 U.S. 661 (2001) where it refused to defer to the defendant's statement that a rule was essential. It said that the PGA's "refusal to consider Martin's personal circumstances in deciding whether to accommodate his disability runs counter to the clear language and purpose of the ADA." The Court stated that the statute "requires an *individualized inquiry* must be made to determine whether a specific modification for a particular person's disability would be reasonable under the circumstances as well as necessary for that person, and yet at the same time not work a fundamental alteration [in the defendant's program]." (Emphasis added).

§ 7.12   ADA TITLES II AND III AND SECTION 504: REASONABLE ACCOMMODATIONS/MODIFICATIONS

In *Alexander v. Choate*, 469 U.S. 287 (1985), the Court interpreted Section 504 and held that, "while a [recipient of federal funds] need not be required to make 'fundamental' or 'substantial' modification to accommodate the handicapped, it may be required to make 'reasonable' ones." The ADA includes a similar balancing test. Title III requires owners and operators of places of public accommodation to make "reasonable modifications" in their practices, policies or procedures *unless* such modifications would "fundamentally alter" the nature of the goods, services, facilities or other benefits offered or would result in an "undue burden." 42 U.S.C.A. § 12182(b)(2)(A)(ii), (iii). The term "undue burden" is defined as encompassing "significant difficulty or expense." 28 C.F.R. § 36.104. When determining whether an action would result in an undue burden, it is necessary to consider: (1) the nature and cost of the required action; (2) the overall financial resources, type of operation, and employment demographics of the covered entity and any applicable parent entity; (3) the impact of the action upon the covered entity; and (4) any legitimate safety concerns.

Similar requirements are found in the ADA Title II regulations which state that a public entity is not required "to take any action that it can demonstrate would result in a fundamental alteration in the nature of a service, program, or activity or in undue financial and administrative burdens." 28 C.F.R. § 35.150(a)(3). The relevant budget of the public entity in the "undue burden" analysis under Title II is the budget for the service, program, or activity at issue. *Pascuiti v. New York Yankees*, 87 F.Supp.2d 221 (S.D.N.Y. 1999)

Courts have used a burden-shifting test for evidence in "fundamental alteration" and "undue burden" cases. First, the plaintiff must "introduc[e] evidence that the requested modification is reasonable in the general sense." *Johnson v. Gambrinus Co./Spoetzl Brewery*, 116 F.3d 1052 (5th Cir. 1997). Once the plaintiff has shown this, the burden shifts to the defendant to prove that the modification would cause an undue burden or fundamentally alter the nature of its service, program or activity. The defendant's proof must focus on the specific circumstances of the case rather than on reasonableness in general. *Id.* As noted above, in *PGA Tour, Inc. v. Martin*, 532 U.S. 661 (2001), the Court stated that the ADA "requires an *individualized inquiry* must be made to determine whether a specific modification for a particular person's disability would be reasonable under the circumstances as well as necessary for that person, and yet at the same time not work a fundamental alteration." (Emphasis added). *See also Crowder v. Kitagawa*, 81 F.3d 1480 (9th Cir. 1996); *Juvelis v. Snider*, 68 F.3d 648 (3d Cir. 1995).

A public accommodation may refer an individual with a disability to another public accommodation if the public accommodation would do so in the normal course of its operation when the person was not disabled. 28 C.F.R. § 36.302(b)(1).

A public accommodation must modify its policies, practices or procedures to permit the use of a service animal (*i.e.*, any animal that assists a disabled person) in any area open to the public. Title III intends that the broadest feasible access be given to service animals. *See, e.g., Johnson v. Gambrinus Co./Spoetzl Brewery*, 116 F.3d 1052 (5th Cir. 1997); *Lockett v. Catalina Channel Express, Inc.*, 496 F.3d 1061 (9th Cir. 2007). However, the DOJ's regulations recognize that in *rare circumstances* accommodation of service animals may not be required if: "(1) The animal is out of control and the animal's handler does not take effective action to control it; or (2) The animal is not housebroken." 28 C.F.R. § 36.302(c)(2).

The Title III regulations were modified in 2010 to define a "service animal" as: "any dog that is individually trained to do work or perform tasks for the benefit of an individual with a disability, including a physical, sensory, psychiatric, intellectual, or other mental disability." 28 C.F.R. § 36.104. In addition, a miniature horse can be a service animal "if the miniature horse has been individually trained to do work or perform tasks for the benefit of the individual with a disability." 28 C.F.R. § 36.302(c)(9). For miniature horses (but not service dogs), an entity is allowed to consider four factors in determining whether it will make a reasonable modification to its policies, practices, or procedures to allow the use of the miniature horse. These factors include: (1) the type, size and weight of the miniature horse, (2) whether the handler has sufficient control of the miniature horse, (3) whether the miniature horse is housebroken, and (4) whether the miniature horse's presence creates a legitimate safety requirement. 28 C.F.R. § 36.302(c)(9)(ii). The Title III service animal regulation has been cited in Title II and Section 504 cases, and courts have rejected the argument that a service animal must be professionally trained or certified and note that there is no requirement in the federal regulations as to the amount or type of work a service animal must provide for the benefit of the disabled person. *See, e.g., Green v. Housing Authority of Clackamas County*, 994 F.Supp. 1253 (D.Or. 1998); *Bronk v. Ineichen*, 54 F.3d 425 (7th Cir. 1995); *but see Access Now, Inc. v. Town of Jasper*, 268 F.Supp.2d 973 (E.D.Tenn. 2003).

Public accommodations must also modify its policies, practices or procedures to allow use of mobility devices. The 2010 regulations added a new definition of "mobility devices." 28 C.F.R. § 36.311. This definition was added because of increased use of motorized devices, such as Segways, that were not designed to be used as mobility aids but which are sometimes used by individuals with mobility impairments. DOJ distinguishes between devices that are "designed for use by individuals with mobility disabilities" and "other power-driven mobility devices." Covered entities must permit the use of the first category of devices. 28 C.F.R. § 36.311(a) & (b). For mobility devices in the second category, the regulations provide five assessment factors for the public accommodation to use in demonstrating that the power-driven mobility device cannot be operated safely. 28 C.F.R. § 36.311(b).

The 2010 regulations also create rules about inquiries directed to people who use mobility devices. For those individuals who use devices that are designed for use by individuals with disabilities, a covered entity can *not* ask questions about the nature and extent of the individual's disability. 28 C.F.R. § 36.311(c)(1). For individuals using other power-driven mobility devices, a covered entity can seek a "credible assurance" that the mobility device is required because of the person's disability. Such credible assurance can include a state-issued disability parking placard or card. "In lieu of a valid, State-issued disability parking placard or card, or State-issued proof of disability, a public accommodation shall accept as a credible assurance a verbal representation, not contradicted by observable fact, that the other power-driven mobility device is being used for a mobility disability." 28 C.F.R. § 36.311(c)(2).

In the 2008 Amendments to the ADA, Congress clarified that entities do not need make "reasonable modifications" under ADA Titles II or III for individuals who are only covered by the ADA by virtue of the "regarded as" definition of disability. *See* 42 U.S.C. § 12201(h). Congress' clarification is unlikely to have much of an impact on the case law in this area because requests for "reasonable modifications" nearly always occurred under ADA Titles II and III by individuals who met the "actually disabled" definition.

§ 7.13   ADA TITLES II AND III AND SECTION 504: INTEGRATED SETTING

Owners and operators of places of public accommodation must allow individuals with disabilities to participate in an equal fashion or to benefit equally from the goods, services, facilities, or other benefits provided by the entity. Further, such goods, services, facilities and other benefits must be provided to disabled individuals in the "most integrated setting appropriate." 42 U.S.C.A. § 12182(b)(1)(B). Thus, while individuals with disabilities may be *offered* a form of modified participation, such modified participation may not be *required*. For example, while an entity might offer specially designed recreational programs for mobility-impaired children, such children must also be free to attend recreational programs made available to nondisabled children. 28 C.F.R. Pt. 36, App. B § 36.203.

The integrated setting requirement also appears in the Title II and Section 504 regulations. 28 C.F.R. § 35.130(d);   28   C.F.R.   § 41.51(d);   45   C.F.R. § 84.4(b)(2). The Supreme Court interpreted the Title II regulations in *Olmstead v. L.C.*, 527 U.S. 581 (1999) and noted that the ADA specifically identifies unjustified "segregation" of persons with disabilities as a form of discrimination. 42 U.S.C. § 12101(a)(2),   (5).   It   concluded   that   undue institutionalization qualifies as discrimination "by reason of . . . disability." The Court also emphasized, however,   that   nothing   in   the   ADA   or   its implementing   regulations   condones   terminating institutional   placements   for   persons   unable   to handle or benefit from community settings. Nor does the statute require that community-based treatment be imposed on patients who do not want it.   The   Court   left   the   determination   of   an individual's eligibility for community treatment in the states' hands. It held that "the State generally may rely on the reasonable assessments of its own professionals in determining whether an individual 'meets the essential eligibility requirements' for habilitation in a community-based program. Absent such qualification, it would be inappropriate to remove a patient from the more restrictive setting."

The *Olmstead* decision is widely credited with assisting   individuals   with   developmental disabilities live in more integrated communities. *See, e.g., Benjamin ex rel. Yock v. Dep't of Pub. Welfare of Pa.*, 701 F.3d 938 (3rd Cir. 2012).

After *Olmstead*, some defendants have argued that the integration mandate found in the regulations for the ADA and Section 504 is not enforceable because it exceeds the scope of the statutory text. Courts have rejected this argument. *See, e.g., Frederick L. v. Department of Public Welfare*, 157 F.Supp.2d 509 (E.D.Pa. 2001); *Lewis v. New Mexico Dept. of Health*, 94 F.Supp.2d 1217 (D.N.M. 2000).

§ 7.14   ADA TITLES II AND III AND SECTION 504: SAFETY DEFENSE

A.   THREAT TO SELF

It is unclear whether a covered entity may bar individuals from participating in an activity because they pose a risk to *themselves*. The Section 504 regulations define a "qualified handicapped person" as one "who, with or without reasonable accommodation, can perform the essential functions of the position in question without endangering the health and safety *of the individual or others*." 29 C.F.R. § 1613.702(f) (emphasis supplied). Under this regulation courts, were split on whether an entity could bar an individual from participating because they posed a risk to *themselves*. *Compare Poole v. South Plainfield Bd. of Educ.*, 490 F.Supp. 948 (D.N.J. 1980) ("Life has risks. The purpose of § 504, however, is to permit the handicapped individual to live life fully as they are able without paternalistic authorities deciding that certain activities are too risky for them.") *with Knapp v. Northwestern Univ.*, 101 F.3d 473 (7th Cir. 1996) (stating that, if a school has examined all the medical evidence on the risk of injury, it has the right "—regardless of whether conflicting medical opinions exist—. . . to determine that an individual is not otherwise qualified to play without violating the Rehabilitation Act").

The ADA does not allude to the risk to anyone in its definition of "qualified individual with a disability." Instead, it creates a defense to a charge of employment discrimination under Title I where a person with a disability is a "direct threat to the health or safety *of other individuals* in the workplace." 42 U.S.C. § 12113(b). There is no mention of persons who present a risk *to themselves*.

An EEOC regulation interpreting this section, however, defines a direct threat as "a significant risk of substantial harm to the health or safety *of the individual or others* that cannot be eliminated or reduced by reasonable accommodation." The Supreme Court upheld this regulation in *Chevron U.S.A. Inc. v. Echazabal*, 536 U.S. 73 (2002), and, thus, a person can be barred from employment if he poses a risk to himself.

The Title III regulations, however, state only that a covered entity may bar a person from participating "when that individual poses a direct threat to the health or safety *of others*." 28 C.F.R. § 36.208(a) (emphasis added). An interpretive guidance in the Title II regulations indicates that these regulations apply equally to public entities. 28 C.F.R. pt. 35.100, subpt. A § 35.104. No court has ruled on the "threat to self" issue under ADA Titles II and III.

The ADA Title III regulations also provide, however, that "[a] public accommodation may impose legitimate safety requirements that are necessary for safe operation. Safety requirements must be based on actual risks and not on mere speculation, stereotypes, or generalizations about individuals with disabilities." 28 C.F.R. Pt. 36, App. B § 36.301(b). For example, height requirements may be justifiable for certain amusement park rides and in a recreational rafting expedition all participants may be required to be able to meet a necessary level of swimming proficiency. *Id.; see, e.g., Larsen v. Carnival Corp., Inc.*, 242 F.Supp.2d 1333 (S.D.Fla. 2003) (holding a cruise line did not violate ADA where the ship's physician concluded that the passenger had to be disembarked for his own safety and well-being because the ventilator which the passenger used every night to treat his sleep apnea was not functioning and the passenger had almost died on five prior occasions; under the cruise line's universal eligibility criteria, sailing could not impose a critical risk to an individual's health, and the decision to disembark the passenger was based upon a reasonable concern for his safety, rather than mere speculation, stereotypes, or generalizations about his disability).

Based on the Court's decision in *Echazabal*, it is likely that the same logic would be applied to cases brought under ADA Title II and III—that a covered entity can act based on the individual's purported risk to himself (rather than others).

B.   RISK TO OTHERS

Entities covered under Titles II and III and Section 504 are not required to permit an individual with a disability to participate in or benefit from their goods, services, facilities or privileges if the individual would pose a direct threat to the health or safety of *others*. A determination that an individual with a disability poses a direct health or safety threat must be made on a case-by-case basis, through consideration of four basic factors: (1) the duration of the risk; (2) the nature and severity of the potential harm; (3) the likelihood that the potential harm will occur; and (4) the imminence of the potential harm. These factors were enumerated by the Supreme Court in *School Board of Nassau County v. Arline*, 480 U.S. 273 (1987) and subsequently adopted in the ADA and other regulations. *See, e.g.,* 28 C.F.R. § 36.208(c). *See also Doe v. Woodford County Bd. of Educ.*, 213 F.3d 921 (6th Cir. 2000); *Theriault v. Flynn*, 162 F.3d 46 (1st Cir. 1998). The existence of a significant health risk from treating or accommodating an individual with a disability must be determined from the viewpoint of the person refusing the treatment or accommodation. That risk assessment, however, must be based on medical or other objective reasons and not just the person's good faith belief a significant threat existed. *Bragdon v. Abbott*, 524 U.S. 624 (1998).

§ 7.15   ADA TITLES II AND III AND
SECTION 504: DISPARATE IMPACT

In *Alexander v. Choate*, 469 U.S. 287 (1985), the Court held that discriminatory intent is not a necessary element of a Section 504 claim but noted that Section 504 could not reach *every* action disparately affecting people with disabilities. Rather, the Court stated that the appropriate question when determining whether an action has an impermissible disparate impact upon people with disabilities is whether the action denies such persons meaningful access to the benefit offered.

Courts interpreting Titles II and III have also applied disparate impact analysis. *See, e.g., Crowder v. Kitagawa*, 81 F.3d 1480 (9th Cir. 1996) (Title II); *Independent Living Resources v. Oregon Arena Corp.*, 1 F.Supp.2d 1159 (D.Ore.1998) (Title III). In *Alexander v. Sandoval*, 532 U.S. 275 (2001), the Court held that plaintiffs could not pursue a private right of action for disparate impact claims under Title VI of the Civil Rights Act of 1964 because that cause of action is not recognized by statute's language; it is only recognized in the regulations promulgated to enforce Title VI. Lower courts have distinguished Title VI from Section 504 and held that disparate impact claims are still viable under Section 504 and ADA Titles II and III. Those courts acknowledge that Congress modeled Section 504 on Title VI, but note that the *Choate* Court rejected the argument that Section 504 only barred intentional discrimination. *See, e.g., Frederick L. v. Department of Public Welfare*, 157 F.Supp.2d 509 (E.D.Pa. 2001);

Robinson v. State of Kansas, 295 F.3d 1183 (10th Cir. 2002).

§ 7.16   ADA TITLES II AND III AND SECTION 504: DISCRIMINATION VIS-À-VIS OTHER PEOPLE WITH DISABILITIES

Access-to-services cases sometimes involve claims that one group of people with disabilities is being discriminated against another group of people with disabilities. There is some conflict over whether such claims fall within the purview of ADA Titles II and III and Section 504. In *Traynor v. Turnage*, 485 U.S. 535 (1988), the Court stated, "There is nothing in the Rehabilitation Act that requires that any benefit extended to one category of handicapped persons also be extended to all other categories of handicapped persons." Lower courts, however, have disagreed regarding whether discrimination claims can be based on disparities in the treatment of groups of people with differing disabilities. *Compare Martin v. Voinovich*, 840 F.Supp. 1175 (S.D.Ohio 1993) (rejecting argument that Section 504 can never apply between persons with different disabilities); *McGuire v. Switzer*, 734 F.Supp. 99 (S.D.N.Y. 1990) (stating that "conclusion that discrimination vis-à-vis other disabled persons is cognizable under § 504 is supported by the bulk of the authority"); *Helen L. v. DiDario*, 46 F.3d 325 (3d Cir. 1995) *with Flight v. Gloeckler*, 68 F.3d 61 (2d Cir. 1995) (finding that the Rehabilitation Act "d[oes] not clearly establish an obligation to meet [a disabled person's] particular needs vis-à-vis the needs of other handicapped individuals, but mandates only that services provided non-handicapped individuals not be denied [to a disabled person] because he is handicapped."); *Parker v. Metropolitan Life Ins. Co.*, 121 F.3d 1006 (6th Cir. 1997) ("The ADA simply does not mandate equality between individuals with different disabilities. Rather, the ADA, like the Rehabilitation Act, prohibits discrimination between the disabled and the non-disabled.")

The Supreme Court's decision in *Olmstead v. L.C.*, 527 U.S. 581 (1999) can be used to argue that the ADA is not limited to claims of discrimination involving the preferential treatment of individuals without disabilities in comparison to individuals with disabilities. In that case, the Court held that the ADA can be violated when the state fails to offer community-based treatment for persons with mental disabilities and thereby fails to follow the Title II regulation which requires that individuals with disabilities be placed "in the most integrated setting appropriate to [their] needs." 28 C.F.R. § 35.130(d). The plaintiffs, who had mental impairments, were treated less favorably than other individuals with disabilities who the state placed in community-based programs rather than institutional settings. Thus, the Court implicitly recognized that the ADA can be used to argue that disability-based discrimination has occurred even if individuals without disabilities are not being treated preferentially.

§ 7.17   ADA TITLE III: PROVISION OF AUXILIARY AIDS AND SERVICES

Unless it would constitute an undue burden or result in a fundamental alteration, owners and operators of places of public accommodation must provide necessary auxiliary aids and services for individuals with disabilities. The DOJ 2010 Title III regulations expanded the definition of "auxiliary aids and services" and added significant language concerning effective communication, telecommunications, and video remote interpreting. *See* 28 C.F.R. § 36.303. The term "auxiliary aids and services" has been amended to include: qualified interpreters on-site or through video remote interpreting (VRI) services, real-time computer-aided transcription services; exchange of written notes; real-time captioning; voice, text, and video-based telecommunications products and systems, including text telephones (TTYs), videophones, and captioned telephones, or equally effective telecommunications devices; videotext displays; and accessible electronic and information technology. 28 C.F.R. § 36.303(b). A public accommodation is not required to provide services of a personal nature, however, such as assistance with toileting, eating or dressing. 28 C.F.R. § 36.306.

The appropriateness of an auxiliary aid or service is measured, in part, by its *effectiveness*. The 2010 ADA Title III regulations provide that the obligation of effectiveness is especially important for determining whether appropriate assistance with communication has occurred. 28 C.F.R.

§ 36.303(c)(1). Effectiveness is determined by the "nature, length, and complexity of the communication involved; and the context in which the communication is taking place." 28 C.F.R. § 36.303(c)(1)(ii). Public accommodations "should consult with individuals with disabilities whenever possible to determine what type of auxiliary aid is needed to ensure effective communication." *Id.* The public accommodation should also protect the "privacy and independence of the individual with a disability" in selecting an auxiliary aid or service *Id.* Although the public accommodation makes the ultimate decision about what type of auxiliary aid or service is offered, the chosen method must result in "effective communication." *Id.*

A public accommodation shall not rely on an adult accompanying an individual with a disability to interpret or facilitate communication except in an emergency or upon the request of the individual with a disability. Similarly, a public accommodation should not rely on a minor child to interpret or facilitate communication except in an emergency. 28 C.F.R. § 36.303(c)(3) & (4).

In its Section-by-Section Analysis, DOJ provides many examples of what kinds of communication methods are appropriate in various contexts. Some of this discussion relates to the health care context. For example, the Section-by-Section Analysis states: "Exchange of notes likely will be effective in situations that do not involve substantial conversation, for example, when blood is drawn for routine lab tests or regular allergy shots are administered. However interpreters should be used when the matter involves more complexity, such as in communication of medical history or diagnoses, in conversations about medical procedures and treatment decisions, or in communication of instructions for care at home or elsewhere." 28 C.F.R. § 36.303 App.

The 2010 ADA Title III regulations expanded the rules about telecommunication. When a public accommodation uses an automatic-attendant system, the system "must provide effective real-time communication with individuals using auxiliary aids and services." 28 C.F.R. § 36.303(d)(1). The DOJ regulations also require that, if a public accommodation customarily offers its customers, clients or participants the opportunity to make outgoing telephone calls on more than an incidental basis, it must make "available public telephones, TTYs, or other telecommunications products and systems for use by an individual who is deaf or hard of hearing, or has a speech impairment." 28 C.F.R. § 36.303(d)(2). Hotels and motels must possess a TTY or similar device at the front desk to permit receipt of calls from guests who use TTYs in their rooms. 28 C.F.R. § 36.303(d)(5). Further, places of lodging that provide televisions in five or more guest rooms and hospitals that provide televisions for patients must provide, on request, a means for decoding closed-captions for a hearing-impaired customer or patient. 28 C.F.R. § 36.303(e).

The 2010 DOJ ADA Title III regulations also provide specific rules regarding the use of video remote interpreting services to assure their quality and that staff have sufficient training to use such services. 28 C.F.R. § 36.303(f).

With the exception of a few specifically mandated accommodations, however, whether a particular auxiliary aid or service must be provided will depend upon whether the "fundamental alteration" or "undue burden" tests are satisfied. If provision of one auxiliary aid or service would result in a fundamental alteration or undue burden, the public accommodation must provide an alternative aid or service that would *not* result in a fundamental alteration or undue burden to the extent that such an accommodation is possible. 28 C.F.R. § 36.303(g).

§ 7.18   ADA TITLE II: PROVISION OF AUXILIARY AIDS AND SERVICES

When DOJ amended its Title II regulations in 2010, it created rules comparable to what were discussed above for Title III entities. The definition of "auxiliary aids and services" was broadened to include a broad range of ways in which assistance with communication can take place. 28 C.F.R. § 35.104 (definition of auxiliary aids and services). Further, as with the ADA Title III regulations, new and broader language was added concerning effective communication. 28 C.F.R. § 35.160. A public entity may not impose a surcharge on persons with disabilities in order to cover the costs of accommodations or auxiliary aids. 28 C.F.R. § 35.130(f). And, as under Title III, public entities are not required to provide personal devices or services of a personal nature. *Id.* § 35.135.

§ 7.19   ADA TITLE III: NEWLY CONSTRUCTED OR ALTERED FACILITIES

All newly constructed places of public accommodation *and* commercial facilities must be readily accessible to and usable by individuals with disabilities. Further, when altering their facilities or portions thereof, public accommodations and commercial facilities must make such alterations in a manner that "to the maximum extent feasible" renders the altered portions readily accessible to and usable by individuals with disabilities.

The DOJ's Title III regulations set forth detailed criteria to be followed when making newly constructed or altered facilities accessible. *See, generally*, 28 C.F.R. §§ 36.401–406. These include the ADA Accessibility Guidelines for Buildings and Facilities (ADAAG), 28 C.F.R. Pt. 36, App. A. Although a detailed discussion of these rules are beyond the scope of this Nutshell, a few significant regulatory provisions deserve explanation:

First, the requirement that a newly constructed facility be accessible applies to the *entire* facility, *including* work areas; it does not just apply to areas open to the public. However, employee work areas need only be designed and constructed so that individuals with disabilities "can approach, enter, and exit them." ADAAG Standard 203.9. While work areas do not need to be fully accessible, the Advisory commentary states that accessibility "at the outset will avoid more costly retrofits when current employees become temporarily or permanently disabled, or when new employees with disabilities are hired." Advisory ADAAG Standard 203.9.

Second, when a commercial facility is located in a private residence, the portion used either exclusively or in part as a commercial facility must be accessible. The portion used exclusively as a residence need not be accessible, but the entrance to the commercial facility and those portions of the residence available to or used by employees or visitors of the commercial facility, including restrooms, must be accessible. 28 C.F.R. § 36.401(b).

Third, full compliance with the requirement that newly constructed places of public accommodation must be accessible is excused if the entity can demonstrate that it is "structurally impracticable" to meet accessibility requirements due to the "unique characteristics of [the] terrain." 28 C.F.R. § 36.401(c)(1). In such a case, the facility shall be made accessible to the extent it is not structurally impracticable to do so.

Fourth, elevators are not required to be installed in a newly constructed or altered facility that has fewer than three stories *or* less than 3,000 square feet per story. This exemption does not apply, however, if the facility is a professional office of a health care provider, a shopping center or a shopping mall. In addition, the Attorney General may determine that a particular category of facilities requires the installation of elevators based on the usage of the facilities. 42 U.S.C.A. § 12183(b). Pursuant to that proviso, the DOJ has issued a regulation mandating that the elevator exemption does not apply to a terminal, depot, or other station used for specified public transportation or to an airport passenger terminal. 28 C.F.R. § 36.404(a).

Fifth, where a public accommodation or commercial facility is undertaking an alteration that affects, or could affect, the usability of or access to an area of a facility that contains a "primary function" (*i.e.*, "a major activity for which the area is intended"), the entity must ensure that, to the maximum extent feasible, "the path of travel to the altered area and the bathrooms, telephones, and drinking fountains serving the altered area" are readily accessible to and usable by individuals with disabilities. 42 U.S.C.A. § 12183(a)(2). An entity does not have to comply with this rule, however, if "the cost and scope of such alteration is *disproportionate* to the cost of the overall alteration." 28 C.F.R. § 36.403(a) (emphasis added).

Alterations will be deemed "disproportionate" when the cost to provide an accessible path to the altered area is greater than 20% of the cost of the alteration to the primary function area. 28 C.F.R. § 36.403(f)(1). When the costs are found to be disproportionate, the path of travel must be made accessible to the extent that can be accomplished without incurring disproportionate costs. In such a case, when choosing which accessible elements to provide, the regulations state that the order of priority should be in providing:

(i) An accessible entrance;

(ii) An accessible route to the altered area;

(iii) At least one accessible restroom for each sex or a single unisex restroom;

(iv) Accessible telephones;

(v) Accessible drinking fountains; and

(vi) When possible, additional accessible elements such as parking, storage, and alarms.

28 C.F.R. § 36.403(g)(2).

§ 7.20   ADA TITLE III: REMOVAL OF BARRIERS FROM EXISTING FACILITIES

Public accommodations are required to remove structural architecture and communication barriers in existing facilities where such removal is "readily achievable." The "readily achievable" standard is much lower than the "undue burden" or "undue hardship" standards and means "easily accomplishable and able to be carried out without much difficulty or expense." 42 U.S.C.A. § 12181(9). Factors to be considered when determining whether barrier removal is readily achievable include 1) the nature and cost of the action needed; 2) the financial resources of, and the number of persons employed at, the facility; 3) the effect of the action on the entity's expenses or resources; 4) the impact of the action upon the operation of the facility; and 5) the size, nature, type and financial resources of the covered entity.

Measures taken to comply with this obligation need not meet the stringent standards required for the accessibility of new facilities. The ADA recognizes that retrofitting existing facilities may be excessively costly and that a less rigorous degree of accessibility should be required with respect to existing facilities than with respect to new facilities—where accessibility fixtures can be economically incorporated. Thus, measures taken to remove barriers in existing facilities are only subject to the technical standards that must be followed when alterations are made to the facilities of a public accommodation to the extent that compliance with such technical requirements is readily achievable. If compliance with those technical requirements is *not* readily achievable, other readily achievable measures that do not fully comply may be taken to achieve accessibility to the extent they do not pose a significant health or safety risk.

When determining the extent to which a public accommodation must remove barriers in existing facilities, the standards for alterations under the ADAAG on new construction or alteration apply. For example, a hotel could satisfy the requirement that it remove structural barriers in existing facilities if it achieved accessibility to the extent required by the ADAAG. There is one exception, however, to the rule that measures taken to remove barriers in existing facilities are subject to the ADAAG technical standards: public accommodations are not required to comply with the path of travel requirements for new construction. 28 C.F.R. § 36.304(d).

The obligation of public accommodations to remove barriers in existing facilities includes the obligation to remove "structural" communication barriers. *Id.* § 36.304(a). This term includes barriers that are an integral part of a facility's physical structure (such as permanent signage and alarm systems, the lack of adequate sound buffers, and the presence of physical partitions that hamper the passage of sound waves between employees and customers).

The obligation to remove architectural barriers includes removal of *any* kind of physical barrier, even those caused by the location of temporary or movable structures, such as furniture, equipment or display racks. To make premises accessible to persons who use wheelchairs, for example, restaurants may need to rearrange tables and chairs and stores may need to reconfigure display racks and shelves. The latter actions are not readily achievable, however, to the extent that they would result "in a significant loss of selling or serving space." *Id.* § 36.304(f).

If barrier removal is not readily achievable, a public accommodation must make its goods or services available to people with disabilities through alternative measures that are readily achievable.

Because entities subject to Title III may lack the resources to remove all existing barriers at a given time, the regulations recommend that public accommodations follow specified priorities for removing barriers in existing facilities. 28 C.F.R. § 36.304(c). The first priority is to provide access to places of public accommodation (such as by installing entrance ramps, widening entrances and providing accessible parking). The second priority is to provide access to areas where goods and services are made available to the public (such as by adjusting the layout of display racks, rearranging tables, widening doors, providing Brailled and raised signage and visual alarms, and installing ramps). The third priority is to provide access to restroom facilities (such as by removing obstructing furniture or vending machines, widening doors, installing ramps, providing accessible signage, widening toilet stalls and installing grab bars). The last priority is to take any other steps necessary to provide access to the goods, services, facilities or other benefits provided.

The obligation to engage in readily achievable barrier removal is continuing. Barrier removal that was initially not readily achievable may, as a result of changed circumstances, become readily achievable. 28 C.F.R. Pt. 36, App. B § 36.304.

Title III creates an exception for historic properties. To the extent that barrier removal would alter the historic nature of a property, such barrier removal is not required. *Id.*

§ 7.21   ADA TITLE III: LANDLORDS/LESSEES

The non-discrimination mandate of Title III applies to "any person who owns, *leases (or leases to),* or operates a place of public accommodation." 42 U.S.C.A. § 12182(a) (emphasis added). The DOJ regulations explain that responsibilities under this proviso will be allocated among owners, lessors and operators; such allocations may be determined by lease or contract. The regulations reflect the principles that: (1) both landlords and tenants are covered by the public accommodation requirements of Title III; and (2) Title III is not intended to change existing responsibilities between landlords and tenants as set forth in leasing agreements. Both the landlord and tenant remain fully liable in a private suit for compliance with ADA provisions relating to that place of public accommodation. *Botosan v. Paul McNally Realty*, 216 F.3d 827 (9th Cir. 2000).

In a proposed version of the accessibility regulations, DOJ considered allocating responsibility for providing auxiliary aids and services solely to the tenant. After receiving commentary, however, DOJ decided not to list specific allocations to specific parties but, rather, to leave the allocation of responsibility to the lease negotiations. *See* 28 C.F.R. § 36.201(a) App. C.

§ 7.22   ADA TITLE III: FRANCHISORS/FRANCHISEES

Courts are divided on the question of whether a franchisor is liable if a franchisee's building is not accessible. For example, in *United States v. Days Inns of Am., Inc.*, 151 F.3d 822 (8th Cir. 1998) the court held that a franchisor will be liable where it has significant degree of control over the final design and construction of a facility. *See also United*

States v. Days Inns of Am., Inc., 997 F.Supp. 1080 (C.D.Ill. 1998) (holding hotel licensing corporation and its parent were liable for ADA violations at franchisee's hotel). *But see United States v. Days Inns of Am., Inc.*, 22 F.Supp.2d 612 (E.D.Ky. 1998) (holding hotel licensing corporation and its parent were not liable under the ADA because they did not "design and construct" the new hotel at issue). And in *Neff v. American Dairy Queen Corp.*, 58 F.3d 1063 (5th Cir. 1995) the court held that Title III liability rested with the franchisee because it, not the franchisor, operated the franchise. *See also Lonberg v. Sanborn Theaters, Inc.*, 259 F.3d 1029 (9th Cir. 2001) (finding architect not liable under ADA Title III).

§ 7.23   ADA TITLE II: NEW CONSTRUCTION OR ALTERATIONS

Public entities are required to follow regulations with respect to new construction and alteration of existing buildings that are similar, but not identical, to those under Title III of the Act. *See, generally*, 28 C.F.R. § 35.151. In *Kinney v. Yerusalim*, 9 F.3d 1067 (3d Cir. 1993), the court held that resurfacing a street constituted an "alteration" and the corresponding obligation to provide curb cuts for wheelchair users.

State and local government facilities must follow the requirements of the 2010 ADA Standards for Accessible Design, including both the Title II regulations at 28 C.F.R. § 35.151; and the 2004 ADAAG Standards at 36 C.F.R. part 1191, appendices B and D. In the few places where requirements between the two differ, the requirements of 28 C.F.R. § 35.151 prevail. If the start date for construction is on or after March 15, 2012, all newly constructed or altered State and local government facilities must comply with the 2010 Standards. Before that date, the 1991 Standards (without the elevator exemption), the Uniform Federal Accessibility Standards (UFAS), or the 2010 Standards may be used for such projects when the start of construction commences on or after September 15, 2010.

It is confusing to have so many choices of standards prior to March 15, 2012, however, those differences will end over time.

There are significant differences between the UFAS and standards, concerning issues such as text telephones for hearing-impaired people; Brailled elevator car control buttons; requirements relating to seating and assistive listening systems in assembly areas; and the number of accessible check out areas in stores.

§ 7.24   ADA TITLE II: EXISTING FACILITIES AND PROGRAMS

Facilities of state and local government entities that are open to the public must be accessible to individuals with disabilities. This includes the requirements to make reasonable accommodations and/or to provide auxiliary aids where necessary, unless a fundamental alteration or undue burden would result. Thus, for example, state and local courts must be fully accessible to people with disabilities, as must state and local government offices.

Title II requires that the services, programs and activities of a public entity must be readily accessible to and usable by individuals with disabilities *when viewed in their entirety*; it does not necessarily require public entities to make *each* of their existing facilities accessible. 28 C.F.R. § 35.150(a)(1). In *Barden v. City of Sacramento*, 292 F.3d 1073 (9th Cir. 2002) the court stated that, rather than determining whether each function of a city can be characterized as a service, program, or activity for purposes of Title II, courts should determine whether it is "a normal function of a governmental entity." It then held that maintaining public sidewalks is a normal function of a city, and thus maintaining their accessibility for individuals with disabilities falls within the scope of Title II.

The standards for accessibility for state and local government entities are higher than the standards for places of public accommodations under Title III. Under Title III existing facilities must only be made accessible to the extent that accessibility is "readily achievable." Under Title II, however, the programs or activities of public entities must be made accessible to people with disabilities unless that would cause a "fundamental alteration" to the program or activity or constitute an "undue financial and administrative burden" to the entity. 28 C.F.R. § 35.150(a)(3). The latter exception is much narrower.

The decision about whether making facilities or programs accessible would constitute a fundamental alteration or an undue burden must be made by the head of the public entity or a high-ranking designee. Further, the burden is on the public entity to show that compliance would be burdensome and to set forth the reasons for that conclusion in writing. *Id.*

Individuals with disabilities should have access to public services and facilities in all but extraordinary circumstances. Thus, if one action would result in a fundamental alteration or undue burden, the public entity must take other actions that would not have such a result. *Id.*

Structural changes are not required if other methods would provide effective accessibility. When an entity selects a method of providing program access, however, priority must be given to the method that results in the most integrated setting appropriate to the circumstances. *Id.* § 35.150(b)(1).

Where non-structural changes or accommodations are at issue, state and local government entities were required to make their programs and facilities accessible to people with disabilities as of January 26, 1992. 28 C.F.R. Pt. 35, App. A § 35.150. Where structural changes in facilities are undertaken to comply with the accessibility obligations, the Act provided public entities with three years to comply. All structural changes to existing facilities must be made by January 26, 1995 at the latest, "but in any event as expeditiously as possible." 28 C.F.R. § 35.150(c).

The DOJ has opined that, because the ADA does not address the issue of *how* public entities are to finance improvements required under Title II, the final determination with respect to payment for improvements is to be made by the taxing entity. 6 NDLR ¶ 32 (1994).

Public entities are not required to ensure program accessibility for a historic property if the result would be to threaten or destroy its historic significance. Where an accommodation is not required because it would threaten or destroy the historic significance of such a property, alternative methods of achieving accessibility must be provided (such as via use of audio-visual materials and devices, guides or other methods). 28 C.F.R. § 35.150(b)(3).

Individuals with disabilities are not required to accept accommodations or special benefits provided by state and local government entities if they choose not to do so. Similarly, if a state or local government entity offers special programs for people with disabilities, disabled people may choose to forgo such special programs and attend "regular" programs (assuming they are qualified for the "regular" programs). 28 C.F.R. § 35.130(b)(2). If a qualified individual with a disability elects to participate in the "regular" program, the government entity is still required to provide reasonable accommodations for that individual. The fact that a special program is offered, however, may be one factor in determining whether the requested accommodation is reasonable. Department of

Justice, *Title II Technical Assistance Manual* § II–3.4400.

§ 7.25   ADA TITLE II: COMMUNICATIONS

State and local government entities have an affirmative obligation to ensure effective communication with disabled individuals, subject to the "fundamental alteration" and "undue burden" exceptions. Public entities are required to furnish appropriate auxiliary aids and services necessary to ensure that communications with hearing- or speech-impaired persons are as effective as communications with other individuals. When determining what type of auxiliary aid or service is necessary, the entity is required to give primary consideration to the requests of the individual with a disability. The public entity must honor that individual's choice unless it can show that another effective means of communication exists or unless it meets its burden of proving that the fundamental alteration/undue burden test is satisfied. Department of Justice, *Title II Technical Assistance Manual* § II–7.1100.

When a public entity "communicates by telephone with applicants and beneficiaries," the entity must provide a TTY or "equally effective telecommunication system" to communicate with individuals who are hearing- or speech-impaired. 28 C.F.R. § 35.161 All telephone emergency services, including 911 services, must provide direct access to individuals who use TTYs or computer modems. Public entities must provide adequate information and signage to ensure that all interested persons, including persons with impaired hearing or vision, can obtain information about the existence and location of accessible services, activities and facilities.

The 2010 ADA Title II regulations emphasize the importance of "effective communication" and say that effective communication "must be provided in accessible formats, in a timely manner, and in such a way as to protect the privacy and independence of the individual with a disability." 28 C.F.R. § 35.160(b)(2). Further, as with the ADA Title III regulations, they provide that adult companions or minors should not be used as interpreters except for reasons of safety. 28 C.F.R. § 35.160(c)(2) & (3).

§ 7.26   DIFFERENCES BETWEEN ADA TITLE II AND SECTION 504

There are a few differences between the obligations of public entities covered under ADA Title II and recipients of federal financial assistance covered under Section 504.

First, with respect to existing facilities, both laws require public entities and recipients to operate their programs, services and activities so that, when viewed in their entirety, they are readily accessible to and usable by persons with disabilities. Neither Act requires that every part of an existing facility be accessible; all that is required is that the program, service or activity be accessible as a whole. And, under both laws, accessibility with respect to existing facilities may be achieved by making nonstructural changes; structural changes must be made only when there is no feasible alternative means of achieving accessibility. Under Title II, when structural changes to existing facilities *are* required, they must be made by January 26, 1995. Such structural changes must satisfy the standards for new construction and alterations under both Title II (28 C.F.R. § 35.151) and Section 504 (34 C.F.R. § 104.23).

For purposes of Section 504, "existing facilities" are those for which construction began prior to June 3, 1977, while "existing facilities" for purposes of ADA Title II are those for which construction began prior to January 26, 1992. Thus, buildings constructed on or after June 3, 1977 but before January 26, 1992 are both "existing facilities" under ADA Title II *and* newly constructed buildings under Section 504. Such buildings, therefore, must meet the ADA Title II standards for existing facilities (28 C.F.R. § 35.150) *and* the Section 504 standards for new construction and alteration (34 C.F.R § 104.23).

Second, neither ADA Title II nor Section 504 require a covered entity to take an action that would result in a fundamental alteration to its program, service or activity, or that would result in undue financial or administrative burdens. The DOJ has noted, however, that the undue burden defense will rarely be satisfied under Title II. 28 C.F.R. Pt. 35, App. A § 35.150. Moreover, unlike the ADA Title II regulations, the Section 504 regulations do not require that the decision that an action would result in an undue burden or a fundamental alteration be made—in writing—by the head of the public entity at issue.

Third, the Title II regulations create an exception for historic properties, pursuant to which covered entities are not required to take action that would threaten or destroy the historic significance of properties classified as historic. The Section 504 regulations, however, do not contain a similar provision, and historic properties covered by both ADA Title II and Section 504 must satisfy Section 504 accessibility requirements despite the Title II exception. It has been held that "Section 504 could be interpreted with enough flexibility to permit recipients to make programs accessible without impairing the integrity of historical facilities." OCR Senior Staff Memo (Dec. 1, 1992), 19 IDELR 694 (1993) [hereafter "OCR Memo"]. But this issue remains problematic.

Fourth, an exception is created to Section 504's program accessibility requirements for entities with fewer than 15 employees. "[S]mall providers *are not* required by to make significant structural alterations to their existing facilities for the purpose of assuring program accessibility, if alternative means of providing the services are available." 29 U.S.C. § 794(c) (emphasis added). The applicable regulations specifically interpret "small providers" as recipients of federal funds having "fewer than fifteen employees." *See, e.g.,* 28 C.F.R. § 42.521(c); 34 C.F.R. § 104.22(c). No such exception is provided under ADA Title II.

Fifth, under ADA Title II public entities having 50 or more employees must develop a transition plan setting forth the steps necessary to make structural changes. 28 C.F.R § 35.150(d). Section 504, however, requires *all* recipients that are required to make structural changes to develop such a plan. 45 Fed. Reg. 30950 (1980). The Title II requirements with respect to transition plans are more specific, however, and require public entities to create a specified number of accessible parking spaces and public entities responsible for streets, roads or walkways to include schedules for providing curb ramps.

§ 7.27   ADA TITLE III: COURSES AND EXAMINATIONS

Any private entity that "offers examinations or courses related to applications, licensing, certification, or credentialing for secondary or postsecondary education, professional, or trade purposes" must offer such examinations or courses in an accessible place and manner or offer alternative accessible arrangements for persons with disabilities. 42 U.S.C.A. § 12189.

Examinations must be selected and administered to ensure that results reflect the aptitude or achievement level of an individual with a disability rather than any impaired sensory, manual or speaking skills. Where necessary, examinations must be modified for people with disabilities. Required modifications may include changes in the length of time permitted to complete the exam or adaptation of the manner in which the exam is given. Examinations specifically designed for people with disabilities must be offered as often and in as timely a manner as other examinations. They must also be offered at locations that are as convenient as the locations of other exams. Such examinations must either be administered in accessible facilities or alternative accessible arrangements must be made. 28 C.F.R. § 36.309(b).

In 2010, DOJ added three new requirements to the testing regulations. First, requests for documentation must be "reasonable and limited to the need for the modification, accommodation, or auxiliary aid or service requested." 28 C.F.R. § 36.309(b)(iv). Second, when considering requests for accommodations, entities must give "considerable weight to documentation of past modifications, accommodations or auxiliary aids or services received in similar testing situations, as well as such modifications, accommodations, or related aids and services provided in response to an Individualized Education Program (IEP) . . . or a plan describing services provided pursuant to a . . . Section 504 Plan." 28 C.F.R. § 36.309(b)(v). Finally, the 2010 regulations provide that an entity must "respond[ ] in a timely manner to requests for modifications, accommodations, or aids to ensure equal opportunity for individuals with disabilities." 28 C.F.R. § 36.309(b)(vi).

Auxiliary aids and services must be provided for test takers with disabilities when necessary, unless offering a particular aid or service would "fundamentally alter the measurement of the skills or knowledge the examination is intended to test or would result in an undue burden." 28 C.F.R. § 36.309(b)(3). An example of such an auxiliary aid or service is the provision of a reader for an individual with a learning disability.

Test administrators for standardized tests such as the SAT have historically "flagged" scores achieved when an accommodation is granted to indicate the tests were given under non-standard conditions. Many of those practices have been recently eliminated through consent decrees. For a more complete discussion on flagged scores and their use in the admissions process, see § 9.2(B) of this *Nutshell*.

Courses must also be modified to accommodate the needs of individuals with disabilities (such as by changing the length of time permitted for completion, substituting alternative requirements or adapting the manner in which the course is conducted). Courses must be administered in accessible locations and auxiliary aids must be provided where appropriate unless that would fundamentally alter the nature of the course. 28 C.F.R. § 36.309(c).

§ 7.28   ADA TITLE II AND SECTION 504: ENFORCEMENT, PROCEDURE AND REMEDIES

The remedies, procedures and rights for Section 504 claims also apply under Title II. 42 U.S.C.A. § 12133. The remedies under Section 504, in turn, are those found in Title VI of the Civil Rights Act. 29 U.S.C.A. § 794a. Those remedies, which include private enforcement by an individual plaintiff, and other issues regarding the enforcement of Section 504 are discussed in § 4.3 of this *Nutshell*. This section will focus on issues which are unique to the enforcement of Title II.

In *Board of Trustees of University of Alabama v. Garrett*, 531 U.S. 356 (2001) the Court held that *state* government employers have Eleventh Amendment immunity from suits for *money damages* under Title I of the ADA. The *Garrett* Court left open the question of whether monetary damages are permitted under ADA Title II. In *Tennessee v. Lane*, 541 U.S. 509 (2004), the Court held that Congress did not exceed its authority in enacting ADA Title II and providing a remedy of monetary damages in a context in which a fundamental right, such as access to the courts, was at stake. The Court did not define what constituted a fundamental right. In *United States v. Georgia*, 546 U.S. 151 (2006), it concluded that an inmate with a disability could use ADA Title II to attain monetary damages when challenging his conditions of confinement. His case included allegations that the Court found would arise to Eighth Amendment violations.

No matter how the Supreme Court ultimately resolves the question of sovereign immunity from *money damages* for *state* governments under ADA Title II with respect to a particular factual allegation, individuals with disabilities can still sue *municipal or local governments*. The principle of sovereign immunity applies to states, not local government.

Moreover, in *Garrett*, the Court suggested in a footnote that employees can still bring suits against state officials in their official capacities for *injunctive relief* under ADA Title II. Some earlier lower court decisions had found such relief was not available, but the courts have subsequently stated that *Garrett* abrogated those decisions. *See, e.g., Bruggeman v. Blagojevich*, 324 F.3d 906 (7th Cir. 2003); *Henrietta D. v. Bloomberg*, 331 F.3d 261 (2d Cir. 2003). Accordingly, it is now clear that injunctive relief is available against state defendants.

Reasonable attorneys' fees—including litigation expenses and costs—may be awarded to the prevailing party (other than the United States) in a court or administrative proceeding under Title II. For a more detailed discussion of the attorney's fees issue, see § 11.5 of this *Nutshell*.

An individual with a disability, or his or her authorized representative, may choose to file an administrative complaint under Title II. The regulations governing such complaints are found at 28 C.F.R. §§ 35.170–35.174. The individual must file the complaint with the appropriate federal agency within 180 days from the date of the alleged discrimination, unless the federal agency extends the time upon a showing of good cause. The "appropriate" federal agency is either the designated agency under Subpart G of the Title II regulations or any federal agency that provides funding to the public entity that is the subject of the complaint. Alternatively, an individual may file a complaint with the Department of Justice for referral to the proper agency. While an individual may file a grievance with the state or local entity at issue, that is not a necessary prerequisite to filing a complaint with the appropriate agency.

After receiving a complaint and determining that it has jurisdiction over the matter, the federal agency must either resolve the complaint or issue a "Letter of Findings" that describes the findings of fact, conclusions of law and remedies for each violation found. To resolve the complaint, the agency should attempt to negotiate a voluntary agreement with the public agency. If that effort fails, the agency must refer the complaint to the Department of Justice for further action, which may include institution of a civil suit.

Individuals with disabilities may also file an action against a public entity in federal court to enforce the provisions on services and program accessibility. It is not necessary to exhaust administrative remedies before filing such an action. *See, e.g., Bogovich v. Sandoval,* 189 F.3d 999 (9th Cir. 1999); *Bledsoe v. Palm Beach Cty. Soil & Water Conserv. Dist.,* 133 F.3d 816 (11th Cir. 1998).

Title II does not contain a specified statute of limitations. Thus, courts will generally borrow the state statute of limitations that is most analogous to the plaintiff's claim.

§ 7.29   ADA TITLE III: ENFORCEMENT AND REMEDIES

Title III may be enforced both privately by an individual plaintiff and publicly by the United States Attorney General.

An individual may file suit under the Act where he was subjected to discrimination on the basis of disability in violation of Title III or has "reasonable grounds" for believing that he or she is "about to be subjected to discrimination" in violation of the provisions relating to the construction or alteration of places of public accommodation. 42 U.S.C.A. § 12188(a)(1). Damages are *not* available in private actions brought under ADA Title III; remedies are limited to injunctive relief. Accordingly, the "standing" issues regarding injunctive relief discussed in § 4.3 of this *Nutshell* also apply to ADA Title III actions.

The remedies and procedures available under Title III are those set forth in Title II of the Civil Rights Act of 1964 (CRA Title II). However, ADA Title III only *specifically* adopts part of the enforcement provisions CRA Title II: "The remedies and procedures set forth in section 2000a–3*(a)* of this title are the remedies and procedures this subchapter provides. . . ." 42 U.S.C.A. § 12188(a)(1) (emphasis added). Section 2000a–3*(a)* [42 U.S.C.A. § 2000a–3(a)] states that an aggrieved person can bring a civil action for injunctive relief. CRA Title II cases, however, are also governed by § 2000a–3*(c)* which requires the exhaustion of state administrative remedies. ADA Title III did not specifically adopt § 2000a–3(c), and courts are split on whether its notice requirement is incorporated in the statute.

For example, some district courts in the Ninth Circuit initially ruled § 2000a–3(c) applies to ADA actions and state administrative remedies must be exhausted or the appropriate state authority must be notified before a Title III suit is filed. *See, e.g., Burkhart v. Asean Shopping Ctr., Inc.*, 55 F.Supp.2d 1013 (D.Ariz. 1999). Other district courts reached similar conclusions. *See, e.g., Daigle v. Friendly Ice Cream Corp.*, 957 F.Supp. 8 (D.N.H. 1997); *Bechtel v. East Penn School Dist.*, 1994 WL 3396 (E.D.Pa. 1994).

In *Botosan v. Paul McNally Realty*, 216 F.3d 827 (9th Cir. 2000), however, the court rejected these decisions and held that the statutory language is clear because ADA Title III only mentions § 2000a–3(a). Accordingly it held that § 2000a–3(c) does not apply to ADA Title III actions, and plaintiffs need not exhaust state administrative remedies or notify the appropriate state authority before filing suit. *See also Iverson v. Comsage, Inc.*, 132 F.Supp.2d 52 (D.Mass. 2001); *Moyer v. Showboat Casino Hotel, Atlantic City*, 56 F.Supp.2d 498 (D.N.J. 1999).

For violations of the provisions requiring newly constructed or altered facilities to be readily accessible to and usable by persons with disabilities, injunctive relief shall include an order that facilities be made readily accessible. Moreover, the Act provides that "[w]here appropriate, injunctive relief shall also include requiring the provision of an auxiliary aid or service, modification of a policy, or provision of alternative methods, to the extent required by [Title III]." 42 U.S.C. § 12188(a)(2).

Since Title III does not contain a statute of limitations setting a time frame in which actions must be filed, the courts will borrow analogous state statutes of limitations. A claim will be held to accrue when the fact of plaintiff's injury becomes reasonably ascertainable, not when the plaintiff determines the injury was unlawful.

The Attorney General has authority to institute "pattern and practice" lawsuits when there is reasonable cause to believe that any person or group of persons is engaged in a pattern or practice of discriminating against individuals with disabilities. He or she can also bring suit when "any person or group of persons has been discriminated against under [Title III] and such discrimination raises an issue of general public importance. . . ." 42 U.S.C.A. § 12188(b)(1)(B). Monetary damages, while not recoverable in private suits, *are* recoverable in suits filed by the Attorney General. Further, with respect to actions filed by the Attorney General, the court has discretion to vindicate the public interest by assessing penalties of up to $50,000 for a first violation and $100,000 for subsequent violations. In determining the amount of any such penalty, however, the court must consider "any good faith effort or attempt to comply with this Act by the entity." *Id*. § 12188(b)(5). Punitive damages are not available under Title III.

The prevailing party may obtain its attorney's fees in a Title III suit. For a more detailed discussion of the attorney's fees issue, see § 11.5 of this *Nutshell*.

§ 7.30   SECTION 504: INDIVIDUAL LIABILITY

Some courts have found that a person can be held liable in an individual capacity under the Rehabilitation Act if he or she was responsible for deciding whether an entity accepted or rejected federal funds. *See, e.g., Johnson v. New York Hosp.*, 903 F.Supp. 605 (S.D.N.Y. 1995); *United States v. Morvant*, 843 F.Supp. 1092 (E.D.La. 1994). In *Davis v. Flexman*, 109 F.Supp.2d 776 (S.D.Ohio 1999), however the court found that a psychologist, who had failed to provide a hearing impaired patient with a sign language interpreter, could not be individually liable under the Rehabilitation Act. The psychologist operated a clinic through a wholly owned corporation. The court held that the Rehabilitation Act only applied to the recipients of federal funds, and the corporate entity received federal funding, not the doctor individually. It also stated that finding there was individual liability under the Rehabilitation Act would be inconsistent with cases holding there was no individual liability for racial or gender discrimination in violation of Title VI of the Civil Rights Act or Title IX of the Education Amendments of 1972. *See also Fitzpatrick v. Commonwealth of Pa. Dept. of Transp.*, 40 F.Supp.2d 631 (E.D.Pa. 1999) (section 504 does not provide for individual liability).

§ 7.31   ADA TITLE III: INDIVIDUAL LIABILITY

There is also some dispute about whether an individual may be held liable under Title III as an operator of a public accommodation. In *Howe v. Hull*, 873 F.Supp. 72 (N.D.Ohio 1994), for example, the court held that an individual could be liable under Title III if he/she was in a position of authority and exercised his/her own discretion to perform potentially discriminatory acts. Other courts have also permitted individual liability under Title III. *See, e.g., Sharrow v. Bailey*, 910 F.Supp. 187 (M.D.Pa. 1995). Still other courts have ruled to the contrary, however. *See, e.g., Aikins v. St. Helena Hospital*, 843 F.Supp. 1329 (N.D.Cal. 1994) (finding no liability for a doctor because he did not have authority to enact or amend hospital policy); *Simenson v. Hoffman*, 7 NDLR ¶ 229 (N.D.Ill. 1995) (finding that "there is no individual liability under Title III of the ADA" because the statute only pertains to "private entities").

§ 7.32   ADA TITLE II: INDIVIDUAL LIABILITY

Several courts have held that suit cannot be brought against a state official in her *individual* capacity to vindicate rights created by Title II of the ADA or section 504 of the Rehabilitation Act. *See, e.g., Vinson v. Thomas*, 288 F.3d 1145 (9th Cir. 2002). And, prior to *Garrett*, some courts had held ADA Title II does not permit suits against state employees in their *official* capacities because it only lists the "state" itself as a covered entity, not a state official. However, courts have subsequently stated that *Garrett* abrogated those decisions. *See, e.g., Bruggeman v. Blagojevich*, 324 F.3d 906 (7th Cir. 2003); *Henrietta D. v. Bloomberg*, 331 F.3d 261 (2d Cir. 2003). Accordingly, it is now clear that injunctive relief is available against state officials in their official capacities.

§ 7.33   SECTION 508: ELECTRONIC AND INFORMATION TECHNOLOGY

In 1998, Congress amended Section 508 of the Rehabilitation Act, 29 U.S.C. § 794d, to require federal agencies to ensure, unless it would pose an undue burden to do so, that electronic and information technology (EIT) must be accessible to federal employees with disabilities and people with disabilities who are members of the public seeking information or services from the agencies. Section 508 only expressly applies to federal government agencies; the Attorney General has stated that it does not require private companies who market technologies to the federal government to modify EIT products used by company employees or to make their Internet sites accessible to people with disabilities. *Information Technology and People With Disabilities: The Current State of Federal Accessibility, Executive Summary & Recommendations*, http://www.justice.gov/crt/executive-summary-recommendations1.

The Architectural and Transportation Barriers Compliance Board ("the Access Board") has issued standards for EIT. 36 C.F.R. Pt. 1194. Agencies procuring an EIT product must ensure it complies with the regulations "when such products are available in the commercial marketplace or when such products are developed in response to a Government solicitation." *Id.* § 1194.2(2)(b). If no product in the marketplace meets all the standards, the agency must procure the product that best meets the standards. If compliance with the standards imposes an undue burden, the agency must provide the information and data involved by an alternative means, and the agency's documentation supporting the procurement must explain why, and to what extent, compliance with each standard creates an undue burden. Section's 508 standards do not require a fundamental alteration in the nature of a product or its components; the installation of specific accessibility-related software or the attachment of an assistive technology device at a federal employee's workstation if he is not an individual with a disability; or that an agency's EIT be available for access and use by individuals with disabilities at a location other than that where it is provided to the public. The standards do not apply to systems critical to the direct fulfillment of military or intelligence missions. *Id.* § 1194.3.

The Section 508 regulations include specific standards for several different types of EIT which are too detailed to discuss in this *Nutshell*. The following are some key provisions:

1. *Software Applications and Operating Systems*

Software designed to run on a system with a keyboard must be written so the function itself, or the result of performing a function, can be discerned textually. Applications must not disrupt or disable 1) a product's accessibility features which are developed and documented according to industry standards or 2) an operating system's accessibility features where those features' programming interface has been documented by the manufacturer and is available to the product developer. When animation is used, the information must be displayable in at least one non-animated presentation mode at the user's option. *Id.* § 1194.21.

2. *Web-based Intranet and Internet Information and Applications*

Web pages must include a text equivalent for every non-text element, and equivalent alternatives for any multimedia presentation must be synchronized with the presentation. Row and column headers shall be identified for data tables, and frames shall be titled with text that facilitates frame identification and navigation. When compliance cannot be accomplished in any other way, the web-site must include a text-only page with equivalent information or functionality which is updated whenever the primary page changes. The Access Board stated that it interpreted these and other requirements for web pages as consistent with the Web Content Accessibility Guidelines published by the Web Accessibility Initiative of the World Wide Web Consortium. *Id.* § 1194.22

3. *Telecommunications Products*

Telecommunications products or systems which allow voice communication but do not themselves provide a TTY functionality must provide a standard non-acoustic connection point for TTYs. Such telecommunication products shall support all commonly used cross-manufacturer non-proprietary standard TTY signal protocols; voice mail, auto-attendant, and interactive voice response telecommunications systems shall be usable by TTY users with their TTYs. Interference with hearing technologies (including hearing aids, cochlear implants, and assistive listening devices) shall be reduced to the lowest possible level. If a product has mechanically operated controls or keys, they must be tactilely discernible without activating the controls or keys, operable with one hand and shall not require tight grasping, pinching, or twisting of the wrist. If key repeat is supported, the delay before repeat shall be adjustable to at least 2 seconds. The status of all locking or toggle controls or keys shall be visually discernible and discernible either through touch or sound. *Id.* § 1194.23

4. *Video and Multimedia Products*

Analog television displays 13 inches and larger, and computer equipment that includes analog television receiver or display circuitry, must be equipped with caption decoder circuitry. Widescreen digital television (DTV) displays measuring at least 7.8 inches vertically, DTV sets with conventional displays measuring at least 13 inches vertically, and stand-alone DTV tuners must meet the same standard by July 1, 2002. Television tuners and tuner cards used in computers must be equipped with secondary audio program playback circuitry. Training and informational video and multimedia productions which support the agency's mission shall be open or closed captioned and be audio described if they contain visual information necessary for the comprehension of the content. *Id.* § 1194.24.

5. *Self-Contained, Closed Products and Desktop and Portable Computers*

Self-contained, closed products such as information kiosks and information transaction machines, copiers, printers, calculators, and fax machines must be usable by people with disabilities without requiring an end-user to attach assistive technology to the product. Personal headsets for private listening are not assistive technology. *Id.* § 1194.25. Desktop and portable computers shall comply with the mechanically operated control or key requirements described above as well as other requirements. *Id.* § 1194.26

§ 7.34   SECTION 504: ACCESS TO TELEVISION

Private television broadcasters are not subject to Section 504 because they are not recipients of

federal financial assistance. And, while public
broadcasting systems are subject to Section 504, the
courts have consistently held that Section 504 does
not compel public broadcasting systems to provide
open or closed-captioned programs for persons who
are hearing-impaired. In *Community Television of
Southern California v. Gottfried*, 459 U.S. 498
(1983), the Court held that Section 504 does not
require the Federal Communications Commission
(FCC) to apply special standards when reviewing a
public television station's license renewal
application. The majority of the Court held that the
FCC has no responsibility for enforcing Section 504,
and that the Commission's duties derive solely from
the Communications Act of 1934.

In 1987, the FCC adopted rules and regulations
pursuant to Section 504. The FCC ruled that a 1978
amendment extending the coverage of Section 504
to include the activities "conducted by" federal
agencies was not intended to apply to the activities
of licensees of federal agencies. Thus, the FCC's
regulations provide that "the programs or activities
of entities that are licensed or certified by the
Commission are not, themselves, covered by this
part." 47 C.F.R. § 1.1830(b)(6). The FCC's rules were
challenged in *California Association of the
Physically Handicapped, Inc. v. Federal
Communications Commission*, 840 F.2d 88 (D.C.Cir.
1988), and the court upheld the validity of the
regulations.

Section 504, therefore, has proven to be of no
assistance to persons with hearing impairments

seeking to compel television broadcasters to caption their programs. Nor do Titles II or III of the ADA apply to television broadcasters. In an effort to provide some assistance in this area, Congress enacted the Television Decoder Circuitry Act of 1990, which amended the Communication Act of 1934 to require all television sets manufactured in— or for use in—the United States having picture screens of at least 13 inches in size to be equipped with "built-in decoder circuitry designed to display closed-captioned television transmissions." 47 U.S.C.A. § 303(u).

Further, the Telecommunications Act of 1996 required the FCC to adopt rules with respect to the closed captioning of video programming (including TV programming). 47 U.S.C.A. § 613. In September 1997, the FCC promulgated final rules which provide a schedule of dates by which programming must be closed-captioned. 47 C.F.R. § 79.1. For example, between Jan. 1, 2002, and Dec. 31, 2003, a broadcaster must close-caption 900 hours or 95% of non-exempt new programming (whichever is less) per calendar quarter; between Jan. 1, 2004, and Dec. 31, 2005, a broadcaster must close-caption 1,350 hours or 95% of non-exempt new programming (whichever is less) per calendar quarter; as of January 1, 2006, 95% of non-exempt video programming must be closed-captioned. In *Zulauf v. Kentucky Educational Television*, 28 F.Supp.2d 1022 (E.D.Ky. 1998), the court held that a closed captioning advocate who sued to have all broadcasts captioned was required to exhaust administrative remedies with the FCC before filing an action under the ADA or Rehabilitation Act.

The Telecommunications Act of 1996 also required the FCC to prepare a report for Congress on "video descriptions"—aural descriptions of a television program's key visual elements (such as the movement of a person in a scene) that are inserted during pauses in the program dialogue. It did not specifically authorize the Commission to adopt regulations implementing video descriptions, but the FCC later did so. Those regulations were struck down as exceeding the Commission's authority in *Motion Picture Ass'n of America, Inc. v. F.C.C.*, 309 F.3d 796 (D.C.Cir. 2002).

CHAPTER 8
HOUSING

§ 8.1 THE FAIR HOUSING ACT AMENDMENTS OF 1988: INTRODUCTION

In 1968, Congress passed the Fair Housing Act (FHA), 42 U.S.C.A. §§ 3601–3631, to prohibit discrimination in both private and public real estate transactions based on race, color, religion, sex or national origin. The Fair Housing Amendments Act of 1988 (FHAA) extend coverage of the 1968 Act to prohibit discrimination against people with disabilities and families with children 18 years of age and younger.

The FHAA uses the same definition of "handicap" used in the Rehabilitation Act and the ADA: a person who (1) has a physical or mental impairment that substantially limits one or more of the individual's major life activities; (2) has a record of such impairment (*e.g.*, someone with a past history of cancer); or (3) is regarded as having such an impairment (*e.g.*, an individual who has been misclassified as disabled or who is treated as being disabled when in fact he or she is not disabled). 42 U.S.C.A. § 3602(h). Thus, Rehabilitation Act and ADA case law on this issue will impact cases arising under the FHAA. Moreover, all three laws treat drug abusers and alcoholics in the same manner. Like the ADA and Rehabilitation Act, the FHAA specifically excludes current users of illegal drugs from protection under the Act, but both the legislative history to the Act and the regulations promulgated under it clearly explain that a drug abuser who is participating in a treatment program—and thus is not currently using illegal drugs—is protected by the FHAA. And, under all three Acts, current alcoholics *are* protected. To be protected under the statute, however, "a recovering drug addict or alcoholic 'must demonstrate [not only] that he [or she] was actually addicted to drugs or alcohol in the past, [but also] that this addiction substantially limit[s] one or more of his [or her] major life activities.'" *Regional Economic Community Action Program, Inc. v. City of Middletown*, 294 F.3d 35 (2d Cir. 2002).

The Department of Housing and Urban Development (HUD) has issued regulations interpreting the FHAA. The regulations prohibit discrimination on the basis of disability by a "person in the business of selling or renting dwellings," which includes private owners as well as real estate agents and brokers. 24 C.F.R. § 100.20. A private owner of a single family dwelling is not subject to any provision of the Act *except* the non-discriminatory advertising provision, however, if: (a) the owner owns three or fewer single family homes, and (b) the dwelling at issue is being sold or rented without the use of a realtor. *Id.* § 100.10(c)(1). The same limitation applies where the dwelling contains four or fewer independent living quarters and the owner occupies one of the living quarters as his residence. *Id.* § 100.10(c)(2).

The FHA also does not cover religious organizations or private clubs which restrict housing to their members. The exemption applies to dwellings they own or operate "for other than a commercial purpose." 42 U.S.C.A. § 3607.

§ 8.2 FHAA: DISCRIMINATION IN THE RENTAL OR SALE OF HOUSING

A. SALE/RENTAL OF DWELLING

It is illegal under the FHAA to discriminate in the sale or rental of a dwelling, or to "otherwise make unavailable or deny" a dwelling, because of the disability of: (a) the buyer or renter, (b) a person who will reside in the dwelling after it is sold or rented, or (c) any person associated with the buyer or renter. The term "dwelling" is defined in the FHA as "any building, structure, or portion thereof which is occupied as, or designed or intended for occupancy as, a residence by one or more families and any vacant land which is offered for sale or lease for the construction or location thereon of any such structure or portion thereof." 42 U.S.C.A. § 3602(b).

The FHAA also bars discrimination with respect to the "terms, conditions, or privileges of sale or rental of a dwelling," or with respect to "the provision of services or facilities in connection with such dwelling," due to the disability of any of the above-named persons. *Id.* § 3604(f)(2). Discrimination includes: (a) the refusal to allow an individual with a disability to make reasonable modifications of existing premises at his or her own expense; (b) the refusal to make reasonable accommodations in rules, practices or services when necessary to allow a person with a disability equal use and enjoyment of the premises; and (c) the failure to design and construct multi-family dwellings so that such dwellings are accessible to people with disabilities. *Id.* § 3604(f)(3). It is *not* illegal, however, to refuse to rent or sell housing to an individual, with or without a disability, "whose tenancy would constitute a direct threat to the health or safety of other individuals or whose tenancy would result in substantial physical damage to the property of others." *Id.* § 3604(f)(9).

When rental of property is involved, the landlord may, under reasonable circumstances, require the renter to restore the premises to their pre-modified existence. Landlords may not increase the required security deposit when renting to a person with a disability, but the landlord may require as part of the restoration agreement that the tenant set aside reasonable funds in an interest-bearing escrow account. 24 C.F.R. § 100.203(a). Moreover, a landlord may require the tenant to provide reasonable descriptions of proposed modifications plus "reasonable assurances that the work will be done in a workmanlike manner and that any required building permits will be obtained." *Id.* § 100.203(b).

B.   MULTI-FAMILY DWELLINGS

The term "multi-family dwelling" is defined as

(1) buildings consisting of 4 or more units if such buildings have one or more elevators; and

(2) ground floor units in other buildings consisting of 4 or more units.

42 U.S.C.A. § 3604(f)(7). Multi-family dwellings built for first occupancy after March 13, 1991, must be designed so that the public and common-use portions are accessible to people with disabilities; all doors are wide enough to allow wheelchair passage; and all premises within such dwellings contain accessible routes into and through the dwelling, accessible light switches and environmental controls, reinforcements in bathroom walls to allow later installation of grab bars, and kitchens and bathrooms that allow an individual in a wheelchair to adequately maneuver. All covered multi-family dwellings must have one building entrance on an accessible route unless it is impractical to do so because of the terrain or unusual characteristics of the site. 24 C.F.R. § 100.205(a), (c). These conditions can be met through compliance with the appropriate requirements of ANSI A117.1–1986 or a state or local law which includes the FHAA requirements.

C.   REPRESENTATIONS AND ADVERTISEMENTS

It is illegal under the FHA to: (1) represent to any person in a statutorily protected class, including people with disabilities, that "any dwelling is not available for inspection, sale, or rental when such dwelling is in fact so available;" or (2) "[f]or profit, to induce or attempt to induce any person to sell or rent any dwelling by representations regarding the entry or prospective entry into the neighborhood . . . " of persons in any of the statutorily protected classes, including persons with disabilities. 42 U.S.C.A. § 3604(d), (e). The HUD regulations detail specific practices that are illegal under these provisions. *See generally* 24 C.F.R. §§ 100.80 and 100.85.

The section of the FHA dealing with discrimination in the rental or sale of housing also prohibits discriminatory advertising practices— namely the indication of "preference, limitation or discrimination" based on any of the protected categories. 42 U.S.C.A. § 3604(c). Thus, for example, owners of apartment houses or developers of housing projects may not advertise in such a manner that would appear to exclude people with disabilities or to reflect a bias against people with disabilities.

§ 8.3   FHA: DISCRIMINATION IN RESIDENTIAL REAL ESTATE-RELATED TRANSACTIONS

Section 3605(a) of the FHA provides:

It shall be unlawful for any person or other entity whose business includes engaging in residential real estate-related transactions to discriminate against any person in making available such a transaction, or in the terms or conditions of such a transaction, because of race, color, religion, sex, handicap, familial status, or national origin.

The term "residential real estate-related transaction" refers to the "making or purchasing of loans or providing other financial assistance" with respect to the purchase, construction, improvement or maintenance of a dwelling, and to the "selling, brokering or appraising of residential real property." 42 U.S.C.A § 3605(b) Again, the HUD regulations list detailed practices that are considered to violate this provision. *See generally* 24 C.F.R. §§ 100.120–100.135.

§ 8.4 FHA: DISCRIMINATION IN THE PROVISION OF BROKERAGE SERVICES

Section 3606 of the FHA prohibits discrimination on the basis of disability, as well as on the basis of race, color, religion, sex, familial status or national origin, in the provision of brokerage services. The HUD regulations provide that prohibited actions under this section include, but are not limited to, setting different fees for membership in a multiple-listing service; denying or limiting benefits accruing to members in real estate brokers' organization; or establishing geographic boundaries, office location or residence requirements for access to, or membership in, any real estate-related organization—based on an individual's membership in any of the statutorily protected categories. 24 C.F.R. § 100.90(b).

§ 8.5   FHA: INTERFERENCE OR COERCION

Section 3617 of the FHA provides that:

it shall be unlawful to coerce, intimidate, threaten or interfere with any person in the exercise or enjoyment of, or on account of his having exercised or enjoyed, or on account of his having aided or encouraged any other person in the exercise or enjoyment of, any right granted under or protected by §§ 3603, 3604, 3605 or 3606 of this [T]itle.

Violence or physical coercion is not a prerequisite to a retaliation claim under the FHA, but the conduct complained of must be of sufficient magnitude to permit a finding of intimidation, coercion, threats, or interference. *Sporn v. Ocean Colony Condominium Ass'n*, 173 F.Supp.2d 244 (D.N.J. 2001).

It is unclear whether a violation of Section 3617 depends upon the validity of a claim under Section 3604 of the Act (prohibiting discrimination in the sale or rental of housing) when the plaintiff files under both sections. Some courts have stated there must be a violation of Section 3604 for a Section 3617 claim to succeed. *See, e.g., Congdon v. Strine*, 854 F.Supp. 355 (E.D.Pa. 1994).

§ 8.6   FHA: DISPARATE IMPACT DISCRIMINATION PROHIBITED

Courts have consistently interpreted the FHA as prohibiting both conduct that is *intentionally* discriminatory and conduct that has a discriminatory *impact* on members of a protected class. As one court noted, "[t]he Act's stated purpose to end discrimination requires a discriminatory effect standard; an intent requirement would strip the statute of all impact on de facto segregation." *Huntington Branch, NAACP v. Town of Huntington*, 844 F.2d 926 (2d Cir. 1988). In order to prove disparate impact under the FHAA, the plaintiff must first show that the defendant's action had a greater adverse impact on people with disabilities than on others. The burden then shifts to the defendant to show that it had a legitimate, non-discriminatory reason for the action and that no less discriminatory alternatives were available. *See, e.g., Lapid-Laurel, L.L.C. v. Zoning Bd. of Adjustment of Tp. of Scotch Plains*, 284 F.3d 442 (3d Cir. 2002).

In the context of a race discrimination claim, the Supreme Court ruled that disparate impact claims are cognizable under the FHA. *Texas Dept. of Housing and Community Affairs,* 135 S.Ct. 2507 (2015). The Court, however, also clarified that disparate impact claims cannot be made on the basis of a statistical disparity, alone. *Id.* at 2522. "A plaintiff who fails to allege facts at the pleading stage or produce statistical evidence demonstrating a causal connection cannot make out a prima facie case of disparate impact." *Id.* at 2523. Further, the Court emphasized that remedial orders entered by courts when there is a finding of disparate impact liability "must be consistent with the Constitution." It emphasized that courts should seek to use race-neutral means to eliminate the disparate impact. *Id.*

at 2524. Those observations reflected that race discrimination claims are subject to strict scrutiny and, therefore, race-specific programs are disfavored. It is not clear if such reasoning would apply to disparate impact liability in the disability context where the Court has found that strict scrutiny does not attach.

§ 8.7   FHAA: ZONING

The FHAA states that it does not limit "the applicability of any reasonable local, State or Federal restrictions regarding the maximum number of occupants permitted to occupy a dwelling." 42 U.S.C.A. § 3607(b)(1). The legislative history to the statute, however, indicates that this proviso is not intended to permit zoning regulations that discriminate against persons with disabilities.

Specifically, the legislative history provides that the FHAA "is intended to prohibit the application of special requirements through land-use regulations, restrictive covenants, and conditional or special use permits that have the effect of limiting the ability of such individuals to live in the residence of their choice in the community." H.R. Rep. No. 711, 100th Cong., 2d Sess. 24 (June 17, 1988). Thus, a vast number of courts have granted preliminary or permanent injunctive relief to plaintiffs with disabilities who sought: (1) special exemptions under applicable zoning regulations; or (2) to have zoning regulations interpreted in a manner that would provide persons with disabilities equal access to housing. Numerous courts have recognized that if persons with disabilities are to have equal access to housing in residential areas, for example, zoning regulations regarding single family residences must be modified to allow small groups of persons with disabilities to live together in one residential home.

In *City of Edmonds v. Oxford House, Inc.*, 514 U.S. 725 (1995) the Court held that a single-family zoning provision did not fall within the exemption for "any reasonable local, state, or federal restrictions regarding the maximum number of occupants permitted to occupy a dwelling." In that case, the City contended that Oxford House, a group home for 10 to 12 adults recovering from alcoholism and drug addiction, violated a zoning regulation which defined "family" as persons related by genetics, adoption of marriage or a group of five or fewer unrelated persons. Oxford House claimed that the City violated the FHAA by refusing to make a reasonable accommodation to allow it to remain in the single-family dwelling at issue. The City contended that the single-family zoning provision was exempt from the FHAA. The Supreme Court disagreed. The Court noted the distinction between land use restrictions and maximum occupancy restrictions as follows: land use restrictions are intended to reserve land for single-family residences to preserve the character of neighbors with respect to family values, quiet, and clean air. Maximum occupancy restrictions, however, are intended to protect health and safety by preventing overcrowding in a single dwelling. The Court held that the City's single-family zoning regulation was not a valid maximum occupancy restriction because it was instead a land use restriction.

§ 8.8 FHAA: REASONABLE ACCOMMODATION

Under the FHAA, discrimination includes "a refusal to make reasonable accommodations in rules, policies, practices, or services, when such accommodations may be necessary to afford [a] person [with a disability] equal opportunity to use and enjoy a dwelling." 42 U.S.C.A. § 3604(f)(3)(B). Congress based the FHAA's reasonable accommodations provision on the "regulations and caselaw dealing with discrimination on the basis of handicap" under Section 504. H.R. Rep. No. 100–711. Accordingly, courts have incorporated the concepts developed under Section 504 that an accommodation need not be made where it would constitute a "fundamental alteration" of or place an "undue burden" on a housing program.

There are several cases which deal with whether allowing a service animal in housing with a "no pets" policy constitutes a reasonable accommodation under the FHAA. These courts have rejected the argument that a service animal must be professionally trained or certified and note that there is no requirement in the federal regulations as to the amount or type of work a service animal must provide for the benefit of the disabled person. *See, e.g., Green v. Housing Authority of Clackamas County,* 994 F.Supp. 1253 (D.Or. 1998); *Bronk v. Ineichen,* 54 F.3d 425 (7th Cir. 1995); *but see Access*

Now, Inc. v. Town of Jasper, 268 F.Supp.2d 973 (E.D.Tenn. 2003) (holding miniature horse was not "service animal" for purposes of ADA; the horse did not assist and perform tasks for the owner's benefit to help her overcome or deal with her disability).

In 2013, HUD issued a notice explaining how service animals should be treated under HUD's FHAA and Section 504 regulations. *See* https://portal.hud.gov/hudportal/documents/huddoc? id=servanimals_ntcfheo2013-01.pdf. Unlike the ADA Title II and III regulations, HUD's policy is not limited to *dogs*. Instead, HUD policy requires accommodations if the animal does "work, provide assistance, perform tasks or services for the benefit of a person with a disability, or provide emotional support that alleviates one or more of the identified symptoms or effects of a persons' existing disability." *Id.* If an animal meets this definition, the request for accommodation can be denied if: (1) the specific assistance animal would "pose a direct threat to the health or safety of others that cannot be reduced or eliminated by another reasonable accommodation" or (2) the specific assistance animal "would cause substantial physical damage to the property of others that cannot be reduced or eliminated by another reasonable accommodation." *Id.*

§ 8.9   FHAA: DIRECT THREAT DEFENSE

Like the Rehabilitation Act and the ADA, the FHAA includes a "direct threat" defense to disability discrimination claims: "Nothing in this subchapter requires that a dwelling be made available to an individual whose tenancy would constitute *a direct threat to the health or safety of other individuals* or whose tenancy would result in substantial physical damages to the property of others." 42 U.S.C. § 3604(f)(9). Courts have required that apartment complexes which attempt to exclude tenants with mental disorders and a history of threatening behavior must first show that there was no "reasonable accommodation" which would have allowed those tenants to live there safely. *See, e.g., Roe v. Housing Authority of the City of Boulder*, 909 F.Supp. 814 (D.Colo. 1995).

The HUD regulation implementing this rule says that a "direct threat" is a "significant risk to the health or safety of others that cannot be eliminated by a modification of policies, practices, or procedures, or by the provision of auxiliary aids or services." 24 C.F.R. § 9.131(b).

Furthermore, where a disabled tenant has requested a reasonable accommodation, HUD regulations provide: "In determining whether an individual poses a direct threat to the health or safety of others, the agency *must* make an individualized assessment, based on reasonable judgment that relies on current medical knowledge or on the best available objective evidence to ascertain: the nature, duration, and severity of the risk; the probability that the potential injury will actually occur; and whether reasonable modifications of policies, practices, or procedures will mitigate the risk" (emphasis added). 24 C.F.R.

§ 9.131(c). *See Boston Housing Authority v. Bridgewaters,* 452 Mass. 833, 898 N.E.2d 848 (2009).

§ 8.10 FHAA: CONFLICTING STATE STATUTES

Section 3615 of the FHAA provides that:

[A]ny law of a state, a political subdivision, or other such jurisdiction that purports to require or permit any action that would be a discriminatory housing practice under [the Act] shall to that extent be invalid.

Thus, it has been held that a statute violated the FHAA when it barred persons found not guilty by reason of insanity in a criminal trial or unfit to be tried on criminal charges from community residences for mentally ill persons. *Matter of Commitment of J.W.,* 672 A.2d 199 (N.J.Super. 1996). The federal law does not preempt a state law regarding housing discrimination, however, except to extent that the state law is itself a "discriminatory housing practice." *Toledo Fair Housing Center v. Farmers Ins. Group of Companies,* 64 F.Supp.2d 703 (N.D.Ohio 1999).

§ 8.11 FHA: ENFORCEMENT AND REMEDIES

Responsibility for enforcing the FHA lies with the Secretary of HUD. 42 U.S.C.A. § 3608. A private individual who is an "aggrieved person" may also sue directly under the Act, however. *Id.* § 3612. An "aggrieved person" under the Act is one who has either been injured by a discriminatory housing practice or believes that he or she will be "injured by a discriminatory housing practice that is about to occur." 24 C.F.R. § 100.20(b). This term has been broadly interpreted by the courts.

A. ADMINISTRATIVE ENFORCEMENT

Procedures for administrative complaints are found at 42 U.S.C.A. § 3610. Basically, an aggrieved party may file an administrative complaint with HUD within one year of the alleged discriminatory conduct. The Secretary of HUD may also file a complaint on his or her own initiative. If the complainant alleges a discriminatory housing practice within the jurisdiction of a state or local public agency that operates under a fair housing law which HUD has certified as being the "substantial equivalent" of the FHA, HUD must refer the complaint to the applicable state or local agency for proceedings in accordance with state law. HUD may take no further action without the consent of such certified agency unless the certified agency fails to institute proceedings within 30 days or fails to carry forward proceedings with reasonable promptness, or unless the Secretary of HUD determines that the certified agency no longer qualifies for certification. If that agency does not institute proceedings (or if there is no certified agency), HUD must administratively proceed with the complaint.

A primary advantage of administrative proceedings is speedy resolution. HUD is required to complete an investigation of the alleged discriminatory housing practice within 100 days and make a determination as to whether "reasonable cause exists to believe that a discriminatory housing practice has occurred or is about to occur, unless it is impracticable to do so, or unless the Secretary has approved a conciliation agreement with respect to the complaint." 42 U.S.C.A. § 3610(g)(1). If it is unable to complete the investigation within the 100-day period, HUD will notify the aggrieved person and the respondent, by mail, of the reasons for the delay. 24 C.F.R. § 103.225.

The HUD regulations promulgated under the Act provide that a decision as to whether reasonable cause exists shall be made by determining, "based solely on the totality of factual circumstances . . . provided by complainant and respondent and otherwise," whether the facts "are sufficient to warrant the initiation of a civil action in Federal court." 24 C.F.R. § 103.400(a)(1).

The Assistant Secretary for Fair Housing and Equal Opportunity is to dismiss all cases in which he or she has determined that no reasonable cause to believe that a discriminatory housing practice has occurred or is about to occur. Only those cases in which reasonable cause has been found by the Assistant Secretary will be sent to the General Counsel for review. Findings of "no violation" are communicated immediately to the complainant, while OCR findings of "violation" must be submitted to the General Counsel for approval. *Id.* § 103.400(a)(2)(i), (ii).

When conducting its investigation, HUD has authority to issue subpoenas, engage in discovery, and pay witness fees. Any person who fails to comply with a HUD subpoena, falsifies documents, or destroys evidence is subject to a fine of up to $100,000 or imprisonment for up to one year. 24 C.F.R. §§ 103.215, 180.545. The regulations promulgated by HUD provide that both HUD and the respondent shall have broad discovery powers; *id.* § 180.500; however, the aggrieved party is *not* provided access to the discovery process.

If the investigation leads to a finding of reasonable cause that the Act has been violated, HUD must immediately charge the respondent and begin prosecution. 42 U.S.C.A. § 3610(g)(2)(A). If reasonable cause is not found, HUD will dismiss the action. HUD has taken the position that the statute does not contemplate a right of appeal from an agency finding that no reasonable cause exists to find that an FHAA violation has occurred, but that the complainant's only recourse is to file a private civil action. 54 Fed. Reg. 3268 (1989). HUD's opinion has not been tested in the courts, however.

When HUD files a charge, the aggrieved person, the respondent or HUD have 20 days to elect to have the matter resolved in federal court (to preserve the right to a jury trial). 42 U.S.C.A. § 3612(a), (*o*). If an election is made to file a civil action, the Attorney General must commence the action in federal district court within 30 days. If no election is made, the matter will be heard at an administrative hearing, during which the parties have the rights to be represented by counsel, to present evidence and cross-examine witnesses, and to issue subpoenas. The administrative hearing must be commenced within 120 days of the issuance of the charge, and a decision must be issued within 60 days of the hearing's conclusion. *Id.* § 3612(b)–(g).

The Administrative Law Judge (ALJ) has the power to award actual damages and/or equitable relief (such as injunctive relief), to award attorneys' fees to the prevailing party, and to assess civil penalties against the violators. *Id.* § 3612(g)(3) The ALJ may *not* award punitive damages. Further, the Amendments do not provide that an ALJ may provide "such affirmative action as may be appropriate," although such a provision *is* included in the relief available from a federal court. *Id.* § 3613(c)(1).

The ALJ's decision may be reviewed by the Secretary of HUD within 30 days after the final order of the ALJ is entered, regardless of whether the party has filed a complaint with HUD. HUD may petition for enforcement in a court of appeals within 60 days. *Id.* § 3612(h)–(j).

At any time after filing a charge, HUD may authorize the Attorney General to bring a civil action for temporary relief. The Attorney General must "promptly" commence the action. *Id.* § 3610(e)(1). The filing of a civil action for temporary relief will not affect the continuation of the administrative proceedings.

B.   PRIVATE ENFORCEMENT

An aggrieved party may also sue directly in federal court within two years of the allegedly discriminatory action without exhausting administrative remedies. The two-year limitations period does not include the time during which HUD administrative proceedings were pending. But an aggrieved party is barred from filing an action if he or she has consented to a conciliation agreement, or if an ALJ has commenced a hearing on the record with respect to the same or a similar charge. If the defendant is found to have violated the Act, the court may award actual and punitive damages, as well as equitable relief—such as injunctive relief or the ordering of "such affirmative action as may be appropriate." 42 U.S.C.A. § 3613(c)(1). In addition, the court may award the prevailing party (other than the United States) reasonable attorneys' fees and costs. Further, the Act provides that "[t]he United States shall be liable for such fees and costs to the same extent as a private person." *Id.* § 3613(c)(2).

The 1988 Amendments greatly expanded the relief available to private plaintiffs. Under the 1968 Act, for example, the limitations period was 180 days, rather than the current two years. Under the 1968 Act punitive damages were limited to $1,000, instead of the unlimited punitive damages currently available. In addition, under the 1968 Act attorneys' fees were only available to a prevailing plaintiff who could not afford to pay those fees; the amended Act has removed this financial restriction.

C.   PATTERN AND PRACTICE LITIGATION

The United States Attorney General may also file suit under the FHAA when he or she "has reasonable cause to believe that any person or group of persons is engaged in a pattern or practice of resistance to the full enjoyment of any of the rights granted by [the Act]. . . ." *Id.* § 3614(a). Such an action must be filed within 18 months of the conduct at issue. A person aggrieved by such an alleged discriminatory practice may apply to intervene in the civil action. In addition, the Attorney General may file suit for breach of any conciliation agreement entered into pursuant to the Act within 90 days of the alleged breach. If the Attorney General's suit is successful, the court may award injunctive relief and monetary damages to the aggrieved party. Further, to vindicate the public interest, the court may assess civil penalties against the violator of up to $50,000 for a first violation and up to $100,000 for any subsequent violation. The court may also award the prevailing party—other than the United States—attorneys' fees and costs to the same extent that such fees and costs could be awarded in a private civil action.

D.   PREEMPTION

Section 3615 of the FHAA provides that the Act shall not

be construed to invalidate or limit any law of a State or political subdivision of a State, or other jurisdiction in which this subchapter shall be effective, that requires dwellings to be designed and constructed in a manner that affords handicapped persons greater access than is required by this subchapter.

Accordingly, it has been held that the FHAA does not preempt a state or local law which addresses the issue of a landlord's obligations to make reasonable accommodations for individuals with disabilities in their residences. *United Veterans v. New York City Commission on Human Rights*, 616 N.Y.S.2d 84 (N.Y.App.Div. 1994).

The FHAA also provides that nothing in the Act "limits any right, procedure, or remedy available under the Constitution or any other Act of Congress not so amended." 42 U.S.C.A. § 3601 note. Accordingly, it has been held that the FHAA does not preempt Section 1983 and Section 1985 remedies for housing discrimination on the basis of disability. *Community Interactions—Bucks County, Inc. v. Township of Bensalem*, 1994 WL 276476 (E.D.Pa. 1994).

§ 8.12 SECTION 504

As noted above, Congress based the FHAA's anti-discrimination provisions on regulations and caselaw under the Rehabilitation Act. Plaintiffs with disabilities often bring claims based on discriminatory housing practices under Section 504 and the ADA in addition to the FHAA. Several courts have held that Section 504 precludes a recipient of federal financial assistance from discriminating against individuals with disabilities with respect to the provision of housing. A plaintiff with a disability may not, however, utilize Section 504 to circumvent the requirements of federal statutes relating to the provision of federally subsidized housing. In other words, Section 504 does not eliminate the requirement that individuals with disabilities must fall within the class of individuals eligible to participate in federally funded housing programs pursuant to laws such as Section 202 of the Housing Act of 1959, 12 U.S.C.A. § 1701q, which provides for supportive housing for the elderly. *See, e.g., Knutzen v. Eben Ezer Lutheran Housing Center*, 815 F.2d 1343 (10th Cir. 1987).

CHAPTER 9
POSTSECONDARY EDUCATION

§ 9.1   INTRODUCTION AND OVERVIEW

Both Section 504 and the ADA prohibit postsecondary educational institutions from discriminating on the basis of disability. Section 504 governs all such institutions that receive federal financial assistance. Title II of the ADA applies to all state-funded or supported institutions. Title III of the ADA covers all private institutions, with the exception of educational institutions that are controlled by religious entities. With a few exceptions, the same principles will apply under all three provisions.

Generally, a postsecondary institution governed by Section 504 or ADA Titles II or III may not exclude an otherwise qualified student from any part of its program or services, or otherwise discriminate against an applicant or student with a disability. The Department of Education (DOE) issued Section 504 regulations in 1977 which prescribe minimum standards for colleges and universities in six areas: (1) admissions and recruitment; (2) treatment of students; (3) academic adjustments, including the provision of auxiliary aids; (4) housing; (5) financial aid and employment assistance and (6) nonacademic services. 34 C.F.R. §§ 104.1–104.54. The Justice Department has overall responsibility for the enforcement of ADA Titles II and III of the ADA but has delegated responsibility for the enforcement of Title II with regard to postsecondary education (other than schools of medicine, dentistry, nursing, and other health-related schools) to the DOE. 28 C.F.R. § 35.190(b)(2). Regulation of schools of medicine, dentistry, nursing, and other health-related schools are delegated to the Department of Health and Human Services. *Id.* § 35.190(b)(3). The Justice Department maintained jurisdiction over the enforcement of Title III, but its regulations concerning public accommodations such as colleges and universities are similar to the § 504 regulations. *Id.* § 36.301–310.

Generally, the DOE's regulations provide that "qualified handicapped persons may not, on the basis of handicap, be denied admission or be subjected to discrimination. . . ." 34 C.F.R. § 104.42(a). Both ADA Titles II and III are premised on similar precepts.

Entities covered by Section 504 or ADA Titles II or III must ensure that students with disabilities are informed about how to access appropriate services. Neither Section 504 nor the ADA require postsecondary educational institutions to have *written* policies and procedures describing how they will provide services for students with disabilities, however, such a practice is recommended.

Claims against a postsecondary educational institution are most likely to be raised in three contexts: (1) admission; (2) the provision of reasonable accommodations for students with disabilities; and (3) access to non-academic programs and services at a postsecondary educational institution. This chapter will address each of these issues.

§ 9.2   ADMISSIONS

Postsecondary educational institutions subject to Section 504 and the ADA are not required to engage in affirmative action with respect to the admission of students with disabilities. The only requirement is that *qualified* individuals with disabilities not be subjected to discrimination in the admissions process. To qualify for a postsecondary educational program, an individual with a disability must be capable of fulfilling the essential functions or requirements of the program, with or without the provision of reasonable accommodations. The DOE's Section 504 regulations provide that to be qualified for a postsecondary educational program an individual must meet the academic and technical requirements of the program. 34 C.F.R. § 104.3(*l*)(3).

A.   PRE-ADMISSION INQUIRIES

The DOE's Section 504 regulations provide that a college or university may not make pre-admission inquiries as to whether an applicant for admission is disabled. 34 C.F.R. § 104.42(b)(4). Exceptions to this rule are made where "a recipient is taking remedial action to correct the effects of past discrimination," or where "a recipient is taking voluntary action to overcome the effects of conditions that resulted in limited participation in its federally assisted program or activity." 34 C.F.R. § 104.42(c). Even in the latter situations, however, the school must clearly state: (1) "that the information requested is intended for use solely in connection with its remedial action obligations or its voluntary action efforts;" and (2) "that the information is being requested on a voluntary basis, that it will be kept confidential, [and] that refusal to provide it will not subject the applicant to any adverse treatment." *Id.*

The prohibition on disability-related preadmission inquiries also applies to questions concerning applicants' mental health and known behavioral problems. The Department of Education's Office of Civil Rights (OCR) has held, however, that an applicant to a counseling program could be asked about past mental health treatment where the purpose of the inquiry was to determine whether the applicant had adequately resolved any personal/therapeutic issues before attempting to counsel others with similar issues. *North Dakota State Univ.*, 2 NDLR ¶ 174 (1991). The bar on preadmission inquiries also does not apply to college or university programs operated specifically for students with disabilities. *Halasz v. University of New England*, 816 F.Supp. 37 (D.Me. 1993).

B. ADMISSIONS TESTS

The DOE's Section 504 regulations provide that a college or university may "not make use of any test or criterion for admission that has a disproportionate, adverse effect" on applicants with disabilities, unless the test or criterion has been validated as predictor of success in the program and alternative tests or criteria that have a less disproportionate adverse effect are not available. 34 C.F.R. § 104.42(b)(2). Admissions tests must be selected and administered so as to ensure that, when a test is administered to an applicant who has impaired sensory, manual or speaking skills, the test does not reflect those impaired skills but actually measures the applicant's aptitude or achievement level. *Id.* § 104.42(b)(3).

ADA Title III provides that an entity that offers examinations related to applications for postsecondary educational programs "shall offer such examinations or courses in a place and manner accessible to persons with disabilities or offer alternative accessible arrangements for such individuals." 42 U.S.C.A. § 12189. DOJ revised its Title III testing regulations in 2010. They currently require that:

(1) Any private entity offering an examination covered by this section must assure that—

(i) The examination is selected and administered so as to best ensure that, when the examination is administered to an individual with a disability that impairs sensory, manual, or speaking skills, the examination results accurately reflect the individual's aptitude or achievement level or whatever other factor the examination purports to measure, rather than reflecting the individual's impaired sensory, manual, or speaking skills (except where those skills are the factors that the examination purports to measure);

(ii) An examination that is designed for individuals with impaired sensory, manual, or speaking skills is offered at equally convenient locations, as often, and in as timely a manner as are other examinations; and

(iii) The examination is administered in facilities that are accessible to individuals with disabilities or alternative accessible arrangements are made.

(iv) Any request for documentation, if such documentation is required, is reasonable and limited to the need for the modification, accommodation, or auxiliary aid or service requested.

(v) When considering requests for modifications, accommodations, or auxiliary aids or services, the entity gives considerable weight to documentation of past modifications, accommodations, or auxiliary aids or services received in similar testing situations, as well as such modifications, accommodations, or related aids and services provided in response to an Individualized Education Program (IEP) provided under the Individuals with Disabilities Education Act or a plan describing services provided pursuant to section 504 of the Rehabilitation

Act of 1973, as amended (often referred as a Section 504 Plan).

(vi) The entity responds in a timely manner to requests for modifications, accommodations, or aids to ensure equal opportunity for individuals with disabilities.

(2) Required modifications to an examination may include changes in the length of time permitted for completion of the examination and adaptation of the manner in which the examination is given.

(3) A private entity offering an examination covered by this section shall provide appropriate auxiliary aids for persons with impaired sensory, manual, or speaking skills, unless that private entity can demonstrate that offering a particular auxiliary aid would fundamentally alter the measurement of the skills or knowledge the examination is intended to test or would result in an undue burden. Auxiliary aids and services required by this section may include taped examinations, interpreters or other effective methods of making orally delivered materials available to individuals with hearing impairments, Brailled or large print examinations and answer sheets or qualified readers for individuals with visual impairments or learning disabilities, transcribers for individuals with manual impairments, and other similar services and actions.

(4) Alternative accessible arrangements may include, for example, provision of an examination at an individual's home with a proctor if accessible facilities or equipment are unavailable. Alternative arrangements must provide comparable conditions to those provided for nondisabled individuals.

28 C.F.R. § 36.309(b).

The rules governing non-discriminatory testing apply not only to pre-admission tests given by a postsecondary educational institution, but to tests given by other entities, such as the Scholastic Aptitude Test (SAT), Graduate Record Exam (GRE), Law School Admissions Test (LSAT) and Medical College Admission Test (MCAT). In *Halasz v. University of New England*, 816 F.Supp. 37 (D.Me. 1993), the court rejected a challenge to the use of standardized tests in the admissions process. It found the SAT did not have a disproportionate, adverse effect on persons with disabilities because it was available in special formats for students with disabilities. The LSAT survived a similar attack because it is also available in special formats. *Mallet v. Marquette Univ.*, 65 F.3d 170 (7th Cir. 1995). In addition, a Department of Justice policy letter states that "unless there is evidence that a tester has failed to administer a test in a manner that complies with the ADA, the ADA does not require law schools to discontinue the use of standardized tests in the admissions process." 9 Nat'l Disab. L. Rep. ¶ 315 (1996).

Before 2001, entities providing accommodations for tests such as the SAT and GRE frequently "flagged" scores on tests taken with accommodations to show that they were taken under non-standard conditions. The "flag" indicates that the test, taken under non-standard conditions, has—in theory—not been validated as a predictor of success in the program at issue. When the test is flagged, the school receiving the test results becomes aware of the likelihood that the applicant has a disability. In February 2001, however, the Educational Testing Service agreed to stop the practice of "flagging" scores on several tests, including the GRE. In July 2002, the College Board announced that it would stop flagging SAT test scores effective September 2003; the ACT's administrators followed suit. The Law School Admission Council entered into a consent decree in May 2014, also agreeing to stop "flagging" test scores taken under conditions of accommodation. Scores on the MCAT are also no longer "flagged" to indicate that they were taken under a non-standard test administration. *See* https://www.aamc.org/students/applying/mcat/accom modations/faq/261842/scorereported.html

C. ELIGIBILITY CRITERIA

A postsecondary educational institution is not required to lower its admissions standards for applicants with disabilities. An applicant with a disability must be qualified for the program at issue. *See, e.g., Mallet v. Marquette University*, 65 F.3d 170 (7th Cir. 1995); *Murphy v. Franklin Pierce Law Center*, 56 F.3d 59 (1st Cir. 1995); *Anderson v.*

University of Wisconsin, 841 F.2d 737 (7th Cir. 1988). *Cf. Telesca v. Long Island Hous. P'Ship*, 443 F.Supp.2d 397 (E.D.N.Y. 2006) (case involving HUD housing).

Courts and the OCR have also held that applicants may be denied admission to clinical programs where they lack physical qualifications deemed essential to participation in the programs. In *Southeastern Community College v. Davis*, 442 U.S. 397 (1979), the Court held an applicant with a serious hearing disability was not qualified for admission to a registered nursing program where the school presented evidence that her hearing limitations could interfere with her safely caring for patients. A state court reached a similar decision concerning a blind medical school applicant. *Ohio Civil Rights Comm'n v. Case Western Reserve Univ.*, 1994 WL 716543 (Ohio Ct.App. 1994). *But see Palmer College of Chiropractic v. Davenport Civil Rights Commission*, 850 N.W.2d 326 (Iowa 2014) (finding that school failed to comply with applicable federal and state disability laws in denying student accommodations for his visual disability).

D.   DISCLOSURE AND DOCUMENTATION OF DISABILITY

An applicant to a postsecondary educational institution may always voluntarily disclose a disability and ask that it be considered in the admissions determination. Further, once accepted, a student who wishes to receive accommodations or adjustments for his or her disability will have to identify the disability. In either situation the educational institution may require documentation of the disability. The applicant is responsible for providing such documentation at his or her own expense. Moreover, the documentation must be fairly recent, come from an appropriate expert, and be sufficiently comprehensive.

It is important to remember that Congress amended the ADA in 2008 to broaden the definition of disability. "Learning", "reading", "concentrating", and "thinking" are now explicitly mentioned as major life activities. *See* 42 U.S.C. § 12102(2). Further, Congress stated that the question of whether an individual is disabled "should not demand extensive analysis." 42 U.S.C. § 12101 NOTE(b)(5). Hence, it is possible that students will be able to attain disability status with less documentation than may have been required by colleges in the past. Further, it would appear that students with learning disabilities and ADHD will now be covered by the ADA even if courts had previously found a lack of coverage for those disabilities.

In its Section by Section analysis on the definition of disability, the EEOC offers these comments about learning disabilities: "The comparison to most people in the general population continues to mean a comparison to other people in the general population, not a comparison to those similarly situated. . . . This does not mean that disability cannot be shown where an impairment, such as a learning disability, is clinically diagnosed based in part of a disparity between an individual's aptitude and that individual's actual versus expected achievement, taking into account the person's chronological age, measured intelligence, and age-appropriate education. Individuals diagnosed with dyslexia or other learning disabilities will typically be substantially limited in performing activities such as learning, reading, and thinking when compared to most people in the general population, particularly when the ameliorative effects of mitigating measures, including therapies, learned behavioral or adaptive neurological modifications, assistive devices (e.g., audio recordings, screen reading device, voice activated software), studying longer, or receiving more time to take a test, are disregarded as required under the ADA Amendments Act." 29 C.F.R. § 1630.2(j)(1)(v) App.

§ 9.3   REASONABLE ACCOMMODATIONS

Generally, postsecondary educational institutions must make reasonable accommodations or adjustments for qualified individuals with known disabilities. An accommodation is not reasonable if it would constitute an undue burden or hardship to provide it or if it would require a fundamental alteration to the program at issue.

The leading case dealing with the "fundamental alteration" issue is *Southeastern Community College v. Davis*, 442 U.S. 397 (1979). In that case, the Supreme Court held that a nursing school did not discriminate against an applicant with a hearing impairment when it refused to admit the applicant to its program. The Court held that Davis was not otherwise qualified for the nursing program because "nothing less than close, individual attention by a nursing instructor would be sufficient to ensure patient safety if [Davis] took part in the clinical portion of the nursing program." The Court concluded that because Davis could not function in clinical courses without close supervision, the nursing school could only allow her to take academic courses. The Court held that "[w]hatever benefits [Davis] might realize from such a course of study, she would not receive even a rough equivalent of the training a nursing program normally gives. Such a fundamental alteration in the nature of a program is far more than the 'modification' [Section 504] requires."

A.   SUGGESTED ACCOMMODATIONS

The DOE's Section 504 regulations suggest three types of accommodations that may be made to assist a student with a disability in obtaining a postsecondary education: academic adjustments, modification or alteration of course examinations, and the provision of auxiliary aids.

With respect to academic adjustments, the regulations provide that a college or university:

shall make such modifications to its academic requirements as are necessary to ensure that such requirements do not discriminate or have the effect of discriminating, on the basis of handicap, against a qualified handicapped applicant or student. Academic requirements that the recipient can demonstrate are essential to the program of instruction being pursued by such student or to any directly related licensing requirement will not be regarded as discriminatory within the meaning of this section. Modifications may include changes in the length of time permitted for the completion of degree requirements, substitution of specific courses required for the completion of degree requirements, and adaptation of the manner in which specific courses are conducted.

34 C.F.R. § 104.44(a).

The DOE's Section 504 regulations also cover the modification or alteration of course examinations. A recipient college or university:

shall provide such methods for evaluating the achievement of students who have a handicap that impairs sensory, manual, or speaking skills as will best ensure that the results of the evaluation represent the student's achievement in the course, rather than reflecting the student's impaired sensory, manual, or speaking skills (except where such skills are the factors that the test purports to measure).

34 C.F.R. § 104.44(c).

The regulations also require that recipient colleges and universities utilize auxiliary aids to ensure that students with impaired sensory, manual or speaking skills are not subject to discrimination in postsecondary educational programs. Specifically, the regulations state that:

Auxiliary aids may include taped texts, interpreters or other effective methods of making orally delivered materials available to students with hearing impairments, readers in libraries for students with visual impairments, classroom equipment adapted for use by students with manual impairments, and other similar services and actions. Recipients need not provide attendants, individually prescribed devices, readers for personal use or study, or other devices or services of a personal nature.

34 C.F.R. § 104.44(d)(2).

Similarly, the Title III regulations provide that a private postsecondary educational institution must ensure that both courses and examinations are accessible to students with disabilities. With respect to courses, the Title III regulations provide that:

(1) Any private entity that offers a course covered by this section must make such modifications to that course as are necessary to ensure that the place and manner in which the course is given are accessible to individuals with disabilities.

(2) Required modifications may include changes in the length of time permitted for the completion of the course, substitution of specific requirements, or adaptation of the manner in which the course is conducted or course materials are distributed.

(3) A private entity that offers a course covered by this section shall provide appropriate auxiliary aids and services for persons with impaired sensory, manual, or speaking skills, unless the private entity can demonstrate that offering a particular auxiliary aid or service would fundamentally alter the course or would result in an undue burden. Auxiliary aids and services required by this section may include taped texts, interpreters or other effective methods of making orally delivered materials available to individuals with hearing impairments, Brailled or large print texts or qualified readers for individuals with visual impairments and learning disabilities, classroom equipment adapted for use by individuals with manual impairments, and other similar services and actions.

(4) Courses must be administered in facilities that are accessible to individuals with disabilities or alternative accessible arrangements must be made.

(5) Alternative accessible arrangements may include, for example, provision of the course through videotape, cassettes, or prepared notes. Alternative arrangements must provide comparable conditions to those provided for nondisabled individuals.

28 C.F.R. § 36.309(c).

Title III regulations pertaining to examinations were discussed in § 9.2(B), *supra*. The Title II regulations do not specifically address the issue of courses and examinations. Nevertheless, the same principles are viewed as applying.

In addition to reasonable accommodations, the Title II and Title III regulations provide generally that covered entities must provide auxiliary aids and services necessary to provide non-discriminatory treatment to persons with disabilities. "Auxiliary aids and services" are defined as

(1) Qualified interpreters, notetakers, transcription services, written materials, telephone handset amplifiers, assistive listening devices, assistive listening systems, telephones compatible with hearing aids, closed caption decoders, open and closed captioning, telecommunications devices for deaf persons (TDD's), videotext displays, or other effective methods of making aurally delivered materials available to individuals with hearing impairments.

(2) Qualified readers, taped texts, audio recordings, Brailled materials, large print materials, or other effective methods of making visually delivered materials available to individuals with visual impairments;

(3) Acquisition or modification of equipment or devices; and

(4) Other similar services and actions.

28 C.F.R. § 35.104. Under both Titles, this list is merely illustrative, rather than exhaustive. Moreover, under both Titles, entities are not required to provide personal aids or services for students with disabilities.

B. SCOPE OF REASONABLE ACCOMMODATIONS

The extent of accommodations to be provided to students with disabilities is often an issue of dispute.

First, courts generally have held that postsecondary institutions do not have to accommodate students by lowering required standards. For example, in *McGregor v. Louisiana State University Board of Supervisors*, 3 F.3d 850 (5th Cir. 1993) a student with orthopedic and neurological disabilities who used a wheelchair was provided with numerous accommodations by the law school, including extra time to take exams, a student assistant during exams, a wheelchair-accessible table and modified class schedules. Despite those accommodations, the student failed to maintain the required grade-point average. The student requested that he be permitted to continue at the law school without having the requisite first-year grade-point average, and that he be allowed to attend law school on a part-time basis and take his examinations at home. The court held that the requested accommodations exceeded the scope of Section 504. *See also, Maczaczyj v. New York*, 956 F.Supp. 403 (W.D.N.Y. 1997) (college not required to excuse a student with a panic disorder from mandatory attendance requirements as that would impermissibly lower the college's academic requirements); *City Univ. of New York (NY)*, 3 NDLR ¶ 104 (1992) (college not required to waive mathematics requirement for student in Associate in Applied Science Program where it showed that class' purpose was to provide students with firm foundation in mathematics for their careers and increasingly technological society); *Indiana Univ. Northwest*, 3 NDLR ¶ 150 (1992) (university did not have to substitute a foreign language requirement with other courses where it demonstrated that foreign language was considered essential to the its undergraduate liberal arts program of instruction).

Second, OCR has required postsecondary educational institutions to provide necessary accommodations, including interpreters for students with hearing impairments. The requirement for the provision of interpreters extends to class-related activities which take place off campus and even to study abroad programs, and it is the school's obligation to provide such interpreters at no cost to the student if they are not available from outside sources. *See, e.g., Naropa Inst. (CO)*, 4 NDLR ¶ 335 (1993) (OCR found that a school violated Section 504 when it required a student to sign a document stating that the provision of an interpreter for 12 credits of course work was a financial hardship to the school and that "unless we can find other sources of income . . . the [school] will not be able to continue this level of service"); *College of St. Scholastica (MN)*, 3 NDLR ¶ 196 (1992) (OCR held that the need to provide an interpreter applied even to study abroad programs).

An issue of dispute involves the extent to which colleges or universities must accommodate students with disabilities by modifying or changing the form of examinations. In *Wynne v. Tufts University School of Medicine*, 932 F.2d 19 (1st Cir. 1991) (*Wynne I*), for example, a dyslexic student claimed that the medical school was obligated under Section 504 to accommodate his cognitive difficulties by testing him by means other than written multiple-choice questions, such as by oral or essay examinations. After noting that Wynne scored much higher scores on "practicum" examinations, the First Circuit stated that Tufts had not met its burden of "demonstrating that its determination that no reasonable way existed to accommodate Wynne's inability to perform adequately on written multiple-choice examinations was a reasoned, professional academic judgment, not a mere ipse dixit."

Subsequently, Tufts submitted additional information explaining why it believed that written multiple-choice tests offer a better means of evaluating student performance than oral or essay examinations. The district court held that Tufts had met its burden of evaluating alternatives for its current testing format and concluded that change was not practical (oral and essay exams were too subjective). Further, the district court found that Tufts had reasonably accommodated the plaintiff by allowing him to retake the first-year curriculum, which he had previously failed, with the provision of accommodations such as notetakers, tutors and typed lectures. Despite those accommodations, plaintiff failed one course. The First Circuit affirmed the district court's decision in favor of the school, stating that "Tufts demythologized the institutional thought processes leading to its determination that it could not deviate from its wonted format to accommodate Wynne's professed disability." *Wynne v. Tufts University School of Medicine*, 976 F.2d 791 (1st Cir. 1992) (*Wynne II*).

C.   INTERACTIVE PROCESS

The ADA and Section 504 contemplate that the student with a disability and the postsecondary educational institution will work together to determine what accommodations can be reasonably provided for that student. *Guckenberger v. Boston University*, 974 F.Supp. 106 (D.Mass. 1997). A student who fails to cooperate in this interactive process could be denied relief under the federal laws.

D.   PAYMENT FOR REASONABLE ACCOMMODATIONS

A university may not deny the provision of auxiliary aids for students with disabilities based on their ability to pay or their enrollment in specific programs. In *United States v. Board of Trustees for University of Alabama*, 908 F.2d 740 (11th Cir. 1990), the court held that requiring hearing-impaired students to show that they lacked the financial means to pay for their own interpreters (or other auxiliary aids) violated Section 504. The court held that the university is required to be the primary provider of auxiliary aids for students, faculty or staff with disabilities. Thus, universities cannot require students or employees with disabilities to request assistance from vocational rehabilitation centers. By implication, the university must contact those centers for assistance in providing the requisite services. The OCR and other courts have followed similar reasoning. A school may charge a special fee, however, where it provides a special program for learning disabled students that is outside the regular curriculum offered to other students. *Halasz v. University of New England*, 816 F.Supp. 37 (D.Me. 1993).

§ 9.4 SAFETY

Both Section 504 and the ADA incorporate a "safety defense." Accordingly, an individual with a disability is not qualified for a postsecondary educational program if his or her participation would pose a direct threat to the health or safety of other individuals. Courts have interpreted the safety defense as applying under Section 504 when an individual with a disability would pose a direct threat to the health or safety of *himself or herself*, as well as to the health or safety *of others*. As discussed more fully in § 7.14 of this *Nutshell*, it is unclear whether the "threat to self" reasoning applies to ADA Titles II and III.

In addition to the Supreme Court's decision in *Davis*, discussed earlier in this chapter, several Section 504 cases have addressed the safety issue in the context of postsecondary educational issues. For example, in *Doe v. New York University*, 666 F.2d 761 (2d Cir. 1981), the court held that a medical school did not discriminate against an applicant with a history of mental illness when it refused to readmit her to its program. The court held that the applicable question in determining whether Doe was otherwise qualified to be readmitted was "the substantiality of the risk that her mental disturbances [would] recur, resulting in behavior harmful to herself and others." The Second Circuit rejected the district court's test that Doe must be found qualified if it appeared "more likely than not" that she could complete her medical training and serve as a doctor without a recurrence of her self-destructive and antisocial behavior. The appellate court reasoned that Congress would not have intended to force colleges to accept students who pose a significant risk of harm to themselves or others even if the chances of harm were less than 50 percent. *But see Pushkin v. Regents of the Univ. of Colorado*, 658 F.2d 1372 (10th Cir. 1981) (holding that university violated Section 504 when it denied a physician with multiple sclerosis admittance to its psychiatric residency program based on incorrect assumptions or inadequate factual grounds; the admissions committee assumed that the plaintiff was angry and so emotionally upset due to his disability that he would be unable to do an effective job as a psychiatrist and that his disability and use of steroids had led to difficulties with mentation, delirium and disturbed sensorium).

The safety issue also arises in the context of university sports. Some courts addressing this issue have held that it was up to the individual and not the school to decide if the risk is acceptable. *See, e.g., Wright v. Columbia Univ.*, 520 F.Supp. 789 (E.D.Pa. 1981) (stating that while school's motives barring student with only one eye from playing football because of risk of injury were "laudabl[e]" they "derogate[d] from the rights secured to plaintiff under Section 504 which prohibits 'paternalistic authorities' from deciding that certain activities are 'too risky' for the handicapped person", and holding school violated Rehabilitation Act when it refused to respect the student's express wishes after he had "reached a rational decision concerning the risk involved"). Other courts, however, have held that the decision of whether it was too risky for a student to play should be made by the school *See, e.g., Knapp v. Northwestern University*, 101 F.3d 473 (7th Cir. 1996) (stating that, if a school has examined all the medical evidence on the risk of injury, it has the right "—regardless of whether conflicting medical opinions exist—. . . to determine that an individual is not otherwise qualified to play without violating the Rehabilitation Act").

§ 9.5   ACADEMIC DEFERENCE

The extent to which courts are willing to defer to the expertise of academic personnel in upholding or rejecting a claim for discrimination may be the decisive factor in any postsecondary education case alleging disability discrimination. In *Pushkin v. Regents of the Univ. of Colorado*, 658 F.2d 1372 (10th Cir. 1981), the court rejected the rule of deference to academic decisions as inconsistent with the plain language of § 504 forbidding discrimination against otherwise qualified individuals with disabilities. *Pushkin*, however, is perhaps the only case which pays no heed to academic judgments. Most courts have granted considerable deference to academic decisions. *See, e.g., Doe v. New York University*, 666 F.2d 761 (2d Cir. 1981).

These courts have concluded that an educational institution's academic decisions are entitled to deference because courts generally are "ill-equipped," as compared with experienced educators, to determine whether a student meets a university's "reasonable standards for academic and professional achievement." *Wong v. The Regents of the University of California*, 192 F.3d 807 (9th Cir. 1999). This deference is not absolute; courts still must ensure that educational institutions are not "disguis[ing] truly discriminatory requirements" as academic decisions; "[t]he educational institution has a 'real obligation . . . to seek suitable means of reasonably accommodating a handicapped person and to submit a factual record indicating that it conscientiously carried out this statutory obligation.' " *Id.* Specifically, the institution has "a duty to make itself aware of the nature of the student's disability; to explore alternatives for accommodating the student; and to exercise professional judgment in deciding whether the modifications under consideration would give the student the opportunity to complete the program without fundamentally or substantially modifying the school's standards." In *Wong*, the court refused to defer to the institution's academic decision because it had not fulfilled this obligation.

§ 9.6 NON-ACADEMIC PROGRAMS AND SERVICES

The DOE Section 504 regulations also govern access to non-academic programs and services:

> No qualified handicapped student shall, on the basis of handicap, be excluded from participation in, be denied the benefits of, or otherwise be subjected to discrimination under any academic, research, occupational training, housing, health insurance, counseling, financial aid, physical education, athletics, recreation, transportation, other extracurricular, or other postsecondary education program or activity.

34 C.F.R. § 104.43(a).

There are also specific regulations governing several areas of non-academic programs and services. For example, a college or university "that provides housing to its nonhandicapped students shall provide comparable, convenient, and accessible housing to handicapped students at the same cost as to others." 34 C.F.R. § 104.45(a). OCR has found that universities which provide some accessible housing may still violate § 504 when it is not sufficient to meet the needs of all disabled students who request it.

The regulations on physical education and athletics provide that a "recipient that offers physical education courses or that operates or sponsors intercollegiate, club, or intramural athletics shall provide to qualified handicapped students an equal opportunity for participation in these activities." 34 C.F.R. § 104.47(a)(1). The regulations further require that college or university "shall operate its programs and activities in the most integrated setting appropriate." *Id.* § 104.43(d). Therefore, physical education and athletic activities that are separate or different may be offered to students with disabilities only if doing so is consistent with that requirement, and "only if no qualified handicapped student is denied the opportunity to compete for teams or to participate in courses that are not separate or different." *Id.* § 104.47(a)(2).

"[P]ersonal, academic, or vocational counseling, guidance, or placement services" must be provided to disabled students to the same extent that such services are provided to non-disabled students. 34 C.F.R. § 104.47(b). And the school "shall ensure that qualified handicapped students are not counseled toward more restrictive career objectives than are non-handicapped students with similar interests and abilities." *Id.*

A college or university that "provides significant assistance to fraternities, sororities, or similar organizations shall assure itself that the membership practices of such organizations do not permit discrimination [on the basis of disability]." *Id.* § 104.47(c).

Schools which provide financial assistance are barred from dispensing less assistance to students with disabilities than to non-disabled students, limiting the eligibility of non-disabled students to such assistance, or otherwise discriminating on the basis of disability. 34 C.F.R. § 104.46(a). Similarly, a college or university that "assists any agency, organization, or person in providing employment opportunities to any of its students shall assure itself that such employment opportunities, as a whole, are made available in a manner [that does not discriminate against students with disabilities]." *Id.* § 104.46(b). Finally, a school that employs any of its students may not do so in a manner that discriminates against students with disabilities. *Id.* § 104.46(c)

§ 9.7   NOTICE AND DOCUMENTATION OF DISABILITY

Under the federal regulations, a student is responsible for identifying his/her disability to the college, requesting academic adjustments, and providing any necessary evidence of a disability-related need for the requested adjustment. 34 C.F.R. § 104.44 and 28 C.F.R. § 35.160(b)(1). *See also* OCR policy regarding the *Application of Section 504 Regulation Provisions Related to Academic Adjustments in Postsecondary Education Institutions.* ("The student is responsible for providing evidence of a condition that requires academic adjustments. In some cases this will require that the student provide the results of medical, psychological, or educational diagnostic tests and professional prescriptions for academic adjustments."). In recent years, the OCR and the courts have frequently found that a college did not violate § 504 or the ADA by denying a student academic adjustments where the student failed to provide the necessary notification or documentation. *See, e.g., Wynne v. Tufts Univ. Sch. of Med.*, 976 F.2d 791 (1st Cir.1992); *Rossomodando v. Board of Regents*, 2 F.Supp.2d 1223 (D. Ne. 1998); *Ferrell v. Howard University*, 1999 WL 1581759 (D.D.C. 1999). More specifically, the student must notify the school of the need for a particular academic adjustment. *See, e.g., Whittier School of Law (CA)*, 4 NDLR ¶ 183 (1993). In addition, the student must provide documentation to support the need for a particular academic adjustment. *See, e.g., State Univ. of New York*, 3 NDLR ¶ 104 (1992).

Generally, a school has no obligation to provide academic adjustment until it has received sufficient specific information to enable it to evaluate the student's needs and the school's ability to provide the needed academic adjustments. If the school has been provided sufficient notice from a qualified professional and then questions the diagnosis, description of limitations, and/or recommendations, the school can require the student to be evaluated by a professional of its choosing, and at its expense, before deciding what would be appropriate academic adjustments for the student. *Temple Univ.*, 8 NDLR ¶ 125 (1995).

The frequency of testing and the qualifications of those giving them was at issue in *Guckenberger v. Boston University*, 974 F.Supp. 106 (D. Mass. 1997). BU required students with learning disabilities to be retested every three years and to provide evaluations only by clinical or licensed psychologists or physicians. The court held that these requirements were unduly restrictive as applied to students required to be retested because tests originally accepted by the university were later deemed to be conducted by unqualified individuals. It was not unduly restrictive, however, as applied to students who had not been tested prior to matriculation at the university. The court also found that the requirement was "necessary" to the process of accommodating students diagnosed with attention deficit disorder (ADD) and attention deficit hyperactivity disorder (ADHD).

The 2008 Amendments draw into question the reasoning *in Guckenberger* because Congress stated that "the question of whether an individual's impairment is a disability under the ADA should not demand extensive analysis." 42 U.S.C. § 12101 NOTE (b)(5). In its 2010 regulations, DOJ added the following documentation language to its Title III regulations:

(1) Any private entity offering an examination covered by this section must assure that—

. . .

(iv) Any request for documentation, if such documentation is required, is reasonable and limited to the need for the modification, accommodation, or auxiliary aid or service requested.

(v) When considering requests for modifications, accommodations, or auxiliary aids or services, the entity gives considerable weight to documentation of past modifications, accommodations, or auxiliary aids or services received in similar testing situations, as well as such modifications, accommodations, or related aids and services provided in response to an Individualized Education Program (IEP) provided under the Individuals with Disabilities Education Act or a plan describing services provided pursuant to section 504 of the Rehabilitation Act of 1973, as amended (often referred to as a Section 504 Plan).

28 C.F.R. § 36.309(b).

§ 9.8   RETALIATION

Section 504 and ADA Titles II and III all prohibit retaliation against individuals who have exercised their rights under those laws. To establish a *prima facie* case of retaliation it must be shown that: (1) the individual was engaged in an activity protected by Section 504 or the ADA; (2) the individual was subjected to some adverse action by the postsecondary educational institution; and (3) there is sufficient evidence of a connection between the protected activity and the adverse action to give rise to an inference of retaliation. Once a *prima facie* case is established, the school may offer a legitimate, non-discriminatory explanation for the adverse action. The student then has an opportunity to show that the institution's proffered reason for the adverse action is a pretext for discrimination.

§ 9.9 HOSTILE LEARNING ENVIRONMENT

A cause of action exists under the ADA and Section 504 for an educational institution's creation of a hostile learning environment for students with disabilities. *See, e.g., Guckenberger v. Boston University*, 974 F.Supp. 106 (D. Mass. 1997) (involving students with learning disabilities).

§ 9.10 INDIVIDUALS WITH LEARNING DISABILITIES

Increasingly, postsecondary educational institutions are confronted with issues pertaining to applicants or students with learning disabilities. More children are being diagnosed as learning disabled and provided with special education services because of the implementation and enforcement of the Individuals with Disabilities Education Act (IDEA), 20 U.S.C.A. §§ 1400–1485, which requires elementary and secondary school districts to provide children with educational disabilities with a free appropriate education. In addition, testing and identification procedures have become more sophisticated, allowing experts to more readily identify learning disabilities.

Regulations promulgated under Section 504 and the ADA specifically list a learning disability as a covered physical or mental impairment under those laws. 29 C.F.R. § 1630.2(h)(2); 34 C.F.R. § 105.3(1)(ii). To state a claim under Section 504 or the ADA, an individual would have to show either that (1) his or her current learning disability substantially limited a major life activity, (2) he or she is regarded as having a learning disability that substantially limits a major activity, or (3) he or she has a record of a learning disability that substantially limited a major life activity. The ability to learn is held to constitute a major life activity. The 2008 Amendments to the ADA make clear the validity of these regulations because "learning" is now listed as a major life activity. *See* 42 U.S.C. § 12102(2)(A). As discussed in § 9.2(D), above, the EEOC has also promulgated guidance on the coverage of learning disabilities, generally, under the ADA.

A.   ADMISSIONS

In the admissions process, the question that often arises is whether an individual with a learning disability is qualified for admission to a given program.

While colleges and universities may not ask an applicant if he or she has a disability, an applicant may always identify a disability and ask that it be considered as a relevant factor in the admissions determination. In such cases, the institution should evaluate the applicant's *entire* file. A learning disability, for example, may serve as evidence of reasons for poor performance in high school or on standardized tests, such as the SAT. If there is evidence that a learning disability has prevented an applicant from performing as well as the applicant is capable of, the admissions committee may look for other evidence of the applicant's ability, such as performance in courses and on standardized tests that were modified to accommodate the learning disability, employment or community experiences, or letters of recommendation from teachers or employers who know the applicant well. The admissions committee may also consider whether there is evidence showing that the applicant is able to perform well when appropriate accommodations are provided.

Safety concerns may also be at issue with respect to an applicant with a learning disability, such as in the case of an applicant to nursing school who has a learning disability that causes him or her to transpose numbers or an applicant to veterinary school who has a learning disability that precludes him or her from being able to perform certain important mathematical computations. There may be legitimate concerns that the applicant to nursing school would be unable to accurately enter or follow information about medications on patients' charts and that the applicant to veterinary school might be unable to accurately prescribe or compile medications. Ultimately, it would have to be determined whether accommodations or adjustments could be made to eliminate those safety concerns, such as by allowing the nursing student to dictate notes into a tape to be transcribed by a secretary.

Another situation that arises in the context of the admission of applicants with learning disabilities to postsecondary educational programs involves special learning-disabilities programs. In *Halasz v. University of New England*, 816 F.Supp. 37 (D.Me. 1993), the university operated a special program for students with learning disabilities, pursuant to which it provided tutorial assistance by learning-disability specialists, training in study skills, notetakers, books on tape and other assistance. A fee was charged for the program. The university agreed to admit some students with learning disabilities with lower than the requisite SAT scores and GPAs on the condition that the students enrolled in the special program. The court upheld the university's program.

The court in *Halasz* noted that colleges and universities are free to set their own standards and requirements for admission. The program at issue in *Halasz* served as an expanded type of accommodation to assist students with learning disabilities who were not already succeeding independently in academic settings. Charging a fee for the program was permissible since, although a university may not charge a student with disabilities for the cost of reasonable accommodations, this program went beyond the reasonable accommodation obligation. So long as the university provided requisite reasonable accommodations for a student with disabilities at no cost, the court indicated—without really deciding—that a fee may be charged for additional services which are beyond the university's obligation. Moreover, the court held that the university could permissibly limit the number of students who would be admitted to the special learning disabilities program as long as: (1) it did not limit the number of students with learning disabilities admitted to the school, and (2) it provided reasonable accommodations (at no charge) to all admitted students with learning disabilities.

B.   ACCOMMODATIONS FOR ACCEPTED STUDENTS

Every learning disability is different. Thus, each individual with a learning disability may require a unique form of assistance or accommodation. And each postsecondary educational program will have different requirements and standards. As a result, it is not possible to devise a generic list of "appropriate" accommodations for students with learning disabilities in postsecondary educational programs. The issue in each case is fact specific. Courts and the OCR have disagreed in different situations, for example, as to what modification should be made to courses or examination procedures for students with learning disabilities. The basic issue is whether the requested accommodations would require the school to fundamentally alter its program or lower its standards. *See, e.g., Guckenberger v. Boston University*, 974 F.Supp. 106 (D.Mass. 1997) (holding that: (i) the ADA and Section 504 do not require a university to modify degree requirements for students with learning disabilities by providing substitutions for courses the university determines are a fundamental part of its academic program; and (ii) a university has a duty under the ADA and Section 504 to consider whether a course substitution would constitute a reasonable accommodation for a student with a learning disability as opposed to requiring substantial program alteration or lowering of academic standards.)

§ 9.11   ENFORCEMENT

Students can file suit in cases involving disability discrimination in postsecondary education. These cases will use the remedies and procedures for enforcing the access to programs and services requirements of the ADA and Rehabilitation Act discussed in §§ 4.3, 7.28 and 7.29 of this *Nutshell*.

As more fully discussed in § 7.28, the doctrine of sovereign immunity may impact the viability of ADA actions against state universities. *See, e.g., Association for Disabled Americans, Inc. v. Florida International University*, 178 F.Supp.2d 1291 (S.D.Fla. 2001) (holding students with hearing impairments were barred from suing the university under the ADA in federal court). Some courts have also applied sovereign immunity principles to conclude that Section 504 cannot be used to obtain monetary damages against a state entity. *See, e.g., Garcia v. S.U.N.Y. Health Sciences Center of Brooklyn*, 280 F.3d 98 (2d Cir. 2001) (court held damages claims under ADA Title II and section 504 barred by sovereign immunity). The Supreme Court's decision in *Tennessee v. Lane*, 541 U.S. 509 (2004) does not entirely resolve this issue. The Court does mention "education" as potentially covered by ADA Title II and not subject to sovereign immunity protections but that issue was not directly before the Court in *Lane* so can only be understood as dicta.

Students may also bring administrative complaints with OCR to remedy disability discrimination in postsecondary education. The Section 504 regulations, 34 C.F.R. § 104.61, state that procedural provisions applicable to Title VI of the Civil Rights Act of 1964 apply to such complaints. Those procedures are found in 34 C.F.R. § 100.6–100.10 and Part 101 and mirror those described for administrative complaints under Title II which are discussed in § 7.28 of this *Nutshell*.

CHAPTER 10
TRANSPORTATION

§ 10.1 MASS GROUND
TRANSPORTATION: OVERVIEW

Before the Americans with Disabilities Act (ADA) was enacted, four federal statutes obligated transit companies to provide accessible mass transit via bus, rail or other means of ground transportation.

First, in 1970 Congress enacted Section 16(a) of the Urban Mass Transportation Act (UMTA) which declares a national policy that persons who are elderly and/or disabled have the same right as other persons to use mass transit. This Act mandates the undertaking of special efforts in the planning and design of facilities and services to ensure that usable mass transit is available to persons who are elderly and/or disabled. The UMTA requires "all Federal programs offering assistance in the field of mass transportation ... [to] contain provisions implementing this policy." 49 U.S.C.A. § 5301(d).

Second, because most transit systems receive some form of federal financial assistance, they are subject to the antidiscrimination mandate of Section 504.

Third, in 1975 Congress amended Section 165(b) of the Federal-Aid Highway Act to provide funding for public transportation projects through federal financial assistance. Projects funded under the Act must be constructed and operated to allow effective use by persons with disabilities. 23 U.S.C.A. § 142 note.

Fourth, in 1982 Congress amended the UMTA to add Section 317(c) of the Surface Transportation Assistance Act of 1982 which required the Secretary of Transportation to promulgate regulations under the three previously named acts establishing 1) minimum criteria for providing transportation services to individuals with disabilities and elderly individuals and 2) procedures for the Secretary to monitor recipients' compliance with those criteria. 49 U.S.C.A. § 5310(f).

Over the years the United States Department of Transportation (DOT) has promulgated several sets of regulations to implement these four laws. Portions of these regulations were subject to a variety of legal challenges, particularly with respect to the Section 504 regulations. Following enactment of the ADA in 1990, however, the DOT issued regulations on September 6, 1991. 49 C.F.R. §§ 27.19 and 27.3. The explanatory section to those regulations states:

The basic relationship between [S]ection 504 and the ADA is that a recipient of DOT funds complies with its [S]ection 504 obligations by complying with its ADA obligations. At the same time, [S]ection 501 of the ADA [42 U.S.C.A. § 12201] provides that nothing in the ADA shall be construed "to apply a lesser standard than [S]ection 504 or agency regulations implementing [S]ection 504."

Further, the Section 504 regulations were amended to provide that:

Recipients subject to this part . . . shall comply with all applicable requirements of the Americans with Disabilities Act (ADA) of 1990 . . . including the Department's ADA regulations (49 CFR parts 37 and 38), [and] the regulations of the Department of Justice implementing Titles II and III of the ADA (28 CFR parts 35 and 36). . . . Compliance with all these regulations is a condition of receiving Federal financial assistance from the Department of Transportation.

49 C.F.R. § 27.19(a). In addition, a new proviso was enacted that states:

(b) Design, construction, or alteration of buildings or other fixed facilities by public entities subject to [49 C.F.R.] part 37 . . . shall be in conformance with Appendix A to part 37. . . . All other entities subject to section 504 shall design, construct or alter a building, or other fixed facilities shall be in conformance with either Appendix A to part 37 . . . or the Uniform Federal Accessibility Standards, 41 CFR part 101–19 subpart 101–19.6, appendix A.

49 C.F.R. § 27.3(b).

With respect to mass ground transportation, therefore, this *Nutshell* will focus on the transportation provisions set forth in the ADA and the DOT's regulations in 49 C.F.R part 37. The transportation provisions of the ADA constitute a major hub of the Act. Congress recognized that opening the doors to employment and places of public accommodation would be of little use to people with disabilities if they were unable to travel beyond their homes.

§ 10.2   ADA TITLE II: PUBLIC ENTITIES

Title II of the ADA, 42 U.S.C.A. §§ 12141–12165, deals with the provision of public transportation by public entities. The term "public entity" is defined as including any state or local government (including any department, agency or other instrumentality of such government), the National Railroad Passenger Corporation and any rail commuter authority. 42 U.S.C.A. § 12131(1).

Congress required the Attorney General to promulgate regulations for carrying out the provisions of Title II and that they were to be consistent with the regulations enacted under Section 504. Moreover, the regulations were to include standards for covered facilities and vehicles that are consistent with the minimum guidelines and requirements issued by the Architectural and Transportation Barriers Compliance Board (Access Board) under the Architectural Barriers Act (ABA). Accordingly, violations of the ADA regulations will generally constitute violations of Section 504 when the covered entity is governed by that Act.

A.   PART I OF DIVISION B OF TITLE II

Part I of Division B of Title II covers "public transportation" provided by bus or by rail or any other conveyance (such as vans or limousines), not including air travel, that furnish the general public with transportation services on a regular basis. This part of the statutes excludes commuter rail services, which are covered by Part II of Division B of Title II, and public school transportation. If a public entity contracts with a private entity for the latter to provide transportation services, the private entity must stand in the shoes of the public entity and must comply with this Part. The major components of Part I provide as follows:

1. *New Vehicles*

All new buses or rail vehicles solicited for purchase or lease by public entities operating fixed route systems (in which vehicles are operated along prescribed routes in accord with fixed schedules) must be "readily accessible to and usable by individuals with disabilities, including individuals who use wheelchairs." 42 U.S.C.A. § 12142(a). Thus, new buses and rail systems must be fitted with lifts or ramps and fold-up seats or other wheelchair spaces with appropriate securement devices. An exception to this rule is made where lifts for new vehicles are unavailable despite good-faith efforts by the public entity to locate them. A public entity must apply for any such exemption to the Secretary of Transportation, however, and any exemption granted will be temporary, limited in duration by a specified date. 49 C.F.R. § 37.71.

2. *Used Vehicles*

A public entity operating a fixed-route system that purchases or leases a used vehicle must demonstrate good-faith efforts to purchase or lease a used vehicle that is readily accessible to and usable by individuals with disabilities. 42 U.S.C.A. § 12142(b).

3. *Remanufactured Vehicles*

A public entity operating a fixed-route system that remanufactures a vehicle so as to extend its life for five years, or purchases or leases such a remanufactured vehicle, shall ensure that "to the maximum extent feasible," the vehicle is readily accessible to and usable by individuals with disabilities. An exception is made for "historic vehicles" if alteration of a vehicle would significantly alter its historic character. *Id.* § 12142(c).

4. *Paratransit Services*

If a public entity operates a public transportation fixed-route system that is not accessible to certain people with disabilities, the entity must provide origin-to-destination paratransit or other special transportation services (*e.g.*, by van, taxi, car or limousine). The paratransit service must provide a "comparable" level of services to people with disabilities and their companions as that provided to non-disabled persons. 42 U.S.C.A. § 12143(a); 49 C.F.R. § 37.121(a).

A commuter bus service (fixed-route bus service predominantly in one direction during peak periods—usually between the central business district and outlying suburbs) is not required to provide paratransit service. 49 C.F.R. § 37.121(c). Further, paratransit services need only be provided in a service area in which a public entity operates a fixed-route service, and not in any portion of the service area in which the entity only provides commuter bus service. *Id.* § 37.131 Public airport shuttle or connector systems and public university transport systems, while considered providers of fixed route systems, are not required to provide paratransit services. 49 C.F.R. Pt. 37, App. D §§ 37.25, 37.33

In providing paratransit services, public entities must only respond to the request of persons with disabilities "*to the extent practicable*" to meet the comparable level of services provided to individuals without disabilities. 42 U.S.C.A. § 12143(a)(2). Further, public entities are required to provide paratransit services for persons with disabilities only in three circumstances: (1) when an individual's disability precludes him or her from boarding, riding, or disembarking on or from accessible transportation vehicles without the assistance of another person; (2) when an individual with a disability requires an accessible transportation vehicle during the hours of operation of the fixed-route service but an accessible vehicle is not being provided during the time that the individual requires transportation services; or (3) when an individual's disability prevents him or her from traveling to a boarding or disembarking location, and he or she is thus unable to utilize public transportation services. *Id.* § 12143(c)(1)(A).

Finally, the requirement that paratransit services be provided to people with disabilities and their companions is limited to *one* companion of the individual; other companions will be permitted to ride with the person with a disability to the extent that space is available. *Id.* § 12143(c)(1)(C). The intent is to allow persons with disabilities to attend functions with non-disabled family members and friends but at the same time refrain from overburdening the paratransit system.

The ADA requires each public entity operating a fixed-route system to submit to the Secretary an annual plan for providing the required paratransit services. *Id.* § 12143(c)(7)(A). The DOT regulations provide specific requirements for paratransit services. *See* 49 C.F.R. Part 37. Specifically, the regulations provide that riders with disabilities must reserve rides at least one day in advance. The fare may not exceed twice the fare that would be charged in the entity's fixed-route system. Restrictions or priorities based on trip purpose are prohibited. Paratransit services must be available during the same days and hours of operation as fixed-route services. Capacity constraints (such as restrictions on the number of trips available to an individual, waiting lists, untimely pickups or a substantial number of trips with excessive trip lengths) are prohibited. 49 C.F.R. § 37.131(b)–(e). *See, e.g., Anderson v. Rochester-Genesee Regional Transp. Authority*, 337 F.3d 201 (2d Cir. 2003) (finding transportation authority violated the ADA and applicable regulations requiring that a paratransit company plan, design, and implement a system to schedule all next-day ride requests from eligible riders).

Paratransit services may include a subscription service component. Subscription service, however, "may not absorb more than fifty percent of the number of trips available at a given time of day, unless there is non-subscription capacity." 49 C.F.R. § 37.133(b).

Entities are free to provide additional paratransit services for people with disabilities. Costs of such additional service, however, do not count when an entity requests a waiver due to undue financial burden, as discussed below.

A transit agency may obtain a waiver from the requirement that it provide paratransit services if it can demonstrate that providing such services would impose an undue financial burden. This undue burden exception appears to expire on January 26, 1997. 49 C.F.R. § 37.151. Decisions on granting such a waiver will be made on a case-by-case basis by the Administrator after considering relevant factors. *Id.* § 37.155(a). Any waivers granted must be for a limited, specified time. Once a waiver is granted, the Administrator will either (a) require the entity to provide complementary paratransit services to the extent that it can do so without incurring an undue financial burden; or (b) require the entity to provide *basic* complementary paratransit services along the corridors of the entity's key routes (*i.e.*, routes along which services are provided at least hourly throughout the day) during core service hours (those encompassing at least peak periods), even if doing so would cause the entity to incur an undue financial burden.

5. *Demand Responsive Systems*

If a public entity operates a "demand responsive system" (any system providing designated transportation other than a fixed route system) for the general public, all vehicles solicited for purchase or lease must be readily accessible to and usable by individuals with disabilities. An exception can be made if the entity can demonstrate that its system, when viewed in its entirety, provides "equivalent" services to persons with disabilities as those provided to nondisabled persons. 42 U.S.C.A. § 12144.

6. *New Facilities*

All new facilities that will be used to provide public transportation services must be made readily accessible to and usable by individuals with disabilities. *Id.* § 12146.

7. *Altered Facilities*

Alterations made to existing facilities or parts of existing facilities must be made so that "to the maximum extent feasible" the altered portions are readily accessible to and usable by individuals with disabilities. *Id.* § 12147(a). The term "to the maximum extent feasible" is meant to apply

> to the occasional case where the nature of an existing facility makes it impossible to comply fully with applicable standards through a planned alteration. In these circumstances, the entity shall provide the maximum physical accessibility feasible. Any altered features of the facility or portion of the facility that can be made accessible shall be made accessible. If providing accessibility to certain individuals with disabilities (*e.g.*, those who use wheelchairs) would not be feasible, the facility shall be made accessible to individuals with other types of disabilities (*e.g.*, those who use crutches, those who have impaired vision or hearing, or those who have other impairments).

49 C.F.R. § 37.43(b).

Alterations made to primary function areas must be made in such a manner to ensure that the path of travel to the altered area, including the restrooms, telephones and drinking fountains serving the altered area, are readily accessible to and usable by individuals with disabilities. "Primary function areas" are those areas that serve to carry out a major activity for which the facility is intended, such as waiting areas, ticket purchase and collection areas, train or bus platforms, baggage checking and return areas, and employment areas. *Id.* § 37.43(d).

If the cost and scope of making alterations to the path of travel and to drinking fountains, telephones and restrooms along that path is "disproportionate" to the cost of the overall alteration, however, an entity is not required to make those portions accessible. *Id.* § 37.43(a)(2). Alterations will be deemed "disproportionate" to the overall alteration "when the cost exceeds 20 percent of the cost of the alteration to the primary function area (without regard to the costs of accessibility modifications)." *Id.* § 37.43(e)(1). When the costs of altering the path of travel are shown to be disproportionate to the cost of the entire alteration, the path of travel must be made "accessible to the maximum extent without resulting in disproportionate costs." *Id.* § 37.43(f)(1). In such a case, alterations should be made in the following order of priority:

(i) An accessible entrance;

(ii) An accessible route to the altered area;

(iii) At least one accessible restroom for each sex or a single unisex restroom (where there are one or more restrooms);

(iv) Accessible telephones;

(v) Accessible drinking fountains;

(vi) When possible, other accessible elements (*e.g.*, parking, storage, alarms).

Id. § 37.43(f)(2).

8. *Key Stations*

"Key stations" of rapid-rail, light-rail, and commuter rail systems must be made readily accessible to and usable by individuals with disabilities "as soon as practicable but in no event later than" July 26, 1993. 42 U.S.C.A. §§ 12147(b)(2)(A), 12162 (e)(2)(A)(ii). A "key station" is one that is designated as such by a light- or rapid-rail operator, through planning and public participation processes set forth in the DOT regulations, and taking into consideration the following criteria:

(1) Stations where passenger boardings exceed average station passenger boardings on the rail system by at least fifteen percent, unless such a station is close to another accessible station;

(2) Transfer stations on a rail line or between rail lines;

(3) Major interchange points with other transportation modes, including stations connecting with major parking facilities, bus terminals, intercity or commuter rail stations, passenger vessel terminals, or airports;

(4) End stations, unless an end station is close to another accessible station; and

(5) Stations serving major activity centers, such as employment or government centers, institutions of higher education, hospitals or other major health care facilities, or other

facilities that are major trip generators for individuals with disabilities.

49 C.F.R. §§ 37.47(b) and 37.51(b). The regulations note an exception to this time frame for New York City and Philadelphia, pursuant to settlement agreements entered into between those cities and the DOT. *Id.* 37.53.

The three-year period within which to comply may be extended up to 30 years by the Secretary for stations that need "extraordinarily expensive structural changes." 42 U.S.C.A. § 12147(b)(2)(B). As of 20 years after enactment of the Act, at least two-thirds of all key stations for light- or rapid-rail systems (but not commuter rail systems) must be readily accessible to and usable by individuals with disabilities. Public entities must develop plans for compliance with these requirements.

9. *Programs and Activities*

Public entities operating transportation programs and activities in existing facilities must do so in such a manner that "when viewed in its entirety" each program or activity is readily accessible to and usable by individuals with disabilities. 42 U.S.C.A. § 12148(a)(1). This is a lower standard than the standard applied to key stations, because in the latter case the "when viewed in its entirety" language is omitted. The ADA further provides that it shall not be construed to require public entities to make facilities wheelchair accessible except to the extent required by the previously discussed sections relating to alteration of existing facilities and key stations. *Id.* § 12148(a)(2).

10. *Light- or Rapid-Rail Systems*

When a public entity operates a light-or rapid-rail train containing two or more cars, at least one vehicle per train must be accessible to individuals with disabilities "as soon as practicable but in no event later" than July 26, 1995. 42 U.S.C.A. § 12148(b)(1). An exception is made, however, for historic vehicles used on a segment of a light- or rapid-rail system which is on the National Register of Historic Places when rendering the train accessible would significantly alter its historic character.

B. PART II OF DIVISION B OF ADA TITLE II

Part II of Division B of ADA Title II deals with public transportation by commuter rail services and intercity rail services provided by the National Railroad Passenger Corporation (Amtrak). 42 U.S.C.A. § 12161. The salient provisions of this part are as follows:

1. *Accessible Cars*

A person or entity that provides intercity or commuter rail transportation must have at least one passenger car per train that is readily accessible to and usable by individuals with disabilities "as soon as practicable" but in no event later than July 26, 1995. *Id.* § 12162(a)(1) and (b)(1).

2. *New Cars*

A person or entity that makes a solicitation for, or purchases or leases, any new rail passenger car for use in intercity or commuter rail transportation must ensure that such cars are readily accessible to and usable by individuals with disabilities. *Id.* § 12162(a)(2)(A) and (b)(2)(A). Generally, the statute requires coach cars to 1) be able to be entered by an individual in a wheelchair, 2) have space to park and secure a wheelchair, 3) have a seat to which a passenger in a wheelchair can transfer, and 4) have a restroom accessible to an individual in a wheelchair. Dining cars are generally not required to be wheelchair accessible from the station; however, single level dining cars must be accessible from within the train. *Id.* § 12162(a)(2)(B)–(a)(4).

However, for new rail passenger cars purchased for use in *commuter rail* transportation, the requirement that new cars be readily accessible

> shall not be construed to require—(i) a restroom usable by an individual who uses a wheelchair if no restroom is provided in such car for any passenger; (ii) space to fold and store a wheelchair; or (iii) a seat to which a passenger who uses a wheelchair can transfer.

Id. § 12162(b)(2)(B).

3. *Used Cars*

A person or entity that purchases a used rail passenger car for use in intercity or commuter rail transportation must make "demonstrated good faith efforts to purchase or lease a used rail car that is readily accessible to and usable by individuals with disabilities. . . ." 42 U.S.C.A. § 12162(c).

4. *Remanufactured Cars*

A person or entity that remanufactures a rail passenger car, or purchases or leases a remanufactured rail passenger car, for use in intercity or commuter rail transportation so as to extend its life for ten years must ensure that the rail car, "to the maximum extent feasible," is made readily accessible to and usable by individuals with disabilities. 42 U.S.C.A. § 12162(d)(1).

5. *New Stations*

A person or entity that builds a new station for use in intercity or commuter rail transportation must ensure that the station is readily accessible to and usable by individuals with disabilities. 42 U.S.C.A. § 12162(e)(1).

6. *Existing Stations in Intercity Rail Transportation*

All existing stations used in intercity rail transportation systems must be made accessible to and usable by persons with disabilities "as soon as practicable" but in no event later than 20 years after the Act's enactment. 42 U.S.C.A. § 12162(e)(2)(A)(ii)(I). The obligation to implement this provision falls upon the statutorily defined "responsible person," which is 1) the public entity if it owns more than 50 percent of a station, 2) the persons providing transportation to a station when more than 50 percent of the station is owned by a private party, or 3) the persons providing transportation and the public owners of a station when no party owns more than 50 percent of the station. *Id.* § 12161(5).

7. *Existing Key Stations in Commuter Rail Transportation*

The responsible person must make existing key stations used in commuter rail transportation systems readily accessible to and usable by individuals with disabilities "as soon as practicable," but in no event later than three years after the Act's enactment. 42 U.S.C.A. § 12162(e)(2)(A)(ii)(II). The Secretary of Transportation, however, may extend this time limit up to 20 years after the Act's enactment "in a case where the raising of the entire passenger platform is the only means available of attaining accessibility or where other extraordinarily expensive structural changes are necessary to attain accessibility." *Id.*

8. *Altered Stations*

Alterations to existing stations or parts thereof used in intercity or commuter rail transportation systems must be made in a manner to ensure that "to the maximum extent feasible" the altered portions are readily accessible to and usable by individuals with disabilities. 42 U.S.C.A. § 12162(e)(2)(B)(i).

9. *Designation of Responsible Persons*

The DOT regulations set forth a mechanism for determining who bears the legal and financial responsibility for accessibility modifications to commuter or intercity rail stations. 49 C.F.R. § 37.49. Basically, the regulations authorize—and encourage—all covered parties to come to their own agreement regarding the allocation of responsibility.

If the parties do not reach an agreement, the regulations allocate responsibility as follows: First, if a single public entity owns more than 50 percent of the station, the public entity is totally responsible. Second, if a private entity owns more than 50 percent of the station, the private entity bears *no* responsibility. Rather, "the persons providing commuter or intercity rail service to the station are the responsible parties, in a proportion equal to the percentage of all passenger boardings at the station attributable to the service of each, over the entire period during which the station is made accessible." 49 C.F.R. § 37.49(c). Third, if no single party owns 50 percent of the station, public entity owners and persons providing intercity or commuter rail service share the responsibility (with 50 percent of the responsibility being allocated between public entity owners in proportion to their ownership, and the remaining 50 percent of the responsibility being allocated between service providers in proportion to the amount of service provided). *Id.* § 37.49(d).

§ 10.3 ENFORCEMENT OF ADA TITLE II

Enforcement of ADA Title II is intended to parallel enforcement under Section 504. Thus, Title II incorporates the remedies, procedures, and rights set forth in Section 505 of the Rehabilitation Act, 29 U.S.C.A. § 794a. These remedies and procedures are discussed in §§ 4.3 and 7.28 of this *Nutshell*.

Both public and private recipients of federal financial assistance are subject to DOT's Section 504 administrative enforcement procedures. 49 C.F.R. § 37.11. Under those procedures, the complainant files an administrative complaint with the DOT's Office of Civil Rights (OCR). The OCR investigates the complaint, and, if a violation is found, attempts to enter into a conciliation agreement with the entity. The procedures used in such an investigation mirror those described for administrative complaints under ADA Title II which are discussed in § 7.28 of this *Nutshell*.

§ 10.4 ADA TITLE III: PRIVATE ENTITIES

Title III of the ADA covers public transportation by private entities. There are different sets of standards for private entities primarily engaged in the business of transporting people and those which only provide transportation as part of their business.

A. PROVISION OF PUBLIC TRANSPORTATION BY PRIVATE ENTITIES PRIMARILY ENGAGED IN THE BUSINESS OF TRANSPORTING PEOPLE

Private entities primarily engaged in the business of transporting people (other than by air travel), and whose operations affect commerce, are prohibited from discriminating on the basis of disability. The most crucial requirements for these entities are as follows:

1. *New Vehicles*

All new vehicles (other than automobiles, vans with seating capacities of fewer than eight passengers, and over-the-road buses—that is buses that have elevated passenger decks over baggage compartments) used to provide specified public transportation services must be readily accessible to and usable by individuals with disabilities. Compliance with this provision is not required, however, if a new vehicle is to be used solely in a demand-responsive system, and the entity can "demonstrate that [such] system, . . . when viewed in its entirety, provides a level of service to [disabled] individuals equivalent to the level of service provided to the general public." 42 U.S.C.A. § 12184(b)(3).

New vans with a seating capacity of fewer than eight passengers must be readily accessible to and usable by persons with disabilities if they are used to provide specified public transportation services. There is an exception, however, if "the entity can demonstrate that the system for which the van is being purchased or leased, when viewed in its entirety, provides a level of service to [disabled] individuals equivalent to the level of service provided to the general public." *Id.* § 12184(b)(5).

2. *New Rail Vehicles*

All new rail passenger cars used to provide specified public transportation must be readily accessible to and usable by individuals with disabilities. 42 U.S.C.A. § 12184(b)(6).

3. *Remanufactured Rail Vehicles*

All rail passenger cars used to provide specified public transportation that are remanufactured so as to extend their life for ten years or more, or any such remanufactured rail car newly purchased or leased, must, to the maximum extent feasible, be readily accessible to and usable by individuals with disabilities. 42 U.S.C.A. § 12184(b)(7).

4. *Over-the-Road Buses*

As enacted, the ADA required the Secretary of Transportation to issue new regulations relating to the accessibility of over-the-road buses (OTRBs). For "small providers" of transportation, the regulations were to take effect seven years after the Act's enactment (July 26, 1997); for "other" providers of transportation, the regulatory provisions were to take effect six years after the Act's enactment (July 26, 1996). The ADA was later amended to state that the dates by which over-the-road buses must be accessible were delayed until three years and two years, respectively, after the date of issuance of final regulations governing over-the-road buses. Congress also specified that the regulations may "not require the installation of accessible restrooms in over-the-road buses if such installation would result in a loss of seating capacity." *Id.* § 12186(a)(2)(C).

The regulations for OTRBs were finally issued in 1998 and became effective for large operators beginning October 30, 2000, and for small operators beginning October 29, 2001. 49 C.F.R. § 37.181. Under these rules, it is discrimination for an OTRB operator to (a) deny transportation to passengers with disabilities unless they engage in violent, seriously disruptive, or illegal conduct; (b) use or request the use of persons (e.g., family members or traveling companions of a passenger with a disability, medical or public safety personnel) other than the operator's employees for routine boarding or other assistance unless the passenger requests or consents to such assistance; (c) require or request a passenger with a disability to reschedule his or her trip, or travel at a time other than the time the passenger has requested; (d) fail to provide reservation services to passengers with disabilities equivalent to those provided other passengers; or (e) fail or refuse to comply with any applicable regulations. *Id.* § 37.207.

Large operators of *fixed-route systems* are required to ensure that any new OTRB they purchase or lease is "readily accessible to and usable by individuals with disabilities, including individuals who use wheelchairs." *Id.* § 37.183(a).

Small operators and private entities not primarily in the business of transporting people which operate fixed-route systems may comply with the law by doing the same or by providing equivalent service to individuals with disabilities; "[t]o meet this equivalent service standard, the service provided by the operator must permit a wheelchair user to travel in his or her own mobility aid." *Id.* §§ 37.183(b), 37.195(a).

Section 37.185 requires that *a large operator of a fixed-route system* must ensure that no less than 50 percent of the buses in its fleet are accessible by October 30, 2006, and that 100 percent of its buses are accessible by October 29, 2012. An operator may apply to the Transportation Secretary for a time extension of the fleet accessibility deadlines. The Secretary will consider the following factors in determining whether to grant such a request: (1) whether the operator has purchased or leased, since October 30, 2000, enough new OTRBs to replace 50 percent of its OTRBs by October 30, 2006, or 100 percent of its OTRBs by October 29, 2012; (2) whether the operator purchased or leased a number of new inaccessible OTRBs between October 28, 1998, and October 30, 2000 which significantly exceeded the number of buses it would normally obtain in such a period; and (3) the operator's compliance with all requirements of the regulations between October 28, 1998, and the request for time extension.

If the general public can purchase a ticket or make a reservation with one operator for a fixed-

route trip of two or more stages where more than
one operator provides service, the regulations
provide that 1) the first operator must arrange for
an accessible bus or equivalent service to be
provided for each stage of the trip, 2) each operator
is responsible for providing the required
transportation for its portion of an interline trip,
and 3) all fixed-route operators involved in interline
service must have the capacity to receive
communications at all times concerning interline
service for passengers with disabilities. 49 C.F.R.
§ 37.187.

Section 37.193 provides interim service
requirements until a fixed-route service has 100
percent of its fleet composed of accessible OTRBs.
Both large and small operators must, within one
year of the effective date of the regulations, ensure
that any individual with a disability who requests
service in an accessible OTRB must receive such
service. Operators may require up to 48 hours'
advance notice to provide this service; if such notice
is not provided, the operator still must provide the
service if it can do so by making a reasonable effort.
The operator has met this requirement if the trip on
which the person with a disability wishes to travel
is already provided by an accessible bus. A small
operator does not need to satisfy this rule if it is
providing equivalent service to its fixed-route
service. The regulation states that some small fixed-
route operators who exclusively or primarily
purchase or lease used buses may never have a fleet
of 100 percent accessible buses. Such an operator
must continue to comply with the regulations with

respect to any service that is not provided entirely with accessible buses.

The regulations for entities that provide *demand-responsive* OTRB service, including private entities not primarily in the business of transporting people, provide that they are not required to purchase or lease accessible buses except as needed to meet the following requirements. First, both large and small operators must ensure that, within one year of the effective date of the regulations, any individual with a disability who requests service in an accessible OTRB must receive such service. Second, operators may require up to 48 hours advance notice to provide this service; if such notice is not provided, the operator still must provide the service if it can do so by making a reasonable effort. Finally, an operator is not required to fundamentally alter its normal reservation policies or to displace another passenger who has reserved a seat on the bus. *Id.* §§ 37.189, 37.195(b).

A special provision applies to small mixed-service operators that provide both fixed-route and demand-responsive service and do not use more than 25 percent of their buses for fixed-route service. Those operators are 1) not required to comply with the accessible bus acquisition/equivalent service obligations for fixed-route system operators and 2) may conduct all their trips, including fixed-route trips, on an advance-reservation basis as provided for demand-responsive trips. *Id.* § 37.191.

If an OTRB is remanufactured to extend its useful life for five years, it shall be considered feasible to do so such that it is readily accessible unless an engineering analysis demonstrates that including accessibility features would have a significant adverse effect on the structural integrity of the vehicle. *Id.* § 37.197.

When an OTRB makes an intermediate or rest stop, passengers with disabilities, including wheelchair users, shall be permitted to leave and return to the bus on the same basis as other passengers. Accordingly, the operator must provide assistance to passengers with disabilities such as operating the lift and assisting with securement. If an OTRB operator owns, leases, or controls the facility where the stop is made (or contracts with the person who owns, leases, or controls such a facility to provide rest stop services), the OTRB operator shall ensure the facility is fully compliant with applicable ADA requirements. If an OTRB with an inaccessible restroom is making an express run of three hours or more without a rest stop, it must make a good faith effort to accommodate a request for an unscheduled rest stop by a passenger with a disability who is unable to use the inaccessible restroom. The operator is not required to make the stop, but it must explain to the passenger making the request the reason for its decision not to do so. *Id.* § 37.201.

OTRB operators must establish a system of regular and frequent maintenance checks to determine if lifts are operative and ensure that vehicle operators report, by the most immediate means available, any lift failure. When a lift is inoperative, the entity shall take the vehicle out of service before the beginning of its next trip and ensure that the lift is repaired before the vehicle returns to service. However, an entity may keep the vehicle in service with an inoperable lift for no more than five days if there is no other vehicle available to replace it and taking the vehicle out of service before its next trip will reduce the transportation service the entity is able to provide. *Id.* § 37.203.

If the number of wheelchair users seeking to travel on a trip exceeds the number of securement locations on the bus, the OTRB operator shall assign the securement locations on a first come-first served basis. The operator must offer passengers who are not assigned a securement location boarding assistance and the opportunity to sit in a vehicle seat. The operator is not required to provide transportation on the bus if the passengers who are not assigned securement locations are unable or unwilling to accept this offer. *Id.* § 37.205.

OTRB operators must also comply with the requirements described in subheadings 8–10 of the section on Accessibility Provisions later in this chapter.

In February 2001, the Department of Justice entered into a settlement with Greyhound Lines, Inc. which details its obligations and plans for compliance with the ADA. http://www.ada.gov/greyhnd.htm. It has subsequently entered settlement agreements with other transportation entities. For example, it entered into a settlement with Virginia Bus Company to ensure accessibility for people with disabilities on December 5, 2014, see http://www.justice.gov/opa/pr/justice-department-an nounces-settlement-virginia-bus-company-ensure-accessibility-people . It has also entered into settlements with transportation companies to ensure that passengers with disabilities can ride with their service animals. *See* http://www. justice.gov/usao-edmi/pr/justice-department-settles-disability-claims-transportation-companies-discrim inated.

B.   PROVISION OF PUBLIC TRANSPORTATION BY PRIVATE ENTITIES NOT PRIMARILY ENGAGED IN THE BUSINESS OF TRANSPORTING PEOPLE

Private entities not primarily engaged in the business of transporting people are subject to somewhat different regulations. Where such an entity operates a fixed-route system and makes a solicitation for the purchase or lease of a vehicle with a seating capacity in excess of 16 passengers (including the driver) for use in that system, it must ensure that the vehicle is readily accessible to and usable by individuals with disabilities. The same requirement applies for vehicles with a seating capacity of 16 or fewer passengers unless the entity can show that its fixed-route system, when viewed in its entirety, ensures a level of service to disabled individuals equivalent to the level of service provided to non-disabled individuals. Similarly, a demand-responsive system operated by a private entity not primarily engaged in the business of transporting people must, when viewed in its entirety, ensure a level of service to disabled individuals equivalent to the level of service provided to non-disabled individuals. 49 C.F.R. § 37.101(b)–(e). The regulations applicable to over-the-road buses operated by private entities not primarily engaged in the business of transporting people are discussed above.

C. ACCESSIBILITY PROVISIONS

The regulations provide minimum guidelines and requirements for the accessibility standards for transportation vehicles covered under the ADA. 49 C.F.R. Part 38.

1. *Accessibility Standards for Buses and Vans*

New, used or remanufactured buses and vans (except over-the-road buses) must comply with specified accessibility rules. When "portions of the vehicle are modified in a way that affects or could affect accessibility, each such portion shall comply, to the extent practicable," with the same accessibility rules; however, this "does not require that inaccessible buses be retrofitted with lifts, ramps or other boarding devices." 49 C.F.R. § 38.21(b).

The accessibility provisions are detailed and technical. They include requirements with respect to mobility-aid accessibility (such as boarding devices, vehicle lifts, securement devices and platform configurations); doors, steps and thresholds; priority seating signs; interior circulation; handrails and stanchions; lighting; fare boxes; public information systems; stop requests; and destination and route signs. 49 C.F.R. §§ 38.23–38.39.

2. *Accessibility Standards for Rapid-Rail Vehicles and Systems*

New, used and remanufactured rapid-rail vehicles must also comply with specified accessibility rules. 49 C.F.R. §§ 38.51–38.63. Again, when "portions of the vehicle are modified in a way that affects or could affect accessibility, each such portion shall comply, to the extent practicable," with the same accessibility rules. *Id.* § 38.51(b). Moreover, existing vehicles that are retrofitted to comply with the requirement that one car of each train must be accessible must comply with accessibility regulations relating to placement of priority seating signs and must have, in new and key stations, at least one accessible doorway. When existing vehicles are retrofitted, however, seat removal is not required.

The detailed technical accessibility requirements with respect to rapid-rail vehicles and systems include requirements with respect to doorways; priority seating signs; interior circulation; handrails and stanchions; floor surfaces; public information systems; and between-car barriers. 49 C.F.R. §§ 38.53–38.63.

3. *Accessibility Standards for Light-Rail Vehicles and Systems*

New, used and remanufactured light rail vehicles are also required to follow specific accessibility rules. 49 C.F.R. §§ 38.71–38.87. These detailed and technical rules pertain to doorways; priority seating signs; interior circulation; handrails and stanchions; floor steps and thresholds; lighting; mobility-aid accessibility; between-car barriers; and public information systems.

Vehicles that are "intended to be operated solely in light-rail systems confined entirely to a dedicated right-of-way, and for which all stations or stops are designed and constructed for revenue service . . . " must provide level boarding, and must comply with accessibility provisions relating to boarding heights and between-car barriers. *Id.* §§ 38.71(b)(1), 38.73(d)(1), 38.85.

Vehicles "designed for, and operated on, pedestrian malls, city streets, or other areas where level boarding is not practicable . . . " must provide wayside or car-borne lifts, mini-high platforms, or other means of access. *Id.* § 38.71(b)(2).

If portions of a light-rail vehicle are "modified in a way that affects or could affect accessibility, each such portion shall comply, to the extent practicable," with the regulatory technical requirements. *Id.* § 38.71(c). Again, however, this provision "does not require that inaccessible vehicles be retrofitted with lifts, ramps or other boarding devices." *Id.*

Existing vehicles that are retrofitted to comply with the requirement that one car on each train must be accessible must comply with the accessibility requirements relating to priority seating signs; interior circulation; handrails and stanchions; floors, steps and thresholds; mobility-aid accessibility requirements relating to level-change mechanisms or boarding devices; and doorways.

4. *Accessibility Standards for Commuter Rail Cars and Systems*

New, used and remanufactured commuter rail cars must also comply with detailed, technical accessibility requirements. 49 C.F.R. §§ 38.91–38.109. These accessibility standards cover doorways; mobility-aid accessibility; interior circulation; handrails and stanchions; floors, steps, and thresholds; lighting; public information systems; priority seating signs; restrooms; and between-car barriers. If a portion of a commuter rail car is "modified in such a way that it affects or could affect accessibility, each such portion shall comply, to the extent practicable," with the specified accessibility requirements. *Id.* § 38.91(b).

Commuter rail cars are required to comply with requirements for level boarding only when compliance is "structurally and operationally practicable." *Id.* § 38.91(c)(1). Where level boarding is not structurally or operationally practicable, level-change mechanisms or other boarding devices (such as a lift, ramp or bridge plate) must be provided.

Existing vehicles that are retrofitted to comply with the requirement that one car per train be accessible must comply with regulatory standards relating to placement of international symbols of accessibility, provision of level-change mechanisms or boarding devices, and the requirement that accessible restrooms be provided where restrooms are provided to the general public. Further, existing vehicles that are retrofitted to comply with the "one accessible car per train" rule must have accessible doors to allow entry from the cars to new and key stations.

5. *Accessibility Standards for Intercity Rail Cars and Systems*

New, used and remanufactured intercity rail cars must comply with accessibility requirements that differ based on the type of car at issue. 49 C.F.R. §§ 38.111–38.127. One set of rules applies to single-level rail passenger coaches and food service cars (other than single level dining cars); another set applies to single-level dining and lounge cars; a third set applies to bi-level dining cars; a fourth set of rules applies to bi-level lounge cars; a fifth set applies to sleeper cars; and a sixth set of rules applies to existing cars retrofitted to comply with regulatory requirements mandating that intercity rail service cars provide spaces to park and store wheelchairs. The rules refer to delineated technical standards dealing with doorways; interior circulation, handrails and stanchions; floors, steps and thresholds; lighting; public information systems; restrooms; mobility-aid accessibility and sleeping compartments.

Again, the regulations provide that if any portion of an intercity rail car is "modified in a way that it affects or could affect accessibility, each such portion shall comply, to the extent practicable," with the applicable rules. *Id.* § 38.111(c) This proviso "does not require that inaccessible cars be retrofitted with lifts, ramps or other boarding devices." *Id.* The rules provide that restrooms complying with accessibility standards must be provided in single-level rail passenger coaches and food service cars adjacent to accessible seating locations. Accessible restrooms are only required in dining or lounge cars, however, if restrooms are provided for other passengers.

6. *Accessible Standards for Over-the-Road Buses and Systems*

New, used and remanufactured over-the-road buses must comply with detailed technical regulations pertaining to doors, steps and thresholds; interior circulation; handrails and stanchions; and lighting. 49 C.F.R. §§ 38.151–38.157.

7. *Accessible Standards for Other Vehicles and Systems*

New, used and remanufactured vehicles and conveyances for systems not covered elsewhere in the regulations must comply with accessibility standards that differ depending upon the nature of the system. 49 C.F.R. § 38.171–38.179. The regulations set forth accessibility standards to be followed by automated guideway transit vehicles and systems (*e.g.,* "people movers" operated in such facilities as airports); high-speed rail cars, monorails and systems; and trains, similar vehicles and systems. Again, when "portions of the vehicle or conveyance are modified in a way than affects or could affect accessibility, each such portion shall comply, to the extent practicable," with the same accessibility rules. *Id.* § 38.171(b). For vehicles and systems not specified in the regulations, the DOT will make a case-by-case determination.

8. *Lift and Securement Use*

An entity is not required to permit wheelchairs to ride in places other than designated securement locations in the vehicle and may require that an individual permit his or her wheelchair to be secured. However, the entity may not deny transportation to a wheelchair or its user because it cannot be secured or restrained satisfactorily by the vehicle's securement system. An entity may recommend to a wheelchair user that the individual transfer to a vehicle seat but may not require the individual to do so. Transportation personnel shall, where necessary or upon request, assist individuals with disabilities with the use of securement systems, ramps and lifts. Individuals with disabilities who do not use wheelchairs, including standees may use a vehicle's lift or ramp to enter the vehicle. *Id.* § 38.165.

9. *Other Service Requirements*

Section 37.167 includes several specific service requirements. On fixed route systems, stops must be announced "at least at transfer points with other fixed routes, other major intersections and destination points, and intervals along a route sufficient to permit individuals with visual impairments or other disabilities to be oriented to their location." Where vehicles for more than one route serve the same stop, "the entity shall provide a means by which an individual with a visual impairment or other disability can identify the proper vehicle to enter or be identified to the vehicle operator as a person seeking a ride on a particular route." Service animals may accompany individuals with disabilities in vehicles and facilities, and the entity must allow a person with a disability to travel with a respirator or portable oxygen supply if it is consistent with applicable DOT rules on the transportation of hazardous materials. The entity must make adequate information concerning transportation services available to individuals with disabilities including using accessible formats and technology, to enable users to obtain information and schedule service. It may not refuse to use a lift to allow a passenger to disembark at any designated stop unless 1) the lift cannot be deployed or will be damaged if it is deployed or 2) temporary conditions, not under the control of the entity, preclude the safe use of the stop by all passengers. Adequate time must be provided to allow individuals with disabilities to complete boarding or disembarking from the vehicle.

When an individual with a disability needs to sit in a seat or occupy a wheelchair securement location, the entity shall ask the following persons to move: (1) individuals other than those with a disability or elderly persons sitting in a location designated as priority seating for those groups (or other seat as necessary); 2) individuals sitting in or a fold-down or other movable seat in a wheelchair securement location. This requirement applies to light rail, rapid rail, and commuter rail systems only to the extent practicable, but the entity is not required to enforce the request that other passengers move. Signage designating priority seating areas for elderly persons and persons with disabilities, or designating wheelchair securement areas, shall include language informing persons that they should comply with requests by transit provider personnel to vacate their seats to make room for an individual with a disability.

10. *Miscellaneous Regulatory Provisions*

The regulations provide that:

(1) providers of transportation services may not charge people with disabilities for the provision of reasonable accommodations, 49 C.F.R. § 37.5(d);

(2) the training for employees of operators of fixed-route and demand responsive systems shall involve training to a level of proficiency concerning the "difference[s] among [the abilities of] individuals with disabilities," 49 C.F.R. § 37.173;

(3) accessibility features must be in working order and accommodations must be provided for travelers with disabilities when accessibility

features break down. 49 C.F.R. § 37.161. *See, e.g., Martin v. Metropolitan Atlanta Rapid Transit Authority*, 225 F.Supp.2d 1362 (N.D.Ga. 2002) (transit authority violated the ADA where it failed to provide adequate training to its bus and rail operators and their supervisors and a pattern of wheelchair lift breakdowns in service resulted in stranded passengers due to failure to inspect inoperable lifts, or failure to repair them in a timely fashion, or failure to provide alternative transportation).

Other significant provisions mandate that:

(1) Notwithstanding the provision of special services for individuals with disabilities, an entity covered under the transportation provisions of the Act may not deny an individual with a disability the opportunity to use services provided to the general public if the individual is capable of using such services. 49 C.F.R. § 37.5(b).

(2) An entity may not require an individual with a disability to use designated priority seats if the individual does not choose to do so or that an individual with a disability be accompanied by an attendant. *Id.* § 37.5(c), (e).

(3) An entity may not refuse to serve an individual with a disability or require anything contrary to the ADA "because its insurance company conditions coverage or rates on the absence of individuals with disabilities or

requirements contrary to [the Act]." *Id.* § 37.5(g). Further, while an entity may refuse service to an individual with a disability who engages in "violent, seriously disruptive or illegal conduct," an entity may not refuse to provide service to such individual "solely because the individual's disability results in appearance or involuntary behavior that may offend, annoy or inconvenience employees of the entity or other persons." *Id.* § 37.5(h).

The DOT has adopted the ADA Accessibility Guidelines (ADAAG) as the standards to be applied when complying with the transportation provisions of the Act.

§ 10.5 ENFORCEMENT OF ADA TITLE III PROVISIONS

The provisions of Title III dealing with transportation provided by private entities are enforced under Title III generally. A discussion of the enforcement remedies under Title III is found in § 7.29 of this *Nutshell*.

§ 10.6 UNIFORM SYSTEM FOR DISABLED PARKING

In 1988, Congress passed legislation requiring the DOT to establish a "uniform system for handicapped parking designed to enhance safety of handicapped individuals. . . ." 23 U.S.C.A. § 402 note. On March 11, 1991, DOT's Federal Highway Administration and National Highway Traffic Safety Administration issued a final rule establishing a

Uniform System for Handicapped Parking. 23 C.F.R. §§ 1235.1–1235.8. The system became effective April 10, 1991.

The purpose of the Uniform System is to eliminate the problems faced by drivers with disabilities who are frequently given parking tickets by law enforcement personnel outside their home states. Law enforcement personnel often do not recognize other states' disabled or handicapped designations on drivers' license plates or permits. Accordingly, the Uniform System requires all states to use the International Symbol of Access (ISA) to identify people with disabilities. In response to an application from a qualified person with a disability, each state shall issue: (1) a special license plate displaying the ISA (the fee for which cannot exceed the fee for a similar license plate for the same class of vehicle); and (2) a removable windshield placard which includes the ISA in white on a blue background measuring 3 inches by 9.5 inches. In addition, temporary removable window windshield placards must be available with the ISA appearing in white on a red background. Each state must recognize other states' special license plates and window placards.

§ 10.7   AIRLINE TRANSPORTATION

A.   SECTION 504 OF THE REHABILITATION ACT AND THE ADA

The Supreme Court ruled in *United States Department of Transportation v. Paralyzed Veterans of America*, 477 U.S. 597 (1986) that commercial airlines are *not* recipients of federal financial assistance and thus are *not* obligated to comply with Section 504. As a result of this decision, airline passengers with disabilities may not assert discrimination claims against airlines under Section 504. Commercial airline carriers are also not governed by the ADA.

B.   THE AIR CARRIER ACCESS ACT OF 1986

1. *Introduction*

In response to the Supreme Court's ruling in *Paralyzed Veterans*, Congress enacted the Air Carrier Access Act of 1986 (ACAA). 49 U.S.C.A. § 41705. The ACAA provides that air carriers, including certain foreign air carriers may not discriminate against an otherwise qualified individual with a disability

2. *Private Right of Action*

Courts are divided on whether there is a private right of action to enforce the ACAA. For example, in *Tallarico v. Trans World Airlines, Inc.*, 881 F.2d 566 (8th Cir. 1989), the court held that Congress intended to create a private cause of action for persons with disabilities seeking a remedy for an airline's violation of the Act. Numerous courts have held the same. Other courts disagree. *See, e.g. Love v. Delta Air Lines*, 310 F.3d 1347 (11th Cir. 2002) (holding that Congress did not create a private right of action to vindicate the ACAA's prohibition against disability-based discrimination by air carriers). A private cause of action under the ACAA will only lie against an air carrier, and not against a contractor of an air carrier. *See, e.g., Wilson v. United Air Lines*, 7 NDLR ¶ 119 (N.D.Ill. 1995) (holding that a contractor who provided wheelchair services for United Airlines was not an air carrier who could be sued under the ACAA).

3. *Damages for Emotional Distress*

Among courts that recognize a private cause of action under the ACAA, there is a split on whether a plaintiff can recover for emotional distress. In *Tallarico*, the Eighth Circuit held that emotional distress damages are available under the ACAA. *See also Shinault v. American Airlines, Inc.*, 936 F.2d 796 (5th Cir. 1991).

In *Americans Disabled for Accessible Public Transportation (ADAPT), Salt Lake Chapter v. SkyWest Airlines*, 762 F.Supp. 320 (D.Utah 1991), however, the court held that damages for emotional distress and punitive damages are not available under the ACAA. The court reasoned that the ACAA was intended to make the provisions of Section 504 applicable to all air carriers regardless of whether they receive federal financial assistance. The court held that, since punitive and emotional distress damages are not available under Section 504, they are not available under the ACAA.

4. *Preemption of State Law Claims for Failure to Accommodate*

Courts are also split on the issue of whether the Airline Deregulation Act of 1978 preempts state common law claims for an airline's failure to provide accommodations. The Deregulation Act includes a provision preempting any state law "*related to* a price, route, or *service* of an air carrier." 49 U.S.C. § 41713(b)(1) (emphasis added). Courts holding accommodation claims are preempted reason that allegations about airline employees' actions (or inactions) "relate to" airline "services." *See, e.g., Williams v. Express Airlines I, Inc.*, 825 F.Supp. 831 (W.D.Tenn. 1993); *Smith v. Comair, Inc.*, 134 F.3d 254 (4th Cir. 1998); *Belgard v. United Airlines*, 857 P.2d 467 (Colo.Ct.App. 1992); *Fitzpatrick v. Simmons Airlines, Inc.*, 555 N.W.2d 479 (Mich.Ct.App. 1996).

Courts rejecting the preemption argument point to dicta in Supreme Court cases interpreting the Deregulation Act which says that tort claims are not preempted. They also reason that allowing tort claims does not interfere with the Deregulation Act's purpose of barring states from regulating airlines. *See, e.g., Knopp v. American Airlines, Inc.*, 938 S.W.2d 357 (Tenn. 1996); *Kelley v. United Airlines, Inc.*, 986 F.Supp. 684 (D.Mass. 1997).

5. *DOT's ACAA Regulations*

The DOT's ACAA regulations are codified at 14 C.F.R. §§ 382.1–382.65. The most significant provision of the regulations are summarized as follows:

(a) The definition of disability is the same as that under Section 504 and the ADA.

(b) A "qualified individual with a disability" with respect to obtaining air transportation is one who (1) purchases or possesses a valid ticket and (2) meets "reasonable, nondiscriminatory contract of carriage requirements applicable to all passengers." 14 C.F.R. § 382.5.

(c) In general, air carriers are prohibited from: (1) discriminating against an otherwise qualified individual with a disability, by reason of such disability, in the provision of air transportation; (2) requiring an individual with a disability "to accept special services (including, but not limited to, preboarding) not requested by the passenger"; (3) excluding a qualified person with a disability from, or denying such person the benefit of, air transportation or related services that are available to non-disabled persons "even if there are separate or different services available" persons with disabilities except when specifically permitted by the regulations; and (4) taking adverse action against an individual because of the individual's assertion of rights protected by the ACAA. *Id*. § 382.7(a).

(d) Contracts between air carriers and service providers (including agents) must include a "[n]ondiscrimination on the basis of disability" clause. *Id.* § 382.9.

(e) Newly purchased aircraft must meet the following accessibility standards: (1) Aircraft having 30 or more passenger seats must have moveable aisle armrests on at least half the aisle seats, and arrangements are to be made to allow individuals with mobility impairment to "readily obtain seating in rows with moveable aisle armrests." *Id.* § 382.21(a)(1)(iii). (2) Aircraft with 100 or more passenger seats must have space in the cabin to store at least one folding wheelchair. (3) Aircraft with more than one aisle in which lavatories are provided must contain at least one accessible lavatory. Air carriers are not required to retrofit existing aircraft, but as existing planes are refurbished accessibility features are required to be added.

The DOT has concluded that Section 504 standards are to apply to implementation of the ACAA. It stated:

> The language of [the ACAA] is essentially similar to that of Section 504, and, even considered in light of the legislative history, does not give rise to an inference that a stricter-than 504 standard is established by the statute.

55 Fed. Reg. 8011(1990). Thus, the DOT concludes that the ACAA regulations "may not impose 'undue financial or administrative burdens' . . . or require fundamental changes in the carrier's programs . . . "

Id. The DOT has held that the provisions cited above codify the requisite "reasonable accommodations" that air carriers must provide for disabled passengers.

(f) Airport facilities (terminal facilities, including parking and ground transportation facilities) must be "readily accessible to and usable by individuals with disabilities, including individuals who use wheelchairs." 14 C.F.R. § 382.23(b). Air carriers are deemed to comply with this obligation if they meet the requirements in the Department of Justice regulations implementing Title III of the ADA.

(g) Air carriers are prohibited from refusing to provide transportation to a qualified individual with a disability on the basis of his or her disability or because "the person's disability results in appearance or involuntary behavior that may offend, annoy, or inconvenience crewmembers or other passengers." 14 C.F.R. § 382.31(b). Carriers may not limit the number of persons with disabilities who may travel on a given flight.

(h) Air carriers *may* refuse to provide transportation to any passenger "on the basis of safety" or to any passenger whose carriage would violate the FAA regulations. 14 C.F.R. § 382.31(d). When exercising this authority, however, carrier personnel are prohibited from discriminating against any qualified individual with a disability on the basis of disability, and the actions of carrier personnel may not be inconsistent with the ACAA regulations. A carrier that refuses to provide transportation to any individual on the basis of disability must set forth reasons for that decision in writing within ten days.

(i) Air carriers *may* require up to 48 hours advance notice and one hour advance check-in for a passenger who wishes to receive: (1) medical oxygen for use on board the flight; (2) carriage of an incubator; (3) hook-up of a respirator; (4) accommodation of a passenger on a stretcher; (5) transportation of an electric wheelchair when the aircraft has fewer than 60 seats; (6) provision of hazardous materials packaging for a battery for a wheelchair; (7) accommodation for a group of ten or more qualified individuals with a disability who make reservations and travel as a group; and (8) provision of an on-board wheelchair on an aircraft that does not have an accessible lavatory. If a passenger does not meet advance notice or check-in requirements, the carrier must still provide the service, equipment, or accommodation if it can do so by making a reasonable effort, without delaying the flight. *Id.* § 382.33.

(j) Air carriers may require that a passenger with a disability be accompanied by an attendant *only* when the passenger is (1) traveling on a stretcher or in an incubator; (2) mentally disabled to such an extent that he or she is unable to comprehend or respond appropriately to safety instructions; (3) so severely mobility-impaired that he or she is unable to assist in his or her own evacuation of the aircraft; or (4) both severely visually-impaired *and* severely hearing-impaired *and* unable to establish "*some* means of communication with carrier personnel." 14

C.F.R. § 382.35(b). If the carrier determines that a passenger with a disability must be accompanied by an attendant for one of the foregoing reasons, but the passenger disagrees, the carrier may not charge for the transportation of the attendant.

(k) Air carriers may only restrict the seating of passengers with disabilities to comply with the requirements of FAA exit-seating regulations, or (1) when necessary to mitigate safety concerns resulting from a passenger's disability that causes involuntary active behavior or (2) to accommodate a service animal (*e.g.*, seeing eye dog or hearing dog). *Id.* § 382.37.

The FAA published exit-seating regulations on the same date the ACAA regulations were published. The exit-row seating regulations provide that a person seated in a row next to an emergency door must be able to: (1) "locate the door and quickly follow the instructions, written and oral, for its use"; (2) "physically ... open the door"; (3) "determine when to open the door"; (4) "go quickly through the open exit"; and (5) "devote full attention to his or her emergency task." Thus, persons with severe visual or hearing-impairments are precluded from sitting in exit rows, as are persons traveling with children, persons unable to read or understand English, persons under the age of 15, or persons who are unable to perform one or more of the specific list of physical tasks without assistance. 14 C.F.R. §§ 121.585, 135.129.

(*l*) Air carriers must accommodate passengers with hearing-impairments by: (1) providing timely access to routine information such as information concerning ticketing, flight delays, schedule changes, connections and gate assignments; (2) maintaining a TDD (telecommunication device for the deaf) reservation and information service; and (3) ensuring that video instructions are captioned or contain an inset for a sign-language interpreter. 14 C.F.R. § 382.47.

(m) Air carriers may not refuse to provide transportation to passengers with communicable diseases, require such passengers to provide medical certificates, or impose upon such passengers any conditions or restrictions not imposed on other passengers. 14 C.F.R. § 382.51(a). A carrier may bar such passengers if their condition poses a direct threat to the health or safety of others which cannot be eliminated by a modification of policies, practices, or procedures, or by the provision of auxiliary aids or services. A carrier must make an individualized assessment in determining whether an individual poses a direct threat and rely on current medical knowledge or the best available objective evidence in doing so. If the carrier's decision postpones a passenger's travel, it shall permit the passenger to travel up to 90 days later at the fare that would have applied to the originally scheduled trip or, at the passenger's discretion, provide a refund. In addition, the carrier must provide, upon the passenger's request, a written explanation for its decision within 10 days of the request. If an individual with a communicable disease or infection presents a medical certificate saying that the passenger is capable of completing a flight safely without requiring extraordinary medical assistance, the carrier must transport the individual unless it is not feasible to implement the conditions listed in the medical certificate to prevent the transmission of the disease or infection to others in the normal course of a flight. *Id.* § 382.51(b).

(n) Air carriers must provide assistance to persons with disabilities in entering and leaving aircraft, in moving to and from seats, in preparing meals (such as by opening packages or identifying food), in moving to and from the lavatory (when the passenger is semi-ambulatory or the plane contains an on-board wheelchair), and in loading and retrieving carry-on items. Air carriers are *not* required to provide assistance with actual eating, to provide restroom assistance, or to provide medical services. *Id.* § 382.39.

(*o*) Certain air carriers and airport facilities must enter into written agreements that allocate responsibility for meeting requirements relating to providing boarding assistance to passengers with disabilities. The regulations prohibit hand-carrying as a means of providing boarding assistance to passengers with disabilities on aircraft with between 19 and 30 seats, but authorize air carriers to require passengers who require the use of a lift to check in one hour before their scheduled departure time. *Id.* § 382.40.

(p) Qualified individuals with a disability must undergo security screening in the same manner as other passengers, and use of an aid for independent travel shall not subject the person or the aid to special screening procedures if they clear the security system without activating it. Security personnel may, however, examine a mobility aid or assistive device which, in their judgment, may conceal a weapon or other prohibited item. If an aid activates the security system, security searches shall be conducted in the same manner as for other passengers. Private security screenings are not allowed for qualified individuals with a disability to a greater extent, or for any different reason, than for other passengers. If passenger with a disability requests a private screening in a timely manner, however, the carrier must provide it in time for the passenger to enplane. The carrier is not required to provide a private screening if it employs technology that can conduct an appropriate screening of an individual with a disability without necessitating a physical search of the person. *Id.* § 382.49. Information about the Transportation Security Administration (TSA) Screening of Persons with Disabilities Program developed after the September 11, 2001, attacks can be accessed at https://www.tsa.gov/travel/special-procedures.

CHAPTER 11
ADA: MISCELLANEOUS

§ 11.1   INTRODUCTION

In addition to Titles I, II and III of the ADA, which prohibit discrimination on the basis of disability by employers, owners and operators of places of public accommodation, and public entities, the ADA contains several significant miscellaneous titles and sections. This chapter will provide a brief overview of those sections.

§ 11.2   TITLE IV: TELECOMMUNICATIONS RELAY SERVICES

There are over 24 million hearing-impaired and 2.8 million speech-impaired individuals in the United States, many of whom are unable to use the telephone, an essential part of modern American life. Title IV of the ADA amended the Communications Act of 1934, 47 U.S.C.A. §§ 151–757, to require that all common carriers (generally, telephone companies) provide "functionally equivalent" telecommunications services to allow individuals with hearing or speech impairments to communicate with hearing people. 47 U.S.C.A. § 225(a)(3) and (b). To fulfill this mandate, providers of telecommunications services are obligated to provide "telecommunications relay services," either "individually, through designees, through a competitively selected vendor, or in concert with other carriers." *Id.* § 225(a)(3).

Telephone relay services work as follows: Persons who are hearing-impaired or speech-impaired may utilize telecommunications devices for the deaf (TDDs) to communicate via the telephone. These devices are also known as TTYs, short for "Teletype," a registered trademark of the Teletype Corporation. DOJ and FCC currently use the term "TTY" in its regulations rather than "TDD." When using a TTY, the telephone receiver is placed into two headset cups in a machine that resembles a small typewriter with a video screen and/or a paper printout. [Note: Some newer TTYs do not have acoustic cups.] The TTY user types a message on a keyboard, which is relayed to a party on the other end of the line with a similar device. The receiver returns his or her message by typing it to the sender, and the conversation proceeds via typewriter and video screen or printout. Because most hearing people do not have TTYs, a relay service is required to allow TTY users to communicate with non-TTY users. Thus, the TTY user calls a relay service, and a relay operator answers via TTY and places the call to the non-TTY user (or vice versa). The operator then relays messages back and forth between the TTY and non-TTY users, typing messages for the TTY user and speaking messages for the non-TTY user.

To ensure the functional equivalence of telecommunication services provided for persons with hearing or speech impairments, Title IV mandates that such relay services shall (1) operate 24 hours a day, every day; (2) cost no more than regular telephone services; (3) prohibit relay

operators from refusing calls or limiting the length
of calls; (4) require relay operators to maintain strict
confidentiality with respect to all telephone
messages relayed; and (5) prohibit relay operators
from intentionally altering relayed conversations.
Relay operators are subject to the same standards of
conduct that other operators are subject to under
the Communications Act. 47 U.S.C.A. § 225(d).

The ADA gives the FCC sufficient enforcement
authority to ensure that relay services are provided
everywhere in the nation and that minimum federal
standards are met by relay service providers. The
Act also provides for procedures to be established
under which individual states may retain
jurisdiction over the provision of intrastate
telecommunications relay services by applying to
the FCC for certification. While complaints
concerning alleged violations relating to the
provision of intrastate services within a state with a
certified program are to be filed with the FCC, the
FCC is required to refer such complaints to
individual certified states. The FCC cannot
thereafter exercise jurisdiction over the complaint
unless final action has not been taken by the
certified state program within 180 days.

The ultimate cost of the requisite relay services is
to be borne by all users of telephone services, not
just users with disabilities. The ADA provides that
the regulations to be promulgated by the FCC

> shall generally provide that costs caused by
> interstate telecommunications relay services
> shall be recovered from all subscribers for every

interstate service and costs caused by intrastate telecommunications relay services shall be recovered from the intrastate jurisdiction.

47 U.S.C.A. § 225(d)(3)(B).

The FCC's regulations promulgated under Title IV are found at 47 C.F.R. §§ 64.601–64.605.

§ 11.3 ADA: PUBLIC SERVICE ANNOUNCEMENTS

The ADA requires amendment of the Communications Act to require closed captioning of all television public service announcements produced or funded by the federal government. 47 U.S.C.A. § 611.

§ 11.4 ELEVENTH AMENDMENT IMMUNITY

The ADA expressly provides that states shall not be immune from actions under the Act pursuant to the Eleventh Amendment. 42 U.S.C.A. § 12202. In *Board of Trustees of University of Alabama v. Garrett*, 531 U.S. 356 (2001), however, the Court held that state government employers have Eleventh Amendment immunity from suits for *money damages* under Title I of the ADA.

The *Garrett* Court left open the question of whether monetary damages are permitted for access and service claims against states under ADA Title II. In *Tennessee v. Lane*, 541 U.S. 509 (2004) and in *United States v. Georgia*, 546 U.S. 151 (2006), the

Court found that monetary damage suits are permitted under ADA Title II where fundamental rights are involved. *Lane* involved access to the judicial system; *Georgia* involved the conditions of confinement for an inmate.

In *Garrett*, the Court suggested in a footnote that employees can still bring suits against state officials in their official capacities for *injunctive relief* under ADA Title II. Some earlier lower court decisions had found such relief was not available, but the courts have subsequently stated that *Garrett* abrogated those decisions. *See, e.g., Bruggeman v. Blagojevich*, 324 F.3d 906 (7th Cir. 2003); *Henrietta D. v. Bloomberg*, 331 F.3d 261 (2d Cir. 2003). Accordingly, it is now clear that injunctive relief is available against state defendants.

Irrespective of these decisions, individuals with disabilities can still sue *municipal or local governments*. The principle of sovereign immunity applies to states, not local government.

§ 11.5   ATTORNEYS' FEES AND COSTS

Courts and agencies have discretion to award attorneys' fees and litigation expenses (including the cost of expert witnesses) to prevailing parties (other than the United States) in actions under the ADA. 42 U.S.C.A. § 12205. While attorneys' fees may be awarded against both plaintiffs and defendants, generally attorneys' fees against a plaintiff will only be awarded if the suit is found to be frivolous.

In *Buckhannon Board and Care Home, Inc. v. West Virginia Dep't of Health and Human Resources*, 532 U.S. 598 (2001), the Court concluded that the "catalyst theory"—where a party is considered prevailing so long as he or she can prove that the pending litigation was a catalyst that brought about the policy change—is not a permissible basis for the award of attorneys' fees. The Court stated:

> A defendant's voluntary change in conduct, although perhaps accomplishing what the plaintiff sought to achieve by the lawsuit, lacks the necessary judicial *imprimatur* on the change. Our precedents thus counsel against holding that the term "prevailing party" authorizes an award of attorney's fees *without* a corresponding alteration in the legal relationship of the parties.

In dicta, the Court also offered guidance on what it means to be the "prevailing party" for the purpose of collecting attorney's fees—a party must secure either a judgment on the merits or a court-ordered consent decree. A closer look at *Buckhannon*, however, reveals that other "material alterations" in the parties' legal relationship exist. For example, the Court indicated that private settlements "incorporated into [an] order of dismissal," qualify as a judicially accepted "material alteration" that warrants a fee award. A concurring opinion also noted that court-approved settlements bore the necessary judicial imprimatur.

Since *Buckhannon,* a split has developed in the lower courts regarding whether a private settlement, without further judicial action, constitutes an "alteration in the legal relationship of the parties" sufficient to make the plaintiff a "prevailing party." *Compare Barrios v. California Interscholastic Fed'n,* 277 F.3d 1128 (9th Cir. 2002) (finding that, because the plaintiff could "enforce the terms of the settlement agreement against the [defendant]," he was a "prevailing party" regardless of the lack of a separate consent decree or specific retention of jurisdiction by the court); *Johnson v. District of Columbia,* 190 F.Supp.2d 34 (D.D.C. 2002) (same) *with New York State Fed'n of Taxi Drivers, Inc. v. Westchester County Taxi & Limousine Comm'n,* 272 F.3d 154 (2d Cir. 2001) (reversing a grant of fees where the parties entered a private settlement, and the district court simply entered an order dismissing the case as moot); *Smyth v. Rivero,* 282 F.3d 268 (4th Cir. 2002) (the court concluded that a settlement agreement failed to reach consent decree status because the court did not explicitly incorporate the settlement terms in the dismissal order, nor did the agreement contain a provision retaining the court's jurisdiction).

Some courts have held that the district court's approval of a settlement, coupled with its explicit retention of jurisdiction to enforce its terms, were the functional equivalent of a consent decree and sufficient to render the plaintiff a "prevailing party" under the ADA. *See, e.g., American Disability Ass'n, Inc. v. Chmielarz,* 289 F.3d 1315 (11th Cir. 2002); *National Coalition for Students with Disabilities v.*

Bush, 173 F.Supp.2d 1272 (N.D.Fla. 2001). No attorney's fees were available, however, where the court retained jurisdiction but "did not review the terms of the Agreement before dismissing the case." *Dorfsman v. Law School Admission Council, Inc.*, 2001 WL 1754726 (E.D.Pa. Nov. 28, 2001) (holding plaintiff had failed to achieve a judicially sanctioned change in the parties' legal relationship where the parties reached the terms and conditions of the settlement without any intervention from the court and "the Court in no way imposed or dictated the substantive provisions of the Stipulation at issue"). *But see Roberson v. Giuliani*, 346 F.3d 75 (2nd Cir. 2003) (holding that district court's retention of enforcement jurisdiction over parties' private settlement provided sufficient judicial sanction to convey prevailing party status on plaintiffs, for purposes of fee-shifting provision of civil rights statute).

§ 11.6   INSURANCE AND BENEFIT PLANS

A.   INSURANCE COVERAGE IN THE EMPLOYMENT SETTING

ADA Title I prohibits an employer from discriminating against a person with a disability "in regard to . . . terms, conditions, and privileges of employment." 42 U.S.C.A. § 12112(a). Further, Title I prohibits an employer from participating in a contractual relationship that would discriminate against to an employee with a disability. 42 U.S.C.A. § 12112(b)(2). The provision of fringe benefits by an employer or the employer's contractor is expressly stated as falling within the coverage of Title I. *Id.*

Prior to discussing specific substantive issues under Title I relating to insurance, a few preliminary matters must be addressed.

1. *Qualifying as an Employee*

Who may assert an action against an employer to protest allegedly discriminatory insurance coverage? To fall within the protection of Title I, an individual must be a job applicant or employee of the defendant. Independent contractors have been found not to be employees for purposes of the ADA. Volunteer workers have been held not to be employees under Title VII of the Civil Rights Act of 1964 ("Title VII"). Since Congress has stated that Title I is to follow Title VII principles, the same reasoning should be held to apply under Title I.

a. *Part-Time Employees*

The Equal Employment Opportunity Commission (EEOC), which is responsible for interpreting and enforcing Title I, takes the position that employers may require *all* employees, including employees with disabilities, to work a stated number of hours to be eligible for health insurance benefits. According to the EEOC, it is not discriminatory to deny health insurance to part-time workers with disabilities as long as part-time workers without disabilities are also denied health insurance coverage. *See also Tenbrink v. Federal Home Loan Bank*, 920 F.Supp. 1156 (D.Kan. 1996) (an employer

who accommodated an employee with chronic
fatigue syndrome by allowing her to work part-time
did not violate the ADA by denying the employee
medical benefits under a policy requiring any
employee to work at least thirty hours a week to be
eligible for group coverage).

b. *Former Employees*

Courts are in dispute over the question of
whether former employees are covered under ADA
Title I when they sue to challenge limitations placed
on post-employment fringe benefits. Some have held
they are. *See, e.g. Ford v. Schering-Plough Corp.*,
145 F.3d 601 (3d Cir. 1998). Others, however, have
held that a former employee who cannot perform the
essential functions of the employment position with
or without reasonable accommodations cannot be a
qualified individual entitled to sue for employment
discrimination under ADA Title I. *See, e.g., Weyer v.
Twentieth Century Fox Film Corp.*, 198 F.3d 1104
(9th Cir. 2000). For further discussion of this issue,
see § 5.4 of this *Nutshell.*

c. *Suits Against Insurance Companies Under ADA Title I*

Courts are also split on the issue of whether
insurance companies can be sued for allegedly
discriminatory policies under ADA Title I. In
E.E.O.C. v. Benicorp Ins. Co., 2000 WL 724004
(S.D.Ind. 2000), the court held an insurance
company could be covered by ADA Title I under
Seventh Circuit authority holding that an

employer's agent who otherwise meets the statutory definition of an employer can be held liable under the ADA. In *Weyer v. Twentieth Century Fox Film Corp.*, 198 F.3d 1104 (9th Cir. 2000), however, the court held that an employee could not sue the administrator of his employer's health insurance plan under ADA Title I because the administrator was not the insured's "employer". *See also Nearhood v. Freestate Health Plan*, 1997 WL 151545 (D.Md. 1997) (holding an insurance companies are not "covered entities" within the meaning of ADA Title I even if they are agents of the employer).

2. *The Substantive Law*

The ADA provides that insurers may underwrite, classify, or administer risks that are consistent with state law and may establish or observe the terms of bona fide benefit plans that are consistent with state law, as long as such insurance programs or benefit plans are not utilized as a subterfuge to circumvent the intent of the ADA. 42 U.S.C.A. § 12201(c). If an insurance provision is based on sound actuarial principles, it will not constitute a subterfuge to circumvent the ADA.

a. *Disability-Based Distinctions*

The first issue to resolve when determining whether a term or provision in a health insurance policy constitutes a subterfuge, and thus violates Title I, is to determine whether it makes a *disability-based distinction*. Not all health-related distinctions discriminate on the basis of disability;

only disability-based distinctions can be discriminatory. The EEOC provided explicit guidance on what constitutes a "disability-based distinction" in an October 3, 2000, transmittal covering the issuance of a section in its Compliance Manual on "Employee Benefits," http://www.eeoc. gov/policy/docs/benefits.html [hereafter, *EEOC Compliance Manual*], and in a 1993 Interim Enforcement Guidance. http://www.eeoc.gov/policy/ docs/health.html [hereafter, *Interim Guidance*]. These guidelines have not been updated by the EEOC since the ADA was amended in 2008.

First, the EEOC has stated that a health-related distinction in a benefit plan *is not* disability-based if: 1) it is a broad distinction which applies to a multitude of dissimilar conditions, *and* 2) it constrains both individuals with and individuals without disabilities. Some courts have applied the EEOC's reasoning. *See, e.g., Krauel v. Iowa Methodist Medical Center*, 95 F.3d 674 (8th Cir. 1996) (holding that an employer did not violate Title I where its health insurance plan did not pay for infertility treatments, since the distinction applied to both persons with and without disabilities and was not a disability-based distinction).

The EEOC also provides guidance on what type of provision *does* constitute a disability-based distinction in a health insurance plan that may be found to violate the ADA. A term or provision is "disability based" if it singles out:

(a) a particular disability (*e.g.*, a disability retirement plan that covers all physical and mental disorders except major depression);

(b) a discrete group of disabilities (*e.g.*, a health insurance plan caps coverage for treatment of cancer at one million dollars but caps coverage for the treatment of all other physical conditions at 20 million dollars); or

(c) disability in general (*e.g.*, an employer requires all employees who are no longer able to work because of a physical or mental disorder to retire on disability retirement, even if they also are eligible to retire under the employer's service retirement plan).

The first issue that must be determined when deciding whether a disability-based distinction is being made is whether a distinction singles out a covered disability under the ADA. This requires a determination of whether a physical or mental condition is recognized as a covered disability under the ADA. A discussion of this issue is found in Chapter 3 of this *Nutshell*.

b. *Physical-Mental Health Distinctions*

A major dispute with respect to disability-based distinctions involves health insurance plans that provide greater coverage for physical health care than for mental health care. The EEOC has opined in its Compliance Manual that "it is not necessarily a disability-based distinction if an employer's health insurance plan provides unequal benefits for mental conditions compared to physical conditions." The EEOC explains that, in the health insurance context, "the term 'mental conditions' covers, for example, not only impairments like schizophrenia and major depression—which likely would be disabilities under the ADA—but also counseling for grief, self-esteem, or marital problems, which are not impairments and so are not ADA disabilities." Accordingly, "a distinction in a health insurance plan's coverage of expenses for treatment of physical, as compared with mental, conditions (a) constitutes a broad distinction that covers a multitude of dissimilar conditions, and (b) limits both individuals with and those without disabilities."

The Commission has taken the position in litigation, however, that distinctions between mental and physical conditions in long-term disability (LTD) plans are disability-based. For example in 1997, the EEOC filed suit alleging that an employer violated ADA Title I since its long term disability plan limited the benefits to be received by individuals with mental disabilities to 18 months while providing benefits to individuals with physical disabilities until age 65. *See generally EEOC v. Staten Island Savings Bank*, 207 F.3d 144 (2d Cir. 2000). Moreover, the *Compliance Manual* notes that an employee generally becomes eligible for LTD benefits when s/he is no longer able to work because of a serious permanent or long-term illness or injury. This means they have impairments which substantially limit their ability to work or to engage in one or more other major life activities.

Accordingly, the EEOC states that, in most instances, employees who are eligible for or are receiving LTD benefits have disabilities as defined by the ADA.

Most courts have disagreed with the Commission's position and have held that treating physical and mental conditions differently in an LTD plan does not violate the ADA. *See, e.g., EEOC v. Staten Island Savings Bank*, 207 F.3d 144 (2d Cir. 2000); *Ford v. Schering-Plough Corp.*, 145 F.3d 601 (3d Cir. 1998) (*en banc*); *Wyer v. Twentieth Century Fox Film Corp.*, 198 F.3d 1104 (9th Cir. 2000); *Witham v. Brigham & Women's Hospital, Inc.*, 2001 WL 586717 (D. N.H. 2001). *But see Boots v. Northwestern Mut. Life Ins. Co.*, 77 F.Supp.2d 211 (D.N.H. 1999) (allowing claim based on such a distinction to proceed).

c. *Benefit Caps*

Another issue with respect to disability-based distinctions involves benefit caps. The EEOC *Interim Guidance* states that yearly or lifetime benefit caps applied to all health or disability plan participants are permissible. It reasons that such caps are not used almost exclusively with respect to treatment for a particular disability and thus are not disability-based. For example, the EEOC opines that a policy that establishes a maximum benefit of $20,000 per year for medical care would not violate the ADA. An annual or lifetime cap tied to a specific disabling condition, such as AIDS, however, is likely to violate the ADA, according to the EEOC. In

McNeil v. Time Ins. Co., 205 F.3d 179 (5th Cir. 2000), however, the court held that an insurer did not violate the ADA by offering an insurance policy that limited the amount of coverage for AIDS to $10,000 over the first two years of policy; the insurer offered the policy to the insured, who was later diagnosed with AIDS, on the same terms as it offered policy to other applicants. Irrespective of whether they violate the ADA, benefit caps can be illegal under the Affordable Care Act. In an issue brief made available by the U.S. Department of Health and Human Services, it was estimated that 105 million Americans no longer face limits on health benefits because of the Affordable Care Act. http://aspe.hhs.gov/health/reports/2012/lifetimelimit s/ib.shtml. The rules created by the Affordable Care Act are beyond the scope of this *Nutshell*.

d. *Disability and Service Retirement Plans*

Another significant issue involves distinctions in employee benefits between service and disability retirement plans. A disability retirement plan provides lifetime income for employees who become unable to work because of illness or injury, without regard to the employee's age. By contrast, service retirement plans provide lifetime income to employees who have reached a minimum age stated in the plan (most commonly age 60 or 65) and/or who have completed specified years of service with the employer.

The EEOC *Compliance Manual* states that an employer does not violate ADA Title I when it only offers a service retirement plan and not a disability retirement plan. An employer which establishes either or both types of plans, however, may not discriminate against employees with disabilities. Specifically, an employer will violate the ADA if it does any of the following:

(1) Excludes employees from participation in a service retirement or disability retirement plan because of their disabilities. For example, an employer violates the ADA if it requires employees covered by the ADA who qualify for both service and disability retirement plans to take the disability retirement benefit.

(2) Requires different lengths of employment for participation by individuals with disabilities and individuals without disabilities in the employer's service retirement or disability retirement plans. For example, it is discriminatory if an employer requires employees with disabilities to complete 12 years of service before being allowed to enroll in its service retirement plan but only requires other employees to complete 10 years of service.

(3) Sets different levels or types of coverage for individuals with and without disabilities in a service retirement plan. For example, an employer violates the ADA if it gives cost-of-living increases every three years to employees without disabilities but only gives such increases to employees with disabilities every five years.

The EEOC states that the ADA does not, however, require that service retirement and disability retirement plans provide the same level of benefits. The EEOC *Compliance Manual* notes that "they are two separate benefits which serve two different purposes. As long as all employees may participate in the service retirement plan on the same terms, regardless of the existence of a disability, an employer will not violate the ADA if it provides lower levels of benefits in its disability than in its service retirement plans."

Some courts have followed the EEOC's reasoning. *See, e.g., Castellano v. City of New York*, 142 F.3d 58 (2d Cir. 1998) (holding the City did not violate the ADA by providing greater benefits to police officers who retired after twenty years of service than for those who retired due to disability; the ADA does not require that service retirement plans and disability retirement plans provide the same level of benefits; rather, it requires only that persons with disabilities have the opportunity to receive the same benefits as non-disabled employees who have given equivalent amount of service).

e. *Dependent Coverage*

An employer-provided insurance plan that provides coverage for an employee's dependents falls within Title I. Thus, the same principles that apply under Title I to insurance coverage for employees also apply to coverage for dependents. Accordingly, a provision in a health insurance plan that limits dependent coverage based on disability would constitute a disability-based distinction that may violate the ADA. *See* 29 C.F.R. Pt. 1630, App. § 1630.8 (stating an employer would violate the ADA by denying health benefits to a disabled dependent of an employee but not to other dependents, even where the provision of benefits to the disabled dependent would result in increased health insurance costs for the employer).

The EEOC's *Interim Guidance* states, however, that the ADA does not require that an employer provide the same level or scope of health insurance for dependents that it provides for employees. Thus, the EEOC opines that an employer-sponsored health insurance plan could permissibly provide prescription drug coverage for employees but not for dependents or could specify a higher benefit cap for employees than for dependents.

3. *Subterfuge*

As noted above, an insurance or benefit plan cannot be a subterfuge to circumvent the ADA's purposes. The EEOC's *Compliance Manual* defines "subterfuge" as "disability-based disparate treatment that is not justified by the risk or costs associated with the disability." The EEOC suggests several ways to prove that a challenged disability-based distinction is not a subterfuge. The employer may prove any of the following:

(1) "it has not engaged in the disability-based disparate treatment alleged;"

(2) "the disability-based disparate treatment is justified by legitimate actuarial data, or by actual or reasonably anticipated experience, and that conditions with comparable actuarial data and/or experience are treated the same way;"

(3) "the disability-based disparate treatment is necessary to maintain the solvency of the plan;"

(4) "the challenged practice or activity is necessary to avoid unacceptable changes in the coverage of, or the premiums for, a benefit plan;"

(5) "that a particular treatment that it has excluded from a health insurance plan provides *no* medical benefit."

Determining exactly what constitutes a subterfuge in violation of the ADA will involve an individualized, case-by-case analysis. There are, however, several existing areas of controversy surrounding the subterfuge issue in the context of Title I.

a. *Date of Plan's Enactment: Part I of Betts Dispute*

The first question is whether insurance plans established prior to the ADA's enactment can be found to constitute a subterfuge in violation of the ADA. In *Public Employees Retirement System of Ohio v. Betts*, 492 U.S. 158 (1989), the Court held that provisions in a state retirement plan did not constitute a subterfuge in violation of the Age

Discrimination in Employment Act of 1967 ("ADEA") because the retirement plan was enacted prior to the enactment of the ADEA.

The EEOC's *Compliance Manual* states it position that the analysis in *Betts* does not apply to claims involving disability-based distinctions in fringe benefits under the ADA because the statute "makes clear that discrimination in fringe benefits is covered, regardless of the date of adoption of the plan, and is unlawful absent an actuarial justification for disability-based distinctions in coverage." Courts are split on the issue. *Compare, e.g., Cloutier v. Prudential Ins. Co. of Am.*, 964 F.Supp. 299 (N.D.Cal. 1997) (holding *Betts* inapplicable to the ADA; to meet defense, insurers must show that underwriting decisions accord with either sound actuarial principles or with actual or reasonably anticipated experience), *with, e.g., Ford v. Schering-Plough Corp.*, 145 F.3d 601 (3d Cir. 1998) (holding *Betts* applies and bars most challenges to LTD plans adopted after enactment of the ADA). The Commission disagrees with cases applying the *Betts* analysis because the ADA makes clear that discrimination in fringe benefits is covered, regardless of the date of adoption of the plan, and is unlawful absent an actuarial justification for disability-based distinctions in coverage.

b. *Analysis of "Subterfuge": Part II of the Betts Dispute*

In *Betts*, the Supreme Court defined subterfuge under the ADEA as requiring a "scheme" used to discriminate "in some non-fringe benefit aspect of the employment relationship." The EEOC's *Interim Guidance* takes the position that the *Betts* rationale does not apply to Title I cases because Title I, unlike the ADEA, expressly provides that employers may not discriminate with respect to the "fringe benefits" of employment.

Some courts have rejected the EEOC's analysis and have applied the *Betts* rationale to insurance cases filed under Title I. For example, in *Krauel v. Iowa Methodist Medical Center*, 95 F.3d 674 (8th Cir. 1996), the court upheld a lower court's determination that an exclusion for the treatment of infertility in a health insurance plan was not a subterfuge to evade the ADA. The court noted that Congress enacted the ADA after the Supreme Court's decision in *Betts* and said if "Congress intended to reject the *Betts* interpretation of subterfuge when it enacted the ADA, it could have done so expressly by incorporating language for that purpose into the bill that Congress voted on and the President signed." Following *Betts*, the Eighth Circuit held that the "subterfuge" test under the ADA requires proof of employment discrimination outside the insurance plan. Since the plaintiff conceded that she suffered no such discrimination, the court held that the infertility exclusion in the insurance plan was not subterfuge.

c. *Burden of Proving Subterfuge*

The EEOC's *Interim Guidance* states that the defendant-employer bears the burden of proving the plan is *not* a subterfuge. This is in accord "with the well-established principle that the burden of proof should rest with the party who has the greatest access to the relevant facts." The EEOC opines that since individual employees or job applicants have no access to the actuarial data of insurers, they are not in a position to bear the burden of proving subterfuge.

In *Betts*, however, the Supreme Court held that a plaintiff who files an action under the ADEA has the burden of proving that a benefit plan is a subterfuge. Courts have not directly addressed whether the *Betts* rationale applies under the ADA. *See, e.g., Modderno v. King*, 82 F.3d 1059 (D.C.Cir. 1996) (apparently placing the burden on the plaintiff to prove subterfuge); *Henderson v. Bodine Aluminum, Inc.*, 70 F.3d 958 (8th Cir. 1995) (apparently placing the burden on the defendant to prove lack of subterfuge).

B. TITLE III—PUBLIC ACCOMMODATIONS

An individual who claims to have been discriminated against by virtue of provisions in an employer-sponsored insurance plan may file suit against the employer (under Title I), the private insurance provider (under Title III), or both. An individual whose health or disability insurance is not provided via an employment relationship, but is provided via contract between the individual and a private insurance carrier, can only file suit against the insurance carrier under Title III.

1. *Coverage Under Title III*

As a preliminary matter, there is a threshold issue of when an insurer falls within the coverage of Title III. As noted in Chapter 7 of this *Nutshell*, Title III of the ADA prohibits discrimination on the "basis of disability in the full and equal enjoyment of the goods, services, facilities, privileges, advantages, or accommodations of any place of public accommodation." 42 U.S.C.A. § 12182(a) Title III contains a list of twelve categories of private entities that are public accommodations governed by the ADA. Several examples of covered entities are listed in each category.

To be covered by Title III, a private entity *must* fall within one of those twelve categories, although the examples given in each category are merely illustrative. One of the covered categories includes service establishments, defined as: "[a] laundromat, dry-cleaner, bank, barber shop, beauty shop, travel service, shoe repair service, funeral parlor, gas station, office of an accountant or lawyer, pharmacy, *insurance office*, professional office of a health care provider, hospital, or other service establishment." 42 U.S.C.A. 12181(7)(F) (emphasis added).

Clearly, Title III applies to insurance offices themselves because insurance offices are expressly listed as being covered. But does Title III apply to services provided by insurers not involving access to insurance offices? Courts are split on the issue of whether the list of twelve categories listed in Title III includes only physical structures that a person enters to obtain goods or services or whether the list also includes services provided by public accommodations even when clients or customers do not enter physical structures to obtain such goods or services.

In *Carparts Distribution Center, Inc. v. Automotive Wholesaler's Association of New England*, 37 F.3d 12 (1st Cir. 1994), which is discussed more fully in § 7.6 of this *Nutshell*, the court held that the plain meaning of Title III evidences that public accommodations are not limited to actual structures and Title III governs the activities of insurance companies, regardless of whether actual physical facilities are involved. Other courts have disagreed, however. In *Parker v. Metropolitan Life Insurance Co.*, 121 F.3d 1006 (6th Cir. 1997), the court held that Title III only prevents discrimination in *physical* places of public accommodations. The Sixth Circuit thus held that Title III does not govern the content of a long-term disability policy offered by an employer's insurance company. Still others have held Title III applies if there is a "nexus" between the physical place of public accommodation (*i.e.*, the insurance office) and the services or privileges denied in a discriminatory manner (*i.e.*, the insurance policy). *See, e.g., Weyer v. Twentieth Century Fox Film Corp.*, 198 F.3d 1104 (9th Cir. 2000).

2. *Substantive Analysis Under Title III*

Unlike the EEOC, which has promulgated comprehensive guidelines to assist in determining whether distinctions or exemptions in health insurance plans violates Title I, the DOJ has issued limited guidance on how Title III applies to health insurance. The DOJ's *ADA Title III Technical Assistance Manual* § III–3.11000, http://www.ada.gov/taman3.html, states:

> [A] public accommodation may offer [an insurance] plan that limits certain kinds of coverage based on classification of risk, but may not refuse to insure, or refuse to continue to insure, or limit the amount, extent, or kind of coverage available to an individual, or charge a different rate for the same coverage solely because of a physical or mental impairment, except where the refusal, limitation, or rate differential is based on sound actuarial principles or is related to actual or reasonably anticipated experience.

See also 28 C.F.R. § 36.212.

Some courts have held, however, that Title III does not govern the content of a long-term disability policy offered by an employer. These courts have noted that Title III prohibits discrimination in the enjoyment of "the *goods, services,* facilities, privileges, advantages, or accommodations of any place of public accommodation." 42 U.S.C.A. § 1218 (emphasis added). They reason that this language does not require a public accommodation to provide different goods or services, just nondiscriminatory enjoyment of those that are provided. The courts cite a provision in the Title III regulations which states that bookstore and video stores must be accessible to individuals with disabilities, but are not required to carry Brailled books or closed-captioned video tapes. 28 C.F.R. pt. 36, app. B § 36.307. "[L]ikewise, an insurance office must be physically accessible to the disabled but need not provide insurance that treats the disabled equally with the non-disabled." *Ford v. Schering-Plough Corp.*, 145 F.3d 601 (3d Cir. 1998); *Weyer v. Twentieth Century Fox Film Corp.*, 198 F.3d 1104 (9th Cir. 2000).

§ 11.7 RETALIATION AND COERCION

Retaliation and coercion against an individual seeking to enforce his or her rights under the ADA is prohibited and subject to the same penalties imposed for other violations of the Act. It is illegal to coerce, intimidate, threaten or interfere with any individual who exercises, or helps another person exercise, his or her rights under the ADA. 42 U.S.C.A. § 12203(a). The Act prohibits retaliation against both persons with disabilities *and* associates of people with disabilities who oppose—or assist in opposing—discriminatory conduct in violation of the ADA.

§ 11.8 RIGHTS UNDER OTHER LAWS

The ADA shall not be construed to invalidate or limit the remedies, rights and procedures of any federal, state or local law that provides protection for individuals with disabilities that is greater than or equal to that provided under the ADA. 42 U.S.C.A. § 12201(b). Moreover, the Act does not preempt a state "disease control law, or any other public health law, which places certain requirements on certain employees, employers or businesses, but which does not discriminate against people with disabilities. . . ." H.R. Rep. No. 101–558, 101st Cong., 2d Sess., 80 (1990).

§ 11.9   RELATIONSHIP TO THE REHABILITATION ACT

Except as otherwise provided, the ADA shall not be construed "to apply a lesser standard" than the standards applied under the Rehabilitation Act of 1973 or the regulations issued thereunder. 42 U.S.C.A. § 12201(a).

§ 11.10   SMOKING

The ADA shall not be construed to "preclude the prohibition of, or the imposition of restrictions on, smoking" in places of employment, public accommodation or transportation covered by the Act. 42 U.S.C.A. § 12201(b).

§ 11.11   APPLICABILITY TO CONGRESS, PRESIDENTIAL APPOINTEES, WHITE HOUSE EMPLOYEES AND PREVIOUSLY EXEMPT STATE EMPLOYEES

The ADA states that the General Accounting Office, the Government Printing Office, and the

Library of Congress are covered with respect to employment and public services accommodations. 42 U.S.C.A. § 12209. In addition, the Congressional Accountability Act of 1995 states that the ADA and Rehabilitation Act apply to "the legislative branch of the Federal Government." 2 U.S.C.A. § 1302(a). Specifically, disability discrimination is now barred in employment, *id.* § 1311(a)(3), and public services and accommodations. *Id.* § 1331.

Presidential appointees are also covered under the ADA. 42 U.S.C.A. § 2000e–16b(a). So are individuals chosen or appointed by state and local officials

(a) to be a member of the elected official's personal staff;

(b) to serve the elected official on the policymaking level; or

(c) to serve the elected official as an immediate advisor with respect to the exercise of the constitutional or legal powers of the office.

Id. § 2000e–16c(a).

On October 26, 1996, President Clinton signed into law the Presidential and Executive Office Accountability Act, which requires the White House to comply with the ADA (and other laws prohibiting discrimination). 3 U.S.C.A. § 402.

§ 11.12   ALTERNATE DISPUTE RESOLUTION

Where appropriate, and to the extent authorized by law, the use of alternate means of dispute resolution (other than litigation) "is encouraged to resolve disputes arising under" the ADA. 42 U.S.C.A. § 12212. The Committee of Conference Report notes that "[u]nder no condition would an arbitration clause in a collective bargaining agreement or employment contract prevent an individual from pursuing [his] rights under the ADA." H.R. Rep. No. 101–8 101st Cong., 2d Sess. (1990), at 85.

In *Wright v. Universal Maritime Service Corp.*, 525 U.S. 70 (1998), the Court held that a *general* arbitration clause in a collective bargaining agreement (CBA) did not require a longshoreman to use an arbitration procedure for an alleged ADA violation. The Court stated this clause could not be considered a clear and unmistakable incorporation of employment-discrimination laws. Accordingly, it found that the cause of action asserted by the longshoreman arose out of the ADA, rather than contract. Moreover, even if there were a contractual right coextensive with the federal statutory right, the ultimate question of what the federal law required was not subject to the presumption of arbitrability accorded claims under a CBA.

The Supreme Court later held, however, that the Federal Arbitration Act (FAA) mandates enforcement of valid, written arbitration agreements which cover employment discrimination claims. *Circuit City Stores v. Adams*, 532 U.S. 105 (2001). And several circuit courts have held that employment discrimination claims arising under Title VII can be referred to arbitration. *See, e.g.,*

Tinder v. Pinkerton Security, 305 F.3d 728 (7th Cir. 2002) (citing cases).

The terms of such arbitration agreements, however, are still a fertile source of litigation, and courts have refused to enforce them when they limit an employee's rights under employment discrimination statutes such as the ADA. *See, e.g., Ingle v. Circuit City Stores, Inc.*, 328 F.3d 1165 (9th Cir. 2003); *Morrison v. Circuit City Stores, Inc.*, 317 F.3d 646 (6th Cir. 2003). *But see Musnick v. King Motor Co. of Fort Lauderdale*, 325 F.3d 1255 (11th Cir. 2003) (holding that the mere existence of a fee-shifting provision in an arbitration agreement providing for mandatory arbitration of employment discrimination claims did not automatically render the agreement unenforceable). This same principle will apply to the ADA.

In addition, the Supreme Court in *Universal Maritime* specifically declined to address the question of whether a union-negotiated waiver of the statutory right to litigate employment claims in federal court can ever be enforceable. In applying *Universal Maritime*, lower courts have concluded that a CBA can achieve the requisite degree of clarity by either 1) drafting an explicit arbitration clause, (i.e., a clear and unmistakable provision under which the employees agree to submit to arbitration all federal causes of action arising out of their employment) or 2), if the arbitration clause is not so clear, a general arbitration clause can be supported by additional provisions mandating explicit incorporation of statutory antidiscrimination requirements which "make[ ] it unmistakably clear that the discrimination statutes at issue are part of the agreement." *Rogers v. New York University*, 220 F.3d 73 (2d Cir. 2000) (holding that CBA's arbitration clause did *not* contain sufficiently clear and unmistakable waiver of employees' right to a federal forum with respect to claims under employment discrimination statutes); *but see Singletary v. Enersys, Inc.*, 2003 WL 264703 (4th Cir. 2003) (holding that collective CBA *did* contain clear and unmistakable language sufficient to waive an employee's right to litigate an ADA claim in federal court).

CHAPTER 12

THE INDIVIDUALS WITH DISABILITIES EDUCATION ACT (IDEA): INTRODUCTION AND OVERVIEW

§ 12.1 INTRODUCTION

The Individuals with Disabilities Education Act (IDEA), 20 U.S.C.A. § 1400 *et seq.*, formerly called the Education of the Handicapped Act and the Education for All Handicapped Children Act, was enacted in 1975 to address the failure of state education systems to meet the educational needs of children with disabilities. Congress's enactment of the IDEA was in part a response to two well-publicized court cases, *Mills v. Board of Education*, 348 F.Supp. 866 (D.D.C. 1972), and *Pennsylvania Association for Retarded Children v. Commonwealth of Pennsylvania (PARC)*, 343 F.Supp. 279 (E.D.Pa. 1972), and the persistent efforts of persons with disabilities and organizations interested in the rights of persons with disabilities. In its findings, Congress noted that in the mid-1970s more than half of the approximately 8 million American children with disabilities were not receiving appropriate educational services, one million were excluded entirely from public school educations, and many in regular school programs were educationally unsuccessful because their disabilities were undetected. 20 U.S.C.A. § 1400(c)(2).

The IDEA was significantly amended and revised in 1997, and these amendments were clarified by substantial regulations issued in 1999. The 1997 IDEA amendments renumbered many of the statute's existing sections. On December 23, 2004, the Individuals with Disabilities Education Improvement Act of 2004 was signed into law by President Bush. In addition to making various changes to the IDEA, this Act sought to align the IDEA with the No Child Left Behind Act.

The purpose of the IDEA is

(A) to ensure that all children with disabilities have available to them a free appropriate public education that emphasizes special education and related services designed to meet their unique needs and prepare them for further education, employment and independent living;

(B) to ensure that the rights of children with disabilities and parents of such children are protected; and

(C) to assist States, localities, educational service agencies, and Federal agencies to provide for the education of all children with disabilities.

Id. § 1400(d)(1).

The 2004 Amendments added the phrase "further education" to the first purpose.

The IDEA contains four subchapters. Part A contains the general provisions of the Act, including definitions. Part B sets forth the formula grant program that requires each state receiving federal financial assistance under the Act to develop a plan to ensure a free appropriate public education (FAPE) to all disabled children.

Part B also contains the "heart" of the IDEA—a set of procedural safeguards intended to protect the interests of children with disabilities from 3 to 21 years of age. Among the most significant of those procedural protections is the requirement that school districts, with the assistance of parents, prepare an Individualized Education Plan (IEP) for each student with a disability. Two crucial components of the IDEA are: (a) the requirement of parental involvement in planning an appropriate educational program for their child with a disability and (b) the intent that a child with a disability is to be removed from the regular educational environment only when "the nature or severity of the disability of a child is such that education in regular classes with the use of supplementary aids and services cannot be achieved satisfactorily." 20 U.S.C. § 1412(a)(5)(A).

Part C of the IDEA authorizes states to receive grants from the federal government to develop and implement statewide systems to provide early intervention services for infants and toddlers (ages 0–3) with disabilities. And Part D provides for state program improvement grants for children with disabilities.

This *Nutshell* will focus on Parts A and B which encompass the basic, substantive portions of the Act.

§ 12.2   FEDERAL ENFORCEMENT

A.   STATE PLANS AND ELIGIBILITY FOR FEDERAL FUNDS

A state seeking to obtain funds pursuant to the IDEA must submit a state plan to the United States Secretary of Education. That plan must set forth goals, timetables and descriptive information concerning the facilities, personnel and services needed to meet the goal of full educational opportunity for all children with disabilities. If the Secretary intends to disapprove any state plan, he or she must provide the state with reasonable notice and an opportunity for a hearing prior to such disapproval.

In order for a state to receive or continue to receive federal funding under the IDEA, it must demonstrate: (1) that it has a policy assuring all children with disabilities the right to a FAPE; (2) that it has submitted a plan to the federal government setting forth policies and procedures designed to assure that monies received are expended in a manner consistent with the IDEA; (3) that its educational plan includes procedural safeguards required by the IDEA; (4) that its plan ensures that funds will be used to supplement rather than supplant state and local funds expended for the education of children with disabilities; (5)

that its plan contains procedures to assure that to the maximum extent appropriate children with disabilities are educated with children who are not disabled; (6) that its plan contains procedures designed to identify, locate and evaluate all children with disabilities residing in the state; and (7) that its plan contains procedures to assure that testing and evaluation materials and procedures are both selected and administered so as not to be racially or culturally discriminatory. The responsibility for ensuring that the eligibility requirements for federal funding are met belongs to the appropriate State Education Agency (SEA), which must determine whether the state's proclaimed standards and plans meet the agency's educational standards and requirements. A state that does not satisfy these requirements will not receive or will lose the right to receive funding for its educational programs.

The state has the ultimate responsibility to ensure that funding is provided for a required placement. Thus, if a Local Educational Agency (LEA) will not or cannot provide a placement, the SEA must provide the required placement.

B. REMEDIES

If the Secretary of Education subsequently finds that the state has failed to comply substantially with the requirements of the IDEA, the Secretary may withhold further payments for certain specified programs "to the extent that funds under such programs are available for the provision of assistance for the education of children with disabilities." 20 U.S.C.A. § 1416(a)(2)(B). In other words, whatever programmatic funds still remain to be disbursed may be withheld. Such a decision by the Secretary of Education is subject to judicial review, but the Secretary's findings of fact may not be overturned unless "good cause" is shown. Good cause is defined as requiring a judicial finding that the Secretary's decision was not supported by substantial evidence. 20 U.S.C.A. § 1416(b)(3).

The Part B regulations provide parents with two means of resolving disputes under the IDEA: (i) an impartial due process hearing system and (ii) a Complaint Resolution Procedure (CRP). The due process procedures are discussed in chapter 15 of this *Nutshell*. The CRP require SEAs to adopt written procedures for receiving and resolving complaints, to conduct necessary on-site investigations and to resolve complaints within 60 days. 34 C.F.R. §§ 300.507–300.515.

Courts are split on whether parents have a private right to enforce CRP regulations. See, e.g., *Virginia Office of Protection and Advocacy v. Virginia Dept. of Educ.*, 262 F.Supp.2d 648 (E.D. Va. 2003) (finding no private right of action); *R.K. v. Hayward Unified Sch. Dist.*, 2007 WL 2778702 (N.D. Cal. 2007) (no private right of action); *Ryan v. Shawnee Mission U.S.D.*, 416 F.Supp.2d 1090 (D. Kan. 2006) (no private right of action); *Beth V. v. Carroll*, 87 F.3d 80 (3d Cir.1996) (finding private right of action); *S.A. v. Tulare County Office of Education*, 2009 WL 30298 (E.D. Calif. 2009) (finding private right of action); *Yolo County Office*

of Education v. California Dept. of Education, 2012
WL 3143904 (E.D. Cal. 2012) (distinguishing *S.A.* to
find no private right of action).

§ 12.3   TERMINOLOGY AND CONCEPTS

A.   CHILDREN WITH DISABILITIES

Not all children with disabilities are covered by
the IDEA; rather, only those children who are
educationally disabled fall within the scope of the
Act. The IDEA lists those disabilities that are
recognizable as educational disabilities. This listing
addresses a child

> (i) with mental retardation, hearing
> impairments (including deafness), speech or
> language impairments, visual impairments
> (including blindness), serious emotional
> disturbance (hereinafter referred to as
> "emotional disturbance"), orthopedic
> impairments, autism, traumatic brain injury,
> other health impairments, or specific learning
> disabilities; and

> (ii) who, by reason thereof, needs special
> education and related services.

20 U.S.C.A. § 1401(3)(A).

Although not specially mentioned in the
definition of "child with a disability," many states
have utilized the term "multiply handicapped" (or a
derivative thereof) to describe children with two or
more recognizable disabilities. The DOE's
regulations define "multiple disabilities" as

"concomitant impairments (such as mental retardation-blindness, mental retardation-orthopedic impairment, etc.), the combination of which causes such severe educational needs that they cannot be accommodated in special education programs solely for one of the impairments. Multiple disabilities does not include deaf-blindness." 34 C.F.R. § 300.8(c)(7).

For children aged three through nine (or any subset of that age range, including ages three through five), a state may, at its discretion, include a child who is not specifically labeled but is experiencing "developing delays":

as defined by the State and as measured by appropriate diagnostic instruments and procedures, in one or more of the following areas: Physical development, cognitive development, communication development, social or emotional development, or adaptive development; and . . . [w]ho, by reason thereof, needs special education and related services.

34 C.F.R. § 300.8(b) This proviso is intended to ensure that eligible preschoolers are provided services and are not inappropriately labeled. The 2004 Amendments added the reference to the ages three through five subset to clarify the existence of the state's discretion for that age range.

By definition, in order to be covered by either Part B or C of the Act a child must require "special education and related services." A child with a minor limb disorder who does not need special attention in the educational setting, for example, would not qualify under this definition.

B. SPECIAL EDUCATION

The term "special education" is defined as "specially designed instruction ... to meet the unique needs of a child with a disability" and includes "instruction conducted in the classroom, in the home, in hospitals and institutions, and in other settings" and physical education instruction. 20 U.S.C.A. § 1401(29). It is a combination of being specially designed and meeting the unique needs of a child that makes special education "special." In most states, special education can be provided only by a certified special education teacher; the IDEA, however, does not contain such a proviso.

Special education cannot be labeled by a precise definition because of its child-specific character. The implications of the statutory definition, however, are significant. One clear ramification is that special education is not limited to traditional academic instruction in the classroom but may be provided in any setting as necessary to meet a child's unique needs.

Special education can be related to, and in support of, regular academic instruction; it can also include vocational instruction, or it can focus upon daily living skills, community living skills, pre-vocational skills or whatever is appropriate for the particular child in question, including transition services to prepare a student for life after public education. Thus, the nature of special education instruction will vary as required to address the individual child's needs.

C.   FREE APPROPRIATE PUBLIC EDUCATION

A "free appropriate public education" (FAPE), as defined under the Act, comprises special education and/or related services provided at public expense that meet the standards of the State Educational Agency (SEA) and that are provided in conformance with the Individualized Education Program (IEP) devised for each disabled child. 20 U.S.C.A. § 1401(9). The student's school district has responsibility for assuring the provision of the FAPE as described in the IEP. The SEA has the responsibility to step in and provide a FAPE when the school district fails to do so.

A FAPE must be available to all children with disabilities between the ages of 3–21, unless providing services to children 3–5 and/or 18–21 is inconsistent with state law or practice.

D.   RELATED SERVICES

"Related services" under the Act are defined as including:

transportation, and such developmental, corrective, and other supportive services (including speech-language pathology and audiology services, interpreting services, psychological services, physical and occupational therapy, recreation, including therapeutic recreation, social work services,

school nurse services designed to enable a child
with a disability to receive a free appropriate
public   education   as   described   in   the
individualized education program of the child,
counseling   services,   including   rehabilitation
counseling,   orientation   and   mobility   services,
and medical services, except that such medical
services shall be for diagnostic and evaluation
purposes only

20 U.S.C. § 1401(26)(A).

The following exception is also included: "The term
does not include a medical device that is surgically
implanted, or the replacement of such device." 20
U.S.C.   § 1401(26)(B).   The   Conference   Report
clarified that related services should include "travel
training instructions." The relate services list is not
an exhaustive list. Services are covered by the IDEA
"as   may   be   required   to   assist   a   child   with   a
disability   to   benefit   from   special   education,   and
includes the early identification and assessment of
disabling   conditions   in   children."   20   U.S.C.
§ 1401(26)(A).

The issue of related services is discussed in
further detail in chapter 13 of this *Nutshell*.

E.   INDIVIDUALIZED EDUCATION PROGRAM

The "individualized educational program" (IEP) is
the cornerstone of the IDEA. This document, which
is   ideally   developed   in   a   collaborative   and
cooperative   effort   between   parents   and   school
personnel, describes the disabled child's abilities

and needs and prescribes the placement and services designed to meet that child's unique needs. The IEP is not only a document—it is also the culmination of a prescribed process. It has thus substantially altered the means by which educators plan programming for disabled children. Educators must work with parents, who are mandatory participants in this planning process and who are provided with procedural safeguards in the event that they disagree with the educators responsible for educating their children.

In order for an IEP to comply with the law, it must have been developed and implemented in accordance with detailed, legally mandated procedures. 34 C.F.R. §§ 300.320–300.328. Those procedures are discussed in § 13.4(A) of this chapter.

F.   LEAST RESTRICTIVE ENVIRONMENT

Each child with a disability must be educated in the least restrictive environment (LRE) appropriate to meet his or her needs. A child with a disability is to be removed from the regular educational environment only when "the nature or severity of the disability is such that education in regular classes with the use of supplementary aids and services cannot be achieved satisfactorily." 34 C.F.R. § 300.114(a)(2)(ii). This LRE concept creates a presumption in favor of the integration of children with disabilities. When segregation can be avoided while still providing an appropriate education for a child with a disability, the Act requires integration.

In 2004, the LRE rule was enhanced by including the following language:

> a State shall not use a funding mechanism by which the State distributes funds on the basis of the type of setting in which a child is served that will result in the failure to provide a child with a disability a free appropriate public education according to the unique needs of the child as described in the child's IEP.

20 U.S.C. § 1412(a)(5).

The purpose of this rule is to make sure that states have a continuum of alternative placements such as instruction in regular classes, special classes, special schools, home instruction, and instruction in hospital and institutions to meet the needs of children with disabilities. *See* 34 C.F.R. § 300.115 (continuum of alternative placement requirement).

The terms "least restrictive environment" and "mainstreaming" are sometimes thought to be synonymous, but such an interpretation is incorrect. The term "mainstreaming," which does not actually appear as a formal term in the IDEA, has become common jargon in the educational community. It is typically accepted as meaning the placement of a disabled child in a regular educational setting. Such mainstreaming can be achieved in all aspects of a child's educational program or in just some portions of that program, such as in a particular academic class, in a special area of instruction—such as art, music or physical education, or simply in the cafeteria at lunchtime.

The concept of "least restrictive environment" is considerably broader than the concept of mainstreaming. A disabled child who can be mainstreamed for only part of the day can be in a less or more restrictive environment than a similarly situated child. If, for instance, one child is mainstreamed for one hour per day and another for two hours per day, the latter child, all other factors being equal, is in a less restrictive environment.

Mainstreaming, therefore, is only part of the larger concept of least restrictive environment. The distinction between mainstreaming and LRE is particularly highlighted whenever parents or educators grapple with incorporating the concept of "integrated education" or "inclusion" into an IEP. This concept involves placement of a disabled child primarily in the regular classroom. In contrast to mainstreaming, however, the disabled child in an integrated educational setting is not expected to keep pace with the nondisabled children in the class; nor is the disabled child expected to achieve all the regular educational requirements in order to be placed into the next grade level. Rather, the disabled child is to be provided an adapted curriculum and to move on to the next grade level if he or she achieves enough success as measured against his or her own IEP.

The relationship between the LRE and the provision of a FAPE is discussed in chapter 13 of this *Nutshell*.

G.   LOCAL EDUCATIONAL AGENCY

Local Educational Agency (LEA) is the term utilized to describe the public board of education or other public authority that exercises administrative control or direction over public elementary and/or secondary schools in a political subdivision. Although each LEA is responsible for ensuring that a FAPE is provided for all children with disabilities residing within its geographical boundaries, the residence of a child is a matter of state, not federal, law.

H.   STATE EDUCATIONAL AGENCY

The state, through its state educational agency (SEA), has the ultimate responsibility for ensuring that eligibility requirements for federal funding are met. The state's obligation can include actually providing an appropriate placement when an LEA is unable to do so. 20 U.S.C.A. § 1413(g)(1)(B).

I.   SPECIFIC LEARNING DISABILITIES

A "specific learning disability" is defined as "a disorder in one or more of the basic psychological processes involved in understanding or in using language, spoken or written, which disorder may manifest itself in imperfect ability to listen, think, speak, read, write, spell, or do mathematical calculations." 20 U.S.C. § 1401(30)(A). That term includes "perceptual disabilities, brain injury, minimal brain dysfunction, dyslexia, and developmental aphasia." *Id.* § 1401(30)(B). It does not include "a learning problem that is primarily the result of visual, hearing or motor disabilities, of mental retardation, of emotional disturbance, or of environmental, cultural, or economic disadvantage." *Id.* § 1401(30)(C).

The 2004 Amendments clarified the definition of "specific learning disability." Congress determined that the "discrepancy" model should not be the only way to determine whether a child has a learning disability. Hence, the IDEA states "when determining whether a child has a specific learning disability . . . a local educational agency shall not be required to take into consideration whether a child has a severe discrepancy between achievement and intellectual ability in oral expression, listening comprehension, written expression, basic reading skill, reading comprehension, mathematical calculation, or mathematical reasoning." 20 U.S.C. § 1414(b)(6). That language, of course, is a negative—it does not say how a school district *should* determine the existence of a learning disability. The mere evidence of a discrepancy between aptitude and achievement, however, does not appear to *require* a school district to conclude that a learning disability exists.

The purpose of the new learning disability rule appears to be to preclude overidentification of learning disabilities. Hence, the 2004 Amendments also provide that "In determining whether a child has a specific learning disability, a local educational agency may use a process that determines if the child responds to scientific, research-based

intervention as part of the evaluation procedures."
20 U.S.C. § 1414(b)(6)(B).

Neither Section 504 nor the IDEA and its
regulations directly address "attention deficit
disorder" (ADD) or "attention deficit hyperactivity
disorder" (ADHD). Rather, they are included under
the IDEA's definition of "other health impairment."
This definition, added in a regulation in 1999, states
that "[o]ther health impairment means having
limited strength, vitality or alertness, including a
heightened alertness to environmental stimuli that
results in limited alertness with respect to the
educational environment, that is due to chronic or
acute health problems such as . . . attention deficit
disorder or attention deficit hyperactivity disorder
. . . and [such limitation] [a]dversely affects a child's
educational performance." 34 C.F.R. § 300.8(c)(9). In
addition, in some situations children with ADD may
satisfy criteria of being learning disabled.

§ 12.4   PROCEDURAL SAFEGUARDS

A.   DEVELOPMENT OF AN INDIVIDUALIZED EDUCATION PROGRAM

The IDEA places considerable weight upon the
process used to develop the IEP. The process
typically commences when a child is suspected of
being disabled. School districts have an affirmative
obligation to seek an evaluation of any child
suspected of having a disability. The LEA must
provide a detailed notice to the child's parents and
seek to obtain consent from the parents to conduct

an evaluation of the child. After this evaluation is complete, a meeting is held to determine whether the child should be classified as disabled and, if so, what placement and services should be provided in order to furnish the child with a FAPE. This information, and more, is included in the child's IEP.

Before conducting an initial evaluation to determine if the child is disabled, the local educational agency must obtain informed consent from the parent of the child. 20 U.S.C. § 1414(a)(1)(D)(i)(1). Special rules apply for children who are wards of the state. *See* 20 U.S.C. § 1414(a)(1)(D)(iii). If the parent does not provide consent for the initial evaluation or the parent fails to respond to a request to provide consent, the local educational agency may pursue the initial evaluation of the child by using due process procedures except to the extent such procedures would be inconsistent with State law relating to such parental consent. 20 U.S.C. § 1414(a)(1)(D)(ii)(I). If the parent refuses to consent to identification or services, the local educational agency cannot be considered to be in violation of the requirement to provide a child with a free and appropriate public education. *See* 20 U.S.C. § 1414(a)(1)(D)(ii)(III).

Before a school district (or educational agency) may propose to initiate or change the identification, evaluation or educational placement of a child, the school district (or agency) must first provide notice, in writing, to the child's parents. Similar notice is required before a school district may refuse to initiate or change the identification, evaluation or educational placement of a child. 20 U.S.C. § 1415(b)(3). The notice must be understandable to the general public and be provided in the native language or other mode of communication used by the parent, unless this is clearly not feasible. 20 U.S.C. § 1415(b)(4). Similar notice is required with respect to a proposal to initiate a change—or refusal to initiate or change—in the provision of a FAPE to a child. The 2004 Amendments added specific procedures regarding surrogates and wards of the state. *See* 20 U.S.C. § 1415(b)(2)(A).

The 2004 Amendments enhanced the requirements for evaluations of disabilities. *See* 20 U.S.C. § 1414(b)(2) & (3). Congress intended the evaluation process to be a comprehensive process using "technically sound instruments that may assess the relative contribution of cognitive and behavioral factors, in addition to physical or developmental factors." Assessments of children "who transfer from one school district to another school district in the same academic year are coordinated with such children's prior and subsequent schools, as necessary and as expeditiously as possible, to ensure prompt completion of full evaluations." 20 U.S.C. § 1414(b)(3)(D).

After the evaluation is concluded, the next step is to hold a meeting attended by certain mandated participants. Both the school district and the child's parents or guardians are to be represented.

Participants on behalf of the school district (or public agency) must include: (i) an individual who is qualified to supervise a specially designed education program for the child, and who is knowledgeable about the general curriculum and about the school district's resources to assist the child (the "LEA representative"); (ii) a regular education teacher (if the child is participating or may participate in regular education); (iii) a special education teacher or representative; and (iv) an individual who can interpret the instructional implications of evaluation results of the child (this person may also be one of the teachers or the LEA representative). 20 U.S.C. § 1414(d)(1)(B). Both the child, where appropriate, and one or both of the child's parents are also to be involved in the IEP meeting. At the discretion of the parents or agency, other persons may also be present. The team deciding the child's placement and IEP is commonly referred to as the multidisciplinary team. The 2004 Amendments clarified that certain members of the IEP team can be excused from attending. 20 U.S.C. § 1414(d)(1)(C). A parent's consent to a member's absence must be in writing.

The public agency must ensure that one or both parents are afforded an opportunity to participate in the IEP meeting. Sufficient notice must be provided to the parents to allow them time to arrange to be present. The meeting must be scheduled at a mutually agreed-upon time and place. In the event the parents cannot otherwise participate in the meeting, telephone conference calls are permissible. The public agency may conduct the meeting without the presence of the parent only if the agency has made and recorded its unsuccessful attempts to arrange a mutually agreed-upon time and place for the meeting. 34 C.F.R. § 300.300

B.   THE IEP DOCUMENT

The IDEA requires that the IEP document must, at a minimum, contain the following information:

(1) The child's present levels of academic and functional performance.

(2) The annual goals for the child, including academic and functional goals.

(3) A description of how the child's progress toward meeting the annual goals will be measured and when periodic reports on the progress the child is making toward meeting the annual goals will be provided.

(4) A statement of the special education, related services, and supplementary aids and related services and supplementary aids and services, based on peer-reviewed research to the extent practicable, to be provided to or for the child.

(5) An explanation of the extent, if any to which the child will not participate with nondisabled children in the regular classroom.

(6) A statement of any individual appropriate accommodations that are necessary to measure the academic achievement and functional

performance of the child on State and districtwide assessments.

(7) The dates on which it is anticipated that the services listed will be initiated, and the expected frequency, location, and duration of those services.

(8) Beginning at age 16, and every year thereafter, a statement of the child's needed transition services related to the child's course of study (to ensure that the child's educational program is planned to help the child reach his or her goals for life after secondary school).

20 U.S.C.A. § 1414(d)(1)(A). In addition, beginning at least one year before the child reaches the age of majority under state law (*i.e.,* 18 or 21 as the state law provides), the IEP must include a statement that the child has been informed of his or her rights under Part B of the IDEA.

With respect to information included in the IEP, the 1997 Amendments, as strengthened by the 2004 Amendments, require the multidisciplinary team to consider (1) the child's strengths, the parents' concerns for enhancing the education of their child, and the results of the child's initial or most recent evaluation, and the academic, developmental, and functional needs of the child; (2) in the case of a child whose behavior impedes the child's learning or that of others, consider the use of positive behavioral interventions and supports, and other strategies, to address that behavior; (3) in the case of a child with limited English proficiency, the language needs of the child as they relate to the IEP; (4) in the case of a child who is blind or visually impaired, provision of instruction in Braille and the use of Braille unless the IEP team determines that instruction in Braille or the use of Braille is not appropriate for the child; (5) the communication needs of the child, and in the case of a child who is deaf or hard-of-hearing, the child's language and communication needs, opportunities for direct communications with peers and professional personnel in the children's language and communication mode, academic level, and full range of needs, including opportunities for direct instruction in the child's language and communication mode; and (6) the child's need for assistive technology devices and services. 20 U.S.C. § 1414(d)(3).

C.   DUE PROCESS HEARINGS

When a parent and a public education agency disagree concerning any of these matters—the identification, evaluation, educational placement or provision of a FAPE—for a disabled child, or for a child suspected of being disabled, either party may initiate a "due process hearing." 20 U.S.C. § 1415(f). The due process hearing will be conducted by either the public agency directly responsible for the child's education (usually the LEA) or the SEA. State law determines which level of government is responsible for conducting the hearing. The hearing should be scheduled to accommodate the scheduling of the parents, child and the LEA. The 2004 Amendments specify that the complaint must set forth an alleged violation that occurred not more than two years before the date the parent or public agency knew or should have known about the alleged action that forms the basis of the complaint unless the state has its own rules on this subject. *See* 20 U.S.C. § 1415(b)(6).

The 2004 Amendments added requirements for the content of these complaints as well as the school district's response to the complaint. The complaint must state the nature of the problem, including facts relating to the problem, as well as a proposed resolution of the problem. *See* 20 U.S.C. § 1415(b)(7)(A)(III). The parent or the local educational agency can be the entity filing a complaint. If it is the parent who filed the complaint, then the local educational agency must send the parent a written notice explaining why the agency "proposes or refuses to take the action and a description of each evaluation procedure, assessment, record, or report the agency used as a basis for the proposed or refused action." 20 U.S.C. § 1415(c)(1)(B). The notice should also describe "other options considered by the IEP Team and the reason why those options were rejected" and "the factors that are relevant to the agency's proposal or refusal." *Id.* at 1415(c)(1)(E) & (F).

Prior to the opportunity for an impartial due process hearing, the local educational agency shall convene a meeting with the parents and the relevant members of the IEP team to resolve the complaint unless the parents and the local educational agency agree in writing to waive such meeting or agree to conduct a mediation. 20 U.S.C. § 1415(f)(1)(B). The mediation process is described extensively at 20 U.S.C. § 1415(e). The 2004 Amendments clarified that the mediation process is confidential and that any agreement reached at mediation is enforceable in state or federal court. *See Id.* at § 1415(e)(2)(F) & (G). The state bears the cost of mediation.

The resolution session requirements, as well as due process rules, create significant timing requirements. The resolution meeting is supposed to occur within 15 days of the local educational agency receiving notice of the parents' complaint. § 1415(f)(1)(B). Irrespective of whether parties elect a resolution session or mediation, the due process hearing is supposed to occur within 30 days of the filing of the complaint. § 1415(f)(1)(B)(ii). Although it can be time consuming to select a mediator, the use of the mediation process is not supposed to "deny or delay a parent's right to a due process hearing." § 1415(e)(2)(A)(ii).

The due process hearing must be conducted by an "impartial" hearing officer. Thus, the hearing officer may not be employed by the public agency involved in educating the child and may not have any other apparent conflict of interest with respect to the proceeding. The parties to the hearing have a right to counsel and traditional due process rights to present evidence, confront and cross-examine witnesses (as well as to compel attendance of witnesses), and obtain a verbatim record of the hearing. Either party may prohibit the production of any evidence that has not been disclosed to that party at least five days before the hearing. The hearing officer's decision must be in writing and must include written findings of fact. 20 U.S.C. § 1415(f).

The hearing officer must reach a final decision within 45 days after receipt of the request for a hearing. 34 C.F.R. § 300.515(a). In those states that provide for a hearing at the local level, the losing party may appeal to the SEA. For those states in which an administrative appeal lies with the SEA, an appellate administrative decision must be rendered within 30 days of receipt of a request for review. 34 C.F.R. § 300.515(b). The decision at the state level (either the hearing officer's decision in a one-tier administrative procedure or the appellate decision in a two-tier administrative procedure) may be appealed by commencing a civil action in either a state or federal court, at which the court may receive additional evidence. The court's decision to affirm or reverse the administrative decision will be based on a preponderance of the evidence. 20 U.S.C. § 1415(i)(2)(C)(iii) When parents prevail through the administrative process and the LEA (or appropriate government agency) fails to implement the decision and does not appeal to court, the parents may seek court enforcement of the administrative decision in federal court via 42 U.S.C. § 1983 which requires compliance with federal laws.

The hearing officer's decision may be based on substantive or procedural grounds. If the hearing rules in the parent's favor based on procedural grounds, then the hearing officer must determine that the procedural inadequacies: (1) "impeded the child's right to a free appropriate public education," (2) "significantly impeded the parents' opportunity to participate in the decisionmaking process," or (3) "caused a deprivation of educational benefits." 20 U.S.C. § 1415(f)(3)(E)(ii). These rules clarify that parents cannot prevail on the basis of minor procedural errors on the part of the school district.

D. THE "STAY-PUT" PROVISION

Recognizing that continuity and stability, although beneficial to all children, are particularly important to children with disabilities, the IDEA includes a mechanism called the "stay-put" provision. If the mere proposal of a change in placement were sufficient to require implementation of the proposed change, the child could become subject to a "yo-yo" effect. Frequent changes would occur, with the possibility that a child could be shuttled back and forth between alternative placements. This type of system would also be unmanageable.

Accordingly, the IDEA provides that "[d]uring the pendency of any proceedings . . . unless the State or local educational agency and the parents otherwise agree, the child shall remain in the then current educational placement of such child." 20 U.S.C.A. § 1415(j). Pursuant to this proviso, when the LEA and the parents of a disabled child disagree about a proposed change in the child's educational placement, the child must remain in his or her present educational placement while an administrative dispute or subsequent judicial proceeding is pending. Particularly difficult problems arise when the "present educational placement" no longer exists, either due to the actions of the public agency or as a result of outside forces.

The 2004 Amendments added one change to this long-standing "stay put" rule to help schools deal with discipline issues. School personnel have the discretion to order a change of placement "for a child with a disability who violates a code of school conduct" and may "remove" a child with a disability (instead of ordering a change of placement) for not more than 10 school days when the student violates a code of conduct from their current placement. 20 U.S.C. § 1415(k)(1). In other words, schools may use the standard discipline rules that apply under the IDEA even when the placement is a source of dispute with the parent.

Despite the stay-put provision, the public agency and parents can always agree to change the placement provided to the child (without prejudice to either party's position) while the parties proceed with their dispute. If the dispute relates to initial admission to the public school, the child, with the consent of the parents, is placed in the regular public school program until completion of all proceedings. *Id.*

There is no language in the IDEA, nor any indication in its legislative history, that the law was intended to limit the traditional deference to parents in making significant decisions for their children. Parental prerogative to decide whether to enroll a child in the local school district or in some other acceptable educational situation remains. Thus, the stay-put provision effectively operates only to limit the actions of the school district, except to the extent that a disabled child's parents are unable to place the child elsewhere due to limited funds or the unavailability of an alternate placement. Parents who make a unilateral placement choice, however, do not thereby create a new stay-put placement that must be funded.

The status quo must be maintained for as long as the review proceedings continue, unless a court directs otherwise. In effect, therefore, the stay-put provision of the IDEA acts as an *automatic* preliminary injunction. It is *automatic* because the mere request for a hearing requires maintaining, not changing, the child's placement. There is no requirement to demonstrate a probability of success on the merits, which is typically a prerequisite to the granting of a preliminary injunction. *See, e.g., Drinker by Drinker v. Colonial School Dist.*, 78 F.3d 859 (3d Cir. 1996). *But see Doe v. Brookline Sch. Comm.*, 722 F.2d 910, 919 (1st Cir. 1983) (stay-put provision entitles the parents to a preliminary injunction unless the School District can demonstrate that the application of the traditional preliminary injunction criteria warrant a different result).

Despite the stay-put proviso, if the parents and education agency otherwise agree, the child may be placed into any mutually agreeable placement while the present dispute continues. This enables educators and parents to consider the best interests of the child without concern for the legal ramifications of such an educational decision. An agreement to maintain the child or to move the child to some particular educational placement while litigation ensues does not create a new status quo, so long as both parties understand and agree that it is for the limited purpose of an interim placement until the dispute is finally resolved. Accordingly, in *Verhoeven v. Brunswick School Committee*, 207 F.3d 1 (1st Cir. 1999) the court held that a disabled student's "current educational placement" at the time of challenge to the proposed IEP for the next school year was not his recently-concluded temporary placement at a private school. Thus, his parents were not entitled to a "stay put" injunction compelling the school district to fund an interim placement at that school during the pendency of the challenge to the IEP. The parties had agreed in a settlement agreement to temporarily place the student at the private school "only through the end of the 1997–1998 school year," and agreed that the purpose of the temporary placement was to transition the student to placement at the public high school in the next school year.

The question of what constitutes a change in educational placement is, necessarily, fact specific. The "then current placement" that must be maintained is the general nature of that placement, not each and every single element of it. For instance, a change in the location of the program, in and of itself, has been held not to constitute a change in the placement. It is the nature of the placement, rather than all of its particulars, that is addressed by the stay-put provision. *See, e.g., J.S. v. Lenape Regional High School Dist. Bd. of Educ.*, 102 F.Supp.2d 540 (D.N.J. 2000). On the other hand, it has been held that a change in the program that will *substantially* or *significantly* affect the programs and services being provided to the child constitutes a change in placement. Such a change is not permitted.

The "then current placement" may not be discontinued by subterfuge or back-door activity. Accordingly, withdrawal of funding, although not a direct change of placement, has generally been held impermissible, since in effect it results in a change in placement. *See, e.g., Drinker v. Colonial School District*, 78 F.3d 859 (3d Cir. 1996).

If the existing placement is in dispute in pending proceedings, the "then current placement" cannot be changed by the expiration of an IEP and the creation of new one. *See, e.g., Board of Educ. of Pawling Cent. School Dist. v. Schutz*, 137 F.Supp.2d 83 (N.D.N.Y. 2001). Courts have adopted the same approach with placements created by expired temporary settlement agreements; the stay put provision keeps in the placement in effect as long as proceedings are pending. *See, e.g., Doe by Doe v. Independent School Dist. No. 9 of Tulsa County*, 938 F.Supp. 758 (N.D.Okl. 1996).

So-called "temporary" changes in placement may become more than temporary, and thereby violate the stay-put requirement. An example involves a suspension of more than ten days, which is discussed in chapter 18 of this *Nutshell*.

§ 12.5   CONFIDENTIALITY OF AND ACCESS TO RECORDS

Parents of children with disabilities are entitled to an opportunity to inspect and review all educational records relating to the identification, evaluation and placement of their child, and all records related to the provision of a FAPE for the child. *See* 20 U.S.C. § 1415(b)(1). The educational agency may charge a reasonable fee for copies, but it may not charge a fee to search for or retrieve information. Courts have held that the failure to disclose certain confidential information to parents can render the district liable. *See, e.g., Savino v. Board of Educ. of School Dist. No. 1, Westbury*, 506 N.Y.S.2d 210 (N.Y. App.Div. 1986).

Any parent who believes that information in his or her child's educational records is inaccurate or misleading, or violates the privacy or other rights of the child, may request that the education agency amend the information. In the event that the agency declines to amend the information, the parent has a right to a hearing conducted by the education agency. If the parent prevails, the records must be amended. If the parent does not prevail, he or she can place a statement in the child's records commenting on the challenged information. *Id.* §§ 300.567–300.569.

Information contained in a child's educational records is confidential. It cannot be shared with outside parties unless the consent of the parents is first obtained or the outside party is a specifically delineated agency such as another school or school system in which the student seeks or intends to enroll, the United States Secretary of Education, or the SEA. *Id.* § 300.571. The access and confidentiality rights promulgated pursuant to the IDEA are very similar in scope and nature to the regulations promulgated pursuant to The Family Educational Rights and Privacy Act (FERPA). 20 U.S.C.A. § 1232g. In *Gonzaga University v. Doe*, 536 U.S. 273 (2002), the Court held that a person whose records were disclosed in violation of FERPA has no right to sue the institution for its violation of the statute. At least one district court, however, has ruled that parents may sue a school district for the release of confidential information during a due process hearing. *Sean R. v. Board of Educ. of Town of Woodbridge*, 794 F.Supp. 467 (D.Conn. 1992).

§ 12.6   "ZERO REJECT" PRINCIPLE

The IDEA was premised on a "zero reject" principle. This concept assumes that *all* children with disabilities, regardless of the severity of their disabilities, are entitled to receive a FAPE. In accord with this precept, in *Timothy W. v. Rochester, New Hampshire, School District*, 875 F.2d 954 (1st Cir. 1989), the First Circuit reversed a lower court ruling holding that the IDEA did not require the school district to provide educational services for a multidisabled child who was allegedly unable to "benefit" from special education. The First Circuit followed the generally acknowledged understanding of the IDEA in holding that the statute "makes clear that a 'zero reject' policy is at the core of the Act", and that there is no requirement under the Act "that a [disabled] child must demonstrate that he or she will 'benefit' from the educational program." *Id.*

The "zero reject" principle has also been extended to children with communicable diseases. The courts have generally held that, in the absence of a significant health hazard, children with communicable diseases should not be excluded from school. *See, e.g., Ray v. School Dist. of DeSoto County,* 666 F.Supp. 1524 (M.D.Fla. 1987) (holding that school children who tested seropositive for HIV should be admitted to normal and regular integrated classroom settings, subject to guidelines adopted by the court, unless and until it could be established that the children posed a real and valid threat to the school population). For more on the safety issue, see § 7.28 of this *Nutshell.*

§ 12.7   EXTRACURRICULAR ACTIVITIES

The IDEA applies to *all* facets of a disabled child's educational program. *See* 20 U.S.C. § 1414(d)(1)(A)(i)(IV)(bb) (stating that special education services must also be provided to allow the child "to participate in extracurricular and other nonacademic activities"). Under this rule, services must be provided for extracurricular and nonacademic activities so long so long as those programs are mentioned as "appropriate activities" in the IEP itself.

Courts have held that a child with a disability would be entitled to participate in an extracurricular activity if that activity is included in the student's IEP as part of his or her special education program. *See, e.g., Dennin v. Connecticut Interscholastic Athletic Conference, Inc.*, 913 F.Supp. 663 (D.Conn. 1996) (holding inclusion of participation of interscholastic sports in an IEP transforms it into a federally protected right, and due process is required before student can be deprived of that right). *But see M.H. v. Montana High Sch. Ass'n*, 929 P.2d 239 (Mont. 1996) (holding that a high school student who did not have a formal IEP under the IDEA, but only an informal one-page letter "IEP" under the Rehabilitation Act did not have a federally protected right to participate in interscholastic sports in high school after reaching age 19). If the activity is not included in an IEP, a child with a disability is only entitled to an equal opportunity for participation. These principles will presumably govern application of the so-called "no pass, no play" rule used by many school districts. This rule conditions participation in extracurricular activities upon a student's maintaining an acceptable grade-point average. If participation in a given extracurricular activity is included in a disabled student's IEP, the IEP would have to be revised—after complying with all the procedural safeguards on the IDEA—before a disabled student could be dropped from that activity.

§ 12.8   INFANTS AND TODDLERS
WITH DISABILITIES

The provisions of Part B of the IDEA apply to children with disabilities ages three to 21 (unless a child with a disability has legally and voluntarily dropped out of school or obtained a diploma). The 1986 amendments provide for incentive grants to those states that submit plans approved by the United States Secretary of Education and provide special education and related services to disabled children ages three to five.

The 1986 amendments also established a Part H (termed Part C by the 1997 Amendments) to the IDEA to protect the interests of infants and toddlers with disabilities 20 U.S.C.A. §§ 1431–1445. Part C requires a statewide system of coordinated, comprehensive, multidisciplinary, interagency programs providing appropriate early intervention services by the beginning of the fifth year of a state's participation under that program. When enacting this legislation, Congress recognized that early intervention enhances the development of infants with disabilities, minimizes their potential for developmental delay, reduces overall educational costs, enhances the capacity of families to meet the special needs of their disabled infants and toddlers, minimizes the likelihood of the institutionalization of such children, and maximizes the potential for individuals with disabilities eventually to live independently in society.

Infants and toddlers with disabilities within the meaning of the IDEA are those children under 3 years of age who require intervention services because they are experiencing developmental delays or have a diagnosed physical or mental condition that has a high probability of resulting in developmental delay. *Id.* § 1432(5). Depending on state law, disabled infants and toddlers may also include children from birth through age two who are at risk of having substantial developmental delays if early intervention services are not provided. The 2004 Amendments specify that states must include a "rigorous definition" to ensure that all eligible children are covered. *See* 20 U.S.C. § 1435(a)(1). The state must also use "scientifically based research, to the extent practicable" in defining appropriate early intervention services. *Id.* at § 1435(a)(2).

Early intervention services under the IDEA are developmental services provided ˙under public supervision that are designed to meet the child's needs in physical development, cognitive development, language and speech development (communication development), psychosocial development (social or emotional development) and/or the development of self-help skills (adaptive development). These services may include the following:

(i) family training, counseling and home visits,

(ii) special instruction,

(iii) speech-language pathology and audiology services, and cued language services;

(iv) occupational therapy,

(v) physical therapy,

(vi) psychological services,

(vii) service coordination services,

(viii) medical services only for diagnostic or evaluation purposes,

(ix) early identification, screening, and assessment services,

(x) health services necessary to enable the infant or toddler to benefit from the other early intervention services,

(xi) social work services,

(xii) vision services,

(xiii) assistive technology devices and assistive technology services, and

(xiv) transportation and related costs that are necessary to enable an infant or toddler and the infant's or toddler's family to receive early intervention services. . . .

20 U.S.C.A. § 1432(4)(C). The 2004 Amendments added "sign language and cued speech services." This list of services is not intended to be exhaustive. The state must provide such services through qualified personnel. If the state fails to provide appropriate services, parents may seek reimbursement for parentally acquired appropriate services. *See, e.g., Still v. DeBuono*, 101 F.3d 888 (2d Cir. 1996).

The law permits the federal or state government to provide for a system of payments by families for such services, including a schedule of sliding fees. 20 U.S.C.A. § 1432(4)(B). Any such state system requiring payment by families is subject to some limitations, however. The regulations enacted pursuant to Part C, 34 C.F.R. §§ 303.520–303.521, prohibit the charging of fees for certain specified services, including those pertaining to evaluations, assessments and case management. Further, although states may establish reasonable standards regarding the ability and inability of parents to pay, such standards may not result in denial of services to an eligible child or the child's family because of inability to pay.

One of these services—service coordination—must be made available to disabled infants and toddlers and their families, although it is not required for school-age children. 20 U.S.C.A. § 1432(4)(E)(vii). "Case management" means activities conducted by a case manager to assist a Part C child and the child's family to receive the rights, procedural safeguards and services available under the state's early intervention program. Under Part C, each eligible child and his or her family must be provided with a case manager who is responsible for: (i) coordinating all services across agency lines; and (ii) serving as the single point of contact in helping parents obtain the services and assistance they need. 34 C.F.R. § 303.23(a)(2).

Case management is an active ongoing process that continuously seeks appropriate services in situations that will benefit the child's development. Case management activities, which are all carried out in conjunction with the family, include:

(1) Coordinating the performance of evaluations and assessments;

(2) Facilitating and participating in the development, review, and evaluation of individualized family service plans;

(3) Assisting families in identifying available service providers;

(4) Coordinating and monitoring the delivery of available services;

(5) Informing families of the availability of advocacy services;

(6) Coordinating with medical and health providers; and

(7) Facilitating the development of a transition plan to pre-school services, if appropriate.

34 C.F.R. § 303.23(b). State law is used to determine how case managers may be employed or assigned. Case managers are required, however, to have demonstrated knowledge and understanding of the services available under Part C and the infants and toddlers who are eligible for such services.

Early intervention services are generally not expected to be provided in center-based programs. The Act provides that such services "to the maximum extent appropriate, [should be] provided in natural environments, including the home, and community settings in which children without disabilities participate. . . ." 20 U.S.C.A. § 1432(4)(G).

Instead of describing programming services to be provided to the child in an IEP (as required for children ages 3 to 21 under the IDEA), Part C requires development of an individualized family service plan (IFSP). An IFSP is to be developed after "a multidisciplinary assessment of the unique strengths and needs of the infant or toddler" and "a family-directed assessment of the resources, priorities and concerns of the family. . . ." *Id.* § 1436(a). This plan must include the following: (1) a statement of the infant's or toddler's present levels of development; (2) a statement of the family's resources, priorities and concerns; (3) a statement of the "measurable results" (instead of "major outcomes") expected to be achieved for the child and family (as well as criteria, procedures and timelines used to determine progress); (4) a statement of specific early intervention services based on peer-reviewed research, to the extent practicable, necessary to meet the unique needs of the child and family; (5) a statement of the natural environments in which early intervention services will be provided including a justification of the extent, if any, to which the services will not be provided in a natural environment; (6) projected dates for initiation, and the anticipated duration, of services; (7) the name of the case manager (service coordinator); and (8) the steps to be taken to support transition services available to 3-year-olds and above. *Id.* § 1436(d). The 2004 Amendments also specified that the measurable results and outcomes should include "preliteracy and language skills, as developmentally appropriate for the child."

A child with an educational disability is entitled to receive a FAPE under Part B of the IDEA as of his or her third birthday. In order to avoid disruption of services to a disabled child who turns three while receiving early intervention services, the Act requires states to ensure a smooth transition to an IEP under Part B. Such a smooth transition includes convening a meeting among the Part C lead agency, the LEA and the family, if the parents approve, at least 90 days before the child's third birthday for the purpose of establishing a transition plan for the child. To assist in this regard, the Act authorizes state policy to permit an LEA and the parents to agree to continued implementation of an IFSP beyond a child's third birthday in order to effectuate a smooth transition to an IEP under Part B of the IDEA. 34 C.F.R. § 303.148.

An IFSP can be continued for a child after his or her third birthday, however, only if it is consistent with the requirements for an IEP. An IFSP may be used to provide a FAPE to three to five year olds if: (1) the State has a policy allowing IFSPs to be used for FAPE; (2) the LEA chooses to have an IFSP instead of an IEP; and (3) the parents or guardian concur. *OSEP Policy Letter*, 18 IDELR 783 (1991). The LEA must ensure that all parties necessary for an IEP meeting attend the IFSP meeting and that the IFSP contains projected dates for initiation of services and the anticipated duration of the services. If a child turns three years old during the summer, the child's IEP team shall determine the date when services under the IEP or IFSP will begin. 34 C.F.R. § 300.121(c)(2).

Part C requires each state system to establish and maintain a central directory of information. This directory must contain information concerning public and private early intervention services, resources, and experts available in the state. It must also provide information about professional and other groups (including parent support groups and advocate associations) that provide assistance to eligible children and their families. Further, each state's early intervention system must include a comprehensive child-find system. In addition to meeting the child-find requirements applicable to Part B of the Act, the child-find system must ensure that:

(1) All infants and toddlers in the State who are eligible for services under this part are identified, located, and evaluated; and

(2) An effective method is developed and implemented to determine which children are receiving needed early intervention services, and which children are not receiving those services.

34 C.F.R. § 303.321(b).

Part C also provides for procedural safeguards. Parental consent is required before the public agency may conduct an initial evaluation and assessment of a child or initiate the provision of early intervention services for the first time. This consent must be in writing and must be based upon the parent being fully informed of all information relevant to the activity for which consent is sought. Parents may later decline such a service after first accepting it, without jeopardizing other early intervention services. *Id.* § 303.404–303.405. As with school-age children, however, the public agency can initiate a due process hearing or other procedure to override a parent's refusal to consent to the initial evaluation of the child. Under Part C the public agency does not have the authority or responsibility to override parental refusal to consent to services.

Part C further provides that there must be a timely administrative resolution of parental complaints before a public agency or service provider initiates or changes, or refuses to initiate or change any Part C services. Each state has two options concerning the administrative resolution procedure it wishes to establish. 34 C.F.R. § 303.420. The first simply involves adopting the due process procedures applicable to school-age students with disabilities. The second is to establish procedures that meet the requirements set forth in the regulations promulgated pursuant to Part C: appointment of an impartial decision maker, application of basic due process rights in an administrative proceeding conducted at a time and place that is reasonably convenient to the parents, and the right to bring a civil action in state or federal court upon conclusion of the administrative process.

These protections are similar to those available to school-age children, with at least four apparent, significant differences. First, the decision written by the impartial decision maker must under Part C regulations be provided no later than 30 days after receipt of a parent's complaint. The school-age due process procedures permit 45 days. Second, while the school-age procedures permit states to establish a two-tier administrative system (a hearing plus appeal), the Part C regulations provide for only one administrative proceeding. Third, while school-age procedural safeguards include the parents' rights to obtain an independent educational evaluation (IEE), Part C does not require that parents be permitted the right to an IEE. Fourth, there is no explicit attorney's fees provision. *Id.* §§ 303.421–303.425.

Strictly similar protections in the two Acts include the stay-put and confidentiality provisions. The stay-put principle applicable under Part C is basically unchanged from Part B. A child who has not yet received any services must receive those services that are not in dispute while a complaint is being pursued. Further, as with school-age youngsters, confidentiality of information is protected.

CHAPTER 13

IDEA: APPROPRIATENESS/ LEAST RESTRICTIVE ENVIRONMENT; CONTINUUM OF EDUCATIONAL OPTIONS; RELATED SERVICES

§ 13.1   APPROPRIATENESS

Every child who is educationally disabled is entitled under the IDEA to receive a free appropriate public education (FAPE). A FAPE is defined in the Act as special education and related services that

(A) have been provided at public expense, under public supervision and direction, and without charge,

(B) meet the standards of the State educational agency,

(C) include an appropriate preschool, elementary, or secondary school education in the State involved, and

(D) are provided in conformity with the individualized education program required under section 1414(d) of this title.

20 U.S.C.A. § 1401(9).

The term "special education" means

[s]pecially designed instruction, at no cost to parents or guardians, to meet the unique needs of a child with a disability, including—

(A) instruction conducted in the classroom, in the home, in hospitals and institutions, and in other settings; and

(B) instruction in physical education.

Id. § 1401(29).

The term "related services" is defined as "transportation, and such developmental, corrective, and other supportive services (including speech-language pathology and audiology services, interpreting services, psychological services, physical and occupational therapy, recreation, including therapeutic recreation, social work services, school nurse services designed to enable a child with a disability to receive a free appropriate public education as described in the individualized education program of the child, counseling services, including rehabilitation counseling, orientation and mobility services, and medical services, except that such medical services shall be for diagnostic and evaluation purposes only) as may be required to assist a child with a disability to benefit from special education . . . " *Id.* § 1401(26). The 2004 Amendments added interpreting services and school nurse services and clarified that the term does not include a medical device that is surgically implanted or the replacement of such a device. *See Id.* § 1401(26)(B).

§ 13.2   THE *ROWLEY* CASE

The Supreme Court was called upon to address the meaning of an "appropriate education" in its first case involving the IDEA. In *Board of Education of the Hendrick Hudson Central School District v. Rowley,* 458 U.S. 176 (1982), the Court attempted to provide some guidance for the lower courts to apply in future cases.

A.   STANDARDS TO BE APPLIED BY COURTS

In *Rowley,* the issue before the Supreme Court was whether the IEP recommended by the LEA for Amy Rowley's first grade educational program was sufficient to provide her with an "appropriate education" as required by the Act. Amy, a deaf student with minimal residual hearing, was an excellent lip-reader. She was in a regular first grade classroom and had been provided with an FM hearing aid. She also received instruction from a tutor of the deaf for one hour each day and speech therapy for three hours per week. Amy's parents were concerned that Amy was missing too much of the classroom instruction by having to rely solely upon lip-reading and hearing aids. Accordingly, they requested that a qualified sign-language interpreter assist Amy in all of Amy's academic classes.

The hearing officer at the due process hearing agreed with the school district's determination that an interpreter was not necessary because " 'Amy was achieving educationally, academically, and socially' without such assistance." Amy's parents filed an administrative appeal with the New York State Commissioner of Education who affirmed the hearing officer's decision.

The federal district court, however, subsequently ruled in favor of the parents. Despite finding that Amy "performs better than the average child in her class and is advancing easily from grade to grade," that court also found that Amy "'understands considerably less of what goes on in class than she could if she were not deaf' and thus 'is not learning as much, or performing as well academically, as she would without her handicap.'" Accordingly, the district court concluded that Amy was not receiving a free appropriate public education, which it defined as "an opportunity to achieve [her] full potential commensurate with the opportunity provided to other children." The Second Circuit affirmed the district court's decision.

In reversing the Second Circuit's decision, the Supreme Court attempted to provide some guidance to the lower courts for the myriad of cases where they would address the question of appropriateness under the IDEA. It rejected the lower courts' holding that the services must be "sufficient to maximize each child's potential 'commensurate with the opportunity provided other children.'" The Supreme Court stated: "We do not think [there was] a congressional intent to achieve strict equality of opportunity or services."

Specifically, the Court in *Rowley* instructed lower courts to make a twofold inquiry in determining if a child's education was "appropriate":

First, has the State complied with the procedures set forth in the Act? And second, is the individualized educational program developed through the Act's procedures reasonably calculated to enable the child to receive educational benefits? If these requirements are met, the State has complied with the obligations imposed by Congress and the courts can require no more.

The Supreme Court cautioned, however, that

[i]n assuring that the requirements of the Act have been met, courts must be careful to avoid imposing their view of preferable educational methods upon the States ... [I]t seems highly unlikely that Congress intended courts to overturn a State's choice of appropriate educational theories in a proceeding conducted pursuant to [the Act].

The first inquiry required by *Rowley* is a procedural one. The Court noted that it had previously cautioned that "courts lack the 'specialized knowledge and experience' necessary to resolve 'persistent and difficult questions of educational policy.'" Accordingly, "once a court determines that the requirements of the Act have been met, questions of methodology are for resolution by the States."

The second prong of the *Rowley* approach, in which courts are to determine whether the IEP is reasonably calculated to enable the child in question to receive educational benefits, has been the subject of much litigation and some confusion. Accordingly, close scrutiny of the Supreme Court's explanation of this standard is essential.

The Court stated that a State satisfies the IDEA's "free appropriate public education" requirement

by providing personalized instruction with sufficient support services to permit the child to benefit educationally from that instruction. . . . In addition, the IEP, and therefore the personalized instruction, should be formulated in accordance with the requirements of the Act and, if the child is being educated in the regular classrooms of the public education system, should be reasonably calculated to enable the child to achieve passing marks and advance from grade to grade.

The Court further stated that there was no substantive standard prescribing the level of education to be accorded children with disabilities included in the Act. Instead, "the intent of the Act was more to open the door of public education to handicapped children on appropriate terms than to guarantee any particular level of education once inside." The Court concluded that the Act establishes a "basic floor of opportunity" consisting of "access to specialized instruction and related services which are individually designed to provide educational benefit to the handicapped child."

In holding that Amy Rowley was not entitled to a sign-language interpreter, the Court relied in large part on the fact that Amy was passing from grade to grade in a public school program. The Court stated:

When the handicapped child is being educated in the regular classrooms of a public school system, the achievement of passing marks and advancement from grade to grade will be one important factor in determining educational benefit.

In *Rowley*, Amy was not only passing from grade to grade; she was in the upper half of her class. The Court noted, however, that

We do not hold today that every handicapped child who is advancing from grade to grade in a regular public school system is automatically receiving a "free appropriate public education."

It also stated: "We do not attempt today to establish any one test for determining the adequacy of educational benefits conferred upon all children covered by the Act." Finally, the Court balanced its statement that the IDEA provides only a basic floor of opportunity guaranteeing a right to educational benefit, by further stating that "[t]he determination of when handicapped children are receiving *sufficient* educational benefits to satisfy the requirements of the Act presents a more difficult problem" and limiting its description of sufficient educational benefit to the circumstances presented by Amy Rowley.

Thus the Supreme Court in *Rowley* set forth a two-pronged test, one procedural and one somewhat substantive, for courts to apply in determining whether children with disabilities have been provided a FAPE. The Court indicated that the individual needs of the child, as determined by an IEP, are the appropriate focus. Further, the Court held that children with disabilities do not have an enforceable right to achieve their maximum potential, but rather are entitled only to receive *some* educational benefit, the sufficiency of which is to be left to a case-by-case analysis.

B. APPLICATION OF THE FEDERAL STANDARD

1. *Procedural Violations as Denial of a FAPE*

The IDEA and its implementing regulations establish procedural safeguards for children and their parents. These procedural protections for families act as mandates upon LEAs, intermediate educational units (IEUs) and SEAs. In *Rowley*, the Supreme Court established the principle that an educational agency's failure to comply with the procedures set forth by the Act constitutes sufficient reason to rule that a child with a disability has been denied a FAPE. The 2004 Amendments clarified that the hearing officer should only find that a child has been denied a FAPE if the procedural inadequacy: (1) impeded the child's right to a free and appropriate public education, (2) significantly impeded the parents' opportunity to participate in the decisionmaking process regarding the provision of a FAPE, or (3) caused a deprivation of educational benefits. *See* 20 U.S.C. § 1415(f)(3)(E)(ii).

2. *Reasonably Calculated to Provide Educational Benefits*

The second prong of the *Rowley* test requires a child's IEP to be reasonably calculated to provide educational benefits. The Supreme Court held that a child with a disability is not entitled to an IEP designed to permit him or her to reach his or her ultimate or optimum potential. Stated another way, the Act does not require a child with a disability to be provided with the best education. The IDEA only entitles a child with a disability to an "appropriate" education.

To determine whether an IEP is reasonably calculated to provide educational benefit for a child, the court must do an analysis of the unique needs of that particular child. This individualized analysis by the court (which the LEA is also required to make in developing the IEP) often provides the significant information necessary to determine whether a particular placement is appropriate. In some situations, such an analysis may show that a particular policy or procedure is an impediment to designing a personalized placement or program. In other instances, refusal by a child and the parents to cooperate with the stipulations in the IEP may render an otherwise appropriate IEP inappropriate, at least insofar as it applies to those conditions sought by the parents.

The extent of educational benefit being received, or to be received, by the child is a significant factor in determining appropriateness. The courts generally interpret *Rowley* as requiring an IEP to provide *"meaningful"* educational benefit. *See, e.g., T.R. v. Kingwood Township Bd. of Educ.*, 205 F.3d 572 (3d Cir. 2000); *Derek B. ex rel. Lester B. v. Donegal School Dist.*, 2007 WL 136670 (E.D. Pa. 2007); *S.H. v. State-Operated School District of the City of Newark*, 336 F.3d 260 (3rd Cir. 2003); *L.G. and E.G. on behalf of E.G. v. Wissahickon School District,* 2011 WL 13572 (E.D. Pa. 2011). The distinction between minimal and sufficient educational benefit cannot be made in a vacuum. A close appraisal of the child's past progress, or lack of progress, frequently can be the strongest indicator of the appropriateness of a particular placement. Thus, courts have felt comfortable in concluding that a child is receiving an appropriate education when he or she has progressed adequately in a given placement and have found the converse when progress has been inadequate.

The 2004 Amendments have arguably raised the standards by emphasizing the "appropriateness" of annual goals and progress towards those goals. *See* 20 U.S.C. § 1414(d)(1)(A)(i)(IV). The IDEA has also tried to integrate its standards with those contained in No Child Left Behind Act of 2001 (NCLB). Both laws emphasize that proficiency in reading, math, and science by 2013–2014 is expected for all students with disabilities along with all other students. *See* 20 U.S.C. § 6301 *et seq.* (No Child Left Behind). Both NCLB and the IDEA focus on the need for peer-reviewed research in setting goals and in determining whether those goals have been met. *See* 20 U.S.C. § 1414(d)(1)(A)(iv).

In addition to a student's progress, another issue that frequently must be considered when assessing whether a child with a disability is receiving an appropriate education is the meaning of the term "education" with respect to that child. Since the IDEA addresses *all* children who are educationally disabled, many different disabilities and different degrees of severity of disability must be addressed. The required starting point for determining what "education" means for a particular child will vary based upon the child's disability and its severity and the individual characteristics of the child. Accordingly, the educational needs of a child with a disability frequently include non-academic as well as academic areas.

For children with such disabilities as emotional problems, for example, addressing the child's needs that result from the disability cannot be limited merely to providing academic services. Similarly, in order for deaf or hearing-impaired children to adapt to the hearing, speaking world, they need to be provided with intensive speech training. In such situations, the term "educational benefit" encompasses more than just academic subjects. For youngsters with very severe disabilities, education is often largely non-academic. In such situations, an appropriate education requires addressing those skills that will assist the child to function as well as is reasonably possible in an independent fashion. The 2004 Amendments, however, emphasize that all children should have academic goals— developmental, behavioral or functional goals are not enough. *See* 20 U.S.C. § 1414(d)(1)(A)(i)(II).

Although LEAs have the initial responsibility to assure that a child with a disability receives a FAPE, the SEA bears the ultimate responsibility. Accordingly, the SEA must step in and take necessary action when an LEA is either unable or unwilling to do so. 20 U.S.C.A. § 1413(h)(1)(B).

§ 13.3 INCORPORATION OF STATE STANDARDS

The definition of a FAPE includes the requirement that the special education and related services provided to a child with a disability must meet the standards of the SEA. 20 U.S.C.A. § 1401(9). This provision recognizes that education has traditionally been considered in the state's domain, rather than in the domain of the federal government. A FAPE, as construed in *Rowley*, consists of a properly developed IEP that is reasonably calculated to provide educational benefits to the child. In *Rowley*, however, the Court emphasized that this standard constitutes a federal floor of opportunity, but *not* a ceiling upon the right to educational services. Accordingly, higher state standards are incorporated into the IDEA whenever they are not inconsistent with the Act.

A State standard that is weaker than the federal requirement must step aside in favor of the basic floor of opportunity guaranteed by the Act. On the other hand, when a state standard is more stringent or demanding than the minimum requirements of the IDEA, the state standard will be applied. The actualization of a higher state standard may assist the parents in some factual circumstances, while in certain limited circumstances it may support the position of the educational officials. In either event, the higher state standard is presumably intended to benefit the child with a disability.

Included in the state standards incorporated in the Act are those addressing licensure and certification of professionals who are to provide special education or related services.

§ 13.4   COST

The Act mandates that special education and related services be provided to children with disabilities without charge. Governmental officials have nonetheless sometimes attempted to create exceptions to this requirement, generally to no avail. Disputes have also arisen when school districts have attempted to obtain payments from parents' private insurance carriers or other third party payors, an issue discussed later in § 14.5 of this *Nutshell*.

In *Cedar Rapids Community School District v. Garrett F.*, 526 U.S. 66 (1999), the Court refused to read an "undue burden" exception into the IDEA. The school district argued it was not required to provide a ventilator-dependent student with certain nursing services during school hours because of the cost involved. The Court acknowledged that the district might have legitimate financial concerns but stated that "[d]efining 'related services' in a manner that *accommodates* the cost concerns Congress may have had, is altogether different from using cost

itself as the definition." *Id*. at 77. (Emphasis in
original). The IDEA does not include "cost" in its
definition of "related services," and the Court said
that "accepting the District's cost-based standard as
the sole test for determining the scope of the
provision would require us to engage in judicial
lawmaking without any guidance from Congress."

Even though it is clear that parents may not be
charged for educational or related services provided
to their children with disabilities, a significant fiscal
issue still remains as to whether educational
officials may consider cost as a factor when making
a placement or other educational decision. Even
after *Garrett F.* courts have held that cost can be
considered without violating the IDEA if the school
district is considering two different programs that
each would provide a FAPE. *See, e.g., L.B. v. Nebo
School Dist.*, 214 F.Supp.2d 1172 (D.Utah 2002),
partially overturned 379 F.3d 966 (10th Cir. 2004);
*J.P. ex rel. Popson v. West Clark Community
Schools*, 230 F.Supp.2d 910 (S.D.Ind. 2002).

§ 13.5   EXTENDED SCHOOL YEAR

The traditional school year continues for
approximately ten months or 180 school days.
Several cases have addressed the issue of whether
this time limitation must be extended for children
with disabilities who would benefit from a longer
school year; most, if not all, of the courts have
answered that question affirmatively.

Some courts have based their rulings upon the
inflexibility of the 180-day rule and its conflict with

the Act's mandate to individualize when determining an appropriate education for each child with a disability. Other courts have based their decisions upon a determination that the children in question had a so-called regression-recoupment problem. This problem occurs when: (1) a child suffers an inordinate or disproportionate degree of regression during that portion of the calendar year in which the 180-day school year is not in session, and (2) it takes an inordinate or unacceptable length of time for the child to recoup those skills that have been lost. Accordingly, the child requires more than the 180-day school year in order to avoid the regression-recoupment problem. The mere fact of likely regression is not a sufficient basis to support an extended school year (ESY) because all students, disabled or not, may regress to some extent during lengthy school breaks. Instead, ESY Services are only required if the regression will substantially thwart the goal of "meaningful progress." *See, e.g., MM v. School District of Greenville County*, 303 F.3d 523 (4th Cir. 2002); *Coleman v. Pottstown School District*, 983 F.Supp.2d 543 (E.D. Pa. 2013).

This analysis has also been applied to non-academic areas, such as those involving emotional, behavioral and social concerns. And, in *Johnson v. Independent School District No. 4 of Bixby*, 921 F.2d 1022 (10th Cir. 1990), the Tenth Circuit opined that *all* the factors that are typically considered when determining a FAPE should also be involved when analyzing the appropriateness of an extended school year. In *Reusch v. Fountain*, 872 F.Supp. 1421

(D.Md. 1994) the court held that: (i) extended school year services cannot be limited to a rigid formula and (ii) at least three factors must be considered in determining whether a student is eligible for such services, including whether the student's progress toward developing emerging skills and critical life skills will be inappropriately interrupted without the provision of an extended school year. Thus, the court held that it is inappropriate to make a determination as to the student's need for an extended school year based solely on regression-recoupment standards.

§ 13.6   CONTINUUM OF EDUCATIONAL OPTIONS

In support of the least restrictive environment (LRE) mandate and the FAPE requirement, the regulations promulgated pursuant to the IDEA require that:

(a) Each public agency must ensure that a continuum of alternative placements is available to meet the needs of children with disabilities for special education and related services.

(b) The continuum required under paragraph (a) of this section must:

(1) Include the alternative placements listed in the definition of special education under § 300.38 (instruction in regular classes, special classes, special schools, home

instruction, and instruction in hospitals and institutions); and

(2) Make provision for supplementary services (such as resource room or itinerant instruction) to be provided in conjunction with regular class placement.

34 C.F.R. § 300.115.

Requiring the existence of a continuum of alternative placements not only helps ensure the availability of an appropriate program for each child with a disability; it provides some protection against a child with a disability being placed in a setting more restrictive than necessary because a less restrictive alternative is unavailable due to a gap in the continuum. Regardless of an LEA's actions, the SEA bears the ultimate responsibility for ensuring that an adequate continuum of placement options exists.

§ 13.7   INTERRELATIONSHIP BETWEEN LRE AND APPROPRIATENESS

Primary attention must be given to providing a child with a disability with a FAPE. Application of the LRE principle (discussed in chapter 12 of this *Nutshell*) although important, is secondary to ensuring appropriateness. The Act requires that every child with a disability must be placed in the least restrictive environment "to the maximum extent *appropriate*." 20 U.S.C. § 1412(a)(5). Thus, not all children are to be educated in a regular education setting. This principle is further evidenced by the requirement that a continuum of alternatives be available—including restrictive settings—as well as by the Act's emphasis upon individualization when determining what is appropriate for each child with a disability.

Thus, when making any placement decision with a respect to a child with a disability, the first criterion that must be satisfied is that the placement is appropriate (or, as stated in *Rowley*, that the placement is reasonably calculated to enable the child to receive educational benefits). As discussed earlier, a child with a disability is not entitled to the best education, but only to an appropriate education. The least restrictive alternative—from among those placements that have been determined to be appropriate—is the placement that must be chosen.

There is no simple rule for LRE that can be easily applied to every child with a disability. This is because a determination of what is appropriate must be made before one can finally apply the LRE principle. Accordingly, courts have ordered institutional or quite restrictive placements for some children because such placements were required to provide an appropriate education. In most cases, residential or institutional placements have only been upheld or ordered where a child has a very severe or profound disability. For other children with disabilities, particularly those with limited physical needs, services can be configured to enable the child to attend the regular school in the child's neighborhood. In all instances, however, an

LEA must adequately inquire into the particular, individualized special education needs of each student to properly arrive at a placement which is both appropriate and the least restrictive alternative.

§ 13.8   APPLYING THE PROPER STANDARD

The courts have not developed a uniform standard to be utilized when determining whether a child is being provided an appropriate education in the LRE. One of the earlier, and oft-cited, cases to address this issue was *Roncker v. Walter*, 700 F.2d 1058 (6th Cir. 1983). In holding that the child should be placed in the regular elementary school, the court stated:

> The Act does not require mainstreaming in every case but its requirement that mainstreaming be provided to the *maximum* extent appropriate indicates a very strong congressional preference. . . . In a case where the segregated facility is considered superior, the court should determine whether the services which make that placement superior could be feasibly provided in a non-segregated setting. If they can, the placement in the segregated school would be inappropriate under the Act.

Roncker has been described as establishing the "portability" test: if the particular services that make a more restrictive setting more appropriate can be transported to a less restrictive setting, such a modification is required by the LRE mandate.

Courts are to (1) compare the benefits the child would receive in special education with those she would receive in regular education; (2) consider whether the child would be disruptive in the non-segregated setting; and (3) consider the cost of mainstreaming.

A second standard was enunciated in *Daniel R.R. v. State Board of Education*, 874 F.2d 1036 (5th Cir. 1989) which declined to follow the *Roncker* test, holding that the portability test impermissibly intrudes upon decisions to be made by school districts. Nonetheless the Fifth Circuit was careful to point out that it did not require all children with disabilities to perform on the same level as nondisabled children. The court further recognized that the benefits of mainstreaming are not limited solely to academics. In recognition of the strong preference in favor of mainstreaming, the Fifth Circuit applied its own two-part test for determining compliance with the mainstreaming requirement of the IDEA.

> First, we ask whether education in the regular classroom, with the use of supplemental aids and services, can be achieved satisfactorily for a given child. . . . If it cannot and the school intends to provide special education or to remove the child from regular education, we ask, second, whether the school has mainstreamed the child to the maximum extent appropriate.

In *Daniel R.R.*, the Fifth Circuit provided further direction for lower courts to follow by setting forth several factors that, although not necessarily constituting an exhaustive list, should be utilized in applying the court's two-part test. The court was careful to point out, however, that no single factor would be dispositive in all cases. Concerning the first stage of the *Daniel R.R.* test, the court said the first factor to be examined is "whether the state has taken steps to accommodate the handicapped child in regular education." Then, if the public agency is providing supplementary aids and services and is modifying its regular educational program, the court must examine whether the educational agency's efforts are sufficient. The question of sufficiency must be viewed in a realistic and practical manner. The court noted that "regular educational instructors [are not required] to devote all or most of their time to one handicapped child or to modify the regular educational curriculum beyond recognition."

The Fifth Circuit next examined whether the child would receive educational benefit from regular education. This task requires focusing "on the student's ability to grasp the essential elements of the regular education curriculum." The inquiry must extend, however, beyond the mere academic benefits the child may receive; the court must also inquire into the child's overall educational experience, and "balanc[e] the benefits of regular and special education for each individual child." Finally, the Fifth Circuit indicated that there should be some focus upon the "effect the handicapped child's presence has on the regular classroom environment and, thus, on the education that the other students are receiving."

If it is determined, after applying this test, that education in the regular classroom cannot be satisfactorily achieved, the second prong of the *Daniel R.R.* test would be applied. Under that prong, the court must determine "whether the child has been mainstreamed to the maximum extent appropriate." Presumably, the same factors would be applied when evaluating the appropriateness of each succeedingly more restrictive alternative. Since school districts are required to offer a continuum of services, the LEA must take intermediate steps where necessary because the absence of an appropriate alternative in the continuum cannot be used as an excuse for not providing appropriate services.

Several courts have followed the reasoning in either *Roncker* or *Daniel R.R.* or some variation thereof. In *Sacramento City Unified School District v. Holland*, 14 F.3d 1398 (9th Cir. 1994), however, the court applied a hybrid of the *Daniel R.R.* and *Roncker* tests. That approach involves a four-factor balancing test, weighing the following factors:

(1) The educational benefits of full-time placement in a regular class;

(2) the non-academic benefits of such placement;

(3) the effect the student with a disability has on the teacher and children in the regular class; and

(4) the cost of mainstreaming the student with a disability.

§ 13.9   PROXIMITY TO HOME

The regulations enacted pursuant to the IDEA require that "[e]ach public agency shall ensure that . . . each [disabled] child's educational placement . . . [i]s as close as possible to the child's home. . . ." 34 C.F.R. § 300.116(b)(3). Courts disagree on whether this regulation creates a presumption that the least restrictive environment is in the child's neighborhood school. *Compare Murray v. Montrose County Sch. Dist.*, 51 F.3d 921 (10th Cir. 1995) (holding the regulations do not create a presumption that the neighborhood school is the least restrictive environment for a child's education) *with Oberti v. Board of Educ.*, 995 F.2d 1204 (3d Cir. 1993) ("There is thus a presumption in favor of placing the child, if possible, in the neighborhood school, and if that is not feasible, as close to home as possible.") As with the other aspects of the LRE principle, however, the primary concern is to provide an appropriate education for each disabled child. Thus, if the neighborhood school cannot provide a FAPE, the LEA is not necessarily required to place the child with a disability in that neighborhood school.

Moreover, the concept of placing a child with a disability as close to home as possible does not override the exercise of proper administrative discretion by school districts in utilizing resources in an efficient manner. School districts may permissibly concentrate resources at particular schools for particular needs and disabilities.

At least one court has held that the needs of a child with a disability, as identified in an IEP, may require an LEA or SEA to enter into an interagency agreement to provide a regional or state program. In *Todd D. v. Andrews*, 933 F.2d 1576 (11th Cir. 1991), the court held that since a child's IEP identified a need to prepare him for transition into the community, an out-of-state residential program was not appropriate for that child. The court concluded that the student "must therefore be placed at a facility close enough to his community to allow implementation of his transition goals."

§ 13.10 INCLUSION

In *Oberti v. Board of Education of Clementon School District*, 801 F.Supp. 1392 (D.N.J. 1992), the district court built upon the LRE requirement to find a presumption in favor of inclusion. The district court required the school district to place a student with Down Syndrome in the regular education classroom, with sufficient supplemental aids and services, rather than in the self-contained setting recommended by the LEA. The district court stated that "School Districts . . . must consider placing children with disabilities in regular classroom settings, with use of supplementary aids and services, including classroom assistants, *before* exploring other, more restrictive, alternatives." The district court relied initially upon the reasoning in *Roncker*, but went beyond that reasoning in stating:

> Success in special school and special classes is unlikely to lead to [this child] functioning successfully either in integrated education settings or in the community. . . . Inclusive

public education for children with disabilities offers substantial benefits for children with disabilities, for their non-disabled peers, as well as for the community at large. This type of education increases the opportunities for individuals with disabilities to become fully-functioning, co-equal members of society.

The district court held that the presumption in favor of inclusion can only be rebutted by the school district's showing that: (1) the child will receive little or no benefit from inclusion; (2) the child is so disruptive that he or she would significantly impair the education of other children in the classroom; or (3) the cost of providing inclusive education would significantly affect other children in the school district. The district court concluded its analysis by stating:

> [This child] should not have to earn his way into an integrated school setting by first functioning successfully in a segregated setting. Inclusion is a right, not a privilege for a select few. Success in special schools and special classes does not lead to successful functioning in integrated society, which is clearly one of the goals of the IDEA. . . . We take particular notice of the potential for harm when a child with a disability is educated in a segregated milieu.

The Third Circuit affirmed the decision of the district court in *Oberti v. Board of Education of Clementon School District*, 995 F.2d 1204 (3d Cir. 1993). The appellate court reached the same result as the district court, but explicitly stated that it was applying the two-part test set forth in *Daniel R.R.* Further, in maintaining that the burden is on an LEA to justify its conclusion that a child with a disability should not be included in the regular classroom, the Third Circuit stated:

> In practical terms, the school has an advantage when a dispute arises under the Act: the school has better access to the relevant information, greater control over the potentially more persuasive witnesses (those who have been directly involved with the child's education), and greater overall educational expertise than the parents.

The Third Circuit thus concluded that the LRE principle "would be turned on its head if parents had to prove that their child was worthy of being included, rather than the school district having to justify a decision to exclude the child from the regular classroom."

Many proponents of inclusion believe that all students with disabilities should be fully educated in the regular education environment (with integrated special education). There are instances, however, where the social benefits of inclusion are outweighed by mainstreaming's effect on the disabled child's academic achievement or its impact on the learning environment for other students in the classroom. *See, e.g., Hartmann v. Loudoun County Bd. of Educ.*, 118 F.3d 996 (4th Cir. 1997) (holding the presumption for an inclusive placement with sufficient supportive services was rebutted by the net negative benefits on the child and the disruptive effects on other children).

§ 13.11   PROVISION OF RELATED SERVICES

The definition of "related services" is set forth in chapter 12.3(D) of this *Nutshell*. This section discusses issues involved in the provision of the related services which are listed in the disabled child's IEP and become part of the appropriate education that must be provided to the child at no cost.

Regardless of whether a related service is or is not specifically listed in the Act or its regulations, it is essential that the service be related to and assist a child with a disability to benefit from special education. Thus the child who is to receive the related service must be classified as educationally disabled. The Supreme Court has noted that "[i]n the absence of a handicap that requires special education, the need for what otherwise might qualify as a related service does not create an obligation under the Act." *Irving Independent School District v. Tatro*, 468 U.S. 883 (1984).

There is one exception to the requirement that a child with a disability must otherwise receive special education so as to be entitled to receive a related service. The federal regulations allow a state to define what would otherwise be a related service (such as occupational therapy or physical therapy) as "special education" itself.   34   C.F.R. § 300.39(a)(2)(i). This is done for financial reasons. Some children are entitled to such services under

Section 504, and, if the state did not classify them as "special education," it would be required to provide them but not be able to receive funding for the services under the IDEA.

A. ISSUES CONCERNING SPECIFIED RELATED SERVICES

Even though a service is listed in the Act or its regulations as a related service, issues of dispute still arise. For example, the Act provides that medical services should be provided as related services (and thus at no cost to the family) *only when* such services serve diagnostic or evaluation purposes. Thus, disputes sometimes arise about whether a medical service is relevant to determine: (1) whether a child should be classified as disabled (or which label of disability should be applied to the child), or (2) what placement or services should be provided to the child. If the medical service is relevant to determining the proper classification or educational placement of a child with a disability, it is held to be a related service. If the medical service is not relevant to determining the proper classification or educational placement of a child with a disability, however, it will not constitute an educationally related service since it was not used for a diagnostic or evaluation purpose. The need to receive what would otherwise be considered educationally related services in a hospital setting does not, by virtue of the provision of services in a hospital, convert those services to medical services.

Another area of controversy involving specified forms of related services concerns transportation. Because transportation is a specifically listed form of related service, it has been held that an LEA must transport a child with a disability to and from school or where services are received even when the school the child attends is a private one or one in another school district. *See, e.g., Union School Dist. v. Smith*, 15 F.3d 1519 (9th Cir. 1994). Transportation is not required, however, where the parent's request for such transportation was made for personal reasons unrelated to the student's educational needs. *See, e.g., Fick v. Sioux Falls School Dist.*, 337 F.3d 968 (8th Cir. 2003). Nor is it required if parents unilaterally place a child in a private school. *See, e.g., Barwacz v. Michigan Dept. of Ed.*, 681 F.Supp. 427 (W.D.Mich. 1988).

At least one court, however, has held that for transportation to be considered a related service, the need for transportation must be specifically related to the unique needs caused by the child's disability. *See, e.g., McNair v. Oak Hills Local Sch. Dist.*, 872 F.2d 153 (6th Cir. 1989) (holding that lack of relationship between student's need for transportation and her hearing impairment precluded imposition of obligation on school district to provide free transportation). In *Donald B. v. Board of School Commissioners of Mobile County*, 117 F.3d 1371 (11th Cir. 1997), however, the court held that the IDEA requires transportation if it is necessary for a child to benefit from special education "even if that child has no ambulatory impairment that directly causes a 'unique need' for some form of specialized transport." In determining whether transportation as a related service was necessary, the court considered:

(1) [the disabled child's] age; (2) the distance he or she must travel; (3) the nature of the area through which the child must pass; (4) his or her access to private assistance in making the trip; and (5) the availability of other forms of public assistance in route, such as crossing guards or public transit.

B. "MEDICAL" SERVICES

Services that address the physical or health condition of a child have been a frequent source of litigation. Such disputes revolve around the question of whether the service at issue is an educationally-related service or a "medical" service that does not constitute a related service under the Act.

The DOE opined that a service will be considered "medical" if a physician is required to provide it—unless the physician is performing the service for diagnostic or evaluation purposes. To the converse, DOE concludes that if the services do not require a physician and can performed by a school nurse (or other properly trained employee) during school hours, such services will not be considered to be "medical."

In *Irving Independent School District v. Tatro*, 468 U.S. 883 (1984), the Supreme Court addressed the question of whether clean intermittent catheterization (CIC) was a "medical" service. The Court concluded that the DOE had reasonably determined that the term "medical services" referred only to services that must be performed by a physician and not to school health services. Accordingly, it held that CIC, which is often, though not always, performed by a nurse, is not an excluded medical service.

The Court revisited the "medical services" issue in *Cedar Rapids Community School District v. Garrett F.*, 526 U.S. 66 (1999), where it refused to read an "undue burden" exception into the IDEA. The school district argued it was not required to provide a ventilator-dependent student with continuous nursing services during school hours because of the cost involved. The Court stated:

> Continuous services may be more costly and may require additional school personnel, but they are not thereby more "medical." Whatever its imperfections, a rule that limits the medical services exemption to physician services is unquestionably a reasonable and generally workable interpretation of the statute. Absent an elaboration of the statutory terms plainly more convincing than that which we reviewed in *Tatro,* there is no good reason to depart from settled law.

Id. at 76.

The Court acknowledged that the district might have legitimate financial concerns but stated that "[d]efining 'related services' in a manner that *accommodates* the cost concerns Congress may have had, is altogether different from using cost *itself* as the definition." *Id.* at 77 (Emphasis in original). The IDEA does not include "cost" in its definition of "related services," and the Court said that "accepting the District's cost-based standard as the sole test for determining the scope of the provision would require us to engage in judicial lawmaking without any guidance from Congress."

When a non-related medical service such as private-duty nursing is necessary to enable a child with a disability to attend school, other sources of funding may be available. For example, a child with a disability receiving nursing services under Medicaid can require such nursing services to be provided outside of the home for normal life activities such as attending school.

Another area of controversy relates to the Act's inclusion of psychological services and counseling services as related services. To some degree, these terms overlap. The term "psychotherapy" does not appear anywhere in the statute or regulations, and courts disagree over whether it is included in the definition of related services. Some courts have held that psychotherapy, even when conducted by a medical doctor, is not necessarily a "medical" service which is not covered by the IDEA. *See, e.g., Max M. v. Thompson*, 585 F.Supp. 317 (N.D.Ill. 1984) (the court included a caveat, however, stating the service would be "medical" if it "can only be provided by a psychiatrist"). To the converse, at least one court has opined that psychotherapy by persons other than physicians—at least for an emotionally disturbed child hospitalized in an acute-care facility—is not a related service when the purpose is primarily to address the child's medical needs. *Clovis Unified School District v. California Office of Administrative Proceedings*, 903 F.2d 635 (9th Cir. 1990). By way of further contrast, at least one court found psychological and counseling services provided as a component of a private psychiatric hospital placement to constitute related services. *Tice v. Botetourt County School Board*, 908 F.2d 1200 (4th Cir. 1990).

C.   ISSUES CONCERNING NON-SPECIFIED RELATED SERVICES

Because of the Act's open-ended language permitting "such developmental, corrective, and other supportive services . . . as may be required to assist a child with a disability to benefit from special education . . . " to be considered related services, 20 U.S.C.A. § 1401(26), each case must be addressed on an individual basis and compared to this definition. Under this approach, both residential placement and summer enrichment activities have been held to be related services. Moreover, the regulatory inclusion of "parent counseling and training" as related services may warrant training in sign language for parents of a deaf child as support for the child's special education program, as well as counseling and training in techniques to address inappropriate child behaviors. Transition services may also be provided as a related service.

Assistive technology devices and services are defined in the Act. An assistive technology device is

any item, piece of equipment, or product system, whether acquired commercially off the shelf, modified, or customized, that is used to increase, maintain, or improve functional capabilities of individuals with disabilities.

20 U.S.C.A. § 1401(1). For example, a calculator could qualify as an assistive technology device for a student with a learning disability in a regular education math class.

The Act defines an assistive technology service as any service that directly assists an individual with a disability in the selection, acquisition, or use of an assistive technology device. Such term includes—

(A) the evaluation of the needs of an individual with a disability, including a functional evaluation of the individual in the individual's customary environment;

(B) purchasing, leasing, or otherwise providing for the acquisition of assistive technology devices by individuals with disabilities;

(C) selecting, designing, fitting, customizing, adapting, applying, maintaining, repairing, or replacing of assistive technology devices;

(D) coordinating and using other therapies, interventions, or services with assistive technology devices, such as those associated with existing education and rehabilitation plans and programs;

(E) training or technical assistance for an individual with disabilities, or, where appropriate, the family of an individual with disabilities; and

(F) training or technical assistance for professionals (including individuals providing education and rehabilitation services), employers, or other individuals who provide services to, employ, or are otherwise substantially involved in the major life functions of individuals with disabilities.

20 U.S.C.A. § 1401(2).

The IDEA regulations provide that assistive technology is available as part of a child's special education, related services or supplementary aids and services to enable the child to remain in the regular educational environment. 34 C.F.R. § 300.114(a)(2)(ii). Further, if assistive technology is required for home use to provide a child with a disability with a FAPE, such technology will need to be provided at home.

CHAPTER 14

IDEA: PRIVATE SCHOOLING; PERSONS IN A PARENTAL ROLE; TESTING AND EVALUATION; THIRD-PARTY PAYMENTS

§ 14.1 PRIVATE SCHOOLING FOR CHILDREN WITH DISABILITIES

Children with disabilities whose parents (as opposed to the school district) place them in private schools without programs designed specifically for special education may still be entitled to receive special education or related services, or both, from their local education agency (LEA). The IDEA requires a state's plan to set forth policies and procedures assuring that:

> to the extent consistent with the number and location of children with disabilities in the State who are enrolled in private elementary and secondary schools, provision is made for the participation of such children in the program assisted or carried out under this subchapter by providing for such children special education and related services. . . .

20 U.S.C.A. § 1412(a)(10)(A)(i). LEAs—as well as intermediate educational units (IEUs)—are required to assure that their school district policies and programs will be administered in the manner required by the state's plan.

A.   CHILDREN WITH DISABILITIES IN NON-RELIGIOUS SCHOOLS

An LEA must be prepared to provide a FAPE to any child with a disability residing within its jurisdiction. Parents of children with disabilities, however, are not required to avail themselves of a proffered placement. They may instead choose to place their children in private schools, even schools that do not adhere to state standards for the education of disabled children. Children with disabilities in such placements are identified as "private school children with disabilities," and those placements are deemed voluntary. 20 U.S.C. § 1412(10). The 1997 Amendments to the IDEA, as well as the DOE's IDEA regulations, provide that the local school district is not required to pay for the education of a child with a disability at a private school when the school district offers an appropriate placement. *Id.* § 1412 (C). For a discussion of what happens if the school district's placement is found *not* to be appropriate, see chapter 16 of this *Nutshell*.

The state education agency (SEA) and the LEA in which the child resides each have some responsibility, however, to ensure that voluntarily placed private school children with disabilities receive appropriate special education and related services. *See generally* 20 U.S.C. § 1412(a)(10).

The DOE has interpreted this provision narrowly. The DOE contends that children with disabilities who are voluntarily enrolled in private school do not have a right to a FAPE. The DOE has stated that the IDEA does not provide children enrolled by their parents in private schools with an individual entitlement to receive special education and related services. Rather, an LEA must follow a process of consultation with representatives of the private school students to determine, among other things, which children with disabilities enrolled in private school should be served.

Under the DOE's view, SEAs and LEAs must provide students enrolled in private schools only with a "genuine opportunity for equitable participation" in programs assisted or carried out under Part B of the IDEA. *See generally* 34 C.F.R. § 300.137 & 300.138.

The DOE does require LEAs to allot a proportionate amount of federal funds for special education and related services for disabled children in private schools based on the number and location of disabled students residing in their jurisdiction. *See* 34 C.F.R. § 300.233. LEAs need not exceed this obligation and are not required to utilize local and state funding for special education and related services. Thus, for example, suppose 300 children with disabilities (covered under the IDEA) reside in "X" school district. Suppose also that 30 of those 300 children with disabilities, or 10%, are voluntarily placed by their parents in private schools. Ten percent of the *federal* money allocated to X school district for the education of those 300 children must be allocated for necessary services for the 30 children voluntarily enrolled in private schools. (Note that the 1997 Amendments do not obligate school districts to spend *state* monies to provide children voluntarily enrolled in private schools with special education and related services.) Under the 1997 Amendments. "[n]o private school child with a disability has an individual right to receive some or all of the special education and related services that the child would receive if enrolled in a public school." 34 C.F.R. § 300.137(a).

The IDEA Amendments of 1997 also state that LEAs *may*, but are not required to, provide services "on the premises of private, including parochial, schools, to the extent consistent with the law." 20 U.S.C. § 1412(a)(10)(A)(i)(III). In *KDM v. Reedsport School Dist.*, 196 F.3d 1046 (9th Cir. 1999), the court stressed the uniformity with which courts have upheld the permissiveness of the IDEA: "Every circuit [court] that has considered whether the IDEA . . . requires services to be provided on site at a private school has concluded it does not."

If services pursuant to the Act are provided at a location other than the private school site, "a parentally-placed private school child with a disability must be provided transportation . . . [f]rom the child's school or the child's home to a site other than the private school . . . and [f]rom the service site to the private school, or to the child's home, depending upon the timing of the services." 34 C.F.R. § 300.139(b)(1)(i)(A)–(B). School districts are not required, however, to provide transportation from the child's home to the private school, and the cost of the transportation may be included in the proportionate amount of federal funds spent on private school students. *Id.* §§ 300.139(b)(1)(ii), (2). For more on the transportation issue, see § 13.11(A) of this *Nutshell*.

B.   CHILDREN WITH DISABILITIES IN RELIGIOUS SCHOOLS

The First Amendment's prohibition against the establishment of religion raises a constitutional issue when a child with a disability attends a religious school. In *Zobrest v. Catalina Foothills School District*, 509 U.S. 1 (1993), however, the court held that the First Amendment does not present a bar to an LEA providing a sign-language interpreter for a deaf student attending a parochial school. The Court observed that the establishment clause does not bar religious groups from receiving general government benefits. Otherwise, "a church could not be protected by the police and fire departments, or have its public sidewalk kept in repair." The Court reasoned:

> government programs that neutrally provide benefits to a broad class of citizens defined without reference to religion are not readily subject to an Establishment Clause challenge just because sectarian institutions may also receive an attenuated financial benefit.

After concluding that the IDEA is such a government program, the Court noted that the availability of interpreter services does not result in additional funding for the religious school. The Court viewed the dynamics of its decision as "according parents freedom to select a school of their choice."

The *Zobrest* Court also addressed another concern—the presence of a public employee (the interpreter) in a religious school assisting a student's religious education. The majority found two factors in *Zobrest* to be significant: (1) the interpreter service did not relieve the parochial school of a cost it otherwise would have borne; and (2) the task of a sign-language interpreter is quite different from that of a teacher or guidance counselor.

As noted above, however, the IDEA Amendments of 1997 state that LEAs *may*, but are not required to, provide services "on the premises of private, including *religious*, schools, to the extent consistent with the law." 20 U.S.C. § 1412(a)(10)(A)(i)(III) (emphasis added). Courts have interpreted that rule so as not to require school district to provide services at religious school so long as state is spending proportionate amounts on special education services for children in private schools. *See, e.g., KDM v. Reedsport School District*, 196 F.3d 1046 (9th Cir. 1999); *Foley v. Special School District of St. Louis County*, 153 F.3d 863 (8th Cir. 1998); *Russman v. Board of Education of City of Watervliet*, 150 F.3d 219 (2nd Cir. 1998). *See also Locke v. Davey*, 540 U.S. 712 (2004) (holding that state did not violate Free Exercise clause by refusing to fund devotional theology instruction).

Another issue involving the First Amendment arises when states treat students with disabilities in religious schools differently than other private school students. In *Peter v. Wedl*, 155 F.3d 992 (8th Cir. 1998), the court found there was a possible violation of the First Amendment's guarantees of free exercise and free speech and the Fourteenth Amendment's equal protection clause if IDEA-eligible students in parochial schools were treated differently than those in other private and home schools. In *KDM v. Reedsport School Dist.*, 196 F.3d 1046 (9th Cir. 1999), however, the court found that an Oregon regulation which permitted IDEA services to be offered to private school students only in a religiously-neutral setting did not impose an impermissible burden on the free exercise of religion or violate either the establishment clause or equal protection clause. The *KDM* decision is arguably consistent with the Supreme Court's decision in *Locke v. Davey*, 540 U.S. 712 (2004) in which it held that state did not violate Free Exercise Clause when it prohibited state aid to any post-secondary student pursuing a degree in theology.

To the extent that an LEA is expected to provide services at a site other than the parochial school, the First Amendment issues concerning separation of church and state should not come into play. Accordingly, as is the case with students attending non-religious schools, a school district would be expected to provide transportation to and from the public school location at which special education services are provided. For more on the transportation issue, see § 13.11(A) of this *Nutshell*.

C. HOME SCHOOLS

According to the DOE, "[s]tates have discretion to determine whether or not home education qualifies as a 'private school or facility' that implicates IDEA requirements." *Letter to Williams*, 18 IDELR 742 (1992). In *Hooks v. Clark Co. Sch. Dist.*, 228 F.3d 1036 (9th Cir. 2000), the court held that "Congress explicitly ratified [this] view that States must define the ambit of 'private schools'" because the amended IDEA provides that "[t]he term 'elementary school' means a nonprofit institutional day or residential school that provides elementary education, *as determined under State law*." The current IDEA's definition of "secondary school" is likewise committed to "State law." *Id.* § 1401(27).

In *Hooks*, a home schooled student's parents sued a school district alleging that its refusal to provide speech therapy services for the student violated the IDEA and the Fourteenth Amendment. The court ruled for the school district, finding that (1) states have discretion to determine whether home education qualifies as a "private school" under the IDEA; (2) the district's refusal of services did not violate the due process clause; and (3) neither the district's refusal of services nor the IDEA's delegation of such a decision to states violated the equal protection clause.

In *Forstrom v. Byrne*, 775 A.2d 65 (N.J. Super. A.D. 2001), the court agreed with *Hooks* regarding the states' discretion and ruled that home schooled children in New Jersey are not entitled to special education and related services under the IDEA. It also found, however, that denying speech therapy services to the child violated his rights under the New Jersey Constitution as applied to the specific child.

Despite these decisions, the hearing officer has the option of awarding reimbursement for a private placement that does not meet state standards when the local educational agency has not provided a free and appropriate public education. *See L.M. v. Evesham Township*, 256 F.Supp.2d 290 (D.N.J. 2003). *See also* 34 C.F.R. § 300.147(c) ("A parental placement may be found to be appropriate by a hearing officer or a court even if it does not meet the State standards that apply to education provided by the SEA and LEAs").

§ 14.2   PERSONS IN A PARENTAL ROLE

Under the IDEA, parents and guardians of children with disabilities play a central role. First, an LEA must encourage the participation of a child's parents or guardian when developing an IEP for a child with a disability. Further, extensive requirements are set forth in the Act to assure that children with disabilities and their parents or guardians are guaranteed procedural safeguards with respect to the provision of free appropriate public education. *See generally* 20 U.S.C.A. § 1415. Thus, parents have standing to challenge alleged violations of procedural safeguards.

The regulations promulgated pursuant to the IDEA define the term "parent" as:

(1) A biological or adoptive parent of a child;

(2) A foster parent;

(3) A guardian but not the State if the child is a ward of the State;

(4) A person acting in the place of a parent (such as a grandparent or stepparent with whom the child lives, or a person who is legally responsible for the child's welfare); or

(5) A surrogate parent who has been appointed in accordance with § 300.519.

34 C.F.R § 300.30(a).

A state may allow a foster parent to act as a parent if:

(1) The biological or adoptive parents' authority to make educational decisions on the child's behalf has been extinguished under State law; or

(2) A judicial decree or order identifies that person to act of the "parent" of a child or to make educational decisions on behalf of the child.

Id. § 300.30(b).

The selection of surrogate parents is governed by 34 C.F.R. § 300.519. Pursuant to that regulation, a surrogate parent should be appointed when no parent can be identified or located or when the child is a ward of the state. The educational agency responsible for assigning an individual to act as surrogate parent must ensure that the individual is not an employee of any other agency involved in the education or care of the child and has "no interest that conflicts with the interest of the child he or she represents" and "knowledge and skills that insure adequate representation of the child." *Id.* § 300.519(d)(2). A surrogate parent's responsibilities are to represent the child with a disability in all matters relating to: "(1) [t]he identification, evaluation and educational placement of the child, and (2) [t]he provision of FAPE to the child." *Id.* § 300.519(g).

§ 14.3   TESTING AND EVALUATION

A.   EVALUATION PROCEDURES

Parents must be provided with written notice when an LEA proposes to initiate an evaluation of a child suspected of being disabled. The requisite notice must explain all of the available procedural safeguards, set forth the proposed action, describe why the agency proposes to take such action, and include any other relevant factors. The notice must be understandable and must be provided in the native language or other mode of communication used by the parent unless it is not feasible to do so.

An LEA must obtain parental consent before conducting a pre-placement evaluation. 34 C.F.R. § 300.300(a). For such consent to be valid, the IDEA regulations require that:

(1) The parent [must have] been fully informed of all information relevant to the activity for

which consent is sought, in his or her native language, or other mode of communication;

(2) The parent understands and agrees in writing to the carrying out of the activity for which his or her consent is sought, and the consent describes that activity and lists the records (if any) which will be released and to whom; and

(3) The parent understands that the granting of consent is voluntary on the part of the parent and may be revoked at any time.

Id. § 300.9.

If the parents refuse to provide the requisite consent, the agency may pursue those evaluations through due process procedures, under §§ 300.300(a)(3)(i) unless doing so is inconsistent with State law on parental consent. Parents have the right to revoke their consent, but "that revocation is not retroactive (i.e., it does not negate an action that has occurred after the consent was given and before the consent was revoked)." *Id.* § 300.9(c)(2).

Parents are entitled to an opportunity to inspect and review all educational records with respect to the identification, evaluation and educational placement of their child. 34 C.F.R. § 300.501. Any testing and evaluation conducted pursuant to the IDEA must be racially and culturally unbiased. To qualify for financial assistance under the Act, each state must establish procedures to ensure that testing and evaluation materials and procedures are not racially or culturally discriminatory. 20 U.S.C.A. § 1412(6)(B).

Before an LEA may take action on the initial placement of a child with a disability, it must make sure that a "full and individual evaluation of the child's educational needs" is conducted. 34 C.F.R. § 300.301. There are specific procedures set forth in the regulations that must be followed when conducting an evaluation. *Id.* § 300.304. The procedures are designed to ensure that a comprehensive and multiperspective evaluation is conducted. Evaluations must use a variety of assessment tools, not use any single measure or assessment as the sole criterion for determining eligibility; and use technically sound instruments. *Id.* § 300.304(b). The child must be assessed in all areas of suspected disability. § 300.204(c)(4). Assessments must be administered by trained and knowledgeable personnel and be used for the purposes for which assessments are valid and reliable. § 300.204(c)(1).

B. REEVALUATIONS

Each child with a disability must be fully reevaluated at least every three years. This triennial evaluation must conform to the evaluation procedures described above. 34 C.F.R. § 300.303. In most respects, therefore, triennial evaluations are performed in the same fashion as initial evaluations. An LEA must obtain informed parental consent before conducting any reevaluation unless it can demonstrate that it had taken reasonable measures to obtain such consent and the child's parent has failed to respond. 20 U.S.C. § 1414(c)(3).

§ 14.4   INDEPENDENT EDUCATIONAL EVALUATIONS

An independent educational evaluation (IEE) is "an evaluation conducted by a qualified examiner who is not employed by the public agency responsible for the education of the child in question." 34 C.F.R. § 300.502(a)(3)(i). Parents of a child with a disability have the right to obtain an IEE. Upon request, each LEA must provide information to parents explaining where an IEE may be obtained. Whenever parents obtain an IEE, the public agency must consider that evaluation when making any decision regarding provision of a FAPE to the disabled child. In the event that there is a due process hearing, the IEE may be presented as evidence. *Id.* § 300.502(c).

The most significant practical issue involving IEEs concerns the question of who must bear the cost of obtaining the evaluation—the public agency or the parents. According to the IDEA regulations:

[a] parent has the right to an independent educational evaluation at public expense if the parent disagrees with an evaluation obtained by the public agency. However, the public agency may initiate a [due process] hearing ... to show that its evaluation is appropriate. If the final decision is that the evaluation is appropriate, the parent still has the right to an

independent educational evaluation, but not at
public expense.

34 C.F.R. § 300.503(b).

Once a parent requests an IEE at public expense,
the public agency must, "without unnecessary
delay," either 1) initiate a due process hearing or 2)
ensure that an IEE is provided at public expense,
unless it can demonstrate in a hearing that "the
evaluation obtained by the parent did not meet
agency criteria." *Id.* § 300.503(b)(2). A parent who
believes an LEA's delay either in paying for an IEE
or initiating a hearing is denying the parent's right
to a publicly funded IEE may request a due process
hearing. Although an LEA cannot be required to
choose between paying for an IEE and initiating a
hearing until after receiving a copy of the IEE, a
parent may initiate a hearing to compel an LEA to
finance an IEE if the unavailability of advance
funding would deny the parent the right to a
publicly funded IEE. *Letter to Anonymous*, 23
IDELR 719 (1995).

Parents are not required to notify the LEA before
obtaining an IEE, and the IEE may be conducted
before the multidisciplinary team meets to develop
the IEP. Whenever a hearing officer requests an
IEE, however, the cost of such an evaluation is at
public expense. *Id.* § 300.503(d).

When determining whether it will pay for an IEE,
an LEA must apply the same criteria utilized when
the LEA initiates an evaluation. *Id.* § 300.503(e).
The DOE has stated, however, that a school district

may establish maximum allowable charges for specific tests to ensure that the cost of a publicly funded IEE is reasonable. The maximum fee cannot be an average of fees customarily charged in the area by qualified professionals; it must allow parents to choose from among those qualified professionals and only eliminate unreasonably excessive fees. However, the district must give the parent an opportunity to demonstrate that unique circumstances justify going outside of the district's fee criteria, and the district must pay that fee if they do. *Letter to Anonymous*, 22 IDELR 637 (1994).

Ultimately, the question of whether an LEA must pay for an IEE of a child with a disability must be resolved on a case-by-case basis. A school district's financial responsibility turns on facts unique to the particular situation being addressed, such as whether the LEA evaluation is appropriate, whether the IEE is appropriate, and whether the IEE merely duplicates or corroborates an already existing LEA evaluation. Further, the nature of the evaluation in question will vary based upon the needs of the child, and upon what is relevant in order to determine a FAPE for the particular child with a disability. Thus, evaluations can take the form of a psychological evaluation, a psychiatric evaluation, or any evaluation designed to determine the nature and extent of special education and related services required, including an assistive technology evaluation.

The 1997 Amendments to the IDEA require that, five days prior to any due process hearing initiated by either parents or school district, each party must disclose all evaluations (and recommendations resulting from such evaluations) completed by that date that are intended to be used at the hearing. 34 C.F.R. § 300.512(b)(1). The 2004 Amendments retained that rule.

§ 14.5   THIRD-PARTY PAYMENTS

A.   PRIVATE INSURANCE

1. *Availability of Insurance Benefits*

The IDEA guarantees every child with a disability a right to a FAPE. The "free" portion of a FAPE is defined as "special education and related services that ... have been provided at public expense." 20 U.S.C.A. § 1401(9). The regulations promulgated pursuant to the IDEA provide:

> "[n]othing in this part relieves an insurer or similar third party from an otherwise valid obligation to provide or to pay for services provided to a child with a disability."

34 C.F.R. § 300.103(b). The purpose of this regulation is not to alleviate school districts' responsibilities to pay for services but simply to prevent insurers from disclaiming applicable responsibility.

Parents may use their insurance benefits to pay for related services or permit public agencies to access those benefits. When parents voluntarily choose to access their private insurance for such purposes, an insurance company cannot disclaim financial responsibility by claiming that the LEA is obligated under the IDEA to provide the services for which payment is being sought. In the event that insurance proceeds pay for only part of the cost of providing an educational service, the LEA must pay the remaining portion of the cost in order to guarantee that the parents and child are provided a FAPE.

A school district cannot condition the provision of special education services on the filing of an insurance claim, including a Medicaid claim. *See, e.g., Letter to Simon*, 17 EHLR 225 (1991). Further, parents must provide explicit consent to the filing of a claim against their insurance policy; the act of purchasing a policy does not, by itself, constitute consent. *See, e.g., Letter to Spinner*, 18 IDELR 310 (1991). States can suggest that families apply for Medicaid but cannot refuse to provide early intervention services if the family will not or does not apply for Medicaid coverage. *Letter to Frymoyer*, 25 IDELR 830 (1996).

Parents may not be *required* to make their insurance benefits available for services for their disabled children. The Department of Education has opined that an agency "may not compel parents to file an insurance claim when filing the claim would pose a realistic threat that the parents of handicapped children would suffer a financial loss not incurred by similarly situated parents of non-handicapped children." 45 Fed. Reg. 86390 (1980). Financial losses include, but are not limited to:

(1) A decrease in available lifetime coverage or any other benefit under an insurance policy;

(2) An increase in premiums or the discontinuation of the policy; or

(3) An out-of-pocket expense such as the payment of a deductible amount incurred in filing a claim.

Id. An agency may insist, however, that parents file a claim when they would incur only minor incidental costs such as the time required to complete the form. "For example, if benefits begin only after a $50.00 deductible, the agency may insist that the parents file a claim if it pays for the services and the deductible in advance." *Id.*

Under the DOE's interpretation, parents may demand reimbursement from the LEA when they have used insurance proceeds to pay for mandated services and such usage has depleted limited insurance benefits. *See, e.g., Raymond S. v. Ramirez*, 918 F.Supp. 1280 (N.D.Iowa 1996) (holding that parents were entitled to reimbursement for payments made by their health insurer for an IEE since the health insurance policy had lifetime cap and payment by insurer would reduce lifetime benefits); *Knable v. Bexley City School Dist.*, 238 F.3d 755 (6th Cir. 2001) (IEP failed to provide a FAPE where it required a behaviorally disabled child's parents to exhaust their own insurance coverage before the school district would pay, and the parents' family medical insurance plan contained a lifetime coverage limit for psychiatric care).

In addition to indicating what *cannot* be required of parents with respect to the use of insurance benefits, the DOE has clarified at least one instance in which an LEA *can* require parental action. The DOE has said that an LEA can compel parents to file a claim with their insurance company if the only financial effect of making such a claim is an increase in the premiums and the LEA offers to pay the increased cost of the premiums. A parent's refusal to file a claim under these circumstances, however, does not release the public agency from its obligation to provide a FAPE. *Letter to Newby*, 16 EHLR 549 (1990).

2. *Exclusionary Clauses*

Many insurance policies contain so-called "exclusionary clauses," which exclude insurance coverage for services or equipment that the insured is entitled to receive under federal law, such as the IDEA. The DOE has stated that the IDEA regulation, 34 C.F.R. § 300.103, does not nullify an insurance contract's exclusionary clause. That interpretation does not answer the question, however, of whether, or to what extent, an exclusionary clause can preclude an insurance carrier from being financially responsible for special education or related services. In *Chester County Intermediate Unit v. Pennsylvania Blue Shield*, 896 F.2d 808 (3d Cir. 1990), the court upheld exclusionary language in an insurance policy, stating that there was no evidence that Congress intended the IDEA to abrogate an exclusionary provision in a privately negotiated contract. Thus, the court held that, in accord with the exclusionary clause, the insurer was not liable to pay for related services (physical therapy) provided to a child with a disability pursuant to the IDEA.

3. *Insurers' Standing*

In situations in which students with disabilities are receiving services that are paid for by insurance policies, some insurance companies have attempted to shift the financial burden to an educational agency. The courts have generally refused such attempts, holding that the insurance companies lacked standing to file actions under the IDEA. *See, e.g., Allstate Ins. Co. v. Bethlehem Area School Dist.,* 678 F.Supp. 1132 (E.D.Pa. 1987); *but see Farmers Ins. Exchange v. South Lyon Community Schools,* 602 N.W.2d 588 (Mich.App. 1999) (holding that an insurance company had standing to seek judicial determination of whether certain benefits were related services "required to be provided" under the IDEA where it sought the determination for purposes of determining its entitlement to a setoff under the state's no-fault act rather than under the IDEA itself and where the school district stipulated to facts that would have been determined in an administrative review process).

B. MEDICAID REIMBURSEMENT

The Medicaid program, authorized under Title XIX of the Social Security Act, is designed to provide medical assistance to individuals whose resources are insufficient to meet the costs of necessary care and services. Under the Medicaid program, states that choose to reimburse certain costs of medical care for qualified needy persons receive federal financial assistance for services specified in a state plan approved by the Secretary of DHHS. Although state participation in the Medicaid program is optional, once a state elects to participate in the program it must comply with the requirements of the law.

In 1986 Congress amended the Medicare Catastrophic Coverage Act of the Social Security Act to state that nothing in Title XIX

shall be construed as prohibiting or restricting, or authorizing the Secretary to prohibit or restrict, payment ... for medical assistance for covered services furnished to a child with a disability because such services are included in the child's individualized education program established pursuant to ... [the IDEA] or furnished to an infant or toddler with a disability because such services are included in the child's individualized family service plan.

42 U.S.C.A. § 1396b(c).

The intent of Congress, as expressly stated when enacting this amendment, was to make it clear that matching federal Medicaid funds are available for the cost of health services covered under a state's Medicaid plan that are furnished to a child pursuant to the IDEA. Congress expressly stated that state Medicaid agencies remain responsible for related services provided pursuant to the IDEA if such services are covered under the state's Medicaid plan. Therefore, Medicaid may be available under the proper circumstances to reimburse educational agencies for the cost of both special education and related services. States can suggest that families apply for Medicaid but cannot refuse to provide early intervention services if the family will not or does not apply. *Letter to Frymoyer*, 25 IDELR 830 (1996).

The Centers for Medicare & Medicaid Services (CMMS) [formerly the Health Care Financing Administration (HCFA)] have promulgated a regulation seeking to limit the availability of Medicaid in some educational situations. The regulation provides that

payments to institutions for the mentally retarded or persons with related conditions and to psychiatric facilities or programs providing inpatient services to individuals under age 21 may not include reimbursement for formal educational services or for vocational services.

42 C.F.R. § 441.13(b).

CHAPTER 15

IDEA: PROCEDURAL ISSUES

§ 15.1 EXHAUSTION OF ADMINISTRATIVE REMEDIES

As discussed in § 12.2 of this *Nutshell*, the IDEA provides for both federal and private enforcement. For private enforcement, the Part B regulations provide parents with two means of resolving disputes under the IDEA: (i) an impartial due process hearing system, and (ii) a complaint resolution procedure (CRP) formerly known as EDGAR (Education Department General Administrative Regulations). This chapter will focus on the due process hearing procedures. Parents of a child with a disability must first follow these due process procedures before filing suit under the IDEA.

Parents who disagree with the IEP proposed for their child can request a due process hearing. 34 C.F.R. § 300.507. Once the hearing officer has rendered a decision, the losing party may seek an appeal of that decision. In those states that provide the initial hearing at the local level, a state-level administrative review is available and required as the next step. In those states in which the initial hearing is provided at the state level, the court is the next step. *Id.* §§ 300.510(b), 300.512.

In either event, the party disappointed at the state level is permitted to seek recourse from the courts. As a general rule, the courthouse doors are not open to an aggrieved party under the IDEA unless and until that party has first sought relief through the administrative process. It is not clear whether following EDGAR procedures or the present CRP, 34 C.F.R. §§ 300.660–300.662, constitutes exhaustion of IDEA remedies. *Compare Hoeft v. Tucson Unified School Dist.*, 967 F.2d 1298 (9th Cir.1992) (suggesting in dicta that a plaintiff could, as to certain types of claims, be required to exhaust the EDGAR procedure and stating that "[w]hether to require or to accept exhaustion of the EDGAR procedure as a substitute for exhausting IDEA procedures in challenges to facially invalid policies, however, is a determination which must be made on a case-by-case basis") *with Jeremy H. by Hunter v. Mount Lebanon School Dist.*, 95 F.3d 272 (3d Cir. 1996) (stating that the text of the CRP procedures and their regulatory history "both evince an expectation that invocation of the complaint procedures they establish will be elective, not mandatory").

Prior to the enactment of the Handicapped Children's Protection Act (HCPA) in 1986, parties attempted to circumvent the exhaustion requirement by alleging a violation of Section 504 of the Rehabilitation Act or of Section 1983 of the Civil Rights Act. Exhaustion of administrative remedies is not required under either of those statutes, nor under the Americans with Disabilities Act (ADA). The HCPA clarified the procedural requirements under the IDEA by explicitly requiring parties to pursue administrative remedies through the IDEA before seeking recourse via Section 504 or other statutes. 20 U.S.C.A. § 1415(*l*). To determine whether a plaintiff should be subjected to the IDEA's exhaustion requirement, courts focus on whether the relief sought by the plaintiff is available under the IDEA; *i.e.* whether it deals with the child's educational placement. While seemingly simple, this analysis can become complex in disability-based discrimination cases because of the significant overlap between the IDEA, the ADA, and the Rehabilitation Act. If the plaintiff is not seeking relief also available under IDEA, he or she would not be required to exhaust administrative remedies. *See, e.g., Hornstine v. Township of Moorestown*, 263 F.Supp.2d 887 (D.N.J. 2003); *J.T. v. Dumont Public Schools,* 438 N.J. Super. 241 (N.J. Superior Ct. App. Div. 2014).

This already complicated problem has become even more complicated by the 2008 Amendments to the ADA (and Section 504) that broadened the definition of disability under those statutes. Under the IDEA, a child is only eligible for services if the child "needs special education and related services." 20 U.S.C. § 1401(3). Under the ADA (and Section 504), a child is disabled if he or she "has a physical or mental impairment that substantially limits one or more major life activities." "Major life activities" include learning and concentrating. *See* 42 U.S.C. § 12102. Hence, a child with ADHD may need classroom accommodations and be covered by the ADA and Section 504 but not need "special education and related services" so not be covered by the IDEA. In that situation, a parent should arguably be able to sue a school district without exhausting the IDEA remedy. It is too early to know if the courts will interpret section 1415(*l*) to permit that possibility.

There are several general exceptions to the exhaustion doctrine that apply under the IDEA. First, a party is not required to exhaust administrative remedies where the administrative remedy is inadequate. Thus, a plaintiff need not exhaust administrative remedies when it would be futile to do so (such as where the relief requested is beyond the authority of the hearing officer). Futility cannot be established, however, by claiming that the administrative process is time consuming nor by a showing that the LEA has repeatedly failed to devise an appropriate IEP. *But see Sabatini v. Corning-Painted Post Area School Dist.*, 78 F.Supp.2d 138 (W.D.N.Y. 1999) (holding that the fact that a school district's administrative appeal from a decision in favor of the student was still pending did not preclude the student's IDEA suit; the time for final decision by the appellate board had passed and there was no indication of the reason for delay or the date when the appeal would be decided). However, other courts have, before deeming exhaustion futile, provided the SRO with one last chance to issue a decision. *Engwiller v. Pine Plains Cent. Sch. Dist.*, 110 F.Supp.2d 236, 245–46 (S.D.N.Y. 2000) (ordering SRO to issue decision within 10 days); *Murphy v. Arlington Cent. Sch. Dist. Bd. of Educ.*, No. 99 Civ. 9294, 1999 WL 1140872, at *4 (S.D.N.Y. Dec.13, 1999) (declining to excuse exhaustion where SRO scheduled to render decision within seven days). *See also Walsh v. King,*

2014 WL 4630691, at *3 (N.D. N.Y. 2014) (ordering the SRO to issue a decision within fourteen days and ruling that, if the SRO fails to comply, and the District's appeal is still undecided fourteen days from the filing of this Decision and Order, the Court will find exhaustion futile and exercise jurisdiction over Plaintiffs' claims).

Second, exhaustion is not required when the practical effect of requiring exhaustion would deny the ultimate relief being sought. This result would usually occur due to the delay that would inevitably be caused by pursuing the administrative process. For example, courts have not required exhaustion where a parent is trying to enforce the stay-put provision. *See, e.g., Murphy v. Arlington Cent. School Dist. Bd. of Educ.*, 297 F.3d 195 (2d Cir. 2002). Third, administrative remedies need not be pursued when the issue in dispute is a pure matter of law. *See, e.g., VanDenBerg v. Appleton Area School Dist.*, 252 F.Supp.2d 786 (E.D.Wis. 2003). Additional exceptions include those in which the legality of the administrative process itself is being challenged, where the adequacy of the administrative remedy is, for all practical purposes, co-extensive with the merits of the claim itself, or where no meaningful administrative process is available.

Other circumstances in which immediate access to the courts has been allowed include instances in which a policy of general applicability is being challenged, a class-action lawsuit is being pursued, systemic violations are alleged, procedural irregularities or deficiencies have affected a parent's ability to pursue administrative remedies, or it is clear that improper injury is occurring or is about to occur.

§ 15.2   STATUTES OF LIMITATION

The IDEA does not specify a statute of limitations that sets forth a time frame within which a party must file suit in court. The general rule is that when a federal statute does not provide for its own statute of limitations the court will look to the most appropriate, or analogous, state statute of limitations. This has led to different statutes of limitations being applied in lawsuits arising under the IDEA depending upon the particular state in which the action arose. Courts have followed the statutes of limitations for statutory causes of action, for administrative appeals, for actions upon liability created by federal statute or unspecified actions, among others, with time periods ranging from 30 days to six years. *See, e.g., Georgia State Dept. of Educ. v. Derrick C.*, 314 F.3d 545 (11th Cir. 2002) (30-day limit under Georgia law); *Murphy v. Timberlane Regional School Dist.*, 22 F.3d 1186 (1st Cir. 1994) (six-year limit under New Hampshire law). Similar reasoning—looking to an analogous state statute of limitations—is usually applied for due process hearings. *See, e.g., Manning v. Fairfax County School Bd.*, 176 F.3d 235 (4th Cir. 1999).

A court's declaration of the appropriate state statute of limitations for IDEA actions may not be sufficient, however, to determine whether a claim is time barred. For example, when a state statute of limitations is applied to the IDEA, other related state rules—such as tolling of the statute of limitations—may also be applicable. *See, e.g., C.M. v. Board of Educ. of Henderson County*, 241 F.3d 374 (4th Cir. 2001) (holding that school authorities did not provide the parents of disabled children with the required notice of the limitations period for requesting a due process hearing under IDEA, as mandated by North Carolina statute, so the 60-day limitations period could not be applied). An action accrues under the IDEA "when the parents know of the injury or the event that is the basis for their claim." *R.R. v. Fairfax County School Bd.*, 338 F.3d 325 (4th Cir. 2003).

Even when the statute of limitations does not prohibit an action, suit may be barred under the equitable doctrine of laches, which forbids unreasonable delays in filing suit. If a court determines that a party has unreasonably delayed commencing a lawsuit and that delay has prejudiced the other party, the court may bar the claim under the theory of laches. *See, e.g., Phillips v. Board of Educ. of Hendrick Hudson School Dist.*, 949 F.Supp. 1108 (S.D.N.Y. 1997).

§ 15.3   JUDICIAL REVIEW

The IDEA specifically provides that any party who is dissatisfied with the final administrative decision concerning a child with a disability may initiate a lawsuit in the appropriate state or federal court. 20 U.S.C.A. § 1415(i)(2)(A). Federal and state courts have been held to have concurrent jurisdiction to hear claims under the IDEA. In some situations, however, federal courts may decline to exercise jurisdiction, and instead defer to state courts. If the plaintiff brings a lawsuit in state court, it has been held that the defendant may remove the action to federal court.

When the LEA fails to implement an administrative order, the parents who have prevailed in the administrative process are not aggrieved parties entitled to judicial review under the IDEA; the parents are not objecting to the decision of the administrative hearing officer *per se*. Judicial review of the LEA's failure to implement the hearing decision may nonetheless be available under Section 1983 of the Civil Rights Act. *See, e.g., Blazejewski v. Board of Education of Allegany Central School District*, 599 F.Supp. 975 (W.D.N.Y. 1985).

The IDEA provides that in a court action under the Act the court

(i) shall receive the records of the administrative proceedings;

(ii) shall hear additional evidence at the request of a party; and

(iii) basing its decision on the preponderance of the evidence, shall grant such relief as the court determines is appropriate.

20 U.S.C.A. § 1415(i)(2)(B).

In *Board of Education of the Hendrick Hudson Central School District v. Rowley*, 458 U.S. 176 (1982), the Supreme Court provided further guidance concerning the role of the courts in actions arising under the IDEA. A court's inquiry is twofold: (1) to determine whether the educational agency has complied with the procedural requirements of the Act; and (2) to determine whether the IEP for the child is reasonably calculated to enable the child to receive educational benefits. The Supreme Court cautioned, however, that although a court should render its decision based upon the preponderance of the evidence, this is not "an invitation to the courts to substitute their own notions of sound educational policy for those of the school authorities which they review." The Court added that, because the Act directs the court to receive the records of the administrative proceedings, this "carries with it the implied requirement that due weight shall be given to these proceedings."

A. SCOPE OF REVIEW

Traditionally, when a court reviews administrative decisions, it gives great deference to the administrative decisionmaker. In such an instance, the court views itself as performing an appellate function. Since the IDEA calls for the court to base its decision upon a preponderance of the evidence, however, it is at least implied that in IDEA cases the court is not sitting in a stereotypical appellate role. Nonetheless, courts have made it clear that due weight must be given to the administrative decision. This standard of review is referred to as "modified *de novo*" review. *See, e.g., S.H. v. State-Operated School Dist. of City of Newark*, 336 F.3d 260 (3d Cir. 2003). The Seventh Circuit, however, has apparently adopted a more deferential standards. In *Dale M. v. Board of Educ. of Bradley-Bourbonnais High School Dist. No. 307*, 237 F.3d 813 (7th Cir. 2001) it stated that court should uphold an examiner's decision unless court is "strongly convinced that the order is erroneous". Purely legal questions, however, are reviewed *de novo. See, e.g., Morton Cmty. Unit Sch. Dist. No. 709 v. J. M.*, 152 F.3d 583 (7th Cir. 1998); *E.D. ex rel. Dukes v. Enterprise City Bd. of Educ.*, 273 F.Supp.2d 1252 (M.D.Ala. 2003).

On evidentiary matters, the trial court has the authority to admit and consider evidence if the additional evidence is necessary and the basic issue or controversy is the same as that addressed in the administrative process. Where the district court hears additional evidence, it is "free to accept or reject the agency findings depending on whether those findings are supported by the new, expanded record and whether they are consistent with the requirements of the Act." *S.H. v. State-Operated School Dist. of City of Newark*, 336 F.3d 260 (3d Cir. 2003); *see also Dale M. v. Board of Educ. of Bradley-Bourbonnais High School Dist. No. 307*, 237 F.3d 813 (7th Cir. 2001) ("When the court has before it evidence that was not before the hearing officers, the amount of deference due the reviewing officer declines, since the latter's decision was based on an incomplete record.").

B.   RIGHT TO TRIAL BY JURY

In *Whitehead By and Through Whitehead v. School Bd. for Hillsborough County*, 918 F.Supp. 1515 (M.D.Fla. 1996), the court held that the parents of a child with a disability were not entitled to a jury trial on an IDEA claim because the statute only allows injunctive relief and equitable damages. As seen in § 16.1 of this *Nutshell*, however, there is actually a split in authority on the availability of compensatory and punitive damages under the IDEA. More importantly, the *Whitehead* court also stated that the parents were entitled to jury trial for their claim based on Section 504 of Rehabilitation Act. For a broader discussion of the issue of jury trials for Section 504 claims, see § 4.3(E) of this *Nutshell*.

C.   DUE WEIGHT—GIVEN FOR WHAT

There is no consensus among the courts as to whom (or to what) "due weight" should be given. The Supreme Court stated in *Rowley* that the Act's requirement that the record of the administrative proceedings be received by the court "carries with it the implied requirement that due weight shall be given to these [administrative] proceedings." The Court's reference to administrative proceedings has resulted in a number of interpretations. In *Burilovich v. Board of Educ. of Lincoln Consol. Schools*, 208 F.3d 560 (6th Cir. 2000), the court noted that "the weight due will vary, depending on whether the court is reviewing procedural or substantive matters and whether educational expertise is essential to the administrative findings." Also, at least one court has held that no deference or weight should be given to administrative decisions when there is a conflict between the local hearing officer and the state hearing officer in a state with a two-tier administrative system. *Bonadonna v. Cooperman*, 619 F.Supp. 401 (D.N.J. 1985). Other courts have held that, where there is a conflict between the local hearing officer and state review officer and the difference is due to the credibility ascribed to a witness, no weight should be given to the state review officer's decision where he did not see or hear the witness testify. *See, e.g., Independent School Dist. No. 283 v. S.D.*, 88 F.3d 556 (8th Cir. 1996).

§ 15.4   BURDEN OF PROOF

The IDEA does not specify which party bears the burden of persuasion at the due process hearing. In *Schaffer v. Weast*, 546 U.S. 49 (2005), the Supreme Court held in a 6–2 decision that the burden of persuasion in an administrative hearing challenging an IEP is properly placed upon the party seeking relief, whether that is the child with a disability or the school district. The petitioner in this litigation recognized that the default rule is for the party seeking relief to have the burden of proof but he argued that that default rule should not apply where the non-moving party has great access to the facts. The Court held, however, that the IDEA gives parents numerous procedural protections to ensure that they have a realistic chance of collecting evidence.

§ 15.5   IMPARTIALITY OF HEARING OFFICERS

The Supreme Court indicated in *Rowley* that considerable reliance should be placed upon the procedures set forth in the IDEA to help ensure that children with disabilities are provided with appropriate educational placements. When a due process hearing is conducted pursuant to the IDEA, the hearing officer must be impartial in order to preserve the integrity of the process. Accordingly, a hearing officer, whether at a local or state level, may not be "an employee of the State educational agency or the local educational agency involved in the education or care of the child." 20 U.S.C.A. § 1415(f)(3). Further, no "person having a personal or professional interest which would conflict with his or her objectivity in the hearing" may serve as a hearing officer. 34 C.F.R. § 300.511(c)(1)(B).

There is some precedent to support the prohibition of an employee of one school district from serving as a hearing officer for another school district. In at least one case, the court recognized a conflict of interest in such a situation. *Mayson v. Teague*, 749 F.2d 652 (11th Cir. 1984). The same court also held that university personnel who had been involved in formulating state policies for special education were not sufficiently impartial to serve as due process hearing officers. Other courts have refused to follow the rationale of *Mayson*, concluding that individuals "who have devoted themselves professionally to the implementation of special education" are not necessarily "biased against the very children they have devoted their lives to helping." *Leon v. State of Michigan Board of Education*, 807 F.Supp. 1278 (E.D. Mich. 1992).

CHAPTER 16
IDEA: REMEDIES

§ 16.1   DAMAGES

There has been considerable litigation concerning whether courts have the authority to award monetary damages to plaintiffs who prevail in actions brought under the IDEA. This dispute revolves around language in the Act providing that

> [a]ny party aggrieved . . . shall have the right to bring a civil action. . . . In any [such] action . . . the court . . . shall grant such relief as the court determines is appropriate. . . .

20 U.S.C.A. § 1415(i)(2)(A), (B).

Until the Supreme Court's decision in *School Committee of the Town of Burlington v. Department of Education of Massachusetts*, 471 U.S. 359 (1985), some courts interpreted the statutory language— "such relief as the court determines is appropriate"—as permitting an award of damages for tuition reimbursement when the court determined that parents' voluntary placement of their child with a disability was necessary for the child to receive a FAPE. The *Burlington* decision clarified the fact that, while reimbursement of tuition for a properly made voluntary placement is permitted under the IDEA, such reimbursement is not considered a form of damages.

The *Burlington* case did not address the question of whether damages are an available remedy under the IDEA when reimbursement is not at issue. The majority of courts that have considered this issue have held that damages are generally not available under the IDEA or via actions to enforce it under 42 U.S.C.A. § 1983. A minority of courts, however, have held that damages are available under the Act and/or through Section 1983 actions.

One court rejecting damages stated that the claim before it was essentially for "educational malpractice" and followed an earlier ruling that damages were unavailable for such a claim. It said "[c]ompensatory or punitive damages would transform IDEA into a remedy for pain and suffering, emotional distress, and other consequential damages caused by the lack of a free appropriate public education" and "[s]uch a result would be inconsistent with the structure of the statute, which so strongly favors the provision of and, where appropriate, the restoration of educational rights." *Sellers v. School Board*, 141 F.3d 524 (4th Cir. 1998); *see also Polera v. Board of Educ. of Newburgh Enlarged City Dist.*, 288 F.3d 478 (2d Cir. 2002). Another court, however, held that nothing in the IDEA's text or history suggested that relief is limited in any way. It cautioned that a district court fashioning a remedy for an IDEA violation "may wish to order educational services, such as compensatory education beyond a child's age of eligibility, or reimbursement for providing at private expense what should have been offered by the school, rather than compensatory damages for generalized pain and suffering," but did not preclude the awarding of monetary damages. *W.B.*

v. Matula, 67 F.3d 484 (3d Cir. 1995); *see also Goleta Union Elementary School Dist. v. Ordway,* 166 F.Supp.2d 1287 (C.D.Cal. 2001).

Even if damages are held not to be available under the IDEA, damages may be available for a violation of other laws. The Handicapped Children's Protection Act (HCPA) amended the IDEA in 1986 to provide that: "[n]othing in this chapter shall be construed to restrict or limit the rights, procedures, and remedies available under the Constitution, title V of the Rehabilitation Act of 1973 . . . , or other Federal statutes protecting the rights of children and youth with disabilities." 20 U.S.C.A. § 1415(f).

Although the HCPA makes it clear that the remedies under the ADA, Section 504 and Section 1983 are not limited by the IDEA, the availability of damages may still be restricted by case law specifically applicable to Section 1983, Section 504 and Title II of the ADA. For a discussion on damages under Section 504 and ADA Title II, see §§ 4.3(A) and 7.28 of this *Nutshell.*

§ 16.2   REIMBURSEMENT

In *School Committee of the Town of Burlington v. Department of Education of Massachusetts,* 471 U.S. 359 (1985), the Court held that parents are entitled to reimbursement for expenses incurred for a unilateral placement that is ultimately determined to have been necessary to provide a FAPE for their disabled child. In *Burlington,* the school district recommended placing a child with a disability in a highly structured class within the school district.

Relying upon evaluations from outside experts, the parents wanted the child placed in a state-approved special education private school. Since the LEA and parents were unable to agree, the parents unilaterally placed their child in the private placement and sought reimbursement from the LEA. The LEA argued that the IDEA does not permit reimbursement.

The Supreme Court disagreed. It held that the statutory language calling for a court to "grant such relief as [it] determines is appropriate" should be given its ordinary meaning, and thus the language gives broad discretion to the court. This conclusion was influenced by the Court's perceptive understanding of the practicalities of implementing the procedural guarantees under the IDEA. The Court stated:

> A final judicial decision on the merits of an IEP will in most instances come a year or more after the school term covered by the IEP has passed. . . . [It] would be an empty victory to have a court tell [parents] several years later that they were right but that these expenditures could not in a proper case be reimbursed by the school officials.

In ruling that reimbursement is available to prevailing parents, however, the Court clarified that such reimbursement does not constitute damages, *per se*, but "merely requires the Town to belatedly pay expenses that it should have paid all along and would have borne in the first instance had it developed a proper IEP." Accordingly, even when an

LEA-proposed placement is not appropriate, if the unilateral placement is *also* not appropriate, the parents are not entitled to reimbursement.

With respect to the LEA's argument that the parents' unilateral placement violated the stay-put requirement and thus rendered the parents ineligible for reimbursement, the Court indicated that the stay-put provision says nothing about financial responsibility or reimbursement. The Court nonetheless pointed out that "parents who unilaterally change their child's placement during the pendency of review proceedings, without the consent of state or local school officials, do so at their own financial risk." Thus, parents who do not prevail in a claim that the school district's proffered placement was not appropriate will be forced to bear the expenses of their unilateral action. Further, caselaw indicates that parents who lose in a court action may also be required to bear the expense of court costs.

While making it clear that reimbursement is available as a remedy under the IDEA, the Supreme Court left open the question of whether reimbursement must be awarded in every instance in which parents prevail. The Court stated in *Burlington* that:

> We do think that [the Court of Appeals] was correct in concluding that "such relief as the court determines is appropriate," within the meaning of § 1415(e)(2) [now § 1415(i)(2)(B)(iii)], means that equitable considerations are relevant in fashioning relief.

Thus, even when the LEA has failed to offer a FAPE, the equities should be considered by a court before automatically awarding full reimbursement.

The expenses for which parents are entitled to reimbursement presumably include all those necessary to enable the child with a disability to receive a FAPE. A variety of expenses have been ordered to be reimbursed, including tuition expense, costs of residential placement, expenses for related services, expenses for other services required to permit a student to receive a FAPE, lost earnings by a parent for time expended relating to protecting the child's rights, and even interest on payments made for a unilateral placement or interest on borrowings in order to make such payments. The balancing of equities can also result in neither party gaining a total victory, but rather in the court imposing a Solomon-like decision concerning who shall bear the costs.

The Supreme Court provided additional guidance on when the school district must pay for the private placement if the private placement selected by the parents is found to be appropriate and the school district's proposed placement to be inappropriate. It held that reimbursement must be made even if the private school does not meet state standards or is not on a list of "state approved" schools. *Florence County School District Four v. Carter*, 510 U.S. 7 (1993).

The 1997 Amendments to the IDEA provide, however, that in order to obtain reimbursement for private school expenses (which would include reimbursement for tuition), parents must have complied with the following requirements: (1) At the last IEP meeting prior to removing their child from public school, the parents must inform the IEP team that they are rejecting the school district's proposed placement and intend to place their child in private school. (2) Alternatively, parents must provide the school with *written* notice of their decision to place the child in private school. 20 U.S.C.A. § 1412(a)(10)(C)(iii)(I). Parents *must* follow one of the above two options or they will be denied reimbursement for private school expenses.

If the school district provides the parents with notice of the district's intent to evaluate the child, the parents must make the child available for such evaluation or the parents may not recover reimbursement for private school expenses. In addition reimbursement for private school expenses will be denied if a court finds that the parents acted unreasonably in placing their child in private school. *Id.* § 1412(a)(10)(C)(iii)(II), (III).

An issue that arose in the wake of *Burlington* was whether a court could order reimbursement of private-education tuition when a child had not previously received special education and related services through the public school. The IDEA states that reimbursement is available for a child "who previously received special education and related services under the authority of a public agency." 20 U.S.C. § 1412(a)(10)(C)(ii). The Supreme Court resolved this issue in *Forest Grove v. T.A.*, 129 S.Ct. 2484 (2009). The Court held that the IDEA does not categorically bar reimbursement of private-education tuition if a child had not previously received special education and related services through the public school. In *Forest Grove*, the school district had refused to find the child eligible for special-education services and declined to offer him an IEP. In such a situation, a parent could seek reimbursement of the cost of private-education tuition even though the child had never received special education services because the parent had given the school district sufficient notice that the child was entitled to special education services by requesting identification of the child as disabled. The Court emphasized that principles of equity should resolve this matter in individual cases. Hence, not all parents will receive reimbursement if they have not given the school district sufficient notice that their child should be receiving publicly-funded services.

At least one court has held that an LEA's reimbursing a parent for the cost of voluntary placing a child in a religious school does not violate the First Amendment because the reimbursement compensates the parent rather than the religious school. Further, the IDEA, a federal statute, would take precedence over a state constitution that prohibits an LEA's reimbursement for educational costs of a parochial school. *Matthew J. v. Massachusetts Dept. of Educ.*, 989 F.Supp. 380 (D. Mass. 1998).

§ 16.3   SOVEREIGN IMMUNITY

The Supreme Court unequivocally held in *Dellmuth v. Muth*, 491 U.S. 223 (1989) that reimbursement against a *state* is barred by the Eleventh Amendment. The holding in *Muth*, however, only affected parents' ability to seek reimbursement from a *state*; it did not affect the ability of parents to seek reimbursement from other parties. Thus, parents could seek reimbursement from school districts. Further, compensatory educational services—which are addressed in the next section of this chapter—were not affected by the *Muth* decision.

The *Muth* decision was overruled by the Education for the Handicapped Act Amendments of 1990 which provides that "[a] State shall not be immune under the eleventh amendment to the Constitution of the United States from suit in Federal court for a violation of this chapter." 20 U.S.C. § 1403(a). Given this provision, most courts have considered a state's acceptance of federal money an unequivocal waiver of sovereign immunity. *See, e.g. John T. v. Iowa Dept. of Educ.*, 258 F.3d 860 (8th Cir. 2001); *Board of Educ. of Oak Park v. Kelly E.*, 207 F.3d 931 (7th Cir. 2000). The Fifth Circuit ruled otherwise in *Pace v. Bogalusa City School Bd.*, 325 F.3d 609 (5th Cir. 2003) but then reconsidered its decision *en banc* and concluded that the state did waive its Eleventh Amendment immunity. *Pace v. Bogalusa City School Bd.*, 403 F.3d 272 (5th Cir. 2005).

The sovereign immunity doctrine generally does *not* apply to local school agencies. *See, e.g. Eason v. Clark County School Dist.*, 303 F.3d 1137 (9th Cir. 2002) (collecting cases); *Mt. Healthy Bd. of Educ. v. Doyle*, 429 U.S. 274 (1977) (holding immunity under Eleventh Amendment covers an "arm of the state" but not a municipal corporation or other political subdivision, so Ohio school board was not able to assert sovereign immunity). *But see Belanger v. Madera Unified Sch. Dist.*, 963 F.2d 248 (9th Cir. 1992) (holding that school districts in California are arms of state)

§ 16.4 COMPENSATORY EDUCATIONAL SERVICES

Compensatory educational services are designed to remedy—in whole or in part—the progress lost by a student with a disability because he or she was previously denied a FAPE. The issue of whether the IDEA provides a right to compensatory educational services has received more attention since the Supreme Court ruled in *Burlington* that reimbursement is available under the IDEA and does not constitute damages.

The courts that have considered the issue of compensatory damages are not uniformly in agreement. The majority has held that compensatory educational services are included in the remedies available under the IDEA. They reason that imposing liability for such services merely requires the school district to pay expenses it should have paid in the first place. At least one court has also concluded that compensatory education serves the purpose of deterring school districts from unnecessarily prolonging litigation in order to decrease potential liability. *Jefferson County Bd. of Educ. v. Breen*, 853 F.2d 853 (11th Cir. 1988).

One issue addressed by the courts has been at what age a student "ages out" of the IDEA for the purpose of being awarded compensatory education as a remedy. The IDEA applies to persons "between the ages of 3 and 21, inclusive." 20 U.S.C. § 1412(a)(1)(A). Does that mean that a student "ages out" of the IDEA when he or she turns 21 or 22? The coverage of students beyond the age of 18 depends, in part, on state law. *See* § 1412(a)(1)(B). The Second Circuit has ruled that, in context, it appears that Congress intended to cover students until their 22nd birthday. *See St. Johnsbury Academy v. D.H.*, 240 F.3d 163 (2nd Cir. 2001).

Even if compensatory education is held not to be an available remedy under the IDEA, such relief may yet be available if a student pursues a claim under Section 504. For example, the official comments to the Section 504 regulations state that "persons beyond the [school] age limits . . . may in appropriate cases be required to be provided services that they were formerly denied because of a recipient's violation of Section 504." 34 C.F.R. Pt. 104, App. A. For more on this issue, see chapter 17 of this *Nutshell*.

As noted in the previous section, pursuant to the 1990 Education of the Handicapped Amendments, states are no longer provided Eleventh Amendment immunity from the remedies available under IDEA. Thus, courts recognizing the availability of compensatory educational services under the IDEA have also held that such a remedy will be available to parents regardless of whether the defendant is the state. *See, e.g., Mrs. C. v. Wheaton*, 916 F.2d 69 (2d Cir. 1990) ("If the district court were to provide an award of compensatory education as a remedy under § 504, the Eleventh Amendment would pose no bar since there is no state immunity for violations of § 504.").

§ 16.5   ATTORNEYS' FEES

Prior to 1984, parties who prevailed under the IDEA often sought reimbursement of attorneys' fees via Section 505 of the Rehabilitation Act of 1973 or Section 1988 of the Civil Rights Attorneys' Fees Award Act. The Supreme Court held in *Smith v. Robinson*, 468 U.S. 992 (1984), however, that the IDEA provides the exclusive statutory remedy for parties who prevail under the Act. The Court opined that the IDEA did not permit either the awarding of attorneys' fees or a remedy of such omission by parental recourse to other federal statutes such as Section 1988 or Section 505.

In 1986, the Handicapped Children's Protection Act (HCPA) amended the IDEA to counteract the ruling in *Smith v. Robinson*. The HCPA permits the awarding of attorneys' fees to a prevailing party under the IDEA by providing:

In any action or proceeding brought under this subsection, the court in its discretion, may award reasonable attorneys' fees as part of the costs to the parents or guardian of a child or youth with a disability who is the *prevailing party.*

20 U.S.C.A. § 1415(i)(3)(B) (emphasis added).

A.   PREVAILING PARTY

In *Buckhannon Board and Care Home, Inc. v. West Virginia Department of Health and Human Resources*, 532 U.S. 598 (2001), the Court limited the scope of the term "prevailing party." It rejected the "catalyst theory" which allowed a party to recover attorney's fees where a court found that the pressure of a lawsuit was a material contributing factor in bringing about extrajudicial relief. Instead, the Court interpreted the term "prevailing party" to require a judgment or similar form of judicially-sanctioned relief as a predicate for attorney's fees. The Supreme Court has applied *Buckhannon* to IDEA litigation. *See Arlington Central School District Board of Education v. Murphy*, 548 U.S. 291 (S.Ct. 2006).

In applying *Buckhannon*, courts look to see if an attorney changes the parents' legal relationships with the school board. A stipulated settlement can confer prevailing party status under certain circumstances where, for example, it is in the form of an order signed by a judge. *See John T. ex rel. Paul T. v. Delaware County Intermediate Unit*, 318 F.3d 545 (3rd Cir. 2003). Settlement of an IDEA administrative proceeding, followed by dismissal of proceeding, however, is not sufficient to attain prevailing party status. *See, e.g., A.R. v. New York City Department of Education*, 407 F.3d 65 (2nd Cir. 2005).

After the *Buckhannon* decision, the District of Columbia Public Schools (DCPS) adopted a policy that it would not pay attorneys' fees incurred by a parent in reaching a settlement agreement on an IDEA claim unless the payment of the fees was a negotiated term of the settlement. Many of the parents who sue DCPS do not have the money to pay an attorney, so eliminating their ability to receive money to pay their attorneys if they decide to settle a case could force parents to choose between legal representation and their child's interests in a quick settlement. In *Johnson v. District of Columbia*, 190 F.Supp.2d 34 (D.D.C. 2002), the court held that, while simultaneous attorney fee and merits settlement negotiations for claims under the IDEA are not per se illegal or unethical, evidence of such a practice could be relevant to show an intent to undermine the plaintiffs' ability to retain "unconflicted" counsel. The plaintiffs presented evidence that DCPS had conditioned settlement offers on the waiver of attorneys' fees. "This could reflect the intentional creation of a conflict of interest between plaintiffs and plaintiffs' counsel in an attempt to deprive plaintiffs of their rights to fees and counsel." "[A]ny policy or practice that intentionally or vindictively denies fees to all settling plaintiffs conflicts with [the IDEA's] fees provision."

B. CALCULATION OF FEES

1. *Scope and Nature of Services Covered*

Courts have awarded attorneys' fees for work performed during administrative proceedings and for work done before (and without recourse to) a due process hearing. Moreover, a prevailing party may be awarded attorneys' fees for the time incurred in making an application to recover those fees. *See, e.g., P.G. v. Brick Tp. Bd. of Educ.*, 124 F.Supp.2d 251 (D.N.J. 2000). The 1997 Amendments preclude an award of attorneys' fees for time spent in preparing for IEP meetings unless the meeting is convened as a result of an administrative proceeding, judicial action, or mediation process conducted before the filing of a complaint. 20 U.S.C. § 1415(i)(3)(D)(ii). It must be noted, however, that the change in the definition of "prevailing party" discussed above will impact the ability to recover attorney's fees for due process hearings and other administrative procedures.

2. *Computation of Awards*

The calculation of attorneys' fee awards:

. . . shall be based on rates prevailing in the community in which the action or proceeding arose for the kind and quality of services furnished. No bonus or multiplier may be used in calculating the fees awarded under this subsection.

20 U.S.C.A. § 1415(i)(3)(C). When Congress enacted the HCPA, it decided to set the IDEA apart from other statutes that have been interpreted to permit the application of bonuses or multipliers.

The size of fees ultimately available to a prevailing party is based on a variety of criteria, including the prevailing billing rate in the community, the number of billable hours expended, the extent to which the plaintiff prevailed, the complexity of the litigation, and the adequacy of the legal representation. Information concerning each of these various criteria must be documented by the attorney for a prevailing party when applying to the court for an award of attorneys' fees. There is no artificial ceiling on the amount of fees recoverable, nor is a fee award limited by any lesser amount set forth in a contingency fee agreement or retainer agreement.

Attorney fee awards do *not* include fees for expert witnesses. *See Arlington Central School District Board of Education v. Murphy*, 548 U.S. 291 (2006).

3. *Publicly Funded Law Offices*

Attorneys' fee awards are not limited to instances in which private counsel is retained; fees may be awarded to publicly funded law offices. *See, e.g., Yankton School Dist. v. Schramm*, 93 F.3d 1369 (8th Cir. 1996). It has been held that nonprofit law firms may recover attorneys' fees at the same hourly rates applicable to profit-making law firms since such was intended by Congress when enacting the HCPA. Congress expressly rejected adoption of a standard that would have computed attorneys' fees for publicly funded attorneys in accordance with a cost-based standard rather than the prevailing rate standard. *See, e.g., Collinsgru v. Palmyra Bd. of Educ.*, 161 F.3d 225 (3d Cir. 1998).

4. *Nonavailability of Attorneys' Fees*

The HCPA explicitly prohibits the awarding of attorneys' fees in situations involving unjustifiable rejection of a properly proposed settlement offer. That Act provides:

(i) Attorneys' fees may not be awarded and related costs may not be reimbursed in any action or proceeding under this section for services performed subsequent to the time of a written offer of settlement to a parent if—

(I) the offer is made within the time prescribed by Rule 68 of the Federal Rules of Civil Procedure or, in the case of an administrative proceeding, at any time more than 10 days before the proceeding begins;

(II) the offer is not accepted within 10 days; and

(III) the court or administrative hearing officer finds that the relief finally obtained by the parents is not more favorable to the parents than the offer of settlement.

20 U.S.C.A. § 1415(i)(3)(D). The statute continues: "Notwithstanding subparagraph (D), an award of attorneys' fees and related costs may be made to a

parent who is the prevailing party and who was
substantially justified in rejecting the settlement
offer." *Id.* § 1415(i)(3)(E). Courts will therefore deny
attorneys' fees to parents who reject a properly
made settlement offer and who ultimately obtain
essentially the same relief as was offered previously.

5. *Reduction of Fees*

The HCPA also permits the court to reduce
attorneys' fees "whenever the court finds that"

(i) the parent or guardian, during the course of
the action or proceeding, unreasonably
protracted the final resolution of the
controversy;

(ii) the amount of the attorneys' fees otherwise
authorized to be awarded unreasonably exceeds
the hourly rate prevailing in the community for
similar services by attorneys of reasonably
comparable skill, experience and reputation; or

(iii) the time spent and legal services furnished
were excessive considering the nature of the
action or proceeding; or

(iv) the attorney representing the parent did
not provide to the school district the
appropriate information in the due process
complaint.

20 U.S.C.A. § 1415(i)(3)(F). In other words, the court
is expected to balance the equities, as well as to
consider what is fair under the circumstances, when
exercising its discretion relative to awarding

reasonable attorneys' fees. Attorneys' fees will not be reduced, however, if the school district unreasonably prolonged resolution of the dispute. *Id.* § 1415(i)(3)(G).

CHAPTER 17

SECTION 504 AND THE ADA: ELEMENTARY AND SECONDARY EDUCATION

§ 17.1   APPLICABILITY OF SECTION 504

Children with disabilities are protected from discrimination in elementary and secondary educational under both Section 504 and the IDEA. As previously explained, the IDEA sets forth very detailed and comprehensive rules for states to follow when providing children with disabilities with a "free appropriate public education" (FAPE). Unlike the IDEA, Section 504 does not set out comprehensive rules for school districts to follow when educating children with disabilities, although the regulations promulgated by the Department of Education (DOE) pursuant to Section 504 do set out some specific criteria for school districts to follow when providing special educational services to such children. *See* 34 C.F.R. §§ 104.31–104.38. The DOE regulations also provide, however, that a school district's compliance with the IDEA is one means of complying with Section 504 with respect to providing a FAPE.

More importantly, the IDEA only protects children who, by virtue of their disabilities, require *special educational* services. Section 504, however, prohibits discrimination against *all* school-age children with disabilities regardless of whether they require special educational services. "Qualified" persons with disabilities with respect to federal funds' recipients who provide elementary and secondary educational services include children who are:

(i) of an age during which nonhandicapped persons are provided such services,

(ii) of any age during which it is mandatory under state law to provide such services to handicapped persons, or

(iii) to whom a state is required to provide a free appropriate education under [the IDEA].

34 C.F.R. § 104.3(*l*)(2).

Congress amended the Americans with Disabilities Act in 2008 as well as Section 504 to expand the definition of disability. These amendments broaden who is covered by Section 504 and will be discussed in Section 18.4, *infra.*

Thus, for example, the IDEA would not apply to an academically gifted student with emotional and behavioral problems, but he would be covered under Section 504. *See, e.g., J.D. v. Pawlet School Dist.,* 224 F.3d 60 (2d Cir. 2000). Several courts have also allowed claims under Section 504 and/or the ADA when a student has been excluded from interscholastic sports. *See, e.g., Cruz v. Pennsylvania Interscholastic Athletic Ass'n, Inc.,* 157 F.Supp.2d 485 (E.D.Pa. 2001). On January 25, 2013, the United States Department of Education issued guidance regarding the participation of students with disabilities in various kinds of school athletic programs. The Guidance emphasizes that schools must make reasonable modifications and provide "aids and services that are necessary to ensure an equal opportunity to participate, unless the school district can show that doing so would be a fundamental alteration to its program." *See* http://www2.ed.gov/about/offices/list/ocr/letters/colle ague-201301-504.pdf.

There are numerous other instances where Section 504, but not the IDEA, might apply to school-age children. One such instance involves a child who suffers from an illness that has not progressed to the point where the child requires special education but whose illness does affect the child to such degree that reasonable accommodations are required to allow the child to continue in the regular classroom. To cite four examples: (1) a child with a moderate case of cystic fibrosis could attend regular classes if reasonably accommodated by the provision of respiratory therapy services during the day; (2) a child with sickle-cell anemia could attend regular classes if reasonably accommodated by providing home or hospital tutoring during infrequent crisis situations that necessitated absence from school; (3) a child with spina bifida might be capable of attending regular classes if reasonably accommodated by providing catheterization services; (4) children who test positive for the HIV virus but are not ill with AIDS or AIDS Related Complex.

Cases involving students who are alcoholics or drug addicts also raise issues under Section 504 but not under the IDEA. While alcoholics are disabled within the meaning of Section 504, they generally will not be classified as children with disabilities protected by the IDEA. Section 504, however, does not prevent a school district from prohibiting students who are alcoholics or drug addicts from complying with rules relating to the possession of alcohol or drugs. The DOE Section 504 regulations note that commenters on the proposed regulations were concerned with the:

> effect the inclusion of drug addicts and alcoholics as [disabled] persons would have on school disciplinary rules prohibiting the use or possession of drugs or alcohol by students. Neither such rules nor their application to drug addicts or alcoholics is prohibited by this regulation, provided that the rules are enforced evenly with respect to all students.

34 C.F.R. Part 104, App. A.

Moreover, the ADA amended Section 504's application to substance abusers in schools by providing:

> For purposes of programs and activities providing educational services, local educational agencies may take disciplinary action pertaining to the use or possession of illegal drugs or alcohol against any student who is an individual with a disability and who currently is engaging in the illegal use of drugs or in the use of alcohol to the same extent that such disciplinary action is taken against

students who are not individuals with disabilities. Furthermore, the due process procedures at section 104.36 of title 34, Code of Federal Regulations (or any corresponding similar regulation or ruling) shall not apply to such disciplinary actions.

29 U.S.C.A. § 705(20)(C)(iv).

§ 17.2 PROCEDURAL AND SUBSTANTIVE ASPECTS OF SECTION 504

School districts have both procedural and substantive obligations towards school-age children deemed disabled under Section 504.

A. PROCEDURAL ASPECTS

The DOE Section 504 regulations require school districts receiving federal financial assistance to establish procedures and standards for evaluating and placing students with disabilities who require either special education or related services. 34 C.F.R. § 104.35. A school district that fails to establish such procedures and to conduct the requisite evaluation of a student with a disability will be held to violate Section 504.

The Section 504 regulations provide that schools:

shall establish and implement, with respect to actions regarding the identification, evaluation, or educational placement of persons who, because of handicap, need or are believed to need special instruction or related services, a system of procedural safeguards that includes notice, an opportunity for the parents or guardian of the person to examine relevant records, an impartial hearing with opportunity for participation by the person's parents or guardian and representation by counsel, and a review procedure.

34 C.F.R. § 104.36. Compliance with the IDEA's procedures satisfies the requirements of Section 504. *Id.* Students who are disabled under both the IDEA and Section 504 might be required to exhaust administrative remedies under the IDEA before filing suit in court. For a discussion of the exhaustion requirement under the IDEA, see § 15.1 of this *Nutshell.* As discussed in § 16.1, this area of the law is in flux due to the broadening of the definition of disability under Section 504 through the 2008 Amendments. If, however, a plaintiff is not seeking relief also available under IDEA, he or she would not be required to exhaust administrative remedies. *See, e.g., Hornstine v. Township of Moorestown,* 263 F.Supp.2d 887 (D.N.J. 2003).

The IDEA's stay-put mandate is not a requirement under Section 504, although many school districts apply similar principles to their Section 504 procedures.

B. SUBSTANTIVE ISSUES

Section 504 obligates school districts receiving federal financial assistance to refrain from discriminating against students with disabilities and to provide reasonable accommodations where necessary. Where Section 504 is at issue, the focus is on non-discrimination in the provision of a FAPE or on the provision of reasonable accommodations.

When reasonable accommodations are necessary to provide non-discriminatory educational services to a child with a disability, the requisite accommodations should be documented in an educational plan for that child. Even where reasonable accommodations are not required, however, a school district may not discriminate against a child classified as disabled under Section 504.

With respect to providing a FAPE for children classified as disabled under *both* the IDEA and Section 504, most courts have concluded that the same standards apply whether the student's claim is brought under the IDEA, ADA, or Section 504. *See, e.g., Brett v. Goshen Community Sch. Corp.*, 161 F.Supp.2d 930 (N.D.Ind. 2001) (citing cases). This reasoning is supported by the fact that the DOE regulations provide in three places that compliance with IDEA requirements with respect to the provision of a FAPE would satisfy the requirements of Section 504. Several courts have also noted that compliance with IDEA standards with respect to providing a FAPE constitutes compliance with Section 504. *But see Lyons v. Smith*, 829 F.Supp. 414 (D.D.C. 1993) (suggesting that Section 504 and the IDEA incorporate different standards). It is not yet known whether the 2008 Amendments to the ADA, broadening the scope of covered individuals, will cause the legal standards between IDEA, ADA and Section 504 to diverge.

While compliance with the IDEA is one means of complying with Section 504, noncompliance with the IDEA will not necessarily indicate noncompliance with Section 504. As the DOE's Office for Civil Rights (OCR) has explained, with respect to providing a FAPE:

> ... the implementation of an IEP that meets [IDEA] standards will also meet the requirements of Section 504: however, implementation of an [IEP] that fails to meet the requirements of the [IDEA] does not necessarily violate Section 504. Instead, OCR will look to see whether the services identified during the evaluation process are being provided to the child.

OCR Senior Staff Memo from LeGree S. Daniels, Ass't. Sec. for Civil Rights, EHLR 307:01–05 (Oct. 24, 1988).

The OCR further explains:

> Since consistency with the [IDEA] is only one means of complying with these three provisions of the Section 504 regulation[s] [dealing with the provision of a FAPE].... *noncompliance* determinations cannot rest solely on a conclusion that a recipient has not met the standards of the [IDEA]. While a recipient may comply with these three sections of the Section 504 regulation[s] by complying with the [IDEA], failure to meet the [IDEA] standards does not necessarily constitute a violation of

Section 504, and must not be the basis for OCR's analytic approach or conclusion.

Id.

For those children who qualify as disabled under Section 504 and who are not classified as disabled under the IDEA, the FAPE requirement under the Section 504 regulations may require something more than under the IDEA. In the Section 504 context, the FAPE requirement is presumably not influenced by the reasonableness of the necessary accommodations. The concept of reasonable accommodation is one that applies when determining whether someone is "otherwise qualified" for a particular program or activity. Insofar as school-aged children are concerned, such children are by definition "otherwise qualified" because they meet the qualification of being the proper age for attending school. Thus, the sole issue would appear to be whether the child is being discriminated against on the basis of his or her disability. If the answer is "yes," the child is entitled to a FAPE in order to address his or her needs.

The OCR has ruled that the Section 504 regulation's mandate that school districts provide a FAPE to all children with disabilities requires school districts to assume costs for furnishing assessments and services to students with disabilities. *Letter to Zirkel*, 16 EHLR 1177 (1990).

§ 17.3 RIGHTS OF PARENTS UNDER SECTION 504

Parents of children with disabilities have also utilized Section 504 in actions to preserve their own rights against school districts. For example, in *Rothschild v. Grottenthaler*, 907 F.2d 286 (2d Cir. 1990), deaf parents of nondisabled children requested that their childrens' school district provide them with sign-language interpreters during meetings with teachers and school administrators to discuss their childrens' programs and at various school functions where parents were asked to participate. When the school district refused, the parents claimed they were being denied equal access to services offered by the school in violation of Section 504. The court agreed. It held that the school district must provide qualified sign-language interpreters for hearing-impaired parents at school conferences relating to the academic and/or disciplinary aspects of their childrens' education. The court further held, however, that the school district did not have to provide an interpreter for the parents when they attended their childrens' extracurricular activities. It reasoned that parents who wish to voluntarily participate in any extracurricular activities that their children may be involved in must, like other parents, do so at their own expense.

§ 17.4   APPLICABILITY OF TITLE II OF THE ADA

As previously discussed in chapter 7 of this *Nutshell*, Title II of the Americans with Disabilities Act (ADA) prohibits all state and local government entities from discriminating on the basis of disability. Thus, Title II governs public schools.

Congress amended the ADA in 2008 to broaden the definition of disability. As before the statute was amended, the definition of disability includes a "physical or mental impairment that substantially limits one or more major life activities of such individual." 42 U.S.C. § 12102(1)(A). The term "major life activities" was amended to specifically include "learning, reading, concentrating, thinking, and communicating." 42 U.S.C. § 12102(2)(A). This broadened definition makes clear that students with ADHD or various kinds of learning disabilities are covered by the ADA (and Section 504).

The DOE issued a guidance in 1995 which provides an overview of Title II as it applies to public elementary and secondary schools. *Compliance with the Americans with Disabilities Act: A Self-evaluation Guide for Public Elementary and Secondary Schools.* http://files.eric.ed.gov/full text/ED401688.pdf. The Guidance outlines five steps, four principles, and three phases for schools to follow.

The five steps for schools to follow include: (i) designating a responsible employee to oversee Title II compliance; (ii) providing notice of ADA requirements; (iii) establishing a grievance procedure; (iv) conducting a self-evaluation; and (v) developing a transition plan.

The DOE recommends that schools follow four basic principles to avoid discrimination on the basis of disability: (i) commitment from the highest level of leadership; (ii) coordinated compliance activities; (iii) involvement of people with disabilities in policy making; and (iv) furtherance of an institutionalized compliance procedure.

The DOE further recommends that schools conduct self-evaluations in three phases. First, a preliminary planning stage to define a compliance process, identify participants and set up procedures for communication and coordination. Second, an evaluative stage where current services, policies and practices are evaluated. Third, a final stage where information is assessed and essential modifications to existing practices are identified.

In some respects Section 504 and the ADA may differ. In that situation, entities covered by both laws must meet the higher standard.

§ 17.5   RIGHTS OF STUDENTS IN PRIVATE SCHOOLS UNDER SECTION 504 AND THE ADA

Section 504 applies to any private school that receives federal financial assistance. The Section 504 regulations pertaining to elementary and secondary education do not apply to private schools, however. Thus, the only obligation of covered private schools is to refrain from discriminating on the basis of disability.

Title III of the Americans with Disabilities Act also imposes a non-discrimination obligation on private schools, regardless of whether such schools receive federal financial assistance, with one exception: ADA Title III does not govern private schools operated by a religious organization. 42 U.S.C. § 12187; 28 C.F.R. Pt. 36, App. B § 36.104. Under Title III, all private schools that are not operated by a religious organization are prohibited from discriminating against children on the basis of disability and must provide reasonable accommodations or reasonable modifications in their programs or services when necessary to avoid discrimination against a child with a disability. The definition of disability under ADA Title III is identical to the definition described in Section 18.4.

Both Section 504 and ADA Title III impose significant obligations upon private schools regarding the removal of architectural barriers. *See* chapter 7 of this *Nutshell*. With respect to non-architectural matters, Section 504 and ADA Title III provide as follows:

Under Section 504 private school programs may not exclude a qualified child with a disability from its program on the basis of disability if an education can be provided to that child with the application of "minor adjustments" to the program. 34 C.F.R. § 104.39. If a private school must incur additional costs to accommodate a child with a disability, the school may not charge more for the child's tuition, etc., unless the school's costs are *substantially* increased. *Id.* Private schools subject to Section 504 must educate children in the least restrictive setting, and may not discriminate in the provision of non-academic and extracurricular services and activities. *Id.* and 34 C.F.R. § 104.37.

Under ADA Title III, private schools must make reasonable modifications in their practices, policies or procedures, and/or provide auxiliary aids for students with disabilities. A school may refrain from this obligation only if it would result in a fundamental alteration of the school's program or would result in an undue burden. 42 U.S.C.A. § 12182(b). *See, e.g., St. Johnsbury Academy v. D.H.*, 240 F.3d 163 (2d Cir. 2001); *Alvarez v. Fountainhead, Inc.*, 55 F.Supp.2d 1048 (N.D.Cal. 1999).

CHAPTER 18

DISCIPLINING STUDENTS WITH DISABILITIES

§ 18.1   IMPACT OF THE IDEA AND SECTION 504

Before the IDEA was enacted, school districts' traditional authority to administer discipline to students had been limited only by particular state statutes specifying the procedures to be followed and, in certain circumstances, by the constitutional requirement of minimum due process. The stay-put provision in the IDEA, however, prohibits a school district from unilaterally changing a disabled child's placement. 20 U.S.C.A. § 1415(j). The stay-put provision is more fully discussed in § 13.4(E) of this *Nutshell*. It was initially unclear whether an expulsion or long-term suspension of a disabled child amounted to a "change of placement" that would trigger the need both to adhere to the IDEA's procedural safeguards and to impose the protections of the stay-put provision. The Supreme Court addressed this issue in *Honig v. Doe*, 484 U.S. 305 (1988).

§ 18.2   *HONIG V. DOE*: PROCEDURAL SAFEGUARDS

The Supreme Court in *Honig* found the language of the IDEA with respect to the stay-put provision to be "unequivocal." The Court stated: "We think it clear ... that Congress very much meant to strip schools of the *unilateral* authority they had traditionally employed to exclude disabled students, particularly emotionally disturbed students, from school." (Emphasis in original). Thus, the Supreme Court held that unilateral expulsion of children with disabilities is no longer permitted because it constitutes a change in placement that cannot be instituted without compliance with the IDEA procedural requirements. Further, the Court held that a suspension in excess of ten days constitutes a change in placement, thus triggering the stay-put provision. In sum, therefore, under the Court's ruling a LEA may temporarily suspend a student with a disability for no more than ten school days without such a temporary suspension being considered a change in placement.

In ruling as it did in *Honig*, the Supreme Court rejected the school district's request that the Court read a "dangerousness" exception into the IDEA. Educators were concerned that a literal reading of the stay-put provision would require a school to keep violent or dangerous students in the classroom during pendency of administrative hearings. The Court disagreed, but it did not leave school districts defenseless to respond to children who present a danger to themselves or others. Noting that critical situations could arise in which a parent would not agree with the school district so as to permit a change in placement considered essential by the district, the Supreme Court made it clear that a district may seek court involvement. The Court stated:

in those cases in which the parents of a truly dangerous child adamantly refuse to permit any change in placement, the 10-day respite gives school officials an opportunity to invoke the aid of the courts under Section 1415(e)(2) [now § 1415(i)(2)(A)], which empowers courts to grant any appropriate relief.

Thus, in *Honig* the Supreme Court indicated that not only do parents have the ability to proceed directly to court in certain circumstances without first exhausting administrative remedies, but school districts also have this opportunity, in limited circumstances. The Court noted that exhaustion of administrative procedures is not required when such exhaustion would be futile or inadequate. The Court stated that the school district has the burden of proving that it would be futile or inadequate to exhaust administrative procedures. After meeting that burden, the district does not have to exhaust administrative remedies prior to seeking court relief to allow long-term denial of access to school to an allegedly dangerous disabled child.

Although the Supreme Court does require the school district to first convince the court that it would be futile or inadequate to seek administrative review, this presumably is not a difficult threshold issue. This requirement will be inextricably intertwined and subsumed by the issue of whether the child before the court is dangerous to himself or others. If the child is in fact dangerous, the administrative process is by definition futile or inadequate. Thus, although the Supreme Court stated that there is no dangerousness exception to the IDEA, in reality the Court has recognized such an exception. The major effect of the Court's ruling is that the person determining dangerousness will not be a hearing officer but rather a court. A court may require the school district to prove both that: (i) the disciplined student with a disability poses a substantial likelihood of harm to himself or others; and (ii) the LEA took all reasonable steps to mitigate the risk of harm.

There is another consequence of the *Honig* decision. If a dangerousness exception had been read into the statute (requiring a hearing officer to make a determination of whether the child was in fact dangerous), parents of the child with a disability would probably have had to petition for such a hearing. In that event, the parents, as petitioners, would presumably have had the burden of proving that the child is *not* dangerous. As a result of the Court's ruling in *Honig*, however, the school district will bear the burden of proving that the child is dangerous when it seeks relief from the court because a child with a disability is believed to pose a danger to himself and/or others.

§ 18.3   INTERPLAY BETWEEN IDEA AND SECTION 504

Courts and federal agencies have generally treated expulsion and suspension issues consistently, regardless of whether they involve the IDEA or Section 504. Indeed, the Office of Special Education and Rehabilitative Services (OSERS)—

the office within the DOE responsible for enforcing the IDEA—and OCR—the office within the DOE responsible for enforcing Section 504—have promulgated a joint memorandum reflecting their commitment "to the principle that interpretations of the [IDEA] and Section 504 should not lead to inconsistent obligations being imposed upon states and other departmental recipients." 13 EHLR 202:395 (1987). Further, the regulations implementing the two statutes, although promulgated by different offices within the DOE, frequently refer to each other and to both statutes. Thus, as a general rule—with a few exceptions referred to later in this chapter—suspension and expulsion matters have been treated the same under both the IDEA and Section 504.

§ 18.4   CHANGE IN PLACEMENT

The determination of what constitutes a "change in placement" is critical to applying the discipline limitations under both the IDEA and Section 504. Under the IDEA, a change in placement, if contested by the parents, triggers the "stay-put" provision which prohibits the school district from removing the student from his or her current placement. 20 U.S.C.A. § 1415(j). The stay-put provision is more fully discussed in § 12.4(E) of this *Nutshell*. To summarize, parents must receive prior notice of a proposed change of placement, including an explanation of available procedural safeguards. Similarly, under Section 504 a significant change in placement may be made only after the child is reevaluated, and the parents are given notice and provided with an opportunity for a hearing. A minor change in program, however, does not give rise to due process concerns and the stay-put provision. In other words, if there is not a change in placement, the only limitation set upon a school district is that it treat a child with a disability in the same way as it would treat a non-disabled child.

No statute, agency or court has provided a comprehensive definition of the term "change in placement." *Honig* establishes only that a suspension of ten or more consecutive school days amounts to a change in placement. The IDEA regulations further state that a change in placement occurs if "[t]he child is subjected to a series of removals that constitute a pattern—(i) because the series of removals total more than 10 school days in a school year; (ii) because the child's behavior is substantially similar to the child's behavior in previous incidents that resulted in the series of removals; and (iii) because of such additional factors as the length of each removal, the total amount of time the child has been removed, and the proximity of the removals to one another." 34 C.F.R. § 300.536(b)(2). The second factor was added by the 2004 Amendments.

In *Parents of Student W. v. Puyallup School Dist., No. 3*, 31 F.3d 1489 (9th Cir. 1994), the court held that a school district's special education suspension guidelines were lawful on their face where they limited suspensions to 15 days per semester, and each suspension triggered a meeting of the pupil's multidisciplinary team to decide whether the current problem was part of pupil's disability or resulted from an inappropriate program. The team also looked at whether the cumulative effect of the short-term suspensions had adversely affected the pupil's program.

§ 18.5   THE 1997 AND 2004 AMENDMENTS

The 1997 and 2004 Amendments to the IDEA address and clarify many issues relating to the discipline of children with disabilities. They provide:

(1) School personnel may consider any unique circumstances on a case-by-case basis when determining whether to order a change in place for a child with a disability who violates a code of student conduct. 20 U.S.C. § 1415(k)(1)(A). This rule was added by the 2004 Amendments.

(2) A school district may remove a child with a disability who violates a code of student conduct from their current placement to an appropriate alternative educational setting or another setting, or may suspend a child with a disability, for not more than 10 school days—to the same extent that such alternatives would be applied to children without disabilities. 20 U.S.C. § 1415(k)(1)(B). The 2004 Amendments replaced "order of change in placement" with "remove."

(3) A child with a disability who: (i) carries a weapon to school or to a school function, or (ii) possesses or uses illegal drugs or sells or solicits the sale of a controlled substance while

at a school or a school function, or (iii) inflicts serious bodily injury upon another person while at school can be placed in an interim alternative educational setting for the same time that a nondisabled child would be placed in such a setting, *up to not more than 45 school days*. *Id.* § 1415(k)(1)(G). (The 2004 Amendments replaced "school days" for "calendar days." The alternative setting is to be determined by the IEP team. During that 45-day period, the parents may request a due process hearing to contest the change of placement, but, unless the parents and the LEA agree otherwise, "the child shall remain in the interim alternative educational setting pending the decision of the hearing officer or until the expiration of the time period." *Id.* § 1415(k)(4)(A). In other words, the IDEA's stay-put provision will not apply, and schools cannot be forced to return the student to his or her original placement during the 45-day period.

(4) Not more than 10 days after taking disciplinary action against a child with a disability, the LEA must either (i) convene an IEP meeting to address the child's problem behavior if a behavior intervention plan was not formerly implemented, or (ii) review any existing behavior intervention plan and modify it, as necessary, to address the behavior. *Id.* § 1415(k)(1)(E).

(5) If a hearing officer determines that the school district has demonstrated by substantial evidence that maintaining the current placement of a child with a disability is likely to result in injury to the child or others, the hearing officer may order the child placed in an "interim alternative educational setting" for not more than 45 days. Prior to reaching such a determination, the hearing officer must consider the appropriateness of the child's current placement, consider whether the school district has made reasonable efforts—including use of supplementary aids and services—to minimize the risk of harm in that current placement, and determine that the interim placement would satisfy necessary requirements, as outlined in the next paragraph. *Id.* § 1415(k)(3)(B)(ii)(II).

(6) The "interim alternative educational" setting must be determined by the team that developed the child's IEP, and must: (i) enable the child to continue to participate in the general curriculum; (ii) allow the child to continue to receive services and modifications that will enable the child to meet the goals set forth in the IEP; and (iii) include services and modifications designed to address the problem behavior. *Id.* § 1415(k)(2).

(7) If disciplinary action is contemplated that will involve a change of placement for more than 10 days (including placement in an interim alternative educational setting), a

"manifestation   determination   review"   is
required. This requires that: (i) as of the date
on which the decision to take action is made,
the child's parents must be notified of the
decision and of all procedural safeguards; and
(ii) no later than 10 school days after the date
on which the decision to take that action is
made, a review must be conducted of the
relationship between the child's disability and
the behavior subject to the disciplinary action.
The review is to be conducted by the IEP team
and   other   qualified   personnel.   *Id.*
§ 1415(k)(1)(E).

(8) If it is determined that the child's behavior
was not a manifestation of the child's disability,
the relevant disciplinary procedure applicable
to children without disabilities may be applied
to the child in the same manner in which they
would   be   applied   to   children   without
disabilities. *Id.* § 1415(k)(1)(C). During this
disciplinary period, however, the child with a
disability *must continue to be provided with a
FAPE*. *Id.* § 1412(a)(1)(A).

(9) If the team determines that the conduct
was a manifestation of the child's disability, the
IEP   team   shall   (i)   conduct   a   functional
behavioral   assessment,   and   implement   a
behavioral intervention plan for such child; (ii)
review   an   existing   behavioral   intervention
plan; and (iii) return the child to the placement
from which the child was removed unless the

team agrees to a change in placement. *Id.* § 1415(1)(F).

(10) Parents who disagree with a determination that their child's behavior was not a manifestation of the disability may request a hearing, and the SEA or LEA must arrange for an expedited hearing. During the appeal, the child is to remain in the interim alternative education setting pending the decision of the hearing officer or until the expiration of the time limit, whichever occurs first, unless the parent and the SEA or LEA otherwise agree. If a child is placed in an interim alternative educational setting and school personnel propose to change the child's placement after the interim placement has expired, the child is to remain in his/her current placement (the placement prior to the interim alternative educational setting) during the pendency of any proceeding to challenge the proposed change in placement. If, however, school personnel maintain that it is dangerous for the child to be in that "current" placement, the LEA may request an expedited hearing. *Id.* § 1415(k)(4)(B).

In *Richland Sch. Dist. v. Thomas P.*, 32 IDELR 233 (W.D.Wis. 2000), the court held that a hearing officer making a "manifestation" determination could consider evidence concerning the student's diagnosis that arose after the IEP team's decision. The school district had argued that the review of the IEP Team's manifestation determination should have taken into account only what was known of the child's disability at the time of its decision—a "snapshot," so to speak. The court disagreed, stating that "a manifestation determination is by its very nature retrospective, for it looks back at the child's behavior and attempts to determine if the child's disability impaired his ability to understand and control his behavior."

§ 18.6   CHILDREN CLASSIFIED AS DISABLED AFTER THE MISBEHAVIOR AT ISSUE

The law, both pre- and post-*Honig v. Doe*, concerning whether the procedural protections of Section 504 and the IDEA attach *prior* to when a child is formally classified as disabled is unclear. It is OCR's position that the lack of formal classification does not necessarily leave students unprotected. OCR's approach turns on whether the school district had sufficient notice to suspect that misconduct may be related to a disability. OSEP's position is consistent with that of OCR's. OSEP has stated that IDEA protections, including stay-put, apply to a student not previously classified as disabled if the LEA "knew or reasonably should have known" that the student is in need of special education.

In *Hacienda La Puente Unified School District of Los Angeles v. Honig*, 976 F.2d 487 (9th Cir. 1992), the Ninth Circuit concluded that the procedural protections of the IDEA attach prior to formal classification of a child as disabled. The Ninth

Circuit interpreted the Supreme Court's ruling in *Honig v. Doe* as applying to all students with disabilities, whether classified as disabled or not. The Ninth Circuit's reasoning has been followed by other courts. *See, e.g., Steldt v. School Board of the Riverdale School District*, 885 F.Supp. 1192 (W.D.Wis. 1995).

Similarly, the 1997 Amendments to the IDEA provide that the Act's protections apply to children not yet classified as disabled if the LEA had knowledge that the child was disabled before the behavior leading to disciplinary action occurred. If the LEA did not have such knowledge, the child may be subjected to the same disciplinary measures as applied to children without disabilities.

Pursuant to the 1997 Amendments, an LEA will be considered to have knowledge of the child's disability if: (1) the parent has expressed concern in writing to personnel of the appropriate educational agency that the child is in need of special education and related services (unless the parent is illiterate or has a disability that prevents compliance); (2) the behavior or performance of the child demonstrates the need for such services; (3) the parent has requested an evaluation of the child; or (4) the teacher or other LEA personnel has expressed concern to agency personnel about the behavior or performance of the child. 20 U.S.C.A. § 1415(k)(5).

§ 18.7   IN-SCHOOL DISCIPLINE

The Supreme Court recognized in *Honig* that normal in-school disciplinary procedures are available to school districts seeking to discipline students with disabilities. The Court stated that "[s]uch procedures may include the use of study carrels, time-outs, detention, or the restriction of privileges." There is also considerable case law, decided before *Honig*, upholding alternative disciplinary actions.

Ideally, issues involving in-school techniques to address behavior should be incorporated into the child's IEP. In any event, it is likely that courts will refrain from intervention when in-school discipline is at issue, unless the school's actions arise to the level of a constitutional violation.

The Tenth Circuit held in *Hayes v. Unified School District No. 377*, 877 F.2d 809 (10th Cir. 1989), however, that the provisions of the IDEA extend beyond suspension and expulsion to encompass discipline of children in the classroom generally, "including short-term suspensions and 'time-out' periods." In that case, school officials disciplined two children by placing them, at various times, in a three-foot by five-foot room for "time-out" periods and in-school suspensions. Relying on the Court's determination in *Honig* that suspensions of less than ten days do not constitute a change in placement, the Tenth Circuit concluded that these short-term disciplinary measures did not constitute a change in placement. The court held, nonetheless, that all disciplinary measures are within the purview of the IDEA, because the IDEA requires that disabled children and their parents be given " 'an opportunity to present complaints with respect to *any matter relating to* . . . the provision of a free appropriate public education.' "

§ 18.8   EXPUNGEMENT OF RECORDS

It has been held that Section 504 provides parents, in appropriate circumstances, with a remedy of expungement of their child's disciplinary records. *See Jonathan G. v. Caddo Parish School Board,* 875 F.Supp. 352 (W.D.La. 1994) (ordering expungement of disciplinary records of a student with emotional disabilities where the student had been repeatedly suspended for conduct relating to his disabilities).

§ 18.9   POLICE INTERVENTION AND JUVENILE COURT

The IDEA states that it shall not "be construed to prohibit an agency from reporting a crime committed by a child with a disability to appropriate authorities or to prevent State law enforcement and judicial authorities from exercising their responsibilities with regard to the application of Federal and State law to crimes committed by a child with a disability." 20 U.S.C. § 1415(k)(9)(A). Accordingly, courts have held that a school district may report criminal conduct of an IDEA-eligible student to the juvenile authorities without conducting a manifestation hearing. *Joseph M. v. Southeast Delco School Dist.,* 2001 WL 283154 (E.D.Pa. 2001). Additionally, a court has rejected the argument that a juvenile prosecution constituted a "change in placement" without appropriate procedural protections. *State v. David F.*, 1998 WL 828117 (Conn. Super. Ct. 1998). The court held that the juvenile court's jurisdiction "will not frustrate the IDEA or its 'stay put' provisions" and "the IDEA does not preempt a delinquency proceeding concerning a crime committed by a child with a disability, but rather, explicitly authorizes such delinquency proceeding."

CONCLUSION

As noted in the introductory chapter to this *Nutshell*, this book serves as only a cursory guide to a very complex area of the law. It should not be used for comprehensive analysis. Individuals should consult with an attorney or conduct their own research before determining the appropriate rules in specific subject areas.

INDEX

References are to Sections

EAHCA
See Education for All Handicapped Children Act

EARLY INTERVENTION SERVICES, §§ 12.1; 12.8

EDUCATION
Elementary and secondary. *See* IDEA, Section 504, and ADA
   Title's II and III
Postsecondary. *See* Postsecondary Education

EDUCATION FOR ALL HANDICAPPED CHILDREN ACT
See IDEA

EDUCATION OF THE HANDICAPPED ACT
See IDEA

ELEVATOR ACCESSIBILITY, § 7.23

ELEVENTH AMENDMENT IMMUNITY
See Constitutional Rights

EMPLOYEE
ADA definition, §§ 5.3; 5.4

EMPLOYER
ADA definition, § 5.2

EMPLOYMENT
ADA, entities subject to, § 5.2
Affirmative action, §§ 4.15; 4.6; 4.11–4.13; 5.1; 5.10
Alcoholics, discrimination against, §§ 3.5; 5.10; 5.16(D)
Associates of disabled people, § 5.2
Discrimination. *See, generally,* chapter 5
   Agent and supervisor liability, §§ 5.19(B); 5.20
   Attendance at the workplace, § 5.7
   Disparate impact, §§ 4.3; 4.5; 5.9; 5.19(A)–(B)
   Disparate treatment, §§ 4.5; 5.9
   Essential functions, § 5.7
   Inconsistent statements, § 5.6
   Insurance, § 11.6
   Laws prohibiting, § 5.1
   Reasonable accommodations, §§ 5.10–5.13
   Remedies for,
      ADA, §§ 5.18; 5.19(B)
      Section 501, § 5.19(A)